AMERICA'S
TEST KITCHEN

ALSO BY THE EDITORS AT AMERICA'S TEST KITCHEN

The America's Test Kitchen New Family Cookbook

The Complete Vegetarian Cookbook

The Complete Cooking for Two Cookbook

The Cook's Illustrated Meat Book

The Cook's Illustrated Baking Book

The Cook's Illustrated Cookbook

The Science of Good Cooking

Pressure Cooker Perfection

The America's Test Kitchen Cooking School Cookbook

The America's Test Kitchen Menu Cookbook

The America's Test Kitchen Quick Family Cookbook

The America's Test Kitchen Healthy Family Cookbook

The America's Test Kitchen Family Baking Book

THE AMERICA'S TEST KITCHEN LIBRARY SERIES

The Best Mexican Recipes

The Make-Ahead Cook

The How Can It Be Gluten Free Cookbook

Slow Cooker Revolution Volume 2:
The Easy-Prep Edition

Slow Cooker Revolution

The Six-Ingredient Solution

Comfort Food Makeovers

The America's Test Kitchen D.I.Y. Cookbook

Pasta Revolution

Simple Weeknight Favorites

The Best Simple Recipes

THE TV COMPANION SERIES

The Complete Cook's Country TV Show Cookbook

The Complete America's Test Kitchen TV Show
Cookbook 2001–2015

America's Test Kitchen: The TV Companion Cookbook
(2009 and 2011–2015 Editions)

Behind the Scenes with America's Test Kitchen

Test Kitchen Favorites

Cooking at Home with America's Test Kitchen

America's Test Kitchen Live!

Inside America's Test Kitchen

Here in America's Test Kitchen

The America's Test Kitchen Cookbook

AMERICA'S TEST KITCHEN ANNUALS

The Best of America's Test Kitchen
(2007–2015 Editions)

Cooking for Two (2010–2013 Editions)

Light & Healthy (2010–2012 Editions)

THE COOK'S COUNTRY SERIES

From Our Grandmothers' Kitchens

Cook's Country Blue Ribbon Desserts

Cook's Country Best Potluck Recipes

Cook's Country Best Lost Suppers

Cook's Country Best Grilling Recipes

The Cook's Country Cookbook

America's Best Lost Recipes

THE BEST RECIPE SERIES

The New Best Recipe

More Best Recipes

The Best One-Dish Suppers

Soups, Stews & Chilis

The Best Skillet Recipes

The Best Slow & Easy Recipes

The Best Chicken Recipes

The Best International Recipe

The Best Make-Ahead Recipe

The Best 30-Minute Recipe

The Best Light Recipe

The Cook's Illustrated Guide to Grilling and Barbecue

Best American Side Dishes

Cover & Bake

Steaks, Chops, Roasts & Ribs

Italian Classics

American Classics

FOR A FULL LISTING OF ALL OUR BOOKS
OR TO ORDER TITLES

CooksIllustrated.com

AmericasTestKitchen.com

or call 800-611-0759

Healthy Slow Cooker

REVOLUTION

ONE TEST KITCHEN. 40 SLOW COOKERS. **200 FRESH RECIPES.**

BY THE EDITORS AT
America's Test Kitchen

AMERICA'S TEST KITCHEN 17 Station Street, Brookline, MA 02445

Library of Congress Cataloging-in-Publication Data

Healthy slow cooker revolution : one test kitchen. 40 slow cookers. 200 fresh recipes. / by the editors at America's Test Kitchen.
    pages cm
 Includes index.
 ISBN 978-1-936493-95-1 -- ISBN 1-936493-95-0
1. Electric cooking, Slow. I. America's Test Kitchen (Firm)
 TX827.H38878 2015
 641.5'884--dc23
                          2014032533

Manufactured in the United States of America
10 9 8 7 6 5 4 3 2 1

Paperback: $26.95 US
Distributed by America's Test Kitchen
17 Station Street, Brookline, MA 02445

EDITORIAL DIRECTOR: Jack Bishop

EDITORIAL DIRECTOR, BOOKS: Elizabeth Carduff

EXECUTIVE FOOD EDITOR: Julia Collin Davison

SENIOR EDITOR: Dan Zuccarello

ASSOCIATE EDITOR: Danielle DeSiato-Hallman

EDITORIAL ASSISTANT: Kate Edeker

TEST COOKS: Lawman Johnson, Sebastian Nava, Russell Selander, and Meaghan Walsh

DESIGN DIRECTOR: Amy Klee

ART DIRECTOR: Greg Galvan

ASSOCIATE ART DIRECTOR: Taylor Argenzio

DESIGNERS: Allison Boales and Jen Kanavos Hoffman

PHOTOGRAPHY DIRECTOR: Julie Cote

ASSOCIATE ART DIRECTOR, PHOTOGRAPHY: Steve Klise

STAFF PHOTOGRAPHER: Daniel J. van Ackere

ADDITIONAL PHOTOGRAPHY: Keller + Keller and Carl Tremblay

FOOD STYLING: Jen Beauchesne, Catrine Kelty, and Marie Piraino

PHOTO SHOOT KITCHEN TEAM:
    ASSOCIATE EDITOR: Chris O'Connor
    TEST COOK: Dan Cellucci
    ASSISTANT TEST COOK: Cecelia Jenkins

PRODUCTION DIRECTOR: Guy Rochford

SENIOR PRODUCTION MANAGER: Jessica Quirk

PRODUCTION AND TRAFFIC COORDINATORS: Britt Dresser

PRODUCTION AND IMAGING SPECIALISTS: Dennis Noble, Heather Dube, and Lauren Robbins

COPYEDITOR: Barbara Wood

PROOFREADER: Ann-Marie Imbornoni

INDEXER: Elizabeth Parson

PICTURED ON FRONT COVER: Sweet and Tangy Pulled Chicken (page 94)

PICTURED OPPOSITE TITLE PAGE: Beet and Wheat Berry Salad with Arugula and Apples (page 216)

PICTURED ON BACK COVER: Warm Southwestern Lentil and Bean Salad (page 210), Braised Steaks with Root Vegetables (page 102), Turkish-Style Eggplant Casserole (page 175), Spaghetti with Meatballs Florentine (page 157), Curried Chicken Thighs with Acorn Squash (page 86), and California-Style Fish Tacos (page 136).

Contents

Welcome to America's Test Kitchen

This book has been tested, written, and edited by the folks at America's Test Kitchen, a very real 2,500-square-foot kitchen located just outside of Boston. It is the home of *Cook's Illustrated* magazine and *Cook's Country* magazine and is the Monday-through-Friday destination for more than four dozen test cooks, editors, food scientists, tasters, and cookware specialists. Our mission is to test recipes over and over again until we understand how and why they work and until we arrive at the "best" version.

We start the process of testing a recipe with a complete lack of conviction, which means that we accept no claim, no theory, no technique, and no recipe at face value. We simply assemble as many variations as possible, test a half-dozen of the most promising, and taste the results blind. We then construct our own hybrid recipe and continue to test it, varying ingredients, techniques, and cooking times until we reach a consensus. The result, we hope, is the best version of a particular recipe, but we realize that only you can be the final judge of our success (or failure). As we like to say in the test kitchen, "We make the mistakes, so you don't have to."

All of this would not be possible without a belief that good cooking, much like good music, is indeed based on a foundation of objective technique. Some people like spicy foods and others don't, but there is a right way to sauté, there is a best way to cook a pot roast, and there are measurable scientific principles involved in producing perfectly beaten, stable egg whites. This is our ultimate goal: to investigate the fundamental principles of cooking so that you become a better cook. It is as simple as that.

If you're curious to see what goes on behind the scenes at America's Test Kitchen check out our daily blog, AmericasTestKitchenFeed.com, which features kitchen snapshots, exclusive recipes, video tips, and much more. You can watch us work (in our actual test kitchen) by tuning in to *America's Test Kitchen* (AmericasTestKitchen.com) or *Cook's Country from America's Test Kitchen* (CooksCountryTV.com) on public television. Tune in to *America's Test Kitchen Radio* (AmericasTestKitchen.com) on public radio to listen to insights, tips, and techniques that illuminate the truth about real home cooking. Want to hone your cooking skills or finally learn how to bake—from an America's Test Kitchen test cook? Enroll in a cooking class at our online cooking school at OnlineCookingSchool.com. And find information about subscribing to *Cook's Illustrated* magazine at CooksIllustrated.com or *Cook's Country* magazine at CooksCountry.com. Both magazines are published every other month. However you choose to visit us, we welcome you into our kitchen, where you can stand by our side as we test our way to the best recipes in America.

FACEBOOK.COM/AMERICASTESTKITCHEN

TWITTER.COM/TESTKITCHEN

YOUTUBE.COM/AMERICASTESTKITCHEN

INSTAGRAM.COM/TESTKITCHEN

PINTEREST.COM/TESTKITCHEN

AMERICASTESTKITCHEN.TUMBLR.COM

GOOGLE.COM/+AMERICASTESTKITCHEN

Preface

In 2011, we published *Slow Cooker Revolution*, and, if I say so myself, it was a book that offered a truly revolutionary look at this appliance. (The cover featured slow-cooker lasagna after all!) We had to solve the problems with using a slow cooker—long cooking times mean that sauces become watery, flavors get washed out, and food can end up tasting dull rather than fresh. We also had to address the differences between different models of slow cookers. But, at the end of the day, we did a solid job of rethinking how to use a slow cooker in exciting new ways. We continued our kitchen work to produce *Slow Cooker Revolution: The Easy-Prep Edition*.

In the last few years, we received letters from home cooks about how to use the slow cooker to prepare healthy recipes. Now, don't get me started on "healthy." There is nothing unhealthy about beef stew or a nice bowl of spaghetti and meatballs. But these missives got us thinking about the very nature of slow cookers.

In effect, a slow cooker steams food since it is a closed environment containing liquid. This requires less fat than other cooking methods, which worked to our advantage in this new book. Of course, building flavor is always an issue in a slow cooker and that means starting out with a flavorful base, using spice rubs, and creating strong flavor combinations.

We also came up with a host of new techniques, including using parchment paper on top of rice recipes in the slow cooker. (The rice doesn't dry out.) We wrapped vegetables in cheesecloth to keep them from overcooking. And we found that low-fat cheese is poorly suited for the slow cooker—it can turn waxy and does not melt well.

Our test kitchen work on this book opened us up to a wider world of slow-cooker recipes, including seafood dishes (Halibut with Warm Bean Salad and California-Style Fish Tacos), vegetarian recipes (Stuffed Spiced Eggplants, Farro Risotto, Miso Soup, and Sweet-and-Sour Braised Swiss Chard), and healthier takes on classics (Country Beef and Vegetable Stew and Chicken with "Roasted" Garlic Sauce). We even found new ways to make salads in the slow cooker, including Beet and Wheat Berry Salad with Arugula and Apples.

I have a fascination with old tools and what the old-timers in my town used to do with them. They could split cedar to make shakes for roofing or split logs for clapboards. Of course, they also made barrels, wagons, whippletrees, and traces. In many cases, the old tools, in the right hand, could do a better job than our modern electric machinery. It's all about practice and skill.

That is a long-winded way of saying that slow cookers started out as a convenient way to cook beans. Here in the test kitchen, we used to view slow cookers as special occasion appliances, but now we think of them like a good tool—in the right hands, with the right experience, you can cook almost anything and cook it well. And, as it turns out, you can also produce wholesome, fresh food.

Practicality is the essence of the slow cooker; there is very little last-minute cooking and it forces you to plan ahead. Plus, one doesn't need a battery of pots and pans—recipes call for either just the slow cooker or perhaps one other pan or appliance (a skillet or microwave). This aligns with one of the key elements of home cooking: an eye for sensible food preparation.

That reminds me of a story about a very practical Vermont farmer. He wanted to purchase a train ticket to Littleton. The ticket agent told him that it would be two dollars. He then asked, "Well, then, how much for a cow?" The answer? Three dollars. "How much for a pig, then?" The answer? One dollar. "Book me as a pig," said the old-timer.

So there you have it—fresh, healthy food from a slow cooker and all with an eye for practical home cooking. We think that you'll be more than happy with the results.

CHRISTOPHER KIMBALL
Founder and Editor,
Cook's Illustrated and *Cook's Country*
Host, *America's Test Kitchen* and
Cook's Country from America's Test Kitchen

Slow Cooker 101

Introduction

After developing hundreds of slow-cooker recipes in our test kitchen and publishing two bestselling books, we have learned a thing or two about making the most of this handy appliance. With this latest book, we narrowed our focus and set what we thought would be a tough hurdle for ourselves: develop a collection of 200 decidedly fresh and healthy recipes packed with vegetables and hearty grains. We also wanted a high percentage of the recipes to be easy prep, meaning that it would take no more than 15 minutes of active time (and no stovetop work) before you could press the start button on your slow cooker and walk away. (Look for the easy prep icons throughout the book for the more than 100 recipes you can get into the slow cooker in a flash.) A plentiful selection of vegetarian recipes was another goal, so throughout the book you will see icons for these options as well.

So what did we learn? First, that making healthy meals, sides, and desserts in a slow cooker isn't as hard as you might think because its moist, gentle heat allows you to cook with less fat. The challenge lies in infusing dishes with bold flavor without relying on fatty ingredients to do so. In some cases, we started by getting out a skillet and building a flavorful sauce or base for a dish rather than simply adding ingredients to the slow cooker; this made all the difference between a recipe that was just OK and one that had deep, rich flavor. We chose leaner cuts of meat and boosted their flavor with spice rubs or glazes and, in some cases, stovetop browning. And we learned how to make flavorful sides that could cook alongside chicken or meat, often adding fresh vegetables, herbs, or a simple vinaigrette for bright flavor.

The slow cooker is great for cooking grains and beans, so it was easy to build hearty dishes with lentils, bulgur, quinoa, polenta, and more as the star ingredient. It is also an excellent way to poach many kinds of fish; the risk of overcooking is minimized, and it allows you to infuse the fish with subtle flavor. Healthy desserts benefit from this steamy environment, too, as it mimics a traditional water bath and ensures that normally finicky custards like flan and cheesecake cook to the perfect creamy and silky texture, with no need to obsessively monitor the oven.

When using this book, you may need to think somewhat differently about the slow cooker and how it fits your lifestyle. Chicken, fish, and leaner cuts of meat just cannot withstand a full day in the slow cooker. There are certainly many recipes that can cook while you are at work, but the majority of the recipes have shorter cooking times; we think the trade-off is worth it if you want to eat more healthfully.

Getting Started

Despite all the testing we have done to make these recipes foolproof, using a slow cooker isn't an exact science; the issue is that heating power varies tremendously among brands of slow cookers. So as you are making the recipes in this book, here are a few things you need to know.

USING THE TIME RANGES

In general, for the recipes in this book we give either 1- or 2-hour ranges (and a wide array of cooking times) as guidelines for how long a recipe should be cooked. More delicate and exacting recipes using fish and leaner cuts of meat have the shorter time range (and shorter cooking times); we found this narrower range to be more reliable. We recommend that the first time you make one of these recipes you check for doneness at the lower end of the range.

GETTING TO KNOW YOUR SLOW COOKER

While all ovens set to 350 degrees will perform the same (assuming all the ovens are properly calibrated), temperatures vary widely among slow cookers. We tested more than a dozen models and prepared every recipe in this book in two different models. Some models run hot and fast, while others heat more slowly and gently. Most models perform best on low, but again it's hard to make blanket statements that apply to all slow cookers. In our testing, we have found that some slow cookers run hot or cool on just one of the settings (either low or high). This is where the cook's experience comes into play. If you have been using a slow cooker for some time, ask yourself if recipes are generally done at the low or high end of the cooking times provided in recipes. The answer should tell you whether you have a "fast" slow cooker or a "slow" model. If you are just getting started with your slow cooker, check all recipes at the beginning of the time range, but allow some extra time to cook food longer if necessary.

MATCHING RECIPES TO SLOW-COOKER SIZES

Slow cookers come in a variety of sizes, from the ridiculously small (1 quart) to the very big (7 quarts or more). In general, we like 6-quart models. That said, we tested our recipes in slow cookers of different sizes. Each recipe in this book includes the size range that will work for that particular recipe, though the majority of the recipes work with 4- to 7-quart slow cookers. Note that some recipes must be made in a large slow cooker (at least 5½ quarts) or you run the risk of overfilling the insert. The shape of the slow cooker also matters for some of our recipes: Oval slow cookers are needed to accommodate some roasts, casseroles, and braised vegetable dishes—they just won't fit in a round slow cooker. If you don't know the size of your slow cooker, check the underside of the insert (where the size is usually stamped), or simply measure how much water it takes to fill the insert to just above the lip.

KEEPING FOOD SAFE

Using a slow cooker is a safe way to cook food, but there are few things to keep in mind to ensure it is a safe process. First, make sure your slow cooker and your utensils have been properly cleaned. Do not let your meat or fish sit out on the counter for any length of time before adding them to the slow cooker. And never put frozen food into your slow cooker as this greatly increases the risk that your food will not reach a safe bacteria-killing temperature. You should also follow our guidelines in recipes where we specify the doneness temperature of meat, fish, or poultry. It is advisable to keep the slow-cooker lid in place as this traps the heat and helps the slow cooker reach the ideal temperature zone.

Making Healthy Food in Your Slow Cooker

To meet our goal of developing healthy recipes using a slow cooker, we had to find ways of building flavor without adding excess fat while also packing more hearty grains and vegetables into our recipes. Here's what we learned.

CHOOSE THE RIGHT CUT AND TRIM CAREFULLY
Once trimmed, cuts like chuck roast, eye-round roast, and blade steaks are good choices when you're trying to eat healthy, especially in recipes with a high ratio of vegetables to meat. Chicken is a great choice, too, and we used boneless, skinless breasts, bone-in breasts, and meaty chicken thighs; make sure to remove the skin from bone-in breasts and thighs, which will drastically reduce fat and calories. Pork loin and pork tenderloins are especially lean when trimmed, though we leave a ⅛-inch fat cap on pork loins for flavor.

GET OUT YOUR SKILLET (SOMETIMES)
When recipes are leaner, building a flavorful base is key. Browning aromatics, vegetables, and meat creates a flavorful fond in the bottom of the pan that, when deglazed with wine or broth, provides the basis for a rich sauce. And browning some roasts like pork loin or eye-round roast adds extra flavor and attractive color. The additional 10 minutes or so it takes to do this will make all the difference in many recipes, such as Country Beef and Vegetable Stew, Old-Fashioned Chicken Stew, and Pork Loin with Warm Spiced Chickpea Salad.

BE SMART ABOUT OIL AND BUTTER
We found that a teaspoon or two of canola oil was all that was necessary to properly sauté aromatics, vegetables, or meat in a skillet. To add richness to a dish at the end of cooking, we often turned to extra-virgin olive oil—drizzling a little over a finished grain, vegetable, or pasta dish made a big impact without tipping the scales. As for butter, there are times when there is no substitute for its nutty richness; by adding just a little to our Garlicky Braised Greens, the dish became creamy and satisfying.

USE THE MICROWAVE
When there is no need to get out a skillet, we used the microwave to soften aromatics and vegetables and bloom spices. This helped us use a minimum of fat because we found that, in general, we needed to add only a teaspoon of vegetable oil; stirring the mixture partway though cooking ensured that everything softened properly. The microwave also came in handy when it was necessary to steam vegetables before adding them to the finished dish; when making simple glazes or sauces; and for heating up last-minute additions to a recipe, like coconut milk.

BUILD LAYERS OF FLAVOR
Lean meats and fish need a flavor boost, especially when they are cooked in a moist heat environment where there is no opportunity for flavorful browning or caramelizing. We found many ways to add flavor: Pungent spice rubs add flavor and appealing color; sauces made by reducing flavorful cooking liquids add richness without much fat; glazes made with fruit preserves and other ingredients coat meat surprisingly well; lively vinaigrettes, relishes, and chutneys can be made while the food cooks and make all the difference in the finished dish without adding much in the way of calories or fat.

WAIT TO ADD FRESH INGREDIENTS

Certain ingredients need just a short stint in the slow cooker to warm through and meld into the dish. Delicate vegetables and other ingredients, such as rice noodles, frozen peas, baby spinach, escarole, and corn, turned mushy or lackluster when cooked for hours in the slow cooker, so we stirred them in at the end, letting them heat briefly until perfectly cooked.

MAKE IT A HEALTHY MEAL

Through extensive testing, we sorted out which sides, such as potatoes, bulgur, quinoa, barley, couscous, and canned beans, could cook alongside proteins or could cook quickly in the cooking liquid left behind (this was true with couscous). In some instances vegetables needed to be wrapped in a foil packet to stay tender, while in others, they cooked in a flavorful broth along with the meat or fish, soaking up big flavor along the way.

CREATE AN ULTRASTEAMY ENVIRONMENT

Some recipes, like Stuffed Sole with Creamy Tomato Sauce, Swordfish with Papaya Salsa, and California-Style Fish Tacos, are more foolproof when made in the slow cooker because they cook more gently. To harness the power of the slow cooker for these and similar recipes for fish, we created a simple and flavorful poaching liquid with wine and aromatics, elevating the fish on slices of citrus. As the slow cooker heated up, the liquid steamed the fish perfectly. For recipes like Mashed Potatoes and Root Vegetables, we took things a step further by placing a sheet of parchment paper over the vegetables to trap the steam and cook them through perfectly. The slow cooker functions as a water bath, too, cooking finicky desserts like flan, cheesecake, and crème brûlée so they emerge with the perfect silky-smooth texture.

GIVE RECIPES A FRESH FINISH

Throughout the book you will find easy-to-make sauces and toppings using healthy and nutritious ingredients. For some recipes, like our Moroccan Lentil Soup with Mustard Greens or Turkish-Style Eggplant Casserole, the difference between a merely good recipe and a great one is the finishing touch, in the form of a healthy but lively sauce or topping that takes just minutes to whip together; for both of these recipes we made a lively topping with Greek yogurt, fresh herbs, and other seasonings.

USE LOWER-FAT CHEESE (SOMETIMES)

Some low-fat cheeses turn grainy in the moist heat of the slow cooker, especially when used as a topping—which is why we sometimes reached for a full-fat cheese when meltability was key. Hard cheeses like Parmesan and Asiago added big flavor with few calories and were a winning choice for many recipes. Fresh cheeses, like feta, goat, and *queso fresco*, are a healthy way to add big flavor and texture to casseroles and many other dishes.

BE MINDFUL OF SODIUM

We understand that many people need to watch their sodium intake, so we used a minimum of salt in our recipes and left the seasoning at the end up to you. But the real culprits in terms of sodium are ingredients like commercial broths, canned tomatoes, and canned beans, all of which tend to have fairly high levels of sodium per cup (see page 25). For recipes including these ingredients, if the sodium level per serving was above 600 mg, we have provided the sodium level should you choose low-sodium or no-salt-added alternatives. Of course you can also choose not to add the salt we specify in the recipes if you want to lower the sodium even further.

The Test Kitchen's Guide to Buying a Slow Cooker

Today's slow cookers come in a wide array of sizes with lots of different features. We wondered whether the new generation of slow cookers, many with jazzy new features promising easier, better food, could really deliver. To find out which models performed best and which features really mattered, we chose seven slow cookers, all digital, 6 to 6½ quarts. We used these models to prepare finicky pasta, meaty chili, and delicate boneless, skinless chicken breasts. None of the new technology impressed us, but we did find a model that improved slow cooking at its core, with more even cooking and a few perks like satisfyingly clickable buttons, brighter lights, helpful beeps, and cool-to-the-touch handles: the KitchenAid 6-Quart Slow Cooker.

In addition to testing large slow cookers, we also tested smaller 4-quart slow cookers; they are handy for recipes scaled for two, though we found in our recipe testing that this size of slow cooker is quite versatile and can actually be used for many of the other recipes throughout this book. Our top slow cookers, both large and small, are listed below in order of preference within each category.

LARGE SLOW COOKERS

HIGHLY RECOMMENDED

	CRITERIA		TESTERS' COMMENTS
 **KITCHENAID 6-Quart Slow Cooker with Solid Glass Lid** MODEL: KSC6223SS PRICE: $99.99 CONTROLS: Digital programmable	COOKING DESIGN	★★★ ★★★	This slow cooker made juicy and tender chicken, turkey, and pork, and chili and caramelized onions were rich and evenly cooked. Testers preferred its bright, intuitive control panel, with tactile buttons and cheerful beeps that alert you to changes. Cool-to-the-touch handles were a bonus, too.

RECOMMENDED

	CRITERIA		TESTERS' COMMENTS
 **CROCK-POT Countdown Touch-screen Digital Slow Cooker** MODEL: SCVT650-PS PRICE: $89.99 CONTROLS: Digital programmable	COOKING DESIGN	★★½ ★★★	Our previous winner performed admirably again with an intuitive and attractive control panel. It made food well, but it runs slightly hot; in a runoff against our new winner, it burned caramelized onions and made acceptable, but drier, chicken breasts.

RECOMMENDED WITH RESERVATIONS

	CRITERIA		TESTERS' COMMENTS
HAMILTON BEACH Set 'n Forget 6 Qt. Programmable Slow Cooker with Spoon/ Lid MODEL: 33967 PRICE: $59.99 CONTROLS: Digital programmable	COOKING DESIGN	★★½ ★★	This model's thermometer sticks through the lid and into meat. You program the type of meat, and once the cut reaches a safe temperature, the cooker switches to warming mode. But because it checks the temperature in only one spot and slow cookers often cook unevenly because of their side-located heating elements, this slow cooker often shut off before the meat was fully cooked. Otherwise, it had a nice control panel and cooked well without the probe.

RECOMMENDED WITH RESERVATIONS	CRITERIA		TESTERS' COMMENTS
 **CROCK-POT Digital Slow Cooker with iStir Stirring System** MODEL: SCCPVC600AS-P PRICE: $69.99 CONTROLS: Digital programmable	COOKING DESIGN	★★ ★★	This slow cooker has a removable stirring system that made rich chili but didn't prevent scorching in a thick pasta dish because it stirs food only in the middle, not at the edges near the heat. It was hard to tell if the machine was on if we weren't using the brightly lit timer.
 **CROCK-POT Slow Cooker featuring Smart Cook Technology** MODEL: SCCPVM650-PS PRICE: $99.99 CONTROLS: Digital programmable	COOKING DESIGN	★½ ★★	This slow cooker has a user-friendly control panel and was the more intuitive of the two machines that rev up the heat faster or slower so your meal is ready when you choose, but we still had mixed results. When we set the time and temperature, this cooker ran slightly hot, and testers noted minor scorching.
 **HAMILTON BEACH IntelliTime 6 Quart Slow Cooker** MODEL: 33564 PRICE: $59.99 CONTROLS: Digital programmable	COOKING DESIGN	★★ ★½	This slow cooker also adjusts the heat to lengthen or shorten recipe cooking times. It cooked food well when we set the time and temperature, but the IntelliTime settings were hit or miss. Its controls are on one round dial that you spin to set, which testers found counter intuitive.

SMALL SLOW COOKERS

RECOMMENDED

	CRITERIA		TESTERS' COMMENTS
 **CUISINART 4-Quart Cook Central 3-in-1 Multicooker** MODEL: MSC-400 PRICE: $129.95 CONTROLS: Digital programmable	COOKING DESIGN	★★★ ★★★	This new "multicooker"—a slow cooker that can also brown, sauté, and steam—produced perfect chicken, steaks, and ribs. Its programmable timer can be set to cook for up to 24 hours, then automatically switches to "keep warm." We liked its lightweight, easy-clean, sturdy metal insert with extra-large handles and its oval shape, clear lid, and intuitive controls. The browning function is a nice plus for searing food or reducing sauces.
 **HAMILTON BEACH Stay or Go 4-Quart Slow Cooker** MODEL: 33246T PRICE: $26.99 CONTROLS: Manual **BEST BUY**	COOKING DESIGN	★★★ ★★	This cooker performed well, producing perfect ribs, steak, and chicken. A gasket and clips on the lid let you take your cooker to a potluck without risking spills. It's comparatively low-tech: The "off," "low," "high," and "warm" settings are on a manual dial—which is its drawback. You can't set it to turn off or switch to "keep warm" on its own.

RECOMMENDED WITH RESERVATIONS

	CRITERIA		TESTERS' COMMENTS
 **WEST BEND 4-Quart Oval Crockery Cooker** MODEL: 84384 PRICE: $29.99 CONTROLS: Manual	COOKING DESIGN	★★ ★½	This model performed fine with chicken and cooked steak to tenderness (although the sauce scorched slightly). But ribs developed a leathery crust wherever they touched the hot bottom of the insert.

Soups

● EASY PREP   ● VEGETARIAN

Beef and Garden Vegetable Soup

Serves 6 • **Cooking Time** 8 to 10 hours on Low or 5 to 7 hours on High • **Slow Cooker Size** 4 to 7 Quarts

✔ **WHY THIS RECIPE WORKS:** It's rare that you find a vegetable-packed soup that also features tender, juicy chunks of beef, but this slow-cooker version does just that. Because the meat simmers for hours in the slow cooker, it infuses the fragrant broth with beefy flavor. We started with lean beef chuck roast (which we found to be the best cut for stews and soups) and trimmed it of all visible fat before cutting it into 1-inch pieces. To build flavor without adding fat, we doctored chicken broth with dried porcini mushrooms, tomato paste, and soy sauce for depth and sweetness. While most beef soups go heavy on the meat and light on the vegetables, we increased the amount of vegetables to add substance to the soup. One final touch perfected our beef and vegetable soup recipe: Steaming green beans in the microwave with a little bit of water and adding them at the end of cooking ensured that they were not overcooked and stayed crisp and green. After trimming the beef, you should have 1 pound of usable meat.

2	onions, chopped fine
3	tablespoons tomato paste
1	tablespoon minced fresh thyme or 1 teaspoon dried
4	garlic cloves, minced
¼	ounce dried porcini mushrooms, rinsed and minced
1	teaspoon canola oil
6	cups chicken broth
4	carrots, peeled and cut into ½-inch pieces
1	(14.5-ounce) can diced tomatoes
2	teaspoons low-sodium soy sauce
	Salt and pepper
1½	pounds boneless beef chuck-eye roast, trimmed of all visible fat and cut into 1-inch pieces
8	ounces green beans, trimmed and cut on bias into 1-inch lengths
¼	cup chopped fresh basil

1. Microwave onions, tomato paste, thyme, garlic, mushrooms, and oil in bowl, stirring occasionally, until onions are softened, about 5 minutes; transfer to slow cooker. Stir in broth, carrots, tomatoes and their juice, soy sauce, and ½ teaspoon salt, then stir in beef. Cover and cook until beef is tender, 8 to 10 hours on low or 5 to 7 hours on high.

2. Microwave green beans with 1 tablespoon water in covered bowl, stirring occasionally, until tender, 4 to 6 minutes. Drain green beans, then stir into soup along with basil. Season with salt and pepper to taste. Serve.

Per 2-cup serving: Cal 200; Fat 4.5g; Sat Fat 1.5g; Chol 50mg; Carb 19g; Protein 24g; Fiber 5g; Sodium 1100mg *To reduce sodium level to 550mg, use unsalted broth and no-salt-added tomatoes.

QUICK PREP TIP
CUTTING CHUCK-EYE ROAST
Pull apart roast at its major seams (delineated by lines of fat and silverskin), using knife as necessary. Then trim off excess fat and silverskin and cut meat into pieces as directed in recipe. If you are unable to find smaller roasts (such as the one in this recipe), the meat can be trimmed, cut, and stored in the freezer for up to one month.

Chicken and Wild Rice Soup

Serves 6 • **Cooking Time** 3 to 5 hours on Low • **Slow Cooker Size** 4 to 7 Quarts

✓ WHY THIS RECIPE WORKS: Building a rich and savory chicken and wild rice soup in our slow cooker with little fat required an additional flavor-building step—getting out our skillet to sauté onion and carrots. The browned vegetables, along with tomato paste, garlic, and thyme, provided us with a deep base, and deglazing the pan with wine captured all the flavorful browned bits in the pan. This simple step made a world of difference in both the flavor and color of our soup, and we needed to use only a small amount of oil. Lean, bone-in chicken breasts worked perfectly here as the bones helped the chicken retain its moisture during the long cooking time. To ensure the perfect balance of moist chicken and tender rice, we removed and shredded the chicken at the end of the cooking time, turned the heat to high, and cooked the rice before adding the shredded chicken. Finishing with a small amount of parsley added freshness to the soup. We like the flavor of wild rice in this soup; however, you can substitute 1 cup of long-grain white rice.

1 teaspoon canola oil
1 onion, chopped fine
3 carrots, peeled and sliced ¼ inch thick
2 tablespoons tomato paste
4 garlic cloves, minced
2 teaspoons minced fresh thyme or ½ teaspoon dried
¼ cup dry white wine
6 cups chicken broth
1 fennel bulb, stalks discarded, bulb halved, cored, and cut into ½-inch pieces
2 bay leaves
 Salt and pepper
2 (12-ounce) bone-in split chicken breasts, skin removed, trimmed of all visible fat
⅓ cup long-grain white rice and wild rice blend
2 tablespoons minced fresh parsley

1. Heat oil in 12-inch skillet over medium heat until shimmering. Add onion and carrots and cook until vegetables are softened and lightly browned, 10 to 12 minutes. Stir in tomato paste, garlic, and thyme and cook until fragrant, about 30 seconds. Stir in wine, scraping up any browned bits; transfer to slow cooker.

2. Stir broth, fennel, bay leaves, and ½ teaspoon salt into slow cooker. Nestle chicken into slow cooker, cover, and cook until chicken is tender, 3 to 5 hours on low.

3. Transfer chicken to carving board, let cool slightly, then shred into bite-size pieces using 2 forks; discard bones. Discard bay leaves. Stir rice into soup, cover, and cook on high until tender, 30 to 40 minutes.

4. Stir in shredded chicken and let sit until heated through, about 5 minutes. Stir in parsley and season with salt and pepper to taste. Serve.

Per 1⅔-cup serving: Cal 200; Fat 3g; Sat Fat 0g; Chol 45mg; Carb 20g; Protein 22g; Fiber 3g; Sodium 1010mg *To reduce sodium level to 630mg, use unsalted broth.

QUICK PREP TIP
SHREDDING MEAT
To shred poultry, beef, or pork into bite-size pieces or large chunks, simply insert 2 forks (tines facing down) into cooked meat and gently pull meat apart.

Asian Chicken Noodle Soup with Bok Choy

Serves 6 • **Cooking Time** 3 to 5 hours on Low • **Slow Cooker Size** 4 to 7 Quarts

☑ **WHY THIS RECIPE WORKS:** To craft our own lean take on Asian chicken soup, we turned to chicken broth and a small amount of soy sauce for the base and infused it with flavor from a hefty dose of aromatics and sesame oil bloomed in the microwave. We used lean, bone-in chicken breasts, which lent good flavor to the soup and stayed tender during hours of slow cooking. We poached the chicken in the broth on low, and it slowly absorbed the assertive flavors of the aromatics. After removing the chicken from the soup to shred it, we added delicate rice noodles, which worked perfectly in the slow cooker, since the soup does not come to a boil and the noodles are able to cook gently. To round out the dish we added shiitake mushrooms and bok choy at the end of cooking with the rice noodles. Using ¼-inch-wide rice noodles is important for the success of this soup; do not substitute other types of noodles. Be sure not to overcook the rice noodles or else they will become mushy.

3   **tablespoons grated fresh ginger**

4   **garlic cloves, minced**

2   **teaspoons toasted sesame oil**

8   **cups chicken broth**

3   **tablespoons low-sodium soy sauce, plus extra for seasoning**

2   **(12-ounce) bone-in split chicken breasts, skin removed, trimmed of all visible fat**

2   **heads baby bok choy (4 ounces each), sliced ½ inch thick**

8   **ounces shiitake mushrooms, stemmed and sliced thin**

4   **ounces (¼-inch-wide) rice noodles**
    Salt and pepper

1. Microwave 2 tablespoons ginger, garlic, and oil in bowl, stirring occasionally, until fragrant, about 1 minute; transfer to slow cooker. Stir in broth and soy sauce. Nestle chicken into slow cooker, cover, and cook until chicken is tender, 3 to 5 hours on low.

2. Transfer chicken to carving board, let cool slightly, then shred into bite-size pieces using 2 forks; discard bones. Stir bok choy, mushrooms, and noodles into soup, cover, and cook on high until noodles are tender, 20 to 30 minutes.

3. Stir in shredded chicken and remaining 1 tablespoon ginger and let sit until heated through, about 5 minutes. Season with salt, pepper, and extra soy sauce to taste. Serve.

Per 2-cup serving: Cal 210; Fat 3.5g; Sat Fat 0.5g; Chol 45mg; Carb 22g; Protein 23g; Fiber 1g; Sodium 1060mg *To reduce sodium level to 560mg, use unsalted broth.

SMART SHOPPING FLAT RICE NOODLES
This delicate pasta, made from rice flour and water, is used in a variety of dishes in Southeast Asia and southern China. Typically these noodles are steeped in hot water to soften them (they overcook quickly, so boiling tends to make them mushy), making them ideal for our Asian-style slow-cooker soups. Flat rice noodles come in several widths; we use ¼-inch-wide noodles in our recipes, which we find cook through the most evenly.

Southwestern Chicken Soup

Serves 6 • **Cooking Time** 3 to 5 hours on Low • **Slow Cooker Size** 4 to 7 Quarts

✓ WHY THIS RECIPE WORKS: To put a Southwestern spin on a healthy slow-cooker chicken soup, we built a flavorful base by skillet-browning our aromatics in a small amount of oil. This gave us the full robust flavor and complexity we were seeking and could not achieve by using the microwave alone. To give this soup a little heat, we sautéed a jalapeño chile with the onions before stirring in smoky chipotle chile, tomato paste, and spices. Deglazing the pan with a little chicken broth ensured that all the rich brown bits ended up in the slow cooker. As we slowly cooked our bone-in skinless chicken breasts, this spicy, tomatoey broth infused the meat with flavor without causing its texture to deteriorate. The addition of hominy contributed to the heartiness of this lean dish and added body to the broth. For fresh flavor and crunch we garnished each bowl with thinly sliced radishes and cilantro.

1 teaspoon canola oil

2 onions, chopped fine

1 jalapeño chile, stemmed, seeded, and minced

3 tablespoons tomato paste

4 garlic cloves, minced

1 tablespoon minced canned chipotle chile in adobo sauce

1 tablespoon minced fresh oregano or 1 teaspoon dried

2 teaspoons ground cumin

4 cups chicken broth

1 (15-ounce) can white or yellow hominy, rinsed

1 (14.5-ounce) can diced tomatoes

1 red bell pepper, stemmed, seeded, and cut into ½-inch pieces
Salt and pepper

2 (12-ounce) bone-in split chicken breasts, skin removed, trimmed of all visible fat

½ cup fresh cilantro leaves

4 radishes, trimmed and sliced thin

1. Heat oil in 12-inch skillet over medium heat until shimmering. Add onions and jalapeño and cook until vegetables are softened, about 5 minutes. Stir in tomato paste, garlic, chipotle, oregano, and cumin and cook until fragrant, about 30 seconds. Stir in 1 cup broth, scraping up any browned bits; transfer to slow cooker.

2. Stir remaining 3 cups broth, hominy, tomatoes and their juice, bell pepper, and ½ teaspoon salt into slow cooker. Nestle chicken into slow cooker, cover, and cook until chicken is tender, 3 to 5 hours on low.

3. Transfer chicken to carving board, let cool slightly, then shred into bite-size pieces using 2 forks; discard bones. Stir shredded chicken into soup and let sit until heated through, about 5 minutes. Season with salt and pepper to taste. Top individual portions with cilantro and radishes before serving.

Per 1⅔-cup serving: Cal 190; Fat 3.5g; Sat Fat 0.5g; Chol 45mg; Carb 19g; Protein 21g; Fiber 4g; Sodium 1040mg *To reduce sodium level to 620mg, use unsalted broth and no-salt-added tomatoes.

SMART SHOPPING HOMINY
Hominy is made from dried corn kernels that have been soaked (or cooked) in an alkaline solution (commonly lime water or calcium hydroxide) to remove the germ and hull. It has a slightly chewy texture and toasted-corn flavor and is widely used in soups, stews, and chilis throughout southern North America and Central and South America. Given its sturdy texture, hominy can easily withstand hours of simmering and is perfectly suited for the slow cooker. It is sold both dried and canned; however, we prefer the convenience of canned hominy, which requires only a quick rinse before using.

Thai-Style Chicken and Coconut Soup

Serves 6 • **Cooking Time** 3 to 5 hours on Low • **Slow Cooker Size** 4 to 7 Quarts

✓WHY THIS RECIPE WORKS: Since the star of this aromatic Thai soup is the broth, we set out to make it rich and flavorful. After some initial testing, we decided to skip over homemade Thai curry paste, which was a time-consuming and ingredient-intensive endeavor, and reached for the store-bought variety. Using a generous amount of curry paste and blooming it with onions and oil in the microwave worked to deepen the base flavors. For our protein, we added chicken and infused it with rich flavor by poaching the breasts on low in the broth before shredding the meat. To round out our Thai-style soup, we included bell peppers, snow peas, and mushrooms. Quickly steaming the vegetables in the microwave with a small amount of water and adding them to the soup just before serving ensured that they remained fresh and crisp. Stirring in light coconut milk at the end preserved the soup's clean, fresh taste and added richness without excess fat.

2 **onions, chopped fine**

3 **tablespoons Thai red curry paste**

1 **teaspoon canola oil**

4 **cups chicken broth**

1 **tablespoon fish sauce, plus extra for seasoning**
   Salt and pepper

2 **(12-ounce) bone-in split chicken breasts, skin removed, trimmed of all visible fat**

2 **red bell peppers, stemmed, seeded, and cut into ½-inch pieces**

8 **ounces snow peas, strings removed, cut into 1-inch pieces**

8 **ounces white mushrooms, trimmed and quartered**

1 **(13.5-ounce) can light coconut milk**

½ **cup fresh cilantro leaves**

1 **tablespoon lime juice, plus extra for seasoning**

1. Microwave onions, curry paste, and oil in bowl, stirring occasionally, until onions are softened, about 5 minutes; transfer to slow cooker. Stir in broth, fish sauce, and ½ teaspoon salt. Nestle chicken into slow cooker, cover, and cook until chicken is tender, 3 to 5 hours on low.

2. Transfer chicken to carving board, let cool slightly, then shred into bite-size pieces using 2 forks; discard bones.

3. Microwave bell peppers, snow peas, and mushrooms with 1 tablespoon water in covered bowl, stirring occasionally, until tender, 4 to 6 minutes. Drain vegetables, then stir into soup.

4. Microwave coconut milk in bowl until hot, about 2 minutes. Stir into soup along with shredded chicken and let sit until heated through, about 5 minutes. Stir in cilantro and lime juice and season with salt, pepper, extra fish sauce, and extra lime juice to taste. Serve.

Per 1⅔-cup serving: Cal 190; Fat 5g; Sat Fat 2.5g; Chol 45mg; Carb 15g; Protein 22g; Fiber 3g; Sodium 1030mg *To reduce sodium level to 780mg, use unsalted broth.

SMART SHOPPING CURRY PASTE
Curry pastes, which can be either green or red, are a key ingredient for adding deep, well-rounded flavor to Thai curries. They are made from a mix of lemon grass, kaffir lime leaves, shrimp paste, ginger, garlic, chiles (fresh green Thai chiles for green curry paste and dried red Thai chiles for red curry paste), and other spices. So it's not surprising that making curry paste at home can be quite a chore. We have found that the store-bought variety does a fine job and saves significant time in terms of both shopping and prep. It is usually sold in small jars next to other Thai ingredients at the supermarket. Be aware that these pastes can vary in spiciness depending on the brand, so use more or less as desired.

Hearty Turkey Soup with Swiss Chard

Serves 6 • **Cooking Time** 6 to 8 hours on Low • **Slow Cooker Size** 4 to 7 Quarts

✔ **WHY THIS RECIPE WORKS:** Here, the hearty turkey delivers a full-flavored soup without requiring a lot of extra steps. Turkey thighs (which we preferred for this soup) have more fat than turkey breast, but we found that the flavor of dark thigh meat was worth the few extra grams of fat. To complement the meaty turkey, we microwaved leeks and colorful chard stems to bring out their sweetness, which added valuable depth to the broth. Chopped chard leaves were added during the last 20 minutes of cooking for an earthy, colorful contrast. Orzo was the perfect addition to this soup, adding substance and cooking in the same amount of time as the chard. You can substitute an equal amount of chicken thighs for the turkey; however, the cooking time will need to be reduced to 4 to 6 hours on low.

8 **ounces Swiss chard, stems chopped, leaves cut into 1-inch pieces**

3 **leeks, white and light green parts only, halved lengthwise, sliced ¼ inch thick, and washed thoroughly**

1 **teaspoon canola oil**

1 **teaspoon minced fresh thyme or ¼ teaspoon dried**

8 **cups chicken broth**

2 **carrots, peeled and cut into ½-inch pieces**

2 **bay leaves**
  Salt and pepper

2 **pounds bone-in turkey thighs, skin removed, trimmed of all visible fat**

¼ **cup orzo**

1. Microwave chard stems, leeks, oil, and thyme in bowl, stirring occasionally, until vegetables are softened, about 5 minutes; transfer to slow cooker. Stir in broth, carrots, bay leaves, and ½ teaspoon salt. Nestle turkey into slow cooker, cover, and cook until turkey is tender, 6 to 8 hours on low.

2. Transfer turkey to carving board, let cool slightly, then shred into bite-size pieces using 2 forks; discard bones. Discard bay leaves. Stir orzo and chard leaves into soup, cover, and cook on high until orzo is tender, 20 to 30 minutes.

3. Stir in shredded turkey and let sit until heated through, about 5 minutes. Season with salt and pepper to taste. Serve.

Per 2-cup serving: Cal 190; Fat 3g; Sat Fat 0.5g; Chol 60mg; Carb 17g; Protein 25g; Fiber 2g; Sodium 980mg *To reduce sodium level to 470mg, use unsalted broth.

QUICK PREP TIP **PREPARING LEEKS**
Trim and discard root and dark green leaves. Cut trimmed leek in half lengthwise, then slice it crosswise into pieces as directed in recipe. Rinse cut leeks thoroughly to remove all dirt and sand using either salad spinner or bowl of water.

Italian Meatball and Escarole Soup

Serves 6 • **Cooking Time** 4 to 6 hours on Low • **Slow Cooker Size** 4 to 7 Quarts

✓ **WHY THIS RECIPE WORKS:** Hearty beans, delicate meatballs, and wilted greens make for a classic Italian soup, but timing the dish in a slow cooker took extra care. While most bean-based soups start with cooking dried beans for hours before adding the meatballs, this just would not work in the slow cooker. So rather than settle for a soup with tough meatballs or undercooked beans, we reached for canned beans and broth. To create our rich Italian-style broth we added some classic ingredients: onion, garlic, and red pepper flakes. For the meatballs we decided to use ground turkey, which was lean but still full of flavor. To protect the lean meat from drying out, we mixed it with a panade (a combination of bread and milk) as well as some Parmesan cheese and an egg yolk for flavor and richness. Searing the meatballs in a skillet before adding them to the slow cooker allowed them to keep their shape and added a browned, meaty flavor to the broth. Since we had the skillet out, we took the opportunity to brown our aromatics to further enhance their flavor. Escarole, stirred in toward the end, rounded out our soup perfectly, adding freshness and color. Be sure to use 93 percent lean ground turkey, not ground turkey breast (also labeled 99 percent fat free).

2   slices hearty white sandwich bread, torn into quarters
¼   cup whole milk
1   pound 93 percent lean ground turkey
1   ounce Parmesan cheese, grated (½ cup)
3   tablespoons minced fresh parsley
1   large egg yolk
4   garlic cloves, minced
1½ teaspoons minced fresh oregano or ½ teaspoon dried
    Salt and pepper
2   teaspoons canola oil
1   onion, chopped fine
¼   teaspoon red pepper flakes
6   cups chicken broth
1   (15-ounce) can cannellini beans, rinsed
1   head escarole (1 pound), trimmed and sliced 1 inch thick

1. Mash bread and milk into paste in large bowl using fork. Mix in turkey, Parmesan, parsley, egg yolk, half of garlic, oregano, and ½ teaspoon pepper using hands. Pinch off and roll mixture into tablespoon-size meatballs (about 24 meatballs total).

2. Heat 1 teaspoon oil in 12-inch nonstick skillet over medium heat until shimmering. Brown half of meatballs well on all sides, about 5 minutes; transfer to slow cooker. Repeat with remaining 1 teaspoon oil and remaining meatballs; transfer to slow cooker.

3. Add onion to fat left in skillet and cook over medium heat until softened, 3 to 5 minutes. Stir in pepper flakes and remaining garlic and cook until fragrant, about 30 seconds; transfer to slow cooker. Stir in broth, beans, and ¼ teaspoon salt. Cover and cook until meatballs are tender, 4 to 6 hours on low.

4. Stir in escarole, cover, and cook on high until tender, 15 to 20 minutes. Season with salt and pepper to taste. Serve.

Per 2-cup serving: Cal 260; Fat 9g; Sat Fat 3g; Chol 80mg; Carb 18g; Protein 26g; Fiber 5g; Sodium 940mg *To reduce sodium level to 450mg, use unsalted broth and low-sodium beans.

SMART SHOPPING ESCAROLE
Escarole is a leafy green that looks much like green leaf lettuce. Its bitter flavor makes it a great choice for peppery salads. But unlike lettuce, escarole stands up well to cooking, which makes it a great addition to this hearty soup. Make sure to slice the escarole before washing it well. Use a salad spinner to wash it, as the fine, feathery leaves tend to hold a lot of soil.

Manhattan Clam Chowder

Serves 6 • **Cooking Time** 8 to 10 hours on Low or 5 to 7 hours on High • **Slow Cooker Size** 4 to 7 Quarts

✔ **WHY THIS RECIPE WORKS:** Manhattan clam chowder has a delicate harmony of briny seafood, acidic notes, and creamy potatoes, all in a rich tomatoey broth. Getting the proper balance of tomato to clam took some ingenuity. After pureeing a large can of whole tomatoes to set up our base, we used a bottle of clam juice along with the juice from canned clams to give us the seafood flavor we were looking for. Since the acidity of the tomatoes slowed the breakdown of starches in the potatoes, we added the potatoes at the beginning to give them enough time to cook all the way through. For a meaty flavor we did something unorthodox: We added uncooked slices of bacon directly to the slow cooker and removed them before serving. This gave the soup a savory depth without the presence of bits of bacon and without the soup tasting overtly like pork. To finish, we added a little sherry for sweetness and parsley for brightness.

1   **(28-ounce) can whole peeled tomatoes**

1   **onion, chopped fine**

2   **tablespoons tomato paste**

4   **garlic cloves, minced**

1½   **teaspoons minced fresh oregano or ½ teaspoon dried**

1   **teaspoon canola oil**

1½   **pounds Yukon Gold potatoes, peeled and cut into ½-inch pieces**

4   **(6.5-ounce) cans chopped clams, drained, juice reserved**

1   **(8-ounce) bottle clam juice**

2   **slices bacon**

2   **bay leaves**

2   **tablespoons minced fresh parsley**

1   **tablespoon dry sherry**

    Salt and pepper

1. Process tomatoes and their juice in food processor until smooth, about 30 seconds; transfer to slow cooker.

2. Microwave onion, tomato paste, garlic, oregano, and oil in bowl, stirring occasionally, until onion is softened, about 5 minutes; transfer to slow cooker. Stir in potatoes, reserved clam juice, bottled clam juice, bacon, and bay leaves. Cover and cook until potatoes are tender, 8 to 10 hours on low or 5 to 7 hours on high.

3. Discard bacon and bay leaves. Stir clams into chowder and let sit until heated through, about 5 minutes. Stir in parsley and sherry and season with salt and pepper to taste. Serve.

Per 1⅔-cup serving: Cal 220; Fat 4.5g; Sat Fat 1.5g; Chol 30mg; Carb 30g; Protein 13g; Fiber 3g; Sodium 950mg *To reduce sodium level to 810mg, use no-salt-added tomatoes.

QUICK PREP TIP **WHEN POTATOES TURN GREEN**

When potatoes are stored over time on the counter, they turn slightly green under the skin. It turns out that when potatoes are exposed to light for prolonged periods, they produce chlorophyll in the form of a green ring under their skin. While the chlorophyll is tasteless and harmless, it can signal the potential presence of solanine, a toxin that can cause gastrointestinal distress. Since solanine develops on or just under the skin of the potato, discarding the peel greatly reduces the risk of becoming ill from a slightly green spud. We've found that potatoes stored in a well-ventilated, dark, dry, cool place stay solanine-free for up to a month, while potatoes left on the counter will begin to exhibit signs of solanine in as little as a week.

Spicy Thai-Style Shrimp Soup

Serves 6 • **Cooking Time** 6 to 8 hours on Low or 4 to 6 hours on High • **Slow Cooker Size** 4 to 7 Quarts

✔ **WHY THIS RECIPE WORKS:** Inspired by the popular *tom yum* soup from Thailand, a sweet and spicy soup packed with herbs and spices, we set out to create a version in our slow cooker that was both light and complex in flavor, balancing hot, salty, sweet, and sour elements. Microwaving our aromatics with sesame oil allowed the ingredients to meld and the scallions to release their flavor once added to the soup. A small amount of chili-garlic sauce provided heat, and the saltiness came via fish sauce. Lemon grass was an essential ingredient in this soup, lending a subtle, fragrant lemon essence without harsh citrus notes. This dish traditionally includes shrimp, which is high in protein and low in fat—fitting right in with the healthy profile we were aiming for here. To ensure that the shrimp didn't overcook, we added them at the end and let them cook through on high for 15 minutes. The sweet and fresh flavors of a papaya salad seasoned with Thai basil and sesame oil made a zesty and bright topping. The final result: an easy, aromatic, and tasty Thai-style soup. If you can't find Thai basil, you can substitute Italian basil.

4	scallions, white parts minced, green parts cut into 1-inch pieces
3	garlic cloves, minced
2	teaspoons sesame oil
7	cups chicken broth
2	lemon grass stalks, trimmed to bottom 6 inches and bruised with back of knife
1	(2-inch) piece ginger, peeled and sliced into ½-inch-thick rounds
1	tablespoon fish sauce, plus extra for seasoning
2	teaspoons Asian chili-garlic sauce
1½	teaspoons sugar
1½	pounds medium shrimp (41 to 50 per pound), peeled, deveined, and tails removed
8	ounces white mushrooms, trimmed and sliced thin
8	ounces cherry tomatoes, quartered
	Salt and pepper
1	green papaya, peeled, seeded, and shredded
⅓	cup chopped fresh Thai basil
1	teaspoon lime juice

1. Microwave scallion whites, garlic, and 1 teaspoon oil in bowl, stirring occasionally, until fragrant, about 1 minute; transfer to slow cooker. Stir in broth, lemon grass, ginger, fish sauce, chili-garlic sauce, and sugar. Cover and cook until flavors meld, 6 to 8 hours on low or 4 to 6 hours on high.

2. Discard lemon grass and ginger. Stir in shrimp and mushrooms, cover, and cook on high until shrimp are opaque throughout, 15 to 20 minutes. Stir in tomatoes and scallion greens. Season with salt, pepper, and extra fish sauce to taste.

3. Combine papaya, basil, lime juice, and remaining 1 teaspoon oil in bowl. Top individual portions with papaya mixture before serving.

Per 2-cup serving: Cal 160; Fat 2.5g; Sat Fat 0g; Chol 120mg; Carb 15g; Protein 19g; Fiber 2g; Sodium 1300mg *To reduce sodium level to 860mg, use unsalted broth.

SMART SHOPPING PAPAYA
Though very different in taste, texture, and appearance, green and orange papayas are actually the same fruit picked at different stages of development. The tender, creamy, orange-fleshed papaya is harvested when fully mature (though the exterior may still be green) and has a sweet, melon-y, and even somewhat cheesy flavor. Immature green papaya has crisp, white flesh with a clean, mild flavor similar to that of cucumber or jícama. It is prized mostly for its crunch and used primarily as a base for salads, where it serves as a backdrop for more powerful flavors.

Spanish Seafood Soup

Serves 6 • **Cooking Time** 6 to 8 hours on Low or 4 to 6 hours on High • **Slow Cooker Size** 4 to 7 Quarts

✓ **WHY THIS RECIPE WORKS:** Just about every country with a coastline has a seafood soup specialty, and this one takes its inspiration from Spain's classic version known as *zarzuela*. Chock full of fish, this tomato-based soup is seasoned with saffron and paprika and topped with a *picada*, a flavorful mixture of ground almonds, bread crumbs, and olive oil. For our healthy slow-cooker version, we began with a *sofrito* of onion, bell pepper, and garlic to which we added tomato paste, a large amount of paprika, plus saffron, red pepper flakes, and bay leaves to create a rich foundation for our broth. A bottle of clam juice added the requisite briny seafood flavor, and a little wine added depth. And since the base of our soup was so rich and fragrant, we found that we could simply add water to achieve the right consistency, which helped keep the sodium level in check. Adding the seafood at the end ensured that it was cooked perfectly. Finished with the picada and a drizzle of olive oil, this seafood soup tasted rich and hearty.

1	onion, chopped fine
1	red bell pepper, stemmed, seeded, and chopped fine
2	tablespoons plus 2 teaspoons extra-virgin olive oil
6	garlic cloves, minced
2	tablespoons tomato paste
1	tablespoon paprika
¼	teaspoon saffron threads, crumbled
⅛	teaspoon red pepper flakes
2	(14.5-ounce) cans diced tomatoes
2	cups water
1	(8-ounce) bottle clam juice
¼	cup dry white wine
2	bay leaves
	Salt and pepper
1	pound skinless cod fillets, 1 to 1½ inches thick, cut into 1-inch pieces
8	ounces squid bodies, sliced crosswise into ½-inch-thick rings
½	cup panko bread crumbs
2	tablespoons slivered almonds, chopped fine
2	tablespoons minced fresh parsley

1. Microwave onion, bell pepper, 1 teaspoon oil, garlic, tomato paste, paprika, saffron, and pepper flakes in bowl, stirring occasionally, until vegetables are softened, about 5 minutes; transfer to slow cooker. Stir in tomatoes and their juice, water, clam juice, wine, bay leaves, and ½ teaspoon salt. Cover and cook until flavors meld, 6 to 8 hours on low or 4 to 6 hours on high.

2. Stir cod and squid into soup, cover, and cook on high until cod flakes apart when gently prodded with paring knife, 20 to 30 minutes.

3. Meanwhile, heat 1 teaspoon oil in 12-inch skillet over medium heat until shimmering. Add panko and almonds and cook, stirring often, until golden brown, 5 to 7 minutes; transfer to bowl and season with salt and pepper to taste.

4. Discard bay leaves. Gently stir in parsley and season with salt and pepper to taste. Top individual portions with panko mixture and drizzle each with 1 teaspoon oil before serving.

Per 1⅔-cup serving: Cal 250; Fat 9g; Sat Fat 1g; Chol 120mg; Carb 20g; Protein 23g; Fiber 4g; Sodium 700mg *To reduce sodium level to 370mg, use no-salt-added tomatoes.

SMART SHOPPING SAFFRON
Sometimes known as "red gold," saffron is the world's most expensive spice. Luckily, a little saffron goes a long way, and we have found that brand isn't important as long as the recipe has other strong flavors, as this one does.
Look for bottles that contain dark red threads—saffron is graded, and the richly hued, high-grade threads yield more flavor than the lighter, lesser-grade threads.

Spring Vegetable and Barley Soup

Serves 6 • **Cooking Time** 4 to 6 hours on Low or 3 to 5 hours on High • **Slow Cooker Size** 4 to 7 Quarts

✔ **WHY THIS RECIPE WORKS:** For a light spring soup, we paired asparagus and summer squash with hearty pearl barley. To build flavor in such a simple soup, we found we needed to get out our skillet and sauté a hefty amount of shallots until softened and just starting to brown, then add the garlic and red pepper flakes before transferring them to the slow cooker along with the broth and the barley. The barley itself added a filling texture and a nutty taste, and as it simmered with the rest of the ingredients, it acquired the flavor of the aromatic broth to which we had added two large strips of lemon zest. A sprinkling of Parmesan before serving added welcome richness to this light, fragrant soup. Do not substitute hulled, hull-less, quick-cooking, or presteamed barley for the pearl barley in this recipe; you may need to read the ingredient list on the package carefully to determine if the barley is presteamed.

1 teaspoon extra-virgin olive oil
4 shallots, minced
4 garlic cloves, minced
¼ teaspoon red pepper flakes
8 cups chicken broth
½ cup pearl barley
2 (2-inch) strips lemon zest
    Salt and pepper
8 ounces thin asparagus, trimmed and cut on bias into 1-inch lengths
1 yellow summer squash, quartered lengthwise and sliced ½ inch thick
2 ounces (2 cups) baby arugula
¼ cup grated Parmesan cheese

1. Heat oil in 12-inch skillet over medium heat until shimmering. Add shallots and cook until softened and lightly browned, about 5 minutes. Stir in garlic and pepper flakes and cook until fragrant, about 30 seconds; transfer to slow cooker. Stir in broth, barley, lemon zest, and ¾ teaspoon salt. Cover and cook until barley is tender, 4 to 6 hours on low or 3 to 5 hours on high.

2. Stir asparagus and squash into soup, cover, and cook on high until tender, 20 to 30 minutes. Stir in arugula and let sit until slightly wilted, about 3 minutes. Season with salt and pepper to taste. Sprinkle individual portions with Parmesan before serving.

Per 1⅔-cup serving: Cal 150; Fat 2.5g; Sat Fat 1g; Chol 5mg; Carb 22g; Protein 11g; Fiber 5g; Sodium 1060mg *To reduce sodium level to 550mg, use unsalted broth.

SMART SHOPPING BARLEY
Barley is a nutritious high-fiber, high-protein, and low-fat cereal grain with a nutty flavor that is similar to that of brown rice. It tastes great in soups and in salads, as risotto, and as a simple side dish. The key thing to know about barley is that it is available in multiple forms. Hulled barley, which is sold with the hull removed and the fiber-rich bran intact, is considered a whole grain and is higher in a few nutrients (iron, magnesium, potassium, thiamine, riboflavin, and fiber) compared to pearl (or pearled) barley, which is hulled barley that has been polished to remove the bran. Then there is quick-cooking barley, which is available as kernels or flakes. Hulled barley, which is hard to find in most supermarkets, takes a long time to cook and should be soaked prior to cooking. Pearl barley cooks much more quickly, making it a more versatile choice when you are adding it to soups or making risotto or a simple pilaf. Use it in dishes where you might ordinarily use rice, such as stir-fries or curries.

ALL ABOUT Broths

An essential ingredient in soups and stews, broths are also a valuable tool in creating other healthy slow-cooker recipes, adding flavor and keeping things moist without adding much in the way of fat or calories. The brands pictured below are all winners of test kitchen tastings. Note that many store-bought broths contain a lot of sodium. Making broth from scratch is a reliable way to limit sodium (see our recipes on pages 45-47), but if you don't have time, we recommend that you buy unsalted broth (see our recommendations below). The sodium information provided with each recipe in this book is based on using our winning brands, but we have also provided the sodium level should you choose our top-rated unsalted alternative.

Chicken Broth

We reach for chicken broth for the bulk of the liquid in our slow-cooker soups and stews. Not surprisingly, while searching for the best-tasting commercial broth, we found that few came close to the rich flavor and consistency of homemade. That said, we preferred brands with short ingredient lists that included vegetables like carrots, celery, and onions. Our favorite? **Swanson Chicken Stock**, which tastes rich and meaty thanks to its relatively high percentage of meat-based protein.

With 510 milligrams of sodium per cup, our winning chicken broth can easily push the sodium level of a serving very high given how much is used when making soup. So if you need to watch your sodium intake, we recommend **Swanson's Unsalted Chicken Stock**, which has only 130 milligrams of sodium per cup.

Beef Broth

We don't often reach for beef broth for the recipes in this book, but when we do, we use our winning brand, **Rachael Ray Stock-in-a-Box All-Natural Beef Flavored Stock** (made by Colavita). This broth has a shorter ingredient list that starts with concentrated beef stock, which means it has more real meat than the other brands. Tasters praised it as "steak-y" and "rich" with "thick, gelatin-like body."

Vegetable Broth

Our favorite is a vegan "chicken-flavored" broth, **Orrington Farms Vegan Chicken Flavored Broth Base & Seasoning**. Tasters preferred its mild savoriness to traditional vegetable broth. This jar of powder makes up to 28 cups of broth. To limit your sodium intake we recommend **Edward & Sons Low-Sodium Not-Chick'n Natural Bouillon Cubes** with 130 milligrams of sodium per cup.

Clam Juice

When we need bold, briny flavor for a seafood chowder or stew, we reach for clam juice, made by briefly steaming fresh clams in salted water and filtering the resulting broth before bottling. Moderation is key with clam juice when you are keeping an eye on sodium intake since 1 cup has 480 milligrams of sodium. Fortunately, a little goes a long way.

Our winning brand, **Bar Harbor Clam Juice**, hails from clam country in Maine and brings a "bright" and "mineral-y" flavor to seafood dishes.

Here is how the sodium levels per cup stack up for the broths we use most often in this book (based on the test kitchen's winning brands).

	STORE-BOUGHT	STORE-BOUGHT (LOW SODIUM)	HOMEMADE
Chicken Broth	510mg	130mg	180mg
Beef Broth	480mg	—	130mg
Vegetable Broth	750mg	130mg	140mg
Clam Juice	480mg	—	—

Vegetarian Pho

Serves 6 • **Cooking Time** 4 to 6 hours on Low or 3 to 5 hours on High • **Slow Cooker Size** 4 to 7 Quarts

☑ **WHY THIS RECIPE WORKS:** *Pho* is perhaps the best-recognized rice noodle soup from Southeast Asia where all the effort is put into building a richly flavored broth that is poured over rice noodles and thinly sliced beef or chicken and then topped with an abundance of fresh herbs and bean sprouts. Creating this soup in a slow cooker certainly presented challenges, and we were after a vegetarian version that was flavorful and satisfying. To produce a broth with the flavor and complexity of the real deal in a slow cooker, we knew we had to create a flavorful base. To a combination of vegetable broth and water we added dried porcini for beefy flavor, onion, garlic, soy sauce, lemon grass, star anise, and cloves to bring complex spice notes. For substance and meaty texture, we added portobellos, which can hold up to the long simmering time in the slow cooker and impart their earthy flavor. For our noodles we preferred classic rice noodles and added them to the soup at the end of the cooking time, turning the temperature to high for 10 to 20 minutes. The must-have garnishes—bean sprouts for crunch, basil (preferably Thai basil, though Italian basil will work), lime wedges, and additional soy sauce—balanced the straightforward meatiness and mellow sweetness of the broth with heat, acidity, and freshness. Using ¼-inch-wide rice noodles is important for the success of this soup; do not substitute other types of noodles. Be sure not to overcook the rice noodles or else they will become mushy.

1 **onion, chopped fine**

6 **garlic cloves, minced**

¼ **ounce dried porcini mushrooms, rinsed and minced**

1 **teaspoon canola oil**

6 **cups water**

4 **cups vegetable broth**

1 **pound portobello mushroom caps, gills removed, caps halved and sliced thin**

3 **stalks lemon grass, trimmed to bottom 6 inches and bruised with back of knife**

¼ **cup low-sodium soy sauce, plus extra for seasoning**

4 **star anise pods**

2 **cloves**

6 **ounces (¼-inch-wide) rice noodles**

1 **teaspoon Sriracha sauce, plus extra for seasoning**
   Salt and pepper

2 **ounces (1 cup) bean sprouts**

½ **cup fresh Thai basil leaves**
   Lime wedges

1. Microwave onion, garlic, porcini mushrooms, and oil in bowl, stirring occasionally, until onion is softened, about 5 minutes; transfer to slow cooker. Stir in water, broth, portobello mushrooms, lemon grass, soy sauce, star anise, and cloves. Cover and cook until portobello mushrooms are tender, 4 to 6 hours on low or 3 to 5 hours on high.

2. Stir noodles into soup, cover, and cook on high until tender, 10 to 20 minutes. Discard lemon grass, star anise, and cloves. Stir in Sriracha and season with salt, pepper, extra soy sauce, and extra Sriracha to taste. Top individual portions with bean sprouts and basil and serve with lime wedges.

Per 2-cup serving: Cal 160; Fat 1g; Sat Fat 0g; Chol 0mg; Carb 35g; Protein 3g; Fiber 2g; Sodium 890mg *To reduce sodium level to 480mg, use low-sodium broth.

QUICK PREP TIP
BRUISING LEMON GRASS
Trim and discard all but bottom 6 inches of stalk. Peel off discolored outer layer, then lightly smash stalk with back of chef's knife.

Miso Soup with Sweet Potatoes

Serves 6 • **Cooking Time** 4 to 6 hours on Low or 3 to 5 hours on High • **Slow Cooker Size** 4 to 7 Quarts

✓ **WHY THIS RECIPE WORKS:** A great miso soup is all about the rich, flavorful broth. For our healthy version of slow-cooker miso soup we set out to create a broth with equal complexity and savory vegetables. We started with water for the liquid base and infused it with a hearty amount of shiitake mushrooms, scallions, ginger, garlic, sesame oil, and red pepper flakes. We tried different types of miso, but tasters preferred the traditional white variety for its mild and slightly sweet flavor. Before adding the miso to the slow cooker, we found it best to thin the thick paste with a small amount of water to ensure that it would be fully incorporated into the soup. For extra protein we bumped up the amount of tofu, which is traditional in miso soup, and selected the extra-firm variety, as it held its shape best during cooking. For an interesting twist we added sweet potatoes for a little sweetness and stirred in watercress for a fresh, peppery finish. You can substitute firm tofu here if desired; avoid silken, soft, or medium-firm tofu as these varieties will break down while cooking.

12 ounces shiitake mushrooms, stemmed and sliced thin

2 scallions, sliced thin

1 (2-inch) piece ginger, peeled and sliced into ¼-inch-thick rounds

4 garlic cloves, minced

2 teaspoons sesame oil

⅛ teaspoon red pepper flakes

6 cups water

½ cup white miso

14 ounces extra-firm tofu, cut into ½-inch cubes

12 ounces sweet potatoes, peeled and cut into ½-inch pieces

1 tablespoon low-sodium soy sauce, plus extra for seasoning
   Salt and pepper

3 ounces (3 cups) watercress, washed and cut into 2-inch pieces

1. Microwave mushrooms, scallions, ginger, garlic, oil, and pepper flakes in bowl, stirring occasionally, until mushrooms are softened, about 5 minutes.

2. Whisk 1 cup water and miso together in slow cooker until miso is fully dissolved. Stir in remaining 5 cups water, mushroom mixture, tofu, potatoes, soy sauce, and ¼ teaspoon salt. Cover and cook until potatoes are tender, 4 to 6 hours on low or 3 to 5 hours on high.

3. Discard ginger. Stir in watercress and let sit until slightly wilted, about 3 minutes. Season with salt, pepper, and extra soy sauce to taste. Serve.

Per 1⅔-cup serving: Cal 180; Fat 6; Sat Fat 0g; Chol 0mg; Carb 23g; Protein 10g; Fiber 3g; Sodium 860mg

SMART SHOPPING MISO

Made from a fermented mixture of soybeans and rice, barley, or rye, miso is incredibly versatile, suitable for use in soups, braises, dressings, and sauces. This salty, deep-flavored paste ranges in strength and color from mild pale yellow (referred to as white) to stronger-flavored red or brownish black, depending on the fermentation method and ingredients.

Carrot-Ginger Soup

Serves 4 • **Cooking Time** 6 to 8 hours on Low or 4 to 6 hours on High • **Slow Cooker Size** 4 to 7 Quarts

WHY THIS RECIPE WORKS: For our slow-cooker version of carrot-ginger soup, we wanted a soup that was packed with the bright flavor of carrots and a noticeable amount of ginger. First we needed to settle on the ratio of carrots to liquid, and while most recipes use equal amounts, we decided to alter this ratio in a big way and cook 2 pounds of carrots in 5 cups of water for a clean carrot taste not muddled by excess liquid. Instead of adding cream to the slow cooker for a smooth texture, we added store-bought carrot juice at the end to thin out the puree and add a fresh flavor. Using a mixture of fresh and crystallized ginger gave this soup a bright, refreshing ginger flavor with a moderate kick of heat. Finally, a little cider vinegar and chopped chives were the crowning touches on our rich and creamy soup.

2	**onions, chopped fine**
1	**tablespoon grated fresh ginger**
2	**garlic cloves, minced**
1	**teaspoon canola oil**
5	**cups water, plus extra as needed**
2	**pounds carrots, peeled and sliced ¼ inch thick**
¼	**cup minced crystallized ginger**
2	**sprigs fresh thyme**
1	**teaspoon sugar**
	Salt and pepper
1½	**cups carrot juice**
1	**tablespoon cider vinegar**
¼	**cup minced fresh chives**

1. Microwave onions, fresh ginger, garlic, and oil in bowl, stirring occasionally, until onions are softened, about 5 minutes; transfer to slow cooker. Stir in water, carrots, crystallized ginger, thyme sprigs, sugar, and 1 teaspoon salt. Cover and cook until carrots are tender, 6 to 8 hours on low or 4 to 6 hours on high.

2. Discard thyme sprigs. Working in batches, process soup in blender until smooth, 1 to 2 minutes. Return soup to slow cooker and stir in carrot juice and vinegar. (Adjust soup consistency with extra hot water as needed.) Cover and cook on high until soup is heated through, 5 to 10 minutes. Season with salt and pepper to taste. Sprinkle individual portions with chives before serving.

Per 2-cup serving: Cal 190; Fat 1.5g; Sat Fat 0g; Chol 0mg; Carb 43g; Protein 3g; Fiber 8g; Sodium 800mg

---

QUICK PREP TIP **GRATING GINGER**

Although we love the floral pungency of fresh ginger, its fibrous texture can be distracting when coarsely grated or minced. What's the best way to avoid ginger's stringy texture? Although fancy kitchen stores sometimes carry porcelain "ginger graters" designed specifically for the job, we prefer to use our rasp-style grater. Its fine blades pulverize the ginger, releasing all of its flavorful juice without any stringy segments. Simply peel a small section of a large piece of ginger, then grate the peeled portion, using the rest of the ginger as a handle. Be sure to work with a large nub of ginger—and watch your knuckles.

Creamy Cauliflower and Potato Soup

Serves 6 • **Cooking Time** 6 to 8 hours on Low or 4 to 6 hours on High • **Slow Cooker Size** 4 to 7 Quarts

WHY THIS RECIPE WORKS: For a healthy but rich cauliflower and potato soup, we started by simmering a hefty amount of cauliflower and a pound of potatoes in a broth infused with garlic and onion. To ensure that the flavor of the cauliflower remained at the forefront, we cooked it in vegetable broth rather than chicken broth since it offered a welcome sweetness to the soup. Yukon Gold potatoes delivered a nice buttery taste and helped thicken the soup when pureed along with the cauliflower. Swapping half-and-half for heavy cream provided richness while still letting the clean vegetable flavors shine through. Pinches of nutmeg for depth and cayenne for heat were all this soup needed. A long cooking time coaxed out the sweet, nutty flavor of the cauliflower. Finally, for a hearty and richly flavored garnish, we sautéed some reserved florets in a small amount of butter until tender.

1	onion, chopped fine
2	garlic cloves, minced
1	teaspoon canola oil
	Pinch ground nutmeg
	Pinch cayenne pepper
6	cups vegetable broth, plus extra as needed
1	large head cauliflower (3 pounds), cored and cut into 1-inch florets
1	pound Yukon Gold potatoes, peeled and cut into ½-inch pieces
	Salt and pepper
2	tablespoons unsalted butter
½	teaspoon sherry vinegar
½	cup half-and-half
2	tablespoons minced fresh chives

1. Microwave onion, garlic, oil, nutmeg, and cayenne in bowl, stirring occasionally, until onion is softened, about 5 minutes; transfer to slow cooker. Stir in broth, all but 2 cups cauliflower, potatoes, and ½ teaspoon salt. Cover and cook until vegetables are tender, 6 to 8 hours on low or 4 to 6 hours on high.

2. Meanwhile, melt butter in 12-inch skillet over medium heat. Add remaining 2 cups cauliflower and cook, stirring frequently, until florets are golden brown and tender and butter is browned and imparts nutty aroma, 8 to 10 minutes. Off heat, stir in vinegar and season with salt and pepper to taste.

3. Working in batches, process soup in blender until smooth, 1 to 2 minutes. Return soup to slow cooker, stir in half-and-half, and let sit until heated through, about 5 minutes. (Adjust soup consistency with extra hot broth as needed.) Season with salt and pepper to taste. Top individual portions with browned cauliflower mixture and sprinkle with chives before serving.

Per 1⅔-cup serving: Cal 180; Fat 7g; Sat Fat 4g; Chol 15mg; Carb 24g; Protein 4g; Fiber 3g; Sodium 980mg *To reduce sodium level to 360mg, use low-sodium broth.

QUICK PREP TIP
PUREEING SOUPS SAFELY
To prevent getting burned by an exploding blender top when pureeing hot soup, fill the blender jar as directed, making sure it is never more than two-thirds full. Hold the lid in place with a folded dish towel and pulse rapidly a few times before blending continuously.

Creamy Butternut Squash and Apple Soup

Serves 4 • **Cooking Time** 6 to 8 hours on Low or 4 to 6 hours on High • **Slow Cooker Size** 4 to 7 Quarts

✓ **WHY THIS RECIPE WORKS:** For soup with intense squash and apple flavor, traditional recipes instruct you to roast the main ingredients to concentrate their flavors. But for our slow-cooker version, we learned that when the apples and squash are simmered long enough, their flavors meld and shine through without the tedious step of roasting. A 2:1 ratio of squash to apples let each ingredient be present without one overpowering the other and without the soup becoming overly sweet. For our aromatics we initially started with onions, but they imparted a sharp taste to this simple soup, so we switched to sweeter, milder shallots. We microwaved these with cayenne and cinnamon to punch up the flavors, and butter to give a richer and deeper flavor. To further enhance the soup's vegetable flavor, we chose vegetable broth and water over chicken broth. We also found that half-and-half added just the right amount of richness—no heavy cream necessary. What really put this soup over the top was steeping a sprig of fresh sage in the soup while it cooked. Once pureed, our soup offered all the rich, creamy, sweet squash and apple flavor we were craving. Serve with Spiced Croutons.

4   **shallots, minced**
1   **tablespoon unsalted butter**
½   **teaspoon ground cinnamon**
    Pinch cayenne pepper
3   **cups vegetable broth, plus extra as needed**
1   **cup water**
2   **pounds butternut squash, peeled, seeded, and cut into 1-inch pieces (5 cups)**
1   **pound Golden Delicious apples, peeled, cored, and cut into 1-inch pieces**
1   **sprig fresh sage**
    Salt and pepper
½   **cup half-and-half**

1. Microwave shallots, butter, cinnamon, and cayenne in bowl, stirring occasionally, until shallots are softened, about 2 minutes; transfer to slow cooker. Stir in broth, water, squash, apples, sage sprig, and ½ teaspoon salt. Cover and cook until squash is tender, 6 to 8 hours on low or 4 to 6 hours on high.

2. Discard sage sprig. Working in batches, process soup in blender until smooth, 1 to 2 minutes. Return soup to slow cooker, stir in half-and-half, and let sit until heated through, about 5 minutes. (Adjust soup consistency with extra hot broth as needed.) Season with salt and pepper to taste. Serve.

Per 2-cup serving: Cal 230; Fat 7g; Sat Fat 4g; Chol 20mg; Carb 44g; Protein 4g; Fiber 7g; Sodium 880mg *To reduce sodium level to 410mg, use low-sodium broth.

ON THE SIDE SPICED CROUTONS
Adjust oven rack to middle position and heat oven to 350 degrees. Spray 4 slices hearty white sandwich bread, crusts removed and cut into ½-inch cubes (about 2 cups), with vegetable oil spray and toss with ¼ teaspoon ground cumin, ¼ teaspoon ground coriander, ⅛ teaspoon paprika, ⅛ teaspoon salt, and pinch cayenne pepper. Spread bread cubes in rimmed baking sheet and bake until golden brown, 20 to 25 minutes, stirring halfway through baking. Let croutons cool to room temperature before serving.

Per ⅓-cup serving: Cal 50; Fat 1.5g; Sat Fat 0g; Chol 0mg; Carb 8g; Protein 1g; Fiber 0g; Sodium 135mg

Spiced Tomato Soup

Serves 4 • **Cooking Time** 4 to 6 hours on Low or 3 to 5 hours on High • **Slow Cooker Size** 4 to 7 Quarts

✔ **WHY THIS RECIPE WORKS:** Classic tomato soup is a great comfort food, but sometimes we grow tired of the simple flavor. Here we jazz it up with the help of five-spice powder, ginger, and cayenne. The spice blend added a complex, warm flavor to the soup, which perfectly complemented the tomatoes. High-quality, straight-from-the-can diced tomatoes were a good starting point for the base of our soup but didn't quite deliver enough flavor. We got a more robust tomato flavor by adding tomato paste, which we microwaved along with the aromatics and spices. Most tomato soups incorporate cream at the end for richness, but it tends to dull the bright acidic tomato flavor, not to mention all the fat it adds. Our solution to getting a creamy tomato soup without cream was an unusual addition: bread. We tore a slice of bread into pieces and simmered it in the soup. As the bread broke down, it thickened the soup to a satisfyingly creamy texture and tempered the acidity of the tomatoes without muting their flavor. Brown sugar stirred in at the end contributed subtle caramel notes, creating a deep, sweet flavor.

1	onion, chopped fine
3	tablespoons tomato paste
1	tablespoon unsalted butter
4	garlic cloves, minced
2	teaspoons grated fresh ginger
1¼	teaspoons five-spice powder
⅛	teaspoon cayenne pepper
3	(14.5-ounce) cans diced tomatoes
1	cup water, plus extra as needed
1	slice hearty white sandwich bread, crusts removed, torn into quarters
2	bay leaves
	Salt and pepper
2	tablespoons packed brown sugar

1. Microwave onion, tomato paste, butter, garlic, ginger, five-spice powder, and cayenne in bowl, stirring occasionally, until onion is softened, about 5 minutes; transfer to slow cooker. Stir in tomatoes and their juice, water, bread, bay leaves, and ½ teaspoon salt. Cover and cook until flavors meld, 4 to 6 hours on low or 3 to 5 hours on high.

2. Discard bay leaves. Working in batches, process soup in blender until smooth, 1 to 2 minutes. Return soup to slow cooker and stir in sugar. (Adjust soup consistency with extra hot water as needed.) Season with salt and pepper to taste. Serve.

Per 2-cup serving: Cal 160; Fat 3.5g; Sat Fat 2g; Chol 10mg; Carb 32g; Protein 4g; Fiber 7g; Sodium 1220mg *To reduce sodium level to 460mg, use no-salt-added tomatoes.

SMART SHOPPING DICED TOMATOES

Unlike most types of canned produce, which pale in comparison to their fresh counterparts, a great can of diced tomatoes offers flavor almost every bit as intense as that of ripe, in-season fruit. We gathered 16 brands and tasted them plain and in tomato sauce to find the best brand. To our surprise, nearly half fell short. Factors such as geography and additives played into whether or not a sample rated highly in our tasting. Our top-ranked tomatoes were grown in California, source of most of the world's tomatoes, where the dry, hot growing season develops sweet, complex flavor. Tasters also favored those with more salt. In the end, we found our winner in **Hunt's Diced Tomatoes**, which were praised for their "fresh," "bright" flavor.

Fire-Roasted Tomato and Fennel Soup

Serves 6 • **Cooking Time** 6 to 8 hours on Low or 4 to 6 hours on High • **Slow Cooker Size** 4 to 7 Quarts

✓ **WHY THIS RECIPE WORKS:** For yet another new spin on tomato soup, we turned to fennel, for its subtle anise flavor, and fire-roasted tomatoes, an easy way to give this dish smoky undertones and a slight but appealing charred flavor. Microwaving the fennel before adding it to the slow cooker ensured that it was perfectly cooked. To reinforce the smoky flavor we added a little smoked paprika for an extra kick. Pureeing only a portion of the soup helped to thicken the base but left it appealingly chunky and rustic in texture. Added at the end of the cooking, brown sugar helped balance the acidity of the tomatoes with some earthy sweetness, and tarragon brightened the soup with fresh herbal flavor. A small drizzle of olive oil before serving added fresh flavor and richness.

2   fennel bulbs, stalks discarded, bulbs halved, cored, and cut into ½-inch pieces

2   tablespoons plus 1 teaspoon extra-virgin olive oil

4   garlic cloves

1   tablespoon tomato paste

2   teaspoons smoked paprika

2   (28-ounce) cans diced fire-roasted tomatoes

2   cups vegetable broth
    Salt and pepper

2   tablespoons minced fresh tarragon

2   tablespoons packed brown sugar

1. Microwave fennel, 1 teaspoon oil, garlic, tomato paste, and paprika in bowl, stirring occasionally, until fennel is softened, about 5 minutes; transfer to slow cooker. Stir in tomatoes and their juice, broth, and ¼ teaspoon salt. Cover and cook until fennel is tender, 6 to 8 hours on low or 4 to 6 hours on high.

2. Process 4 cups soup in blender until smooth, about 1 minute; return to slow cooker. Stir in tarragon and sugar and season with salt and pepper to taste. Drizzle each portion with 1 teaspoon oil before serving.

Per 1⅔-cup serving: Cal 170; Fat 6g; Sat Fat 1g; Chol 0mg; Carb 26g; Protein 4g; Fiber 7g; Sodium 1010mg *To reduce sodium level to 460mg, use low-sodium broth and no-salt-added tomatoes.

QUICK PREP TIP
TRIMMING AND CUTTING FENNEL
After cutting off stems and feathery fronds, cut off thin slice from base of bulb. Remove any tough or blemished layers and cut bulb in half through base. Using small, sharp knife, remove pyramid-shaped core, then either slice each half into thin strips with chef's knife or cut into pieces as directed in recipe.

Classic Corn Chowder

Serves 6 • **Cooking Time** 6 to 8 hours on Low or 4 to 6 hours on High • **Slow Cooker Size** 4 to 7 Quarts

✔ WHY THIS RECIPE WORKS: Corn chowder is a summertime favorite, highlighting fresh corn that is bursting with sweetness. But though it sounds like a healthy option, most versions are weighed down with pork and cream, making them decidedly unhealthy. For our base we started with frozen corn for its convenience and availability year-round. But the real trick to making a creamy and rich soup was how we handled the corn. Processing 4 cups of the corn with some of the broth helped give our chowder a creamy texture without the cream. We then added this mixture to the slow cooker with our aromatics and potatoes to allow the flavors to really blend and balance the sweetness of the corn. But we still needed the richness that comes from dairy. We ultimately settled on a two-part solution. Cooking the soup with a cup of low-fat milk gave us a thicker broth, and stirring in a small amount of half-and-half at the end provided extra richness. We finished the soup by adding the remaining corn along with some parsley for texture and bright, fresh flavor.

1	onion, chopped fine
2	garlic cloves, minced
1	teaspoon canola oil
1	teaspoon minced fresh thyme or ¼ teaspoon dried
	Pinch cayenne pepper
6	cups frozen corn, thawed
3	cups vegetable broth
1	pound red potatoes, unpeeled, cut into ½-inch pieces
1	cup 1 percent low-fat milk
1	bay leaf
	Salt and pepper
½	cup half-and-half
2	tablespoons minced fresh parsley

1. Microwave onion, garlic, oil, thyme, and cayenne in bowl, stirring occasionally, until onion is softened, about 5 minutes; transfer to slow cooker.

2. Process 4 cups corn and 2 cups broth in blender until smooth, about 1 minute; transfer to slow cooker. Stir in remaining 1 cup broth, potatoes, milk, bay leaf, and ¾ teaspoon salt. Cover and cook until potatoes are tender, 6 to 8 hours on low or 4 to 6 hours on high.

3. Discard bay leaf. Stir in remaining 2 cups corn and half-and-half and let sit until heated through, about 5 minutes. Stir in parsley and season with salt and pepper to taste. Serve.

Per 1⅔-cup serving: Cal 270; Fat 5g; Sat Fat 2g; Chol 10mg; Carb 50g; Protein 8g; Fiber 3g; Sodium 710mg *To reduce sodium level to 400mg, use low-sodium broth.

SMART SHOPPING FROZEN CORN

There's no arguing that freshly picked corn is superior to frozen; unfortunately, it is typically available for only a short period of time. We enjoy cooking with corn year-round, not just during the summer months, so we regularly head to the freezer aisle for frozen corn kernels (not frozen corn on the cob, which generally has a poor texture). Frozen corn is consistently sweet and a convenient option for a variety of dishes, such as our Classic Corn Chowder.

Red Lentil Soup

Serves 6 • **Cooking Time** 7 to 9 hours on Low or 4 to 6 hours on High • **Slow Cooker Size** 4 to 7 Quarts

✓ **WHY THIS RECIPE WORKS:** For this lentil soup, we were after a vegetable-packed version that was exotically spiced and deeply satisfying. Mild, slightly nutty-tasting red lentils were the best starting point, as they broke down when cooked and thickened the soup to a rich consistency without the need for cream. To achieve deep, intense flavor, we added vibrant spices—curry powder, cinnamon, and spicy cayenne—to enhance the lentils and add complexity. Diced canned tomatoes and carrots added sweetness to the soup, and orange zest contributed bright citrus notes. Stirring in steamed green beans, although unconventional, added a nutritional boost and bright flavor. A small amount of mint was all the soup needed for a crisp finish. Do not substitute other types of lentils for the red lentils here; red lentils produce a very different texture.

2 onions, chopped fine

6 garlic cloves, minced

1 tablespoon curry powder

1 teaspoon canola oil

½ teaspoon ground cinnamon

⅛ teaspoon cayenne pepper

6 cups vegetable broth

1 (14.5-ounce) can diced tomatoes, drained

1 (14-ounce) can chickpeas, rinsed

3 carrots, peeled and cut into ½-inch pieces

1 cup red lentils, picked over and rinsed

3 (2-inch) strips orange zest plus 2 tablespoons juice
Salt and pepper

8 ounces green beans, trimmed and cut on bias into 1-inch lengths

2 tablespoons minced fresh mint

1. Microwave onions, garlic, curry powder, oil, cinnamon, and cayenne in bowl, stirring occasionally, until onions are softened, about 5 minutes; transfer to slow cooker. Stir in broth, tomatoes, chickpeas, carrots, lentils, orange zest, and ¼ teaspoon salt. Cover and cook until lentils are tender, 7 to 9 hours on low or 4 to 6 hours on high.

2. Discard orange zest. Microwave green beans and 1 tablespoon water in covered bowl, stirring occasionally, until tender, 4 to 6 minutes. Drain green beans, then stir into soup along with mint and orange juice. Season with salt and pepper to taste. Serve.

Per 2-cup serving: Cal 240; Fat 2.5g; Sat Fat 0g; Chol 0mg; Carb 43g; Protein 13g; Fiber 11g; Sodium 1110mg *To reduce sodium level to 280mg, use low-sodium broth and chickpeas and no-salt-added tomatoes.

SMART SHOPPING CANNED CHICKPEAS
Think all brands of canned chickpeas taste the same? So did we—until we tried six brands in a side-by-side taste test. Once we drained and rinsed the beans, we found that many of them were incredibly bland or, worse yet, had bitter and metallic flavors. Tasters preferred those that were well seasoned and had a creamy yet "al dente" texture. **Pastene Chickpeas** came out on top for their clean flavor and firm yet tender texture.

15-Bean Soup with Sausage and Spinach

Serves 6 • **Cooking Time** 9 to 11 hours on Low or 6 to 8 hours on High • **Slow Cooker Size** 4 to 7 Quarts

✔WHY THIS RECIPE WORKS: With 15-bean soup mix as our inspiration, we set out to make an easy bean soup with meaty undertones, a bright flavor, and an appealingly chunky texture. Our first step was to ditch the flavoring packets that come with these soup mixes because their dried seasonings and bits of vegetables offered up zero flavor and a lot of sodium. Instead, a combination of onion, garlic, thyme, and red pepper flakes provided a nice balance of oniony aromatics and herbs, and fresh white mushrooms (for mild mushroom flavor) rounded out the flavor of this simple soup. We kept sodium levels down by using water along with savory broth. For heartiness we added precooked chicken sausage, which held up during the long cooking time and has fewer calories and fat than pork sausage. We stirred in spinach at the end of cooking and allowed it to wilt slightly, adding a fresh, bright element to the soup.

8	ounces cooked hot or sweet Italian chicken sausage, sliced ½ inch thick
1	onion, chopped fine
6	garlic cloves, minced
1	tablespoon minced fresh thyme or 1 teaspoon dried
¼	teaspoon red pepper flakes
6	cups chicken broth
2	cups water
8	ounces white mushrooms, trimmed and quartered
8	ounces (1¼ cups) 15-bean soup mix, flavoring packet discarded, picked over and rinsed
2	bay leaves
	Salt and pepper
4	ounces (4 cups) baby spinach

1. Microwave sausage, onion, garlic, thyme, and pepper flakes in bowl, stirring occasionally, until onion is softened, about 5 minutes; transfer to slow cooker. Stir in broth, water, mushrooms, beans, bay leaves, and ¼ teaspoon salt. Cover and cook until beans are tender, 9 to 11 hours on low or 6 to 8 hours on high.

2. Discard bay leaves. Stir in spinach and let sit until slightly wilted, about 5 minutes. Season with salt and pepper to taste. Serve.

Per 1⅔-cup serving: Cal 230; Fat 3g; Sat Fat 1g; Chol 30mg; Carb 31g; Protein 20g; Fiber 5g; Sodium 860mg *To reduce sodium level to 480mg, use unsalted broth.

QUICK PREP TIP STORING SPINACH
Baby spinach is sold in bags and plastic containers of various sizes. If you happen to have leftover spinach, store it either in its original bag with the open end folded over and taped shut, or in its original plastic container, as long as it has holes that allow air to pass through. These specially designed breathable bags and containers keep the spinach fresh as long as possible; if you transfer the spinach to a sealed airtight bag or container, it will spoil prematurely.

Moroccan Lentil Soup with Mustard Greens

Serves 6 • **Cooking Time** 7 to 9 hours on Low or 4 to 6 hours on High • **Slow Cooker Size** 4 to 7 Quarts

✔ **WHY THIS RECIPE WORKS:** Lentil soup is one of the easiest soups to make in a slow cooker, yet all too often it turns into a hodgepodge of lentils, canned tomatoes, and whatever assortment of vegetables happens to be available. To create a cohesive, fresh-tasting, and healthy recipe in the slow cooker, we started by microwaving aromatics with Moroccan spices—coriander, garam masala, and cayenne—for a deep, round flavor. For our base we used vegetable broth for its light and slightly sweet flavor. As for the type of lentils, we found that French green and brown lentils did the best job of retaining their texture, shape, and flavor through the long simmer. To finish, we wanted a new and interesting flavor. Dates are a common Moroccan ingredient, and we found that they imparted a nutty, sweet flavor to the broth. Also added at the end, mustard greens offered the perfect balance to the warm spices in this dish, adding a subtle peppery bitterness. To add a little acidity and tang we topped the soup with a mixture of Greek yogurt, parsley, and lemon juice for a perfect balance. We prefer French green lentils, or *lentilles du Puy*, for this recipe, but it will work with any type of lentil except red or yellow. If you can't find mustard greens, you can substitute kale.

1	onion, chopped fine
2	garlic cloves, minced
1	teaspoon canola oil
1	teaspoon garam masala
¾	teaspoon ground coriander
⅛	teaspoon cayenne pepper
8	cups vegetable broth
1	cup French green lentils, picked over and rinsed
	Salt and pepper
12	ounces mustard greens, stemmed and sliced ½ inch thick
4	ounces pitted dates, chopped (¾ cup)
½	cup 2 percent Greek yogurt
¼	cup chopped fresh parsley
1	tablespoon lemon juice

1. Microwave onion, garlic, oil, garam masala, coriander, and cayenne in bowl, stirring occasionally, until onion is softened, about 5 minutes; transfer to slow cooker. Stir in broth, lentils, and ¼ teaspoon salt. Cover and cook until lentils are tender, 7 to 9 hours on low or 4 to 6 hours on high.

2. Stir mustard greens and dates into soup, cover, and cook on high until greens are tender, 20 to 30 minutes. Season with salt and pepper to taste.

3. Combine yogurt, parsley, lemon juice, and ⅛ teaspoon pepper in bowl. Season with salt and pepper to taste. Top individual portions of soup with yogurt mixture before serving.

Per 1⅔-cup serving: Cal 210; Fat 2g; Sat Fat 0g; Chol 0mg; Carb 42g; Protein 10g; Fiber 8g; Sodium 1110mg *To reduce sodium level to 290mg, use low-sodium broth.

SMART SHOPPING LENTILS

Lentils come in various sizes and colors, and the differences in flavor and texture are surprisingly distinct. Lentilles du Puy are smaller than the more common brown and green varieties and take their name from the city of Puy in central France. They are dark olive green in color and boast a "rich, earthy flavor" and "firm yet tender texture." Brown lentils are larger and have a uniform brown color and a "light and earthy flavor"; green lentils are similar in size to the brown but are greenish brown in color and have a very "mild flavor." Red lentils are very small, have an orange-red hue, and disintegrate completely when cooked; yellow lentils are also small, brightly colored, and break down completely when cooked. Red and yellow lentils are frequently used in Indian and Middle Eastern cuisines.

Spicy Cajun Red Bean and Rice Soup

Serves 6 • **Cooking Time** 9 to 11 hours on Low or 6 to 8 hours on High • **Slow Cooker Size** 5½ to 7 Quarts

✔️ **WHY THIS RECIPE WORKS:** This New Orleans dish balances the sweetness of the beans with a spicy flavor built on a base of vegetables and herbs. To create a vegetarian slow-cooker version that was lean but still had all the heartiness and flavor of the classic, we started by flavoring the broth with the trinity of Cajun cooking: onions, bell peppers, and celery. Softening the onions and celery in the microwave with a hefty amount of herbs and spices punched up the flavor. For the liquid base, a blend of water and vegetable broth proved best, as using all vegetable broth made the soup too sweet. Green bell peppers and rice were stirred in and cooked at the end to ensure that the rice was perfectly cooked and the peppers did not become slimy. For a little sweetness, corn was the perfect last-minute addition. We finished with a little hot sauce to enhance the spices and pack a little extra heat.

2	onions, chopped fine
3	celery ribs, cut into ½-inch pieces
6	garlic cloves, minced
1	tablespoon paprika
1	tablespoon minced fresh thyme or 1 teaspoon dried
2	teaspoons canola oil
2	teaspoons minced fresh oregano or ½ teaspoon dried
⅛	teaspoon cayenne pepper
4	cups water
4	cups vegetable broth
8	ounces (1¼ cups) dried small red beans, picked over and rinsed
2	bay leaves
	Salt and pepper
1	green bell pepper, stemmed, seeded, and cut into ½-inch pieces
⅓	cup long-grain white rice
1½	cups frozen corn, thawed
¼	cup minced fresh parsley
2	tablespoons hot sauce

1. Microwave onions, celery, garlic, paprika, thyme, oil, oregano, and cayenne in bowl, stirring occasionally, until onions are softened, 5 to 7 minutes; transfer to slow cooker. Stir in water, broth, beans, bay leaves, and ½ teaspoon salt. Cover and cook until beans are tender, 9 to 11 hours on low or 6 to 8 hours on high.

2. Stir in bell pepper and rice, cover, and cook on high until rice is tender, about 40 minutes.

3. Discard bay leaves. Stir in corn and let sit until heated through, about 5 minutes. Stir in parsley and hot sauce and season with salt and pepper to taste. Serve.

Per 2-cup serving: Cal 310; Fat 3g; Sat Fat 0g; Chol 0mg; Carb 59g; Protein 16g; Fiber 12g; Sodium 910mg *To reduce sodium level to 500mg, use low-sodium broth.

QUICK PREP TIP
SORTING DRIED BEANS
Before cooking any dried beans, you should pick them over to remove any small stones or debris and then rinse them. The easiest way to check for small stones is to spread the beans on a large plate or rimmed baking sheet.

Chipotle Black Bean and Squash Soup

Serves 6 • **Cooking Time** 9 to 11 hours on Low or 6 to 8 hours on High • **Slow Cooker Size** 4 to 7 Quarts

☑ **WHY THIS RECIPE WORKS:** For a black bean soup full of sweet, spicy, and smoky flavors, our first mission was to find a smoky pork product without all of the fat and sodium that typically come along with it. Linguiça, a Portuguese smoke-cured pork sausage, offered the perfect balance of leaner pork and smokiness—packing the soup with flavor without going overboard on fat. With this smoky and savory base, all we needed to do to accomplish the complex flavor we wanted was to enhance a mixture of broth and water with aromatics and a hefty dose of smoky chipotle chile. Dried beans were used for their firm and creamy texture and lower sodium, and the long cooking time meant there was no need to presoak them. For sweetness and color we added butternut squash, wrapping it in a foil packet to ensure that the soup included tender but distinct (not mushy or black) pieces of squash. We finished with lime juice because when we added it at the beginning, the acidity prevented the beans from cooking through fully. For information on making a foil packet, see page 51.

8 ounces linguiça sausage, quartered lengthwise and sliced ½ inch thick
2 onions, chopped fine
6 garlic cloves, minced
1½ tablespoons minced canned chipotle chile in adobo sauce
1½ teaspoons ground cumin
5 cups chicken broth
2 cups water
1 pound (2½ cups) dried black beans, picked over and rinsed
2 bay leaves
Salt and pepper
1½ pounds butternut squash, peeled, seeded, and cut into ¾-inch pieces (4 cups)
1 tablespoon lime juice

1. Microwave linguiça, onions, garlic, chipotle, and cumin in bowl, stirring occasionally, until onions are softened, about 5 minutes; transfer to slow cooker.

2. Stir broth, water, beans, bay leaves, and ½ teaspoon salt into slow cooker. Wrap squash in foil packet; lay packet on top of soup. Cover and cook until beans are tender, 9 to 11 hours on low or 6 to 8 hours on high.

3. Transfer foil packet to plate. Discard bay leaves. Transfer 1 cup cooked beans to bowl and mash with potato masher until smooth. Carefully open packet (watch for steam) and stir squash along with any accumulated juice and mashed beans into soup. Stir in lime juice and season with salt and pepper to taste. Serve.

Per 1⅔-cup serving: Cal 420; Fat 6g; Sat Fat 2.5g; Chol 25mg; Carb 64g; Protein 27g; Fiber 9g; Sodium 970mg *To reduce sodium level to 650mg, use unsalted broth.

SMART SHOPPING CHIPOTLE CHILES IN ADOBO
Canned chipotle chiles are jalapeños that have been ripened until red, then smoked and dried. They are sold as is, ground to a powder, or packed in a tomato-based sauce. We prefer the latter because the chiles are already reconstituted by the sauce, making them easier to use. These chiles will keep for two weeks in the refrigerator, or they can be frozen for up to two months. To freeze, puree the chiles and quick-freeze teaspoonfuls on a plastic wrap–covered plate. Once the teaspoons of chiles are hard, peel them off the plastic and transfer them to a zipper-lock freezer bag. Thaw what you need before use.

All-Purpose Chicken Broth

Makes 3 quarts   •   **Cooking Time** 6 to 8 hours on Low or 4 to 6 hours on High   •   **Slow Cooker Size** 4 to 7 Quarts

✓ WHY THIS RECIPE WORKS: Chicken broth is one of the most versatile and often-used ingredients in any kitchen. But while making a successful broth on the stovetop can be a tedious task, an equally tasty slow-cooker version is a breeze. Searching for a broth with unadulterated chicken flavor, we tested many combinations of chicken parts, finding a whole cut-up chicken too fussy and chicken backs, legs, and necks too liver-y. Chicken wings were the surprise winner—the resulting broth was remarkably clear and refined, and the long simmering time eked out every last bit of flavor from the chicken bones. Roasting the chicken wings was an easy way to incorporate dark color and pleasantly deep caramelized flavor. Additionally, we found that an onion, a little garlic, and some salt were all we needed to complement, and not distract from, the chicken.

3	**pounds chicken wings**
1	**onion, chopped**
3	**quarts water**
3	**garlic cloves, peeled and smashed**
½	**teaspoon salt**

1. Adjust oven rack to lower-middle position and heat oven to 450 degrees. Line rimmed baking sheet with aluminum foil and lightly spray with vegetable oil spray. Roast chicken and onion on prepared sheet until golden, about 40 minutes; transfer to slow cooker.

2. Stir water, garlic, and salt into slow cooker. Cover and cook until broth is deeply flavored and rich, 6 to 8 hours on low or 4 to 6 hours on high.

3. Strain broth through fine-mesh strainer into large container, pressing on solids to extract as much liquid as possible. Using large spoon, skim excess fat from surface of broth. (Broth can be refrigerated for up to 4 days or frozen for up to 2 months.)

Per 1-cup serving: Cal 20; Fat 0g; Sat Fat 0g; Chol 0mg; Carb 0g; Protein 5g; Fiber 1g; Sodium 180mg

---

QUICK PREP TIP DEFATTING BROTHS

Defatting a broth is important or else it will add unwelcome grease and fat to your finished dishes. If you do not own a fat separator, simply give the strained broth 10 minutes to settle, then use a large flat spoon to skim the fat off the top. Be sure to hold the spoon parallel to the surface of the soup; you want to collect as little broth as possible.

All-Purpose Beef Broth

Makes 3 quarts • **Cooking Time** 4 to 6 hours on Low • **Slow Cooker Size** 4 to 7 Quarts

✔ **WHY THIS RECIPE WORKS:** Rich, deep beef broth is a must-have in any cook's kitchen, and with the help of the slow cooker, it can be whipped up with ease. Hoping to avoid the work involved in cutting up beef chuck or dealing with beef bones, we turned to ground beef since we had success in the past using it as the foundation for a quicker beef broth—its increased surface area enables more beef flavor to be absorbed by the liquid. For additional meaty undertones, we included a full pound of white mushrooms, which we sautéed with onions and tomato paste before browning the beef and soy sauce (both tomato paste and soy sauce add depth of flavor without calling attention to themselves). Finally, we discovered that the broth needed to cook on low heat, and only for a relatively short period of time (4 to 6 hours). Any longer (or higher) and the mushroom flavor took over and the broth became cloudy. To round out our broth, we added red wine for color and acidity, and an onion, carrot, and celery rib for sweetness.

2	teaspoons canola oil
1	pound white mushrooms, trimmed and halved
1	onion, chopped
3	tablespoons tomato paste
1½	pounds 85 percent lean ground beef
¾	cup dry red wine
3	quarts water
1	carrot, peeled and chopped
1	celery rib, chopped
2	tablespoons low-sodium soy sauce
3	bay leaves

1. Heat oil in 12-inch skillet over medium heat until shimmering. Add mushrooms, onion, and tomato paste, cover, and cook until mushrooms are softened, 5 to 10 minutes. Uncover and continue to cook until mushrooms are dry and browned, 5 to 10 minutes.

2. Stir in ground beef and cook, breaking up any large pieces with wooden spoon, until no longer pink, about 5 minutes. Stir in wine, scraping up any browned bits, and cook until nearly evaporated, 5 to 7 minutes; transfer to slow cooker.

3. Stir water, carrot, celery, soy sauce, and bay leaves into slow cooker. Cover and cook until broth is deeply flavored and rich, 4 to 6 hours on low.

4. Strain broth through fine-mesh strainer into large container, pressing on solids to extract as much liquid as possible. Using large spoon, skim excess fat from surface of broth. (Broth can be refrigerated for up to 4 days or frozen for up to 2 months.)

Per 1-cup serving: Cal 20; Fat 0g; Sat Fat 0g; Chol 0mg; Carb 0g; Protein 3g; Fiber 1g; Sodium 130mg

---

SMART SHOPPING BAY LEAVES

There are two kinds of bay leaves: Turkish and Californian. We prefer the milder flavor of the more common Turkish bay leaves. To test the effect of this ingredient, we prepared three batches of a simple chicken broth, one using two bay leaves (as the recipe indicated), one using no bay leaves, and one using four bay leaves. The broth made without bay leaves was panned as "bland" and "watery," with "no flavor." Too many bay leaves, however, left the broth "bitter," "piney," and "sour." Just the right amount produced a broth that was "balanced," "nicely seasoned," and "herby."

All-Purpose Vegetable Broth

Makes 3 quarts • **Cooking Time** 9 to 11 hours on Low or 6 to 8 hours on High • **Slow Cooker Size** 4 to 7 Quarts

VEGETARIAN

✓ **WHY THIS RECIPE WORKS:** Vegetable broth is essential to full-flavored vegetarian cooking, enhancing meat-free dishes with clean vegetal flavor. It needs gentle cooking, and the slow cooker is the perfect medium in which to bring out the subtlety of many types of vegetables. We knew that in order to create a balanced, intensely flavored broth we needed a precise mix of ingredients. First, we found that a base of onions, scallions, carrots, and celery along with a generous dose of garlic provided a strong background to the broth that was neither too vegetal nor too sweet. The addition of half a head of cauliflower, cut into florets and added with the water, gave our broth pleasant earthiness and nuttiness. Finally, a single tomato added acidic balance, and thyme, bay leaves, and peppercorns rounded out the flavors. To cook our broth, we initially wanted to be able to dump all the vegetables into the cooker raw, but we found that we needed the additional flavor developed from browning the aromatics. We chose a longer cooking time than our meat-based broths so that the flavor of all the different vegetables could shine through. To prevent the broth from looking cloudy, do not press on the solids when straining.

2 teaspoons canola oil

3 onions, chopped

4 scallions, chopped

2 carrots, peeled and chopped

2 celery ribs, chopped

15 garlic cloves, peeled and smashed

3 quarts water

½ head cauliflower (1 pound), cored and cut into 1-inch florets

1 tomato, cored and chopped

8 fresh thyme sprigs

½ teaspoon salt

1 teaspoon black peppercorns

3 bay leaves

1. Heat oil in 12-inch skillet over medium heat until shimmering. Add onions, scallions, carrots, celery, and garlic and cook until vegetables are softened and lightly browned, 8 to 10 minutes. Stir in 1 cup water, scraping up any browned bits; transfer to slow cooker.

2. Stir remaining 11 cups water, cauliflower, tomato, thyme sprigs, salt, peppercorns, and bay leaves into slow cooker. Cover and cook until broth is deeply flavored and rich, 9 to 11 hours on low or 6 to 8 hours on high.

3. Strain broth through fine-mesh strainer into large container, without pressing on solids. (Broth can be refrigerated for up to 4 days or frozen for up to 2 months.)

Per 1-cup serving: Cal 20; Fat 0g; Sat Fat 0g; Chol 0mg; Carb 3g; Protein 2g; Fiber 1g; Sodium 140mg

Stews, Chilis, and Curries

● **EASY PREP**   ● **VEGETARIAN**

Country Beef and Vegetable Stew

Serves 6 • **Cooking Time** 9 to 11 hours on Low or 6 to 8 hours on High • **Slow Cooker Size** 4 to 7 Quarts

✔ **WHY THIS RECIPE WORKS:** For a beef stew packed with fresh vegetables, we limited the amount of beef to 4 ounces per person (using beef chuck roast, which is the best cut for stew) and added plenty of extra vegetables—this kept the portion sizes ample but allowed us to trim fat and calories substantially. And for a simple, classic stew like this, developing a deep flavor base is paramount, which is why we decided to brown the meat before adding it to the slow cooker; we found, however, that we needed to brown only half the meat to create a flavorful fond in the pan, which saved us time. We then browned the mushrooms and aromatics with tomato paste to further build our flavorful base. Covering the pan while cooking the mushrooms and onions allowed them to develop their flavor and color while keeping the fat to a minimum. A little flour cooked in this mixture thickened the stew, and deglazing the pan with wine added richness. After trimming the beef, you should have 1½ pounds of usable meat.

2 pounds boneless beef chuck-eye roast, trimmed of all visible fat and cut into 1½-inch pieces

1 teaspoon canola oil

1 pound cremini mushrooms, trimmed and quartered

2 onions, chopped fine

3 tablespoons tomato paste

4 garlic cloves, minced

1 tablespoon minced fresh thyme or 1 teaspoon dried

½ cup all-purpose flour

1 cup dry red wine

3 cups chicken broth, plus extra as needed

1 tablespoon low-sodium soy sauce

2 bay leaves
  Salt and pepper

1 pound red potatoes, unpeeled, cut into 1-inch pieces

1 pound carrots, peeled, halved lengthwise, and sliced 1 inch thick

1 cup frozen peas

¼ cup minced fresh parsley

1. Pat beef dry with paper towels. Heat oil in 12-inch skillet over medium-high heat until just smoking. Brown half of beef on all sides, about 8 minutes; transfer to slow cooker along with remaining beef.

2. Add mushrooms and onions to fat left in skillet, cover, and cook over medium heat until softened, about 5 minutes. Uncover and continue to cook until mushrooms are dry and browned, about 5 minutes. Stir in tomato paste, garlic, and thyme and cook until fragrant, about 1 minute. Stir in flour and cook for 1 minute. Slowly stir in wine, scraping up any browned bits, and simmer until almost completely evaporated, 5 to 7 minutes. Stir in 1 cup broth, smoothing out any lumps; transfer to slow cooker.

3. Stir remaining 2 cups broth, soy sauce, bay leaves, and ¾ teaspoon salt into slow cooker, then stir in potatoes and carrots. Cover and cook until beef is tender, 9 to 11 hours on low or 6 to 8 hours on high.

4. Discard bay leaves. Stir in peas and let sit until heated through, about 5 minutes. (Adjust stew consistency with extra hot broth as needed.) Stir in parsley and season with salt and pepper to taste. Serve.

Per 1⅔-cup serving: Cal 380; Fat 6g; Sat Fat 2g; Chol 75mg; Carb 40g; Protein 34g; Fiber 6g; Sodium 860mg *To reduce sodium level to 670mg, use unsalted broth.

North African Beef Stew

Serves 6 • **Cooking Time** 9 to 11 hours on Low or 6 to 8 hours on High • **Slow Cooker Size** 4 to 7 Quarts

☑ **WHY THIS RECIPE WORKS:** For a unique take on slow-cooker beef stew, this recipe matches rich beef with the intriguing flavors of Tunisia and Morocco. We created our own mixture of North African spices to serve as the heart of our stew. The traditional blend of warm spices can be challenging to find in a grocery store, and chances are you have coriander, cinnamon, cloves, and cayenne in your pantry already. The addition of orange zest rounded out the deep flavor of the dish. The vibrant combination of spices allowed us to skip browning the meat, saving us time and mess without sacrificing any flavor. Swiss chard and sweet potatoes were delicious and traditional pairings with the stew, and better yet, both are nutritional powerhouses. To thicken the stew we mashed some of the sweet potatoes, which we had cooked separately in a foil packet. Removing the stems from the Swiss chard, and cutting the leaves into 1-inch pieces, allowed the leafy green to become tender when added for the last 20 minutes of the cooking time. After trimming the beef, you should have 1½ pounds of usable meat.

2	onions, chopped fine
4	garlic cloves, minced
¾	teaspoon ground coriander
½	teaspoon ground cinnamon
¼	teaspoon ground cloves
⅛	teaspoon cayenne pepper
1	teaspoon canola oil
4	cups chicken broth, plus extra as needed
3	(2-inch) strips orange zest Salt and pepper
2	pounds boneless beef chuck-eye roast, trimmed of all visible fat and cut into 1½-inch pieces
1½	pounds sweet potatoes, peeled and cut into 1-inch pieces
12	ounces Swiss chard, stemmed and cut into 1-inch pieces

1. Microwave onions, garlic, coriander, cinnamon, cloves, cayenne, and oil in bowl, stirring occasionally, until onions are softened, about 5 minutes; transfer to slow cooker.

2. Stir broth, orange zest, and ½ teaspoon salt into slow cooker, then stir in beef. Wrap potatoes in foil packet; lay packet on top of stew. Cover and cook until beef is tender, 9 to 11 hours on low or 6 to 8 hours on high.

3. Transfer foil packet to plate. Discard orange zest. Carefully open packet (watch for steam). Transfer 1½ cups potatoes to bowl and mash with potato masher until smooth. Gently stir remaining potatoes with any accumulated juice, mashed potatoes, and Swiss chard into stew. Cover and cook on high until chard is tender, about 20 minutes. (Adjust stew consistency with extra hot broth as needed.) Season with salt and pepper to taste. Serve.

Per 1⅔-cup serving: Cal 270; Fat 6g; Sat Fat 2g; Chol 75mg; Carb 24g; Protein 30g; Fiber 5g; Sodium 730mg *To reduce sodium level to 480mg, use unsalted broth.

QUICK PREP TIP
MAKING A FOIL PACKET
It is sometimes necessary to wrap vegetables in an aluminum foil packet to keep them from overcooking. To make foil packet, place vegetables on 1 side of large sheet of aluminum foil. Fold foil over vegetables and crimp 3 open edges to seal. Place packet on top of ingredients in slow cooker, pressing it gently to fit.

Pork and White Bean Stew with Kale

Serves 6 • **Cooking Time** 6 to 8 hours on Low or 4 to 6 hours on High • **Slow Cooker Size** 4 to 7 Quarts

✔**WHY THIS RECIPE WORKS:** For a real stick-to-your-ribs meal, we used a classic white bean stew as a starting point and incorporated meaty pork and earthy kale. Boneless country-style pork ribs required minimal prep work, and thanks to plenty of intramuscular fat, they were moist and fall-apart tender after several hours in the slow cooker. Dried beans were still undercooked by the time the pork was done, but canned white beans cooked through perfectly in the same amount of time and required little preparation. To give the stew body, we pureed a portion of them with broth before adding them to the slow cooker. To boost the fresh flavor of the stew and complement the rich pork and beans, we added 2 tablespoons of whole-grain mustard after the kale had cooked through. Cutting the kale into 1-inch pieces allowed the hearty green to become tender in just 20 minutes of cooking time.

2 onions, chopped fine

4 garlic cloves, minced

1 tablespoon minced fresh thyme or 1 teaspoon dried

1 teaspoon canola oil

3 (15-ounce) cans cannellini beans, rinsed

4 cups chicken broth, plus extra as needed
Salt and pepper

1½ pounds boneless country-style pork ribs, trimmed of all visible fat and cut into 1½-inch pieces

8 ounces kale, stemmed and cut into 1-inch pieces

2 tablespoons whole-grain mustard

1. Microwave onions, garlic, thyme, and oil in bowl, stirring occasionally, until onions are softened, about 5 minutes; transfer to slow cooker.

2. Process one-third of beans and 1 cup broth in blender until smooth, about 30 seconds; transfer to slow cooker. Stir in remaining beans, remaining 3 cups broth, and ¼ teaspoon salt, then stir in pork. Cover and cook until pork is tender, 6 to 8 hours on low or 4 to 6 hours on high.

3. Stir in kale, cover, and cook on high until tender, 20 to 30 minutes. (Adjust stew consistency with extra hot broth as needed.) Stir in mustard and season with salt and pepper to taste. Serve.

Per 1⅔-cup serving: Cal 340; Fat 8g; Sat Fat 2.5g; Chol 85mg; Carb 29g; Protein 36g; Fiber 8g; Sodium 990mg *To reduce sodium level to 410mg, use low-sodium beans and unsalted broth.

SMART SHOPPING COUNTRY-STYLE PORK RIBS
Country-style pork ribs aren't actually ribs at all. They're well-marbled pork chops cut from the upper side of the rib cage, from the fatty blade end of the loin. Because they are leaner than pork butt (a common cut used in long-simmered pork dishes) but still contain a good amount of intramuscular fat, they are a great choice when you want to have tender, juicy chunks of pork and be mindful of fat and calories. Butchers usually cut them into individual ribs and package several together.

Spanish Chicken and Quinoa Stew

Serves 6 • **Cooking Time** 3 to 5 hours on Low • **Slow Cooker Size** 4 to 7 Quarts

✔ **WHY THIS RECIPE WORKS:** For a weeknight meal with a Mediterranean edge, we took inspiration from the classic saffron-infused sauces used in Spanish dishes to make a hearty stew. Our starting point was saffron microwaved with tomato paste, smoked paprika, onions, and garlic to intensify their flavors. We added this flavorful mixture to the slow cooker along with chicken broth, bone-in chicken breasts with the skin removed, and canned diced tomatoes. To thicken the stew, we added the powerhouse grain quinoa, which is both flavorful and nutrient dense. After hours of cooking, the spices infused the stew with rich flavor, and the quinoa absorbed the cooking liquid. For a final touch of freshness and acidity, we served the stew with a relish of ripe avocado, red bell pepper, and chopped fresh parsley seasoned with sherry vinegar. If you buy unwashed quinoa (or if you are unsure if it's washed), rinse it before cooking.

2	onions, chopped fine
¼	cup tomato paste
3	garlic cloves, minced
1½	tablespoons smoked paprika
1	teaspoon canola oil
¼	teaspoon saffron threads, crumbled
5	cups chicken broth, plus extra as needed
1	(14.5-ounce) can diced tomatoes
¾	cup prewashed quinoa
	Salt and pepper
3	(12-ounce) bone-in split chicken breasts, skin removed, trimmed of all visible fat
1	cup frozen corn
1	avocado, halved, pitted, and cut into ½-inch pieces
1	red bell pepper, stemmed, seeded, and chopped fine
2	tablespoons chopped fresh parsley
1	tablespoon sherry vinegar

1. Microwave onions, tomato paste, garlic, paprika, oil, and saffron in bowl, stirring occasionally, until onions are softened, about 5 minutes; transfer to slow cooker. Stir in broth, tomatoes and their juice, quinoa, and ½ teaspoon salt. Nestle chicken into slow cooker, cover, and cook until chicken and quinoa are tender and stew is thickened, 3 to 5 hours on low.

2. Transfer chicken to carving board and let cool slightly. Cut chicken into 1-inch pieces; discard bones.

3. Stir chicken and corn into stew and let sit until heated through, about 5 minutes. (Adjust stew consistency with extra hot broth as needed.) Season with salt and pepper to taste.

4. Combine avocado, bell pepper, parsley, and vinegar in bowl. Top individual portions with avocado mixture before serving.

Per 2-cup serving: Cal 360; Fat 10g; Sat Fat 1.5g; Chol 70mg; Carb 35g; Protein 33g; Fiber 8g; Sodium 1020mg *To reduce sodium level to 530mg, use unsalted broth and no-salt-added tomatoes.

SMART SHOPPING QUINOA
Quinoa originated in the Andes Mountains of South America, and while it is generally treated as a grain, it is actually the seed of the goosefoot plant. Sometimes referred to as a "supergrain," quinoa is high in protein and possesses all of the amino acids in the balanced amounts that our bodies require. Beyond its nutritional prowess, we love quinoa for its addictive crunch and nutty taste. Unless labeled as "prewashed," quinoa should always be rinsed before cooking to remove its protective layer (called saponin), which is unpleasantly bitter.

Old-Fashioned Chicken Stew

Serves 6 • **Cooking Time** 3 to 5 hours on Low • **Slow Cooker Size** 4 to 7 Quarts

✓ **WHY THIS RECIPE WORKS:** For a healthy chicken stew with rich flavor and vibrant vegetables, we started with bone-in chicken breasts but removed the skin to keep the fat count down (and ensure that the stew would not be greasy). To make a deeply flavored broth without adding calories or fat, we sautéed aromatics in just a teaspoon of oil with a little tomato paste, which we have found adds richness and color without a noticeable tomatoey presence. In early tests we discovered that our chunky potatoes and carrots were just not tender when the chicken was cooked. So after building a flavorful base for our stew in a skillet, we added part of the chicken broth and the potatoes and carrots, letting the vegetables simmer gently for 10 minutes before adding them to the slow cooker. This ensured that the vegetables and chicken were perfectly cooked through at the same time.

1 teaspoon canola oil

2 onions, chopped fine

3 tablespoons tomato paste

3 garlic cloves, minced

2 teaspoons minced fresh thyme or ½ teaspoon dried

⅓ cup all-purpose flour

½ cup dry white wine

4 cups chicken broth, plus extra as needed

8 ounces red potatoes, unpeeled, cut into ½-inch pieces

3 carrots, peeled and sliced ½ inch thick

8 ounces white mushrooms, stemmed and halved if small or quartered if large

2 bay leaves
   Salt and pepper

3 (12-ounce) bone-in split chicken breasts, skin removed, trimmed of all visible fat

1 cup frozen peas

2 tablespoons minced fresh parsley

1. Heat oil in 12-inch skillet over medium heat until shimmering. Add onions and cook until softened and lightly browned, 5 to 7 minutes. Stir in tomato paste, garlic, and thyme and cook until fragrant, about 1 minute. Stir in flour and cook for 1 minute. Slowly whisk in wine, scraping up any browned bits. Whisk in 2 cups broth, smoothing out any lumps. Stir in potatoes and carrots and bring to simmer. Cover, reduce heat to medium-low, and cook until vegetables just begin to soften, about 10 minutes; transfer to slow cooker.

2. Stir remaining 2 cups broth, mushrooms, bay leaves, and ¾ teaspoon salt into slow cooker. Nestle chicken into slow cooker, cover, and cook until chicken is tender, 3 to 5 hours on low.

3. Transfer chicken to carving board and let cool slightly. Cut chicken into 1-inch pieces; discard bones. Discard bay leaves.

4. Stir chicken and peas into stew and let sit until heated through, about 5 minutes. (Adjust stew consistency with extra hot broth as needed.) Stir in parsley and season with salt and pepper to taste. Serve.

Per 2-cup serving: Cal 280; Fat 4g; Sat Fat 0.5g; Chol 70mg; Carb 26g; Protein 31g; Fiber 4g; Sodium 860mg *To reduce sodium level to 610mg, use unsalted broth.

ALL ABOUT Slow-Cooker Stews, Chilis, and Curries

It's hard enough to make healthy, hearty stews and chilis on the stovetop, where you have the benefit of browning and reduction to develop big, bold flavors, not to mention complete control of temperature to ensure that everything is cooked properly. But in the slow cooker, achieving this is even harder. Sure, the moist, gentle heat of the slow cooker helps cook lean proteins without much additional fat, but it took some test kitchen creativity to develop slow-cooker stews and chilis that were both healthy and worthy of the dinner table. Here is what we have learned. For information on chicken and vegetable broths and their sodium contents, see page 25.

Microwave and Use Less Fat

Over the years, we've learned that the microwave is a great ally when creating slow-cooker recipes. In many (but not all) recipes it can eliminate the need to get out a skillet, especially if you are just softening aromatics and blooming spices. As an added benefit, this method usually requires less fat—just a teaspoon or two of oil. Throughout this book, when we add delicate fresh vegetables at the end of a long cooking time, we often simply "steam" them in the microwave with a little water before adding them to the slow cooker. This helps the vegetables cook without any loss of flavor and ensures that they remain bright and crisp-tender.

Adjust the Ratio of Meat to Vegetables

Meat stews are traditionally heavy on the meat and light on the vegetables. In order to create healthier stews, we limited the amount of meat to 4 ounces (once trimmed) per person and added plenty of extra vegetables—this kept portion sizes ample but trimmed fat and calories substantially.

Finish with Fresh Flavors

The moist heat environment and long cooking times that come with the slow cooker are notorious for muting flavors, so many stews need a flavor boost before serving. You'll see that we often finish our stews (and other dishes) with fresh herbs, citrus juice, vinegar, or other flavorful ingredients, like brown sugar and coconut milk.

Think Differently About Thickeners

Since there is no opportunity for stews to reduce and thicken naturally in the moist environment of the slow cooker, thickeners are often necessary. Classic fat- and flour-based roux add unwanted work (and fat) because they require extra stovetop cooking to remove the raw flour taste. So when possible, we try to use ingredients already in the stew to help thicken it. We have found success processing portions of canned beans and frozen corn before building the stew base, or finishing a stew by mashing some of the cooked beans and vegetables. If all else fails, we typically grab instant tapioca, which we have found over the years to be a great no-fuss thickener that can be stirred in at the start.

Handle Vegetables with Care

We worked hard to pack our stews with interesting combinations of vegetables, so naturally we also focused a lot of attention on ensuring that they were perfectly cooked. For stews that had a short stay in the slow cooker, sturdier vegetables like potatoes and carrots, depending on how large they were cut, just could not cook through properly. In these instances, we parcooked them before adding them to the slow cooker. For longer-cooking stews, the opposite was often the case, with vegetables turning mushy, colorless, and flavorless. In these instances, we often needed to slow down their cooking by insulating them in a foil packet and placing it on top of the stew.

Southern-Style Shrimp and Corn Stew

Serves 6 • **Cooking Time** 3 to 5 hours on Low or 2 to 4 hours on High • **Slow Cooker Size** 4 to 7 Quarts

✓ **WHY THIS RECIPE WORKS:** To achieve a hearty and healthy shrimp and corn stew, we started with the trinity of Southern cooking: onion, bell pepper, and celery. We microwaved the aromatics with the sausage and tomato paste along with Old Bay seasoning. And since the sausage rendered some of its fat when microwaved, there was no need for additional oil. Short-grain brown rice was nutrient-rich and held its shape in the slow cooker. Cooking it in the flavorful broth made the stew even more satisfying while slightly thickening it. We added the corn at the end of the cooking time to ensure that it retained its vibrant color and a satisfying crunch. Also, stirring in the shrimp at the end of the cooking time and letting them cook on high for 15 minutes ensured that they did not overcook. Long-grain brown rice can be substituted for the short-grain rice, if desired; however, the rice will not hold it's shape as well.

8   ounces andouille sausage, halved lengthwise and sliced ½ inch thick
2   onions, chopped fine
3   celery ribs, sliced ¼ inch thick
2   red bell peppers, stemmed, seeded, and chopped fine
2   tablespoons tomato paste
4   garlic cloves, minced
1   teaspoon Old Bay seasoning
2½ cups water
2   cups chicken broth, plus extra as needed
½   cup short-grain brown rice
2   tablespoons instant tapioca
    Salt and pepper
12 ounces medium shrimp (41 to 50 per pound), peeled, deveined, and tails removed
4   cups frozen corn, thawed
1½ teaspoons hot sauce, plus extra for seasoning

1. Microwave andouille, onions, celery, bell peppers, tomato paste, garlic, and Old Bay in covered bowl, stirring occasionally, until vegetables are softened, 8 to 10 minutes; transfer to slow cooker. Stir in water, broth, rice, tapioca, and ¼ teaspoon salt. Cover and cook until flavors meld and rice is tender, 3 to 5 hours on low or 2 to 4 hours on high.

2. Stir shrimp and corn into stew, cover, and cook on high until shrimp are opaque throughout, 15 to 20 minutes. (Adjust stew consistency with extra hot broth as needed.) Stir in hot sauce and season with salt, pepper, and extra hot sauce to taste. Serve.

Per 1⅔-cup serving: Cal 350; Fat 8g; Sat Fat 2g; Chol 75mg; Carb 53g; Protein 20g; Fiber 5g; Sodium 910mg *To reduce sodium level to 780mg, use unsalted broth.

QUICK PREP TIP DEVEINING SHRIMP
To devein shrimp, hold shrimp firmly in 1 hand, then use paring knife to cut down back side of shrimp, about ⅛ to ¼ inch deep, to expose vein. Using tip of knife, gently remove vein. Wipe knife against paper towel to remove vein and discard.

Hearty Farro and Butternut Squash Stew

Serves 6 • **Cooking Time** 10 to 12 hours on Low or 7 to 9 hours on High • **Slow Cooker Size** 4 to 7 Quarts

✔ **WHY THIS RECIPE WORKS:** For a vegetarian stew that was so flavorful and substantial even carnivores would be satisfied, we began with sweet, nutty farro and added mushrooms for meaty depth and butternut squash for substance. To start, we microwaved the mushrooms and aromatics with just a teaspoon of oil until the mushrooms softened, released some of their moisture, and were flavored by the aromatics. Vegetable broth worked well for the cooking liquid and provided a subtly sweet backbone. To give it a boost, we stirred in some white wine, which contributed complexity and brightness to our hearty stew. We cooked the squash in a foil packet on top of the stew to make sure it would retain its sweet flavor and bright color. Fresh, peppery arugula provided color and freshness. Do not substitute pearl, quick-cooking, or presteamed farro for the whole farro in this recipe; you may need to read the ingredient list on the package carefully to determine if the farro is presteamed. Serve with grated Parmesan, if desired. For information on making a foil packet, see page 51.

1½ **pounds cremini mushrooms, trimmed and quartered**

1 **onion, chopped fine**

2 **tablespoons tomato paste**

3 **garlic cloves, minced**

2 **tablespoons plus 1 teaspoon extra-virgin olive oil**

6 **cups vegetable broth, plus extra as needed**

1 **cup whole farro**

¼ **cup dry white wine**

2 **bay leaves**

Salt and pepper

1½ **pounds butternut squash, peeled, seeded, and cut into ½-inch pieces (4 cups)**

5 **ounces (5 cups) baby arugula**

1. Microwave mushrooms, onion, tomato paste, garlic, and 1 teaspoon oil in covered bowl, stirringly occasionally, until vegetables are softened, 8 to 10 minutes; transfer to slow cooker.

2. Stir broth, farro, wine, bay leaves, and ½ teaspoon salt into slow cooker. Wrap squash in foil packet; lay packet on top of stew. Cover and cook until farro is tender, 10 to 12 hours on low or 7 to 9 hours on high.

3. Transfer foil packet to plate. Discard bay leaves. Carefully open packet (watch for steam) and stir squash along with any accumulated juice into stew. Stir in arugula, 1 handful at a time, and let sit until wilted, about 5 minutes. (Adjust stew consistency with extra hot broth as needed.) Season with salt and pepper to taste. Drizzle each portion with 1 teaspoon oil before serving.

Per 2-cup serving: Cal 330; Fat 7g; Sat Fat 1g; Chol 0mg; Carb 58g; Protein 10g; Fiber 7g; Sodium 1010mg *To reduce sodium level to 390mg, use low-sodium broth.

SMART SHOPPING FARRO

Farro is a whole-grain form of wheat that has been enjoyed for centuries in Tuscany and central Italy. Thanks to praise for farro from scores of culinary magazines and top chefs, it is gaining favor with home cooks and is more widely available in supermarkets. We love it for its slightly sweet, big, nutty flavor and chewy texture, not to mention its health benefits (it is high in fiber and protein). Italians traditionally cook farro in the same manner as Arborio rice to create a creamy dish called *farrotto*, though we find it has great potential in slow-cooker dishes, where it benefits from the gentle simmer and turns perfectly tender. Like many other grains, farro is available in multiple quicker-cooking varieties, including pearl, quick-cooking, and presteamed. While the quicker-cooking varieties are convenient in other applications, we prefer the taste and texture of traditional whole farro in our slow-cooker recipes.

French Lentil Stew

Serves 6 • **Cooking Time** 7 to 9 hours on Low or 4 to 6 hours on High • **Slow Cooker Size** 4 to 7 Quarts

✓ **WHY THIS RECIPE WORKS:** For a warming lentil stew with a deep flavor profile and hearty texture, we turned to French green lentils. Also known as *lentilles du Puy*, these legumes retain some of their texture during cooking without getting too soft, and since they are high in fiber, they make for a healthy and filling stew. Caramelizing the onions required getting out a skillet, but our patience was rewarded with a richly flavored foundation. For a truly satisfying stew, we added brown rice to the mix, which added depth of flavor and broke down slightly as it cooked, helping to thicken the stew. Searching for a hearty green to offer a colorful contrast to the dark lentils, we settled on shredded Brussels sprouts, which we added at the end of the cooking time. A little sherry vinegar stirred in just before serving helped to brighten the stew. While we prefer French green lentils for this recipe, any type of lentil will work except red or yellow. Short-grain brown rice can be substituted for the long-grain rice, if desired.

2	slices bacon, chopped fine
3	onions, chopped
½	teaspoon brown sugar
3	garlic cloves, minced
1	tablespoon minced fresh thyme or 1 teaspoon dried
1	tablespoon mustard seeds
1½	teaspoons ground coriander
	Pinch cayenne pepper
8	cups chicken broth, plus extra as needed
4	carrots, peeled, halved lengthwise, and sliced ½ inch thick
1	cup lentils, picked over and rinsed
½	cup long-grain brown rice
	Salt and pepper
8	ounces Brussels sprouts, trimmed, halved, and sliced thin
2	tablespoons sherry vinegar

1. Cook bacon in 12-inch skillet over medium heat until crisp, 5 to 7 minutes. Add onions and sugar, cover, and cook over medium heat until softened, about 5 minutes. Uncover, reduce heat to medium-low, and continue to cook, stirring often, until onions are caramelized, about 20 minutes. Stir in garlic, thyme, mustard seeds, coriander, and cayenne and cook until fragrant, about 1 minute. Stir in 1 cup broth, scraping up any browned bits; transfer to slow cooker.

2. Stir remaining 7 cups broth, carrots, lentils, rice, and ½ teaspoon salt into slow cooker. Cover and cook until lentils are tender, 7 to 9 hours on low or 4 to 6 hours on high.

3. Stir Brussels sprouts into stew and let sit until softened, about 5 minutes. (Adjust stew consistency with extra hot broth as needed.) Stir in vinegar and season with salt and pepper to taste. Serve.

Per 1⅔-cup serving: Cal 290; Fat 5g; Sat Fat 1.5g; Chol 5mg; Carb 47g; Protein 17g; Fiber 10g; Sodium 990mg *To reduce sodium level to 480mg, use unsalted broth.

QUICK PREP TIP PICKING THYME
Picking minuscule leaves off fresh thyme can really pluck at your nerves. In the test kitchen, we rely on some tricks to make this job go faster. If the thyme has very thin, pliable stems, just chop the stems and leaves together, discarding the tough bottom portions as you go. If the stems are thicker and woodier, run your thumb and forefinger down the stems to release the leaves and smaller offshoots. The tender tips can be left intact and chopped along with the leaves once the woodier stems have been sheared clean and discarded.

Weeknight Chili

Serves 6 • **Cooking Time** 6 to 8 hours on Low or 4 to 6 hours on High • **Slow Cooker Size** 4 to 7 Quarts

WHY THIS RECIPE WORKS: Chili is a slow-cooker favorite, but coming up with a recipe that was both healthy and easy to prepare was a bit of a challenge. We microwaved the aromatics with a blend of chili powder, cumin, and oregano and a little oil to bloom the spices, which eliminated the need for any prep time spent on the stovetop. As for the beef, for this leaner take on classic ground beef chili we turned to 93 percent lean ground beef, which we found stayed moist during cooking without producing an oil slick on the surface of the finished chili. Microwaving the beef made it firm enough to break into coarse crumbles that didn't turn grainy during cooking. The addition of crushed tomatoes brought thickening power and rich tomatoey flavor to our beefy chili. Adding two cans of black beans made the chili feel hearty and satisfying without any additional meat. Serve with your favorite chili garnishes.

1	pound 93 percent lean ground beef
2	onions, chopped fine
2	red or green bell peppers, stemmed, seeded, and cut into ½-inch pieces
6	garlic cloves, minced
2	tablespoons chili powder
1	tablespoon ground cumin
2	teaspoons canola oil
1½	teaspoons minced canned chipotle chile in adobo sauce
1	teaspoon dried oregano
2	(28-ounce) cans crushed tomatoes
2	(15-ounce) cans black beans, rinsed
	Salt and pepper
4	scallions, sliced thin
1	tablespoon packed brown sugar

1. Microwave ground beef in bowl, stirring occasionally, until beef is no longer pink, about 5 minutes; transfer to slow cooker, breaking up any large pieces of beef. Microwave onions, bell peppers, garlic, chili powder, cumin, oil, chipotle, and oregano in bowl, stirring occasionally, until vegetables are softened, 5 to 7 minutes; transfer to slow cooker.

2. Stir tomatoes, beans, and ½ teaspoon salt into slow cooker. Cover and cook until beef is tender, 6 to 8 hours on low or 4 to 6 hours on high.

3. Break up any remaining large pieces of beef with spoon. Stir in scallions and sugar and season with salt and pepper to taste. Serve.

Per 2-cup serving: Cal 340; Fat 8g; Sat Fat 2.5g; Chol 50mg; Carb 42g; Protein 26g; Fiber 11g; Sodium 1000mg *To reduce sodium level to 580mg, use no-salt-added tomatoes and low-sodium beans.

SMART SHOPPING CHILI POWDER
To see what the difference was among the various brands of chili powder found at the market, we gathered up seven widely available brands and pitted them against one another in a taste-off. To focus on the flavor of the chili powders, we tasted them sprinkled over potatoes and cooked in beef-and-bean chili. Many brands included unusual ingredients, but our top picks stuck with classic flavorings: cumin, oregano, and garlic. We also liked the addition of paprika, which gave our top two picks a nice complexity. In the end, tasters concluded that **Morton & Bassett Chili Powder** was the clear winner. Tasters found that it had a deep, roasty, complex flavor; subtle sweetness; and just the right amount of heat.

Green Chicken Chili

Serves 6 • **Cooking Time** 3 to 5 hours on Low • **Slow Cooker Size** 4 to 7 Quarts

WHY THIS RECIPE WORKS: To achieve a deeply flavored green chicken chili in the slow cooker, we needed to build flavor every step of the way. We started by choosing bone-in chicken breasts to ensure that our chili had big chicken flavor and that the meat would remain moist and tender in the slow cooker; removing the chicken skin ensured that the chili would not be greasy and of course kept the fat and calories to a minimum. We used both poblano chiles and canned chipotle chile to emphasize the chili flavor. Then, to take the flavors up a notch and build the base of the chili, we broiled the chiles along with the aromatics and spices to concentrate their flavor. We pureed some of our broiled chile-onion mixture to give body to the base and left some of the mixture coarsely ground to add texture. Fresh cilantro and lime juice stirred into the slow cooker at the end of cooking added freshness. Serve with your favorite chili garnishes.

2	pounds poblano chiles, stemmed, halved, and seeded
2	onions, chopped
6	garlic cloves, minced
4	teaspoons ground cumin
2	teaspoons ground coriander
2	teaspoons canola oil
1½	teaspoons minced canned chipotle chile in adobo sauce
3	cups chicken broth
1	(14.5-ounce) can diced tomatoes Salt and pepper
3	(12-ounce) bone-in split chicken breasts, skin removed, trimmed of all visible fat
2	tablespoons minced fresh cilantro
1	tablespoon lime juice, plus extra for seasoning

1. Adjust oven rack 6 inches from broiler element and heat broiler. Toss poblanos, onions, garlic, cumin, coriander, oil, and chipotle together in bowl. Spread poblano mixture in aluminum foil–lined rimmed baking sheet. Broil vegetables until poblanos are spotty black and vegetables begin to soften, about 15 minutes, flipping poblanos halfway through broiling.

2. Transfer half of vegetable mixture to food processor and pulse until coarsely ground, about 8 pulses; transfer to slow cooker. Process remaining vegetable mixture in now-empty processor until smooth, about 30 seconds, scraping down sides of bowl as needed; transfer to slow cooker.

3. Stir broth, tomatoes and their juice, and ½ teaspoon salt into slow cooker. Nestle chicken into slow cooker, cover, and cook until chicken is tender, 3 to 5 hours on low.

4. Transfer chicken to carving board, let cool slightly, then shred into bite-size pieces using 2 forks; discard bones. Stir shredded chicken into chili and let sit until heated through, about 5 minutes. Stir in cilantro and lime juice and season with salt, pepper, and extra lime juice to taste. Serve.

Per 1⅔-cup serving: Cal 250; Fat 6g; Sat Fat 1g; Chol 85mg; Carb 17g; Protein 34g; Fiber 5g; Sodium 890mg *To reduce sodium level to 530mg, use unsalted broth and no-salt-added tomatoes.

SMART SHOPPING POBLANOS
Poblano chiles are medium-size Mexican chiles. They taste slightly bitter, similar to green bell peppers but with a spicier finish. They are sold both fresh and dried (the dried are called anchos). If you can't find them, you can substitute a medium green bell pepper and half of a jalapeño chile per poblano.

Cuban White Bean and Plantain Chili

Serves 6 • **Cooking Time** 9 to 11 hours on Low or 6 to 8 hours on High • **Slow Cooker Size** 4 to 7 Quarts

✔ **WHY THIS RECIPE WORKS:** This satisfying vegetarian chili brings the flavors of Cuba home to your slow cooker. White beans, a dietary staple in Havana, are tender and rich, especially when you use dried beans, which are suited to low-and-slow cooking. To replicate the intricate spice profiles of Latin cuisine, we used a combination of citrusy coriander, earthy cumin, warm oregano, and a fresh jalapeño for complexity. Added to the chili, plantains became tender during the cooking process, and when we mashed a portion with some of the beans, they became a natural thickener. Seasoning with cider vinegar at the end of cooking brought fresh acidity to the finished chili. We prefer the softer texture and added sweetness of ripe plantains in this dish. Green plantains can be substituted; however, they will have a much firmer texture and more starchy flavor.

2	**onions, chopped fine**
6	**garlic cloves, minced**
1	**jalapeño chile, stemmed, seeded, and minced**
1½	**tablespoons ground cumin**
1	**tablespoon ground coriander**
2	**teaspoons canola oil**
1	**teaspoon dried oregano**
6	**cups vegetable broth**
3	**cups water**
2	**pounds ripe plantains, peeled, quartered lengthwise, and sliced 1 inch thick**
1	**pound (2½ cups) dried small white beans, picked over and rinsed**
2	**bay leaves**
	Salt and pepper
1½	**cups frozen corn, thawed**
¼	**cup minced fresh cilantro**
1	**tablespoon apple cider vinegar, plus extra for seasoning**

1. Microwave onions, garlic, jalapeño, cumin, coriander, oil, and oregano in bowl, stirring occasionally, until onions are softened, about 5 minutes; transfer to slow cooker. Stir in broth, water, plantains, beans, bay leaves, and ½ teaspoon salt. Cover and cook until beans are tender, 9 to 11 hours on low or 6 to 8 hours on high.

2. Discard bay leaves. Transfer 1 cup cooked beans and plantains to bowl and mash with potato masher until mostly smooth. Stir mashed bean mixture and corn into chili and let sit until heated through, about 5 minutes. Stir in cilantro and vinegar and season with salt, pepper, and extra vinegar to taste. Serve.

Per 2-cup serving: Cal 490; Fat 3.5g; Sat Fat 0.5g; Chol 0mg; Carb 100g; Protein 20g; Fiber 24g; Sodium 980mg *To reduce sodium level to 360mg, use low-sodium broth.

QUICK PREP TIP PEELING PLANTAINS
A plantain is a large, starchy variety of banana that is popular in Latin American, African, and Asian cuisines. Plantains mature from green (under-ripe) to yellow (ripe) to black (overripe). Though fully ripe plantains can be eaten out of hand, it is more common to cook them before eating. Their flavor is reminiscent of squash and potato, and they have a dense, spongy texture. Plantains are not as easy to peel as bananas. After trimming the ends, cut the plantain in half and make a slit in the peel of each piece with a paring knife, from one end to the other end. Then peel away the skin with your fingers.

Spicy Pork Chili with Black-Eyed Peas

Serves 6 • **Cooking Time** 6 to 8 hours on Low or 4 to 6 hours on High • **Slow Cooker Size** 4 to 7 Quarts

✓ **WHY THIS RECIPE WORKS:** For a slow-cooker chili that was both healthy and out of the ordinary, we looked for a way to pair sweet potatoes with a Southern staple: earthy black-eyed peas. A spicy, smoky flavor profile seemed like a natural fit for these ingredients, and we added country-style pork ribs, which are lean and become meltingly tender in the slow cooker. A hefty dose of bold aromatics, including chili powder and chipotle chile, ensured that this chili made a statement. And to preserve the bright color and flavor of the chunks of sweet potato, we wrapped them in an insulating foil packet. Stirring in the cilantro at the last minute maintained its color and fresh flavor. Serve with your favorite chili garnishes. For information on making a foil packet, see page 51.

2	onions, chopped fine
6	garlic cloves, minced
2	tablespoons chili powder
2	tablespoons tomato paste
2	teaspoons canola oil
1½	teaspoons minced canned chipotle chile in adobo sauce
3	(15-ounce) cans black-eyed peas, rinsed
3	cups chicken broth
	Salt and pepper
1½	pounds boneless country-style pork ribs, trimmed of all visible fat and cut into 1½-inch pieces
1½	pounds sweet potatoes, peeled and cut into ½-inch pieces
2	tablespoons minced fresh cilantro

1. Microwave onions, garlic, chili powder, tomato paste, oil, and chipotle in bowl, stirring occasionally, until onions are softened, about 5 minutes; transfer to slow cooker.

2. Process one-third of peas and 1 cup broth in blender until smooth, about 30 seconds; transfer to slow cooker. Stir in remaining peas, remaining 2 cups broth, and ½ teaspoon salt, then stir in pork. Wrap potatoes in foil packet; lay packet on top of stew. Cover and cook until pork is tender, 6 to 8 hours on low or 4 to 6 hours on high.

3. Transfer foil packet to plate. Carefully open packet (watch for steam) and stir potatoes with any accumulated juice into chili. Stir in cilantro and season with salt and pepper to taste. Serve.

Per 2-cup serving: Cal 390; Fat 9g; Sat Fat 2.5g; Chol 85mg; Carb 42g; Protein 35g; Fiber 10g; Sodium 690mg *To reduce sodium level to 500mg, use unsalted broth.

SMART SHOPPING SWEET POTATO OR YAM?
You often hear "yam" and "sweet potato" used interchangeably, but they actually belong to completely different botanical families. Yams, generally found in Latin and Asian markets, are often sold in chunks (they can grow to be several feet long) and are available in dozens of varieties, with flesh ranging from white to light yellow to pink, and skin from off-white to brown. They all have very starchy flesh. Sweet potatoes are also found in several varieties and can have firm or soft flesh, but it's the soft varieties that have in the past been mislabeled as "yams," and the confusion continues to this day. In an attempt to remedy this, the USDA now requires labels with the term "yam" to be accompanied by the term "sweet potato" when appropriate. We typically buy the conventional sweet potato, a longish, knobby tuber with dark, orangey-brown skin and vivid flesh that cooks up moist and sweet. The buttery-sweet Beauregard is our favorite variety.

Indian-Style Vegetable Curry with Tofu

Serves 6   •   **Cooking Time** 9 to 11 hours on Low or 6 to 8 hours on High   •   **Slow Cooker Size** 4 to 7 Quarts

WHY THIS RECIPE WORKS: Curries are a perfect match for the slow cooker. When the ingredients have the opportunity to cook for hours, the flavors meld and the result is a bold-tasting and complex dish. Although many curries rely on chicken or shrimp for their protein, swapping in tofu ensured an equally satisfying curry. For a flavor-packed dish, we included 2 tablespoons of curry powder and an additional 2 tablespoons of grated fresh ginger. Blooming the curry and half of the ginger (we added the rest later for a zingy punch) in the microwave helped to intensify their flavors and season the onions and garlic. We included tomato paste for a savory depth. Dried chickpeas cooked through perfectly in the slow cooker and absorbed the flavor of the curry. Mashing a portion of the chickpeas gave the curry substantial body. For a rich, velvety sauce, we stirred in light coconut milk; adding it at the end preserved its flavor. Finally, minced cilantro offered a touch of color and freshness. You can substitute firm tofu here if desired; avoid silken, soft, or medium-firm tofu as these varieties will break down while cooking. Serve with rice.

2	onions, chopped fine
6	garlic cloves, minced
2	tablespoons grated fresh ginger
2	tablespoons curry powder
2	tablespoons tomato paste
2	teaspoons canola oil
5	cups vegetable broth
14	ounces extra-firm tofu, cut into ¾-inch cubes
8	ounces (1¼ cups) dried chickpeas, picked over and rinsed
	Salt and pepper
12	ounces cauliflower florets, cut into 1-inch pieces
1	(13.5-ounce) can light coconut milk
2	cups frozen peas, thawed
¼	cup minced fresh cilantro

1. Microwave onions, garlic, 1 tablespoon ginger, curry powder, tomato paste, and oil in bowl, stirring occasionally, until onions are softened, about 5 minutes; transfer to slow cooker. Stir in broth, tofu, chickpeas, and ½ teaspoon salt. Cover and cook until chickpeas are tender, 9 to 11 hours on low or 6 to 8 hours on high.

2. Transfer 2 cups cooked chickpeas to bowl and mash with potato masher until mostly smooth.

3. Microwave cauliflower and 1 tablespoon water in covered bowl, stirring occasionally, until tender, about 6 minutes. Drain cauliflower, then stir into curry. Microwave coconut milk in bowl until hot, about 2 minutes. Stir into curry along with mashed chickpeas, peas, and remaining 1 tablespoon ginger and let sit until heated through, about 5 minutes. Stir in cilantro and season with salt and pepper to taste. Serve.

Per 2-cup serving: Cal 320; Fat 10g; Sat Fat 2g; Chol 0mg; Carb 44g; Protein 18g; Fiber 13g; Sodium 900mg *To reduce sodium level to 380mg, use low-sodium broth.

ON THE SIDE EASY WHITE RICE
Bring 4 quarts water to boil in large saucepan. Stir in 2¼ cups long-grain white rice and 2 teaspoons salt and return to boil. Reduce to simmer and cook gently until rice is tender, 12 to 17 minutes. Drain rice thoroughly and season with salt and pepper to taste. Serves 6.

Per serving: Cal 250; Fat 0g; Sat Fat 0g; Chol 0mg; Carb 55g; Protein 5g; Fiber 1g; Sodium 100mg

Root Vegetable Tagine with Dried Cherries

Serves 6 • **Cooking Time** 8 to 10 hours on Low or 5 to 7 hours on High • **Slow Cooker Size** 4 to 7 Quarts

WHY THIS RECIPE WORKS: For a vegetarian take on tagine, we turned to root vegetables as our starting point since they would be most likely to withstand hours in a slow cooker. Carrots were a must for their sweet, earthy flavor as were parsnips. To round out the mix we turned to rutabaga, which helped offset the sweetness of the other vegetables. To create just the right broth with warm spices, we microwaved an aromatic mixture of onions, garlic, and garam masala with fresh ginger to provide most of the tagine's flavor. We then added dried cherries and fresh cilantro at the end of cooking to bring freshness and vibrancy to the dish. Topping individual portions with Greek yogurt and toasted almonds tamed the spices of the stew and added contrast and crunch. Serve with rice or couscous.

- 2 onions, chopped fine
- 4 garlic cloves, minced
- 1½ tablespoons garam masala
- 2 teaspoons canola oil
- 2 teaspoons paprika
- 1½ teaspoons grated fresh ginger
  Pinch cayenne
- 1½ pounds carrots, peeled, halved lengthwise, and sliced 1 inch thick
- 1 pound parsnips, peeled, halved lengthwise, and sliced 1 inch thick
- 1 pound rutabaga, peeled and cut into ½-inch pieces
- 4 cups vegetable broth
- 2 (2-inch) strips orange zest
- 2 tablespoons instant tapioca
  Salt and pepper
- ½ cup dried cherries, chopped
- 2 tablespoons minced fresh cilantro
- ½ cup 2 percent Greek yogurt
- ⅓ cup slivered almonds, toasted

1. Microwave onions, garlic, garam masala, oil, paprika, ginger, and cayenne in bowl, stirring occasionally, until onions are softened, about 5 minutes; transfer to slow cooker. Stir carrots, parsnips, rutabaga, broth, orange zest, tapioca, and ½ teaspoon salt into slow cooker. Cover and cook until vegetables are tender, 8 to 10 hours on low or 5 to 7 hours on high.

2. Discard orange zest. Stir cherries and cilantro into tagine and season with salt and pepper to taste. Top individual portions with yogurt and almonds before serving.

Per 1⅔-cup serving: Cal 250; Fat 5g; Sat Fat 0g; Chol 0mg; Carb 48g; Protein 6g; Fiber 11g; Sodium 780mg *To reduce sodium level to 370mg, use low-sodium broth.

QUICK PREP TIP
MAKING ZEST STRIPS
Use vegetable peeler to remove long, wide strips of zest from lemons and oranges. Try not to remove any of white pith beneath zest, as it is bitter.

Moroccan Fish Tagine with Artichoke Hearts

Serves 6 • **Cooking Time** 4 to 6 hours on Low or 3 to 5 hours on High • **Slow Cooker Size** 4 to 7 Quarts

✔ WHY THIS RECIPE WORKS: Making a slow-cooker fish tagine with moist and tender cod, an aromatic broth, and perfectly cooked vegetables seemed like a tall order. Our testing revealed that if we built the brothy base of the tagine first and let it and the vegetables simmer for a few hours, all we needed to do was add the fish at the end of the cooking time so it could absorb the tagine's flavors and poach gently until perfectly cooked through. The broth started with white wine, diced tomatoes, and chicken broth. Microwaving the onions and garlic with tomato paste and warm spices developed a complex Moroccan flavor for the tagine. We simmered this mixture with the artichoke hearts until the broth was deeply flavorful and the artichokes tender. Then we added the cod and allowed it to cook gently in the savory liquid for 30 minutes. Stirring in the olives with the cod allowed them to warm through and lightly flavor the broth. All the tagine needed was a sprinkle of fresh parsley to finish. Serve with rice or couscous.

- 2 **onions, chopped fine**
- 2 **tablespoons tomato paste**
- 4 **garlic cloves, minced**
- 2 **teaspoons garam masala**
- 2 **teaspoons canola oil**
- 1½ **teaspoons paprika**
- ¼ **teaspoon cayenne pepper**
- 18 **ounces frozen artichoke hearts, thawed, patted dry, and halved lengthwise**
- 2 **cups chicken broth**
- 1 **(14.5-ounce) can diced tomatoes, drained**
- ¼ **cup dry white wine**
  Salt and pepper
- 1½ **pounds skinless cod fillets, 1 to 1½ inches thick, cut into 2-inch pieces**
- ½ **cup pitted kalamata olives, chopped coarse**
- 2 **tablespoons minced fresh parsley**

1. Microwave onions, tomato paste, garlic, garam masala, oil, paprika, and cayenne in bowl, stirring occasionally, until onions are softened, about 5 minutes; transfer to slow cooker. Stir in artichokes, broth, tomatoes, wine, and ½ teaspoon salt. Cover and cook until flavors meld, 4 to 6 hours on low or 3 to 5 hours on high.

2. Stir cod and olives into tagine, cover, and cook on high until cod flakes apart when gently prodded with paring knife, about 30 minutes. Season with salt and pepper to taste. Sprinkle with parsley and serve.

Per 1⅔-cup serving: Cal 230; Fat 6g; Sat Fat 0.5g; Chol 50mg; Carb 19g; Protein 25g; Fiber 8g; Sodium 870mg *To reduce sodium level to 580mg, use unsalted broth and no-salt-added tomatoes.

SMART SHOPPING FROZEN ARTICHOKES
Artichokes boast a sweet, earthy, nutty flavor that works well in a variety of dishes, but fresh artichokes can be a hassle to prep and cook. Luckily, frozen artichoke hearts are widely available and simply need to be thawed and patted dry to remove excess moisture prior to cooking.

Thai Eggplant Curry

Serves 6 • **Cooking Time** 2 to 4 hours on Low • **Slow Cooker Size** 4 to 7 Quarts

✔ **WHY THIS RECIPE WORKS:** To create a healthy, vegetable-packed Thai curry in the slow cooker, we turned to eggplant as the star ingredient. Our first attempts, however, resulted in bland, mushy eggplant. Clearly we needed to drive off excess moisture before adding the eggplant to the moist heat environment of the slow cooker. A quick spin under the broiler did the trick and further deepened the eggplant's flavor in the process. To achieve great flavor without the need for gathering up a laundry list of ingredients we turned to store-bought green curry paste, which contained all the ingredients of classic Thai curries and added big flavor and depth to this dish in record time. A combination of chicken broth and light coconut milk (added at the end) gave us a rich, creamy base for our curry without adding excess calories or fat. Snow peas and red bell pepper were the perfect accents to the eggplant, and to ensure that they were perfectly crisp and tender, we microwaved them with a little water, then added them to the finished curry. Serve with rice.

Vegetable oil spray

2 pounds eggplant, cut into 1-inch pieces

4 shallots, minced

3 tablespoons Thai green curry paste

1 tablespoon sugar

4 cups chicken broth

2 tablespoons fish sauce, plus extra for seasoning

2 tablespoons instant tapioca
   Salt and pepper

1 pound snow peas, strings removed, cut into 1-inch pieces

1 red bell pepper, stemmed, seeded, and cut into 2-inch-long matchsticks

1 (13.5-ounce) can light coconut milk

¼ cup chopped fresh cilantro

1 tablespoon lime juice, plus extra for seasoning

1. Adjust oven rack 6 inches from broiler element and heat broiler. Line rimmed baking sheet with aluminum foil and spray with oil spray. Toss eggplant, shallots, curry paste, and sugar together in bowl. Spread eggplant mixture evenly in prepared sheet and lightly spray with oil spray. Broil vegetables until softened and beginning to brown, 10 to 12 minutes, rotating sheet halfway through broiling; transfer to slow cooker. Stir in broth, fish sauce, tapioca, and ¼ teaspoon salt. Cover and cook until flavors meld and eggplant is tender, 2 to 4 hours on low.

2. Microwave snow peas, bell pepper, and 1 tablespoon water in covered bowl, stirring occasionally, until crisp-tender, 4 to 6 minutes. Drain vegetables, then stir into curry. Microwave coconut milk in bowl until hot, about 2 minutes. Stir into curry and let sit until heated through, about 5 minutes. Stir in cilantro and lime juice. Season with salt, pepper, extra fish sauce, and extra lime juice to taste. Serve.

Per 1⅔-cup serving: Cal 170; Fat 3.5g; Sat Fat 2g; Chol 0mg; Carb 28g; Protein 8g; Fiber 7g; Sodium 860mg *To reduce sodium level to 600mg, use unsalted broth.

QUICK PREP TIP
CUTTING EGGPLANT
Cutting up an awkwardly shaped vegetable like eggplant can sometimes be a challenge. To cut eggplant into even cubes, simply cut eggplant crosswise into 1-inch-thick rounds, then cut rounds into tidy 1-inch cubes.

Chicken and Turkey

● **EASY PREP**

Easy Cranberry-Orange Chicken

Serves 4 • **Cooking Time** 1 to 2 hours on Low • **Slow Cooker Size** 4 to 7 Quarts

WHY THIS RECIPE WORKS: Boneless, skinless chicken breasts are a great option when you're trying to eat healthfully, but they can be easily overcooked, which is a good reason to reach for your slow cooker, whose gentle heat ensures moist tender results. To turn these simply cooked chicken breasts into an interesting entrée, we decided to use canned whole-berry cranberry sauce, which we livened up with orange juice and zest and fresh thyme, nestling the chicken in this mixture so that as it cooked, it took on the sweet flavors of the sauce base. But we found this sauce to be just a little too sweet and one dimensional, so we added red wine vinegar to cut the sweetness and a tablespoon of soy sauce for depth of flavor. When the chicken was perfectly cooked, we removed it from the slow cooker and poured the sauce into a saucepan, simmering it briefly until it was slightly thickened. After spooning this vibrant sauce over the chicken, we topped it with toasted sliced almonds for an appealing crunchy finish. Check the chicken's temperature after 1 hour of cooking and continue to monitor until it registers 160 degrees. You will need an oval slow cooker for this recipe. Serve with rice or mashed potatoes.

1   **(14-ounce) can whole-berry cranberry sauce**
1   **tablespoon low-sodium soy sauce**
2   **teaspoons red wine vinegar**
1   **teaspoon minced fresh thyme or ¼ teaspoon dried**
½   **teaspoon grated orange zest plus ¼ cup juice**
    Pinch cayenne pepper
4   **(6-ounce) boneless, skinless chicken breasts, trimmed of all visible fat**
    Salt and pepper
⅓   **cup sliced almonds, toasted**

1. Combine cranberry sauce, soy sauce, vinegar, thyme, orange zest and juice, and cayenne in slow cooker. Season chicken with salt and pepper and nestle into slow cooker. Cover and cook until chicken registers 160 degrees, 1 to 2 hours on low.

2. Transfer chicken to serving platter and tent loosely with aluminum foil. Transfer sauce to medium saucepan, bring to simmer over medium heat, and cook until slightly thickened, about 5 minutes. Season with salt and pepper to taste. Spoon sauce over chicken and sprinkle with almonds. Serve.

Per serving: Cal 400; Fat 8g; Sat Fat 1.5g; Chol 110mg; Carb 39g; Protein 38g; Fiber 1g; Sodium 490mg

---

QUICK PREP TIP OVAL VERSUS ROUND SLOW COOKERS

Slow cookers come in a variety of shapes and sizes, and in general we found that the majority of our recipes work in both round and oval slow cookers. In some cases, however, an oval slow cooker, which has a greater surface area in the base of the insert, is important to the success of the recipe. This is often the case for large roasts that need extra room to fit properly or for more delicate chicken and fish dishes that require laying the breasts or fillets in the bottom of the slow cooker, without overlapping, to cook through evenly.

Thai Chicken with Coconut Curry Sauce

Serves 4 • **Cooking Time** 1 to 2 hours on Low • **Slow Cooker Size** 4 to 7 Quarts

✔ **WHY THIS RECIPE WORKS:** For juicy and tender chicken breasts with a complexly aromatic Thai curry sauce, we developed a technique that resulted in big flavor, with just a small amount of hands-on time. We added unsweetened coconut flakes to a small amount of Thai red curry paste, shallots, garlic, and chicken broth to flavor the chicken and create a wonderful sauce for our dish. As the coconut cooked, it became tender and added richness to the cooking liquid. Pureeing the coconut mixture after cooking gave us a vibrant and flavorful accompaniment with the perfect consistency. We stirred a small amount of fresh basil into the sauce at the end, which helped to bring the flavors to life. Using flaked coconut will yield a thicker sauce. Check the chicken's temperature after 1 hour of cooking and continue to monitor until it registers 160 degrees. You will need an oval slow cooker for this recipe. Serve with rice.

2	shallots, chopped
1½	tablespoons Thai red curry paste
1	teaspoon canola oil
1	garlic clove, minced
½	cup chicken broth
½	cup water
⅓	cup unsweetened shredded coconut
4	(6-ounce) boneless, skinless chicken breasts, trimmed of all visible fat
	Salt and pepper
2	tablespoons chopped fresh basil

1. Microwave shallots, curry paste, oil, and garlic in bowl, stirring occasionally, until shallots are softened, about 2 minutes; transfer to slow cooker. Stir in broth, water, and coconut. Season chicken with salt and pepper and nestle into slow cooker. Cover and cook until chicken registers 160 degrees, 1 to 2 hours on low.

2. Transfer chicken to serving platter, brushing any coconut that sticks to breasts back into slow cooker. Process cooking liquid in blender until almost smooth, about 30 seconds. Stir basil into sauce and season with salt and pepper to taste. Spoon sauce over chicken and serve.

Per serving: Cal 280; Fat 10g; Sat Fat 5g; Chol 110mg; Carb 6g; Protein 38g; Fiber 2g; Sodium 630mg

---

ON THE SIDE SIMPLE ROASTED CARROTS
Adjust oven rack to middle position and heat oven to 425 degrees. Peel 2½ pounds carrots and halve crosswise; cut halves lengthwise if necessary to create even pieces. Toss carrots with 2 tablespoons melted butter, ¼ teaspoon salt, and ¼ teaspoon pepper. Spread carrots evenly on aluminum foil–lined rimmed baking sheet. Cover sheet tightly with foil and roast for 15 minutes. Remove foil and continue to roast, stirring twice, until carrots are well browned and tender, 20 to 25 minutes. Season with salt and pepper to taste. Serves 4.

Per serving: Cal 150; Fat 6g; Sat Fat 3.5g; Chol 15mg; Carb 23g; Protein 2g; Fiber 7g; Sodium 310mg

Chicken with "Roasted" Garlic Sauce

Serves 4 • **Cooking Time** 2 to 3 hours on Low • **Slow Cooker Size** 4 to 7 Quarts

WHY THIS RECIPE WORKS: It's often the very simplest meals that are the hardest to re-create in the slow cooker; tender, perfectly cooked bone-in chicken with a garlicky gravy is no exception. For a richly flavored and satisfying gravy without all the calories, we turned to 15 whole cloves of garlic plus a shallot to lend a roasted flavor and body to our sauce while keeping additional fat to a minimum. To end up with aromatics soft enough to puree into a smooth gravy, we found it necessary to jump-start their cooking by sautéing them on the stovetop until lightly browned. Giving the shallots and garlic time to brown also added to the subtle roasted taste and deepened their overall flavor, which became sweeter and mellower after hours in the slow cooker. With the aromatics already in a skillet, adding a small amount of flour was a quick and easy way to thicken the sauce, and deglazing with wine and broth ensured that the flavorful browned bits in the bottom of the pan ended up in the slow cooker. The addition of low-sodium soy sauce helped to round out the overall flavor of the sauce. Rosemary and chives enlivened the gravy with fresh flavors. Check the chicken's temperature after 2 hours of cooking and continue to monitor until it registers 160 degrees. You will need an oval slow cooker for this recipe. Serve with egg noodles or mashed potatoes.

2	teaspoons canola oil
15	garlic cloves, peeled
1	shallot, peeled and quartered
3	tablespoons all-purpose flour
⅔	cup dry white wine
½	cup chicken broth
1	tablespoon low-sodium soy sauce
½	teaspoon minced fresh rosemary or ⅛ teaspoon dried
4	(12-ounce) bone-in split chicken breasts, skin and ribs removed, trimmed of all visible fat
	Salt and pepper
1	tablespoon minced fresh chives

1. Heat oil in 12-inch skillet over medium-low heat until shimmering. Add garlic and shallot and cook until fragrant and lightly browned, 8 to 10 minutes. Stir in flour and cook for 1 minute. Slowly whisk in wine and broth, scraping up any browned bits and smoothing out any lumps; transfer to slow cooker.

2. Stir soy sauce and rosemary into slow cooker. Season chicken with salt and pepper and nestle into slow cooker. Cover and cook until chicken registers 160 degrees, 2 to 3 hours on low.

3. Transfer chicken to serving platter. Process cooking liquid in blender until smooth, about 30 seconds. Stir chives into sauce and season with salt and pepper to taste. Slice chicken and serve with sauce.

Per serving: Cal 380; Fat 8g; Sat Fat 1.5g; Chol 130mg; Carb 22g; Protein 47g; Fiber 3g; Sodium 590mg

---

QUICK PREP TIP **TRIMMING BONE-IN CHICKEN BREASTS**

To allow multiple bone-in chicken breasts to uniformly fit in a slow cooker and cook through evenly, we find it's best to trim away the rib bones. Using kitchen shears, trim off the rib section from each breast, following the vertical line of fat from the tapered end of the breast up to the socket where the wing was attached.

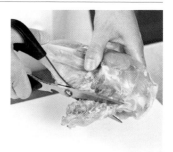

Latin-Style Chicken with Tomatoes and Olives

Serves 4 • **Cooking Time** 2 to 3 hours on Low • **Slow Cooker Size** 4 to 7 Quarts

✔ WHY THIS RECIPE WORKS: This classic Latin-style chicken features tender chicken braised in a chunky tomato sauce; gently simmering the chicken in the sauce helps it to remain moist while enriching the flavors of both. Most slow-cooker recipes result in a dull, waterlogged tomato sauce, so we looked to give our dish a richer texture with a bright and assertive tomato flavor. Our testing revealed that canned diced tomatoes with their juice had the fresh tomato taste we wanted but created too much liquid during cooking. Compounded with the juices from the chicken, they created a thin, dull sauce. Draining the diced tomatoes, plus adding tomato paste and a small amount of tapioca, created the thickened sauce we were after. Finishing the sauce with green olives gave our dish a briny contrast, and a sprinkling of fresh cilantro and lime juice tied it all together. Check the chicken's temperature after 2 hours of cooking and continue to monitor until it registers 160 degrees. You will need an oval slow cooker for this recipe. Serve with rice.

1	onion, halved and sliced thin
4	garlic cloves, sliced thin
1	tablespoon tomato paste
2	teaspoons minced fresh oregano or ½ teaspoon dried
1	teaspoon canola oil
¼	teaspoon ground cumin
1	(14.5-ounce) can diced tomatoes, drained
1	teaspoon instant tapioca
4	(12-ounce) bone-in split chicken breasts, skin and ribs removed, trimmed of all visible fat
	Salt and pepper
⅓	cup pitted large brine-cured green olives, chopped coarse
2	tablespoons chopped fresh cilantro
1	tablespoon lime juice

1. Microwave onion, garlic, tomato paste, oregano, oil, and cumin in bowl, stirring occasionally, until onion is softened, about 5 minutes; transfer to slow cooker. Stir in tomatoes and tapioca. Season chicken with salt and pepper and nestle into slow cooker. Cover and cook until chicken registers 160 degrees, 2 to 3 hours on low.

2. Transfer chicken to serving platter. Stir olives, cilantro, and lime juice into sauce and season with salt and pepper to taste. Spoon sauce over chicken and serve.

Per serving: Cal 300; Fat 8g; Sat Fat 1g; Chol 130mg; Carb 12g; Protein 45g; Fiber 3g; Sodium 840mg *To reduce sodium level to 590mg, use no-salt-added tomatoes.

SMART SHOPPING OLIVES
Jarred olives come in three basic types at the supermarket: brine-cured green (left), brine-cured black (middle), and salt-cured black (right). Curing is the process that removes the bitter compound oleuropein from olives to make them suitable for eating. Brine-cured olives are soaked in a salt solution; salt-cured olives are packed in salt and left to sit until nearly all their liquid has been extracted, then covered in oil to replump. Both processes traditionally take weeks or even months. For canned California olives, on the other hand, producers use lye, which "ripens" the olives artificially in a matter of days, then further process the olives to turn their green flesh black.

ALL ABOUT Chicken and Turkey in the Slow Cooker

Given that it is one of the leanest proteins you'll find, chicken is a valuable option for those watching calories, fat, and cholesterol. But like most lean proteins, chicken can be a challenge to keep moist and flavorful—especially in the slow cooker, where you have less control over temperature. It's not uncommon to see simple recipes result in chicken that is dry, bland, and unappealing. Here is what we've learned about getting juicy, flavorful chicken from the slow cooker.

One-Hour Ranges Are Key

We found that the only way to cook chicken (and turkey) in a slow cooker is on the low setting and for a relatively short amount of time. We recommend that until you have experience cooking chicken in your slow cooker, start checking the temperature of chicken breasts (boneless and bone-in), whole chicken, and turkey breasts at the low end of the temperature range to ward off dry, over-cooked poultry. Chicken thighs, on the other hand, are more forgiving, making them especially well suited to the slow cooker because their dark meat becomes meltingly tender during the long cooking time; for this reason, we cook them longer than bone-in or boneless breasts, and we don't check their temperature. Longer cooking times are also needed in soups or casseroles where the meat is insulated by other ingredients.

Type of Poultry	Cooking Time*
Boneless, Skinless Chicken Breasts	1 to 2 hours on Low
Bone-in Split Chicken Breasts	2 to 3 hours on Low
Chicken Thighs	3 to 4 hours on Low
Whole Chicken	4 to 5 hours on Low
Turkey Breast	5 to 6 hours on Low

*Note that cooking times vary in our "Cooking for Two" chapter.

Remove the Skin

Chicken can be a healthy option as long as you remove the skin and trim away any unwanted fat. One (12-ounce) bone-in split chicken breast with skin has almost 23 grams more fat than its skinless equivalent, which has only 9 grams of fat—that's a difference worth dealing with. Chicken skin is often slippery, so using a paper towel provides extra grip. For whole chickens with skin that is more difficult to remove, we wait until they are fully cooked and carved before removing the skin.

Positioning a Whole Chicken

When cooking a whole chicken in the slow cooker, our testers discovered that placing the chicken breast side down yields a moister bird because the juices from the dark meat render down into the breast, keeping it from becoming overcooked as the dark meat reaches the proper temperature.

Dress It Up with a Sauce or Side

While in some recipes chicken is smothered in heavy sauces, we found that savory sides and bright vinaigrettes bring dishes to life without excessive fat and calories. Heartier vegetables like carrots and bell peppers can cook right alongside the chicken. They help to season the chicken as it cooks and keep the final meal packed with flavor. For a big-flavor finish, we like to drizzle chicken with simple vinaigrettes created with sunny citrus juice and fresh herbs like mint and cilantro.

Greek-Style Chicken with Warm Tabbouleh

Serves 4 • **Cooking Time** 2 to 3 hours on Low • **Slow Cooker Size** 4 to 7 Quarts

✔ **WHY THIS RECIPE WORKS:** Attempting to cook whole grains in a slow cooker along with a lean chicken breast is a tall order. Most grains need to cook for much longer than chicken to become tender enough to eat. Looking for bright and fresh flavors to pair with our Greek-inspired chicken, we turned to the classic tabbouleh salad. Fortunately, our testing revealed that medium-grind bulgur is one of the few hearty grains that can cook in the slow cooker without breaking down and becoming gummy. Rubbing the chicken with an aromatic mixture of garlic, oregano, and lemon zest seasoned not only the chicken but also the bulgur as it cooked. We drained the bulgur at the end of cooking to remove excess liquid and seasoned it with olive oil, lemon juice, parsley, and tomatoes to turn the hearty grain into a vibrant salad. When shopping, don't confuse bulgur with cracked wheat, which has a much longer cooking time and will not work in this recipe. Check the chicken's temperature after 2 hours of cooking and continue to monitor until it registers 160 degrees. You will need an oval slow cooker for this recipe.

1	cup medium-grind bulgur, rinsed
1	cup chicken broth
	Salt and pepper
2	tablespoons extra-virgin olive oil
4	teaspoons minced fresh oregano
1¼	teaspoons grated lemon zest plus 3 tablespoons juice
1	garlic clove, minced
4	(12-ounce) bone-in split chicken breasts, skin and ribs removed, trimmed of all visible fat
½	cup 2 percent Greek yogurt
½	cup chopped fresh parsley
3	tablespoons water
8	ounces cherry tomatoes, quartered

1. Lightly spray inside of slow cooker with vegetable oil spray. Combine bulgur, broth, and ¼ teaspoon salt in slow cooker.

2. Microwave 1 teaspoon oil, 3 teaspoons oregano, 1 teaspoon lemon zest, and garlic in bowl until fragrant, about 30 seconds; let cool slightly. Rub chicken with oregano mixture and season with salt and pepper. Nestle chicken into slow cooker. Cover and cook until chicken registers 160 degrees, 2 to 3 hours on low.

3. Meanwhile, whisk yogurt, 1 tablespoon parsley, water, ⅛ teaspoon salt, remaining 1 teaspoon oregano, and remaining ¼ teaspoon lemon zest together in bowl. Season with salt and pepper to taste.

4. Transfer chicken to serving platter, brushing any bulgur that sticks to breasts back into slow cooker. Drain bulgur mixture, if necessary, and return to now-empty slow cooker. Add tomatoes, lemon juice, remaining 5 teaspoons oil, and remaining 7 tablespoons parsley and fluff with fork to combine. Season with salt and pepper to taste. Serve chicken with tabbouleh and yogurt sauce.

Per serving: Cal 460; Fat 14g; Sat Fat 2.5g; Chol 130mg; Carb 32g; Protein 52g; Fiber 7g; Sodium 750mg *To reduce sodium level to 650mg, use unsalted broth.

SMART SHOPPING BULGUR
Adding bulgur to your repertoire is a great way to add fiber, protein, iron, and magnesium to your diet. A product of the wheat berry, bulgur has been steamed, dried, ground, and sorted by size (fine-grain, medium-grain, and coarse-grain). The result of this process is a fast-cooking, highly nutritious grain that can be used in a variety of applications. Medium-grind bulgur is the most widely available size and our preferred choice for slow-cooker recipes because it cooks evenly and maintains its shape. Don't confuse bulgur with cracked wheat, which is often sold alongside bulgur but is not parcooked. Be sure to rinse bulgur to remove excess starches that can turn the grain gluey.

Spiced Chicken with Carrot Couscous

Serves 4 • **Cooking Time** 2 to 3 hours on Low • **Slow Cooker Size** 4 to 7 Quarts

WHY THIS RECIPE WORKS: Looking for an alternative to the classic pairing of chicken and rice, we turned to the flavors and ingredients of Morocco for inspiration. We made a Moroccan spice rub by blooming garlic, garam masala, and turmeric with a small amount of olive oil in the microwave. For a paste thin enough to spread on the chicken we whisked 1 tablespoon of orange juice into the mixture, which also added great flavor. To complete our meal with an easy but flavorful side, we stirred couscous, shredded carrots, and some of our spiced cooking liquid into the slow cooker while the chicken rested. After just 10 minutes, the couscous had cooked through and was ready to be served. A quick vinaigrette brought freshness and acidity when drizzled over both the chicken and couscous. Check the chicken's temperature after 2 hours of cooking and continue to monitor until it registers 160 degrees. You will need an oval slow cooker for this recipe.

1   cup chicken broth, plus extra as needed

2   tablespoons extra-virgin olive oil

3   garlic cloves, minced

1   teaspoon garam masala

¼   teaspoon ground turmeric

½   cup orange juice

4   (12-ounce) bone-in split chicken breasts, skin and ribs removed, trimmed of all visible fat

     Salt and pepper

2   carrots, peeled and shredded

1   cup couscous

3   tablespoons minced fresh cilantro

1   tablespoon sherry vinegar

2   tablespoons sliced almonds, toasted

1. Pour broth into slow cooker. Microwave 1 teaspoon oil, garlic, garam masala, and turmeric in bowl until fragrant, about 30 seconds. Stir in 1 tablespoon orange juice and let mixture cool slightly. Rub chicken with spice mixture and season with salt and pepper. Nestle chicken into slow cooker. Cover and cook until chicken registers 160 degrees, 2 to 3 hours on low.

2. Transfer chicken to serving platter and tent loosely with aluminum foil. Strain cooking liquid into 2-cup liquid measuring cup. Reserve 1 cup strained cooking liquid and discard remaining liquid; or add extra hot broth as needed to measure 1 cup. Stir reserved liquid, carrots, and couscous into now-empty slow cooker, cover, and cook on high until couscous is tender, about 10 minutes.

3. Meanwhile, whisk remaining 5 teaspoons oil, remaining 7 tablespoons orange juice, cilantro, vinegar, and ⅛ teaspoon salt together in bowl. Add almonds and 3 tablespoons dressing to cooked couscous and fluff with fork to combine. Season with salt and pepper to taste. Serve chicken with couscous and remaining dressing.

Per serving: Cal 510; Fat 14g; Sat Fat 2.5g; Chol 130mg; Carb 42g; Protein 51g; Fiber 4g; Sodium 610mg *To reduce sodium level to 520mg, use unsalted broth.

QUICK PREP TIP TOASTING NUTS AND SEEDS
Toasting nuts and seeds maximizes their flavor and takes only a few minutes. To toast 1 cup or less of nuts or seeds, add to dry skillet over medium heat. Shake skillet occasionally to prevent scorching and toast until lightly browned and fragrant, 3 to 8 minutes. Watch nuts closely because they can go from golden to burnt very quickly. To toast more than 1 cup of nuts, spread nuts in single layer in rimmed baking sheet and toast in 350-degree oven. Toast, shaking baking sheet every few minutes, until nuts are lightly browned and fragrant, 5 to 10 minutes.

Chicken with Warm Potato and Radish Salad

Serves 4 • **Cooking Time** 2 to 3 hours on Low • **Slow Cooker Size** 5½ to 7 Quarts

✔ **WHY THIS RECIPE WORKS:** For a fresh take on the classic chicken and potato dinner, we wanted tender bone-in chicken paired with a warm potato salad. We had to make sure that the potatoes and meat cooked through in the same amount of time, as the lean chicken can quickly overcook and turn dry. We seasoned the breasts simply with a mix of fresh thyme, salt, and pepper. To get the potatoes to cook at the same rate, we quartered small potatoes and gave them a head start in the microwave before adding them to the slow cooker along with the chicken. While the chicken rested, we turned the tender potatoes into a delicious side dish by tossing them with a simple zesty dressing flavored with minced shallot, Dijon mustard, and parsley. Fresh radishes added great color and crunch. Look for potatoes measuring 1 to 2 inches in diameter; do not substitute full-size Yukon Gold potatoes or they will not cook through properly. Check the chicken's temperature after 2 hours of cooking and continue to monitor until it registers 160 degrees. You will need an oval slow cooker for this recipe.

1¾ **pounds small Yukon Gold potatoes, unpeeled, quartered**

4 **(12-ounce) bone-in split chicken breasts, skin and ribs removed, trimmed of all visible fat**

1 **tablespoon minced fresh thyme or 1 teaspoon dried**
 Salt and pepper

3 **tablespoons extra-virgin olive oil**

3 **tablespoons minced fresh parsley**

1 **shallot, minced**

1 **tablespoon Dijon mustard**

2 **teaspoons grated lemon zest plus 2 tablespoons juice**

¼ **teaspoon sugar**

5 **radishes, trimmed and sliced thin**

1. Microwave potatoes and ¼ cup water in covered bowl, stirring occasionally, until almost tender, about 15 minutes; transfer to slow cooker. Season chicken with thyme, salt, and pepper and nestle into slow cooker. Cover and cook until chicken registers 160 degrees, 2 to 3 hours on low.

2. Transfer chicken to serving platter. Whisk oil, parsley, shallot, 2 tablespoons water, mustard, lemon zest and juice, sugar, and ⅛ teaspoon salt together in large bowl. Measure out and reserve ¼ cup dressing. Drain potatoes and transfer to bowl with remaining dressing. Add radishes and toss to combine. Season with salt and pepper to taste. Serve chicken with potato salad and reserved dressing.

Per serving: Cal 510; Fat 16g; Sat Fat 2.5g; Chol 130mg; Carb 39g; Protein 48g; Fiber 3g; Sodium 570mg

---

SMART SHOPPING RADISHES

There's a whole world of radishes out there, but we typically stick to the classic Cherry Belle radishes; they are the most widely available variety you see at the supermarket. They are harvested in both spring and fall, so they can be sold year-round, and their relatively sweet flavor and mild spiciness make them a go-to radish for all kinds of dishes—not just salads. With these and other thin-skinned radishes, good things come in small packages: Large specimens may be tough, woody, and hollow.

Curried Chicken Thighs with Acorn Squash

Serves 4 • **Cooking Time** 3 to 4 hours on Low • **Slow Cooker Size** 5½ to 7 Quarts

✔ WHY THIS RECIPE WORKS: Meaty chicken thighs are a perfect match for the slow cooker as they become meltingly tender in its moist heat environment and the risk of overcooking is slim. Here we opted to pair them with acorn squash, which is hearty enough to withstand a few hours in the slow cooker and still hold its shape. And arranging the squash along the bottom of the slow cooker ensured that the large wedges were perfectly tender by the end of cooking. To give this dish a distinct flavor profile we rubbed the chicken with curry powder that we bloomed in the microwave with a little bit of oil. To finish, we microwaved a mixture of honey and cayenne to which we added lime juice, then drizzled the mixture over the chicken and squash. This simple step tied together the flavors of this easy one-dish meal, perfect for a fall night. You will need an oval slow cooker for this recipe.

2	small acorn squashes (1 pound each), quartered pole to pole and seeded
2	teaspoons curry powder
1	teaspoon canola oil
8	(6-ounce) bone-in chicken thighs, skin removed, trimmed of all visible fat
	Salt and pepper
3	tablespoons honey
⅛	teaspoon cayenne pepper
1	tablespoon lime juice
¼	cup fresh cilantro leaves

1. Shingle squash wedges cut side down into slow cooker, then add ½ cup water. Microwave curry powder and oil in bowl until fragrant, about 30 seconds; let cool slightly. Rub chicken with curry mixture and season with salt and pepper. Place chicken on top of squash in slow cooker. Cover and cook until chicken is tender, 3 to 4 hours on low.

2. Transfer chicken and squash to serving platter; discard cooking liquid. Microwave honey and cayenne in bowl until heated through, about 30 seconds. Stir in lime juice. Drizzle chicken and squash with honey mixture and sprinkle with cilantro. Serve.

Per serving: Cal 400; Fat 10g; Sat Fat 2.5g; Chol 195mg; Carb 37g; Protein 41g; Fiber 4g; Sodium 340mg

---

QUICK PREP TIP

PREPARING ACORN SQUASH

Set squash on damp kitchen towel to hold in place. Position chef's knife on top of squash and strike with mallet to drive it into squash. Continue to hit knife with mallet until it cuts completely through squash. After scooping out seeds with spoon, place squash halves cut side down on cutting board and cut in half, pole to pole, using mallet if necessary.

Chicken Thighs with Black-Eyed Pea Ragout

Serves 4 • **Cooking Time** 3 to 4 hours on Low • **Slow Cooker Size** 5½ to 7 Quarts

✔ **WHY THIS RECIPE WORKS:** Juicy chicken, tender black-eyed peas, and earthy kale are a great combination for a healthy and comforting supper. Sturdy kale is a perfect match for the slow cooker; after a quick spin in the microwave (along with onion, garlic, and oil) it can be added to the slow cooker to fully soften and cook through. To complement the bitter kale, we wanted rich, slightly spicy black-eyed peas. We found that a combination of dry mustard and hot sauce was the key to getting the right balance between heat and spice. Dry mustard added to the slow cooker at the beginning of cooking infused the chicken with a subtle flavor, and finishing the peas with hot sauce punched up the heat and acidity of the dish. Pureeing a portion of the peas also helped to thicken the juices released from the chicken during cooking.

1 **pound kale, stemmed and chopped coarse**

1 **onion, chopped fine**

4 **garlic cloves, minced**

1 **teaspoon canola oil**

1 **teaspoon dry mustard**

2 **teaspoons minced fresh thyme or ½ teaspoon dried**

2 **(15-ounce) cans black-eyed peas, rinsed**

½ **cup chicken broth**

8 **(6-ounce) bone-in chicken thighs, skin removed, trimmed of all visible fat**

Salt and pepper

2 **teaspoons hot sauce**

1. Microwave kale, onion, garlic, oil, mustard, and thyme in covered bowl, stirring occasionally, until vegetables are softened, 5 to 7 minutes; transfer to slow cooker.

2. Process one-third of beans with broth in food processor until smooth, about 30 seconds; transfer to slow cooker. Stir in remaining beans. Season chicken with salt and pepper and nestle into slow cooker. Cover and cook until chicken is tender, 3 to 4 hours on low.

3. Transfer chicken to serving platter. Stir hot sauce into kale and bean mixture and season with salt and pepper to taste. Serve.

Per serving: Cal 410; Fat 10g; Sat Fat 2g; Chol 195mg; Carb 30g; Protein 48g; Fiber 6g; Sodium 950mg *To reduce sodium level to 480mg, use low-sodium peas and unsalted broth.

QUICK PREP TIP

PREPARING HEARTY GREENS

To prepare kale, Swiss chard, and collard greens, cut away leafy green portion from either side of stalk or stem using chef's knife. Stack several leaves on top of one another and either slice leaves crosswise or cut them into pieces as directed in recipe. After they are cut, wash leaves and dry using salad spinner.

Chinese Barbecued Chicken Thighs

Serves 4 • **Cooking Time** 3 to 4 hours on Low • **Slow Cooker Size** 4 to 7 Quarts

WHY THIS RECIPE WORKS: Chinese barbecued chicken is not something most people would associate with a slow cooker, but this dish comes surprisingly close to the labor-intensive classic. The process for making it in a slow cooker is quite simple: First, we made a quick sauce layered with Asian flavors including five-spice powder, hoisin, honey, soy sauce, sesame oil, and ginger. Cooking the chicken in the slow cooker with half of the sauce helped to tenderize the meat and infused it with the sauce's flavors. And since this classic's hallmark lies in its deeply caramelized exterior, we moved our chicken from the slow cooker to the broiler. We brushed the meat with the remaining sauce and gave it a few minutes under a hot broiler to caramelize. In the end we were left with beautiful mahogany barbecued chicken.

2	tablespoons hoisin sauce
2	tablespoons ketchup
2	tablespoons honey
1	tablespoon low-sodium soy sauce
1	tablespoon dry sherry
1½	teaspoons toasted sesame oil
1½	teaspoons grated fresh ginger
1	garlic clove, minced
½	teaspoon five-spice powder
8	(6-ounce) bone-in chicken thighs, skin removed, trimmed of all visible fat

1. Combine hoisin, ketchup, honey, soy sauce, sherry, oil, ginger, garlic, and five-spice powder in bowl. Place chicken in slow cooker and pour half of hoisin mixture over top. Turn chicken to coat evenly with mixture. Cover and cook until chicken is tender, 3 to 4 hours on low.

2. Adjust oven rack 6 inches from broiler element and heat broiler. Set wire rack inside aluminum foil–lined rimmed baking sheet. Gently transfer chicken to prepared rack and arrange in single layer. Brush chicken with remaining hoisin mixture and broil until lightly caramelized, 3 to 5 minutes. Serve.

Per serving: Cal 320; Fat 10g; Sat Fat 2.5g; Chol 195mg; Carb 16g; Protein 40g; Fiber 0g; Sodium 680mg

---

ON THE SIDE NAPA CABBAGE SALAD

Whisk 2 tablespoons orange juice, 2 tablespoons rice vinegar, 1 tablespoon toasted sesame oil, 1 teaspoon grated fresh ginger, and 1 minced garlic clove together in large bowl. Add ½ head napa cabbage, cored and sliced thin (6 cups), and 2 peeled and shredded carrots and toss to coat. Season with salt and pepper to taste. Serves 4.

Per serving: Cal 60; Fat 3.5g; Sat Fat 0.5g; Chol 0mg; Carb 4g; Protein 2g; Fiber 2g; Sodium 15mg

Whole "Roast" Chili-Rubbed Chicken with Bean Salad

Serves 4 • **Cooking Time** 4 to 5 hours on Low • **Slow Cooker Size** 5½ to 7 Quarts

✓ **WHY THIS RECIPE WORKS:** A fantastic method for making a whole "roast" chicken in the slow cooker comes in handy year-round, but it's especially useful in the summer when turning on the oven is just not an appealing option. For this flavorful chicken recipe, a spice rub was the perfect way to give the chicken layers of flavor. We rubbed the mix under the skin to give it direct contact with the meat while it cooked. To add a smoky flavor to the black beans, we cooked them with a small amount of chipotle chile. Check the chicken's temperature after 4 hours of cooking and continue to monitor until the breast registers 160 degrees and the thighs register 175 degrees. You will need an oval slow cooker for this recipe.

1 **(15-ounce) can black beans, rinsed**

1 **teaspoon minced canned chipotle chile in adobo sauce**

5 **teaspoons extra-virgin olive oil**

1 **teaspoon ground cumin**

1 **teaspoon paprika**

2 **teaspoons grated lime zest plus ¼ cup juice (2 limes)**

1½ **teaspoons packed brown sugar Salt and pepper**

1 **(4-pound) whole chicken, giblets discarded**

1 **red bell pepper, stemmed, seeded, and chopped fine**

1 **cup frozen corn, thawed**

2 **scallions, sliced thin**

1. Combine beans and chipotle in slow cooker. Microwave 2 teaspoons oil, cumin, and paprika in bowl until fragrant, about 30 seconds. Let cool slightly, then stir in lime zest, sugar, ¼ teaspoon salt, and ¼ teaspoon pepper.

2. Using your fingers, gently loosen skin covering breast and thighs of chicken. Place half of spice mixture under skin, directly on meat in center of each side of breast and on thighs. Gently press on skin to distribute paste over meat. Rub entire exterior surface of chicken with remaining mixture and place breast side down in slow cooker. Cover and cook until breast registers 160 degrees and thighs register 175 degrees, 4 to 5 hours on low.

3. Transfer chicken to carving board, tent loosely with aluminum foil, and let rest for 15 minutes. Using large spoon, skim any white foam from surface of bean mixture. Drain beans and transfer to large bowl. Stir in bell pepper, corn, scallions, lime juice, and remaining 1 tablespoon oil. Season with salt and pepper to taste. Carve chicken and discard skin. Serve.

Per serving: Cal 430; Fat 13g; Sat Fat 2.5g; Chol 150mg; Carb 23g; Protein 52g; Fiber 4g; Sodium 540mg

---

QUICK PREP TIP CHICKEN RUB-DOWN
Distributing a flavorful rub both over and under the skin of the chicken ensures the best flavor. To do this, loosen skin from over thighs and breast and rub half of spice mixture directly on meat. Rub remaining mixture on skin of entire chicken.

Whole "Roast" Chicken with Lemon-Herb Jus

Serves 4 • **Cooking Time** 4 to 5 hours on Low • **Slow Cooker Size** 4 to 7 Quarts

✓ WHY THIS RECIPE WORKS: Making a perfectly cooked whole chicken with a satisfyingly flavorful jus in a slow cooker is actually much easier than it sounds. Placing the chicken in the slow cooker upside down is the key: As the juices and fat render from the meat, they travel over and through the breast (which can be notoriously dry), helping to maintain moistness. Additionally, as the juices pool in the bottom of the cooker, they submerge the breast, which then retains more moisture. To boost the flavor of our jus, we pulled out the skillet to brown the aromatics, which we deglazed with a bit of broth. This gave deep color and complex flavor to the juices released from the chicken during cooking. Check the chicken's temperature after 4 hours of cooking and continue to monitor until the breast registers 160 degrees and the thighs register 175 degrees. You will need an oval slow cooker for this recipe. Serve with mashed potatoes.

1	teaspoon canola oil
2	onions, chopped
6	garlic cloves, lightly crushed and peeled
5	sprigs fresh thyme
2	tablespoons all-purpose flour
¼	cup chicken broth
1	teaspoon low-sodium soy sauce
1	(4-pound) whole chicken, giblets discarded
	Salt and pepper
1	tablespoon lemon juice
1½	teaspoons chopped fresh tarragon

1. Heat oil in 12-inch skillet over medium heat until shimmering. Add onions and cook until softened and lightly browned, 5 to 7 minutes. Stir in garlic and thyme sprigs and cook until fragrant, about 30 seconds. Stir in flour and cook for 1 minute. Slowly whisk in broth and soy sauce, scraping up any browned bits and smoothing out any lumps; transfer to slow cooker.

2. Season chicken with salt and pepper and place breast side down in slow cooker. Cover and cook until breast registers 160 degrees and thighs register 175 degrees, 4 to 5 hours on low.

3. Transfer chicken to carving board, tent loosely with aluminum foil, and let rest for 15 minutes. Strain sauce into fat separator and let sit for 5 minutes; discard solids. Combine defatted sauce, lemon juice, and tarragon in now-empty slow cooker and season with salt and pepper to taste. Carve chicken and discard skin. Serve.

Per serving: Cal 310; Fat 8g; Sat Fat 2g; Chol 150mg; Carb 11g; Protein 48g; Fiber 2g; Sodium 390mg

---

QUICK PREP TIP CARVING A WHOLE CHICKEN
Using chef's knife, remove leg quarters by cutting through joint that connects leg to carcass. Remove skin from legs, then cut through joint that connects drumstick to thigh. Cut breast meat away from breast bone. Remove wing from breast by cutting through wing joint. Remove skin from breasts, then slice breasts crosswise.

Turkey Breast with Cherry-Orange Sauce

Serves 10 • **Cooking Time** 5 to 6 hours on Low • **Slow Cooker Size** 5½ to 7 Quarts

WHY THIS RECIPE WORKS: We often think of turkey as being reserved for big holiday dinners, but some hands-off cooking in the slow cooker makes turkey breast a weeknight-friendly dinner. The bone-in turkey breast is prep free, and the gentle heat of the slow cooker produces juicy and tender meat every time. For a fresh accompaniment to roast turkey, a cherry-orange sauce seemed like the perfect choice. To keep it simple, we started with frozen cherries, which we chopped, then added orange zest and a little thyme for aroma. By the time the turkey was fully cooked, the cherries were tender and the juices of the turkey had melded with the aromatics to create a flavorful sauce. To give it a thicker consistency, we added a small amount of instant tapioca. If the turkey breast's backbone and wings are still intact, you will need to remove them before proceeding with this recipe. Check the turkey's temperature after 5 hours of cooking and continue to monitor until it registers 160 degrees. You will need an oval slow cooker for this recipe.

12 ounces frozen sweet cherries, thawed and chopped

2 (2-inch) strips orange zest

1 teaspoon instant tapioca

½ teaspoon minced fresh thyme or ⅛ teaspoon dried
Salt and pepper

1 (6-pound) bone-in whole turkey breast, trimmed

½ cup apple butter

2 tablespoons unsalted butter

2 tablespoons lemon juice

1. Combine cherries, orange zest, tapioca, thyme, and ¼ teaspoon salt in slow cooker. Season turkey with salt and pepper and nestle skin side up into slow cooker. Cover and cook until turkey registers 160 degrees, 5 to 6 hours on low.

2. Transfer turkey to carving board, tent loosely with aluminum foil, and let rest for 20 minutes. Whisk apple butter, butter, and lemon juice into cherry mixture until combined. Season with salt and pepper to taste. Carve turkey and discard skin. Serve.

Per serving: Cal 310; Fat 3.5g; Sat Fat 2g; Chol 140mg; Carb 12g; Protein 53g; Fiber 1g; Sodium 220mg

---

ON THE SIDE COUSCOUS FOR A CROWD

Toast 3 cups couscous with 2 tablespoons extra-virgin olive oil in 12-inch skillet over medium heat, stirring occasionally, until lightly browned, 3 to 5 minutes; transfer to medium bowl. Stir in ¼ teaspoon salt and 4 cups boiling water, cover, and let sit until couscous is tender, about 12 minutes. Fluff couscous with fork and season with salt and pepper to taste. Serves 10. (Recipe can be halved.)

Per serving: Cal 220; Fat 3g; Sat Fat 0g; Chol 0mg; Carb 40g; Protein 7g; Fiber 3g; Sodium 65mg

EASY PREP

CHICKEN AND TURKEY **93**

Sweet and Tangy Pulled Chicken

Serves 4 • **Cooking Time** 2 to 3 hours on Low • **Slow Cooker Size** 4 to 7 Quarts

✓ **WHY THIS RECIPE WORKS:** A simple spice mixture and an easy-to-assemble homemade barbecue sauce make it easy to turn slow-cooked bone-in chicken into tangy, silky shredded chicken—perfect for piling onto buns for an easy dinner. Quickly microwaving the aromatics together with the chili powder, paprika, and cayenne softened the onions and infused them with layers of barbecue flavor while blooming the spices. We found that simply seasoning the chicken with salt and pepper before nestling the breasts into our quick sauce mixture of ketchup, molasses, and the aromatics was enough to infuse the chicken with the rich essence of the sauce. Stirring in vinegar at the beginning of cooking made the sauce too thin and dulled its acidity, but adding 2 tablespoons of vinegar at the end of cooking along with a small amount of mustard ensured that the sauce was the perfect consistency and retained its bright flavors. Check the chicken's temperature after 2 hours of cooking and continue to monitor until it registers 160 degrees. Serve on hamburger buns with pickle chips and Sweet and Tangy Coleslaw.

1	onion, chopped fine
¼	cup tomato paste
1	tablespoon chili powder
2	teaspoons canola oil
1	teaspoon paprika
⅛	teaspoon cayenne pepper
¼	cup ketchup
2	tablespoons molasses
2	(12-ounce) bone-in split chicken breasts, skin and ribs removed, trimmed of all visible fat
	Salt and pepper
2	tablespoons cider vinegar
2	teaspoons Dijon mustard

1. Microwave onion, tomato paste, chili powder, oil, paprika, and cayenne in bowl, stirring occasionally, until onion is softened, about 5 minutes; transfer to slow cooker. Stir in ketchup and molasses. Season chicken with salt and pepper, place in slow cooker, and turn to coat with sauce. Cover and cook until chicken registers 160 degrees, 2 to 3 hours on low.

2. Transfer chicken to carving board, let cool slightly, then shred into bite-size pieces using 2 forks; discard bones.

3. Stir vinegar and mustard into sauce. (Adjust sauce consistency with hot water as needed.) Stir in shredded chicken and season with salt and pepper to taste. Serve.

Per serving: Cal 220; Fat 5g; Sat Fat 1g; Chol 65mg; Carb 20g; Protein 23g; Fiber 2g; Sodium 680mg

---

ON THE SIDE CAROLINA-STYLE COLESLAW

Toss 4 cups shredded red or green cabbage and 1 small shredded carrot with 1 teaspoon salt and let drain in colander until wilted, about 1 hour. Rinse cabbage and carrot with cold water, then dry thoroughly with paper towels. Whisk 2 tablespoons cider vinegar, 2 tablespoons sugar, 1 tablespoon extra-virgin olive oil, 1 tablespoon minced fresh parsley, and pinch celery seeds together in large bowl. Add rinsed cabbage mixture and toss to combine. Season with extra vinegar, extra sugar, and salt to taste and refrigerate until chilled.

Per serving: Cal 90; Fat 3.5g; Sat Fat 0g; Chol 0mg; Carb 12g; Protein 1g; Fiber 2g; Sodium 610mg

Shredded Chicken Tacos with Pineapple Salsa

Serves 4 • **Cooking Time** 2 to 3 hours on Low • **Slow Cooker Size** 4 to 7 Quarts

✔ **WHY THIS RECIPE WORKS:** These spicy, smoky shredded chicken soft tacos with Mexican flavors are a far cry from their bland counterparts that are all too common north of the border. Bone-in chicken breasts boast an intense chicken flavor and remain lean and moist after slow cooking, making them the ideal cut for these tacos. We braised the chicken in a rich chipotle-infused tomato sauce made by simply enhancing canned tomato sauce with aromatics, a handful of spices, and a chipotle chile in adobo sauce, which added charred flavor and deep complexity. A squeeze of fresh lime juice enlivened the flavors at the end, leaving us with a chicken filling that was smoky, spicy, and complex. A quick salsa of fresh pineapple with lime, red onion, and cilantro was the perfect counterpoint to the smoky chicken. Check the chicken's temperature after 2 hours of cooking and continue to monitor until it registers 160 degrees.

2 cups ¼-inch pineapple pieces
5 tablespoons lime juice (3 limes)
¼ cup finely chopped red onion
2 tablespoons chopped fresh cilantro
1 tablespoon canola oil
1 tablespoon chili powder
4 garlic cloves, minced
1 teaspoon minced canned chipotle chile in adobo sauce
1 teaspoon ground coriander
1 teaspoon ground cumin
1 cup canned tomato sauce
2 teaspoons sugar
2 (12-ounce) bone-in split chicken breasts, skin and ribs removed, trimmed of all visible fat
Salt and pepper
12 (6-inch) corn tortillas, warmed

1. Combine pineapple, ¼ cup lime juice, onion, and cilantro in bowl; set aside until ready to serve.

2. Microwave oil, chili powder, garlic, chipotle, coriander, and cumin in bowl until fragrant, about 30 seconds; transfer to slow cooker. Stir in tomato sauce and sugar. Season chicken with salt and pepper, place in slow cooker, and turn to coat with sauce. Cover and cook until chicken registers 160 degrees, 2 to 3 hours on low.

3. Transfer chicken to carving board, let cool slightly, then shred into bite-size pieces using 2 forks; discard bones.

4. Stir remaining 1 tablespoon lime juice into sauce. (Adjust sauce consistency with hot water as needed.) Stir in shredded chicken and season with salt and pepper to taste. Divide shredded chicken among warm tortillas and top with pineapple salsa. Serve, passing remaining sauce separately.

Per serving: Cal 400; Fat 9g; Sat Fat 1g; Chol 65mg; Carb 55g; Protein 27g; Fiber 7g; Sodium 720mg *To reduce sodium level to 300mg, use no-salt-added tomato sauce.

ON THE SIDE MEXICAN STREET CORN
Adjust oven rack 6 inches from broiler element. Spray 4 ears peeled corn with vegetable oil spray and place in aluminum foil–lined rimmed baking sheet. Broil corn until tender and well browned on both sides, 5 to 10 minutes per side. In large bowl, mix together 2 tablespoons light mayonnaise, 2 tablespoons plain whole-milk yogurt, ¼ cup queso fresco cheese, 2 tablespoons minced fresh cilantro, 1 tablespoon lime juice, 1 minced garlic clove, 1 teaspoon chili powder, ¼ teaspoon salt, and pinch pepper. Roll broiled corn in mayonnaise mixture to coat thoroughly and transfer to serving platter. Spoon remaining mayonnaise mixture over corn. Serve with lime wedges. Serves 4.

Per serving: Cal 140; Fat 6g; Sat Fat 1g; Chol 5mg; Carb 20g; Protein 5g; Fiber 2g; Sodium 230mg

Italian Braised Turkey Sausages

Serves 4 • **Cooking Time** 3 to 4 hours on Low • **Slow Cooker Size** 5½ to 7 Quarts

✔ **WHY THIS RECIPE WORKS:** For this hearty dinner, a simple combination of sausage, peppers, onions, and potatoes is transformed into a rich, satisfying meal by the gentle and moist heat of the slow cooker. For the main components of the dish, we chose creamy red potatoes, red bell peppers, onions, and Italian turkey sausage, which was packed with spices like fennel and caraway that would flavor the dish. We microwaved tomato paste, garlic, oregano, and red pepper flakes with the vegetables, both to give the potatoes, peppers, and onions a head start and to infuse them with layers of flavor. Some fresh basil stirred in right before serving brightened up this comforting dish. Italian chicken sausage can be substituted for the turkey sausage.

12	ounces red potatoes, unpeeled, quartered and sliced ¼ inch thick
3	red or green bell peppers, stemmed, seeded, and cut into ¼-inch-wide strips
1	onion, halved and sliced ½ inch thick
¼	cup tomato paste
2	tablespoons water
3	garlic cloves, minced
2	teaspoons minced fresh oregano or ½ teaspoon dried
¼	teaspoon red pepper flakes
¼	cup chicken broth
1½	pounds hot or sweet Italian turkey sausage
2	tablespoons chopped fresh basil
	Salt and pepper

1. Microwave potatoes, bell peppers, onion, tomato paste, water, garlic, oregano, and pepper flakes in covered bowl, stirring occasionally, until vegetables are almost tender, about 15 minutes; transfer to slow cooker. Stir in broth. Nestle sausage into slow cooker. Cover and cook until sausage and vegetables are tender, 3 to 4 hours on low.

2. Transfer sausage to serving platter. Stir basil into vegetable mixture and season with salt and pepper to taste. Spoon vegetable mixture over sausage and serve.

Per serving: Cal 280; Fat 11g; Sat Fat 2.5g; Chol 75mg; Carb 28g; Protein 23g; Fiber 5g; Sodium 1040mg

ON THE SIDE CUTTING A BELL PEPPER
To cut bell pepper, slice off top and bottom, remove core, then slice down through side of pepper. Lay pepper flat on cutting board, cut away any remaining ribs, then cut pepper into pieces as directed in recipe.

Glazed Meatloaf

Serves 8 • **Cooking Time** 2 to 3 hours on Low • **Slow Cooker Size** 5½ to 7 Quarts

☑ **WHY THIS RECIPE WORKS:** It might come as a surprise that you can cook meatloaf in a slow cooker, but we've found that the gentle and moist heat is the ideal cooking environment for this comfort food classic. Using ground turkey instead of the standard mix of pork and beef made this meatloaf lower overall in both calories and fat. Adding coarsely chopped mushrooms gave us the deep meaty flavor of using a combination of meats, without the additional fat. Be sure to use 93 percent lean ground turkey, not ground turkey breast (also labeled 99 percent fat free). Check the meatloaf's temperature after 2 hours of cooking and continue to monitor until it registers 160 degrees. You will need an oval slow cooker for this recipe.

1	shallot, minced
2	garlic cloves, minced
1	teaspoon vegetable oil
1	teaspoon minced fresh thyme or ¼ teaspoon dried
¼	teaspoon cayenne pepper
3	slices hearty white sandwich bread, crusts removed, torn into quarters
6	tablespoons milk
2	tablespoons Worcestershire sauce
1	teaspoon salt
¾	teaspoon pepper
4	ounces white mushrooms, trimmed
1	large egg
2	pounds 93 percent lean ground turkey
6	tablespoons ketchup
2	tablespoons molasses

1. Fold sheet of aluminum foil into 12 by 9-inch sling. Microwave shallot, garlic, oil, thyme, and cayenne in large bowl, stirring occasionally, until shallot is softened, about 2 minutes; let cool slightly.

2. Process bread, milk, Worcestershire, salt, and pepper in food processor until paste forms, about 20 seconds, scraping down bowl as needed. Add mushrooms and pulse until coarsely chopped, about 6 pulses; transfer to bowl with cooled shallot mixture. Stir in egg until combined. Mix in ground turkey using hands until uniform.

3. Shape turkey mixture into 9 by 4-inch loaf across center of foil sling. Using sling, transfer meatloaf to slow cooker. Cover and cook until meatloaf registers 160 degrees, 2 to 3 hours on low.

4. Adjust oven rack 6 inches from broiler element and heat broiler. Whisk ketchup and molasses together in bowl. Using sling, transfer meatloaf to rimmed baking sheet, allowing juices to drain back into slow cooker; discard juices. Press edges of foil flat and brush meatloaf with ketchup mixture. Broil meatloaf until spotty brown, 5 to 7 minutes. Let cool for 15 minutes before slicing and serving.

Per serving: Cal 230; Fat 9g; Sat Fat 2.5g; Chol 90mg; Carb 14g; Protein 24g; Fiber 0g; Sodium 620mg

---

QUICK PREP TIP **MAKING A FOIL SLING FOR MEATLOAF**
To make it easy to get the meatloaf in and out of the slow cooker, we use a foil sling. To make sling, fold sheet of aluminum foil into 12 by 9-inch rectangle, then shape meatloaf across center of sling into 9-inch-long loaf. Be sure to pack meat mixture well so it doesn't break apart while cooking.

Steaks, Chops, Roasts, and More

● **EASY PREP**

Braised Steaks with Root Vegetables

Serves 4 • **Cooking Time** 8 to 9 hours on Low or 5 to 6 hours on High • **Slow Cooker Size** 5½ to 7 Quarts

WHY THIS RECIPE WORKS: Steak with roasted vegetables is a classic pairing that we wanted to bring to the slow cooker. Blade steaks, which can be tough if poorly prepared, turn meltingly tender when cooked in the slow cooker. They were also a great choice for a healthy yet flavor-packed dish, since they are relatively lean but full of flavor. This left us with tender, juicy steaks and a robust, meaty sauce. Our next challenge was getting the steak and vegetables to cook through in the same amount of time. The key to success turned out to be a crafty one: a cheesecloth bundle. Placing a mixture of potatoes, carrots, and parsnips in the bundle on top of the steaks elevated the vegetables above the braising liquid and allowed them to steam gently. This also kept our vegetable side dish from taking on the flavor of our braising liquid, maintaining the vegetables' sweet and fresh taste. Just a tablespoon of butter added moisture and richness to our tender vegetables, and we tossed in parsley for bright flavor.

1	onion, chopped fine
1	tablespoon tomato paste
2	garlic cloves, minced
1	teaspoon canola oil
1	teaspoon minced fresh thyme or ¼ teaspoon dried
¾	cup beef broth
1	tablespoon Worcestershire sauce
2	teaspoons instant tapioca
4	(6-ounce) beef blade steaks, ¾ to 1 inch thick, trimmed of all visible fat
	Salt and pepper
12	ounces red potatoes, unpeeled, cut into 1-inch pieces
4	carrots, peeled, halved lengthwise, and sliced 1 inch thick
4	parsnips, peeled, halved lengthwise, and sliced 1 inch thick
2	tablespoons minced fresh parsley
1	tablespoon unsalted butter, melted

1. Microwave onion, tomato paste, garlic, oil, and thyme in bowl, stirring occasionally, until onion is softened, about 5 minutes; transfer to slow cooker. Stir in broth, Worcestershire, and tapioca. Season steaks with salt and pepper and nestle into slow cooker.

2. Loosely tie potatoes, carrots, and parsnips in cheesecloth bundle; lay bundle on top of steaks. Cover and cook until beef is tender, 8 to 9 hours on low or 5 to 6 hours on high.

3. Transfer vegetables to large bowl. Transfer steaks to serving platter, tent loosely with aluminum foil, and let rest for 5 minutes.

4. Meanwhile, toss vegetables with parsley and melted butter and season with salt and pepper to taste. Season sauce with salt and pepper to taste, spoon over steaks, and serve with vegetables.

Per serving: Cal 410; Fat 14g; Sat Fat 6g; Chol 105mg; Carb 42g; Protein 33g; Fiber 9g; Sodium 510mg

---

QUICK PREP TIP
CHEESECLOTH BUNDLES
To make cheesecloth bundle, place vegetables in center of large, double-layered sheet of cheesecloth. Bring four corners of cheesecloth over vegetables and tie together to form loose bundle. Place bundle over steaks.

Whiskey-Braised Steaks with Chipotle Sweet Potatoes

Serves 4 • **Cooking Time** 8 to 9 hours on Low or 5 to 6 hours on High • **Slow Cooker Size** 5½ to 7 Quarts

✔ **WHY THIS RECIPE WORKS:** For a unique take on steak and potatoes, we braised blade steaks in a whiskey-infused sauce and paired them with sweet and smoky chipotle mashed sweet potatoes. We started with a mix of onion, tomato paste, coriander, and Worcestershire for a flavor-packed sauce base. To get meltingly tender meat, we needed to ensure that there was enough liquid in the slow cooker to almost submerge the steaks. We found that ¾ cup was the right amount to properly braise the meat, even though it resulted in a little extra sauce per serving. Swapping out a portion of the beef broth for whiskey added depth and a hint of smokiness to the sauce. To get perfectly steamed sweet potatoes, we placed them in a cheesecloth bundle above the steaks. While the steaks rested, we mashed the sweet potatoes with a bit of lime and chipotle in adobo. The acidity of the lime and the kick of the chipotle perfectly complemented the sweetness of the potatoes, without the need for extra fat. For information on making a cheesecloth bundle, see page 102.

1	onion, chopped fine
1	tablespoon tomato paste
1	teaspoon canola oil
½	teaspoon ground coriander
½	cup beef broth
¼	cup whiskey
1	tablespoon Worcestershire sauce
2	teaspoons instant tapioca
4	(6-ounce) beef blade steaks, ¾ to 1 inch thick, trimmed of all visible fat
	Salt and pepper
2	pounds sweet potatoes, peeled and cut into 1-inch pieces
1½	teaspoons minced canned chipotle chile in adobo sauce
1	teaspoon grated lime zest plus 2 teaspoons juice

1. Microwave onion, tomato paste, oil, and coriander in bowl, stirring occasionally, until onion is softened, about 5 minutes; transfer to slow cooker. Stir in broth, whiskey, Worcestershire, and tapioca. Season steaks with salt and pepper and nestle into slow cooker.

2. Loosely tie potatoes in cheesecloth bundle; lay bundle on top of steaks. Cover and cook until beef is tender, 8 to 9 hours on low or 5 to 6 hours on high.

3. Transfer potatoes to large bowl. Transfer steaks to serving platter, tent loosely with aluminum foil, and let rest for 5 minutes.

4. Meanwhile, mash potatoes with potato masher until mostly smooth. Stir in chipotle and lime zest and juice and season with salt and pepper to taste. Season sauce with salt and pepper to taste, spoon over steaks, and serve with potatoes.

Per serving: Cal 420; Fat 10g; Sat Fat 4g; Chol 100mg; Carb 42g; Protein 33g; Fiber 7g; Sodium 510mg

---

SMART SHOPPING BLADE STEAKS
One of our favorite cuts for the slow cooker, this surprisingly tender steak is a small cut from the cow's shoulder, or chuck, where most other cuts are quite tough. We love blade steaks because they are inexpensive and turn fall-apart tender when made in the slow cooker, yielding a richly flavored, beefy steak.

Braised Pork Chops with Campfire Beans

Serves 4 • **Cooking Time** 2 to 3 hours on Low • **Slow Cooker Size** 5½ to 7 Quarts

✓ **WHY THIS RECIPE WORKS:** Beans are a classic accompaniment to pork dishes, and we wanted to complement our meaty pork chops with a side of hearty barbecued beans. But to keep the calorie count under control, we needed to minimize the sugary ingredients found in most barbecue sauces. To create a deeply flavored sauce without a lot of sugar, we used a small amount of ketchup and amped up the flavor with onion, chili powder, and liquid smoke. Just 1 tablespoon of molasses added the sweetness and viscosity our sauce needed. Canned pinto beans turned creamy and tender in the slow cooker while they absorbed the smoky flavor of the sauce and helped to braise the chops. We chose blade-cut pork chops, which provided a balance of dark and light meat, and the moderate amount of fat kept the chops tender throughout braising while also keeping this dish in healthy territory. To really wake up the flavor of the beans before serving, we stirred in cider vinegar and Dijon mustard for a hit of piquant freshness.

4	(8-ounce) bone-in blade-cut pork chops, ¾ inch thick, trimmed
½	teaspoon onion powder
½	teaspoon garlic powder
	Salt and pepper
1	onion, chopped fine
1	teaspoon chili powder
1	teaspoon canola oil
2	(15-ounce) cans pinto or navy beans
¼	cup ketchup
1	tablespoon molasses
½	teaspoon liquid smoke
1	tablespoon cider vinegar
1	tablespoon Dijon mustard

1. Season chops with onion powder, garlic powder, salt, and pepper and nestle into bottom of slow cooker.

2. Microwave onion, chili powder, and oil in large bowl, stirring occasionally, until onion is softened, about 5 minutes. Stir in beans, ketchup, molasses, and liquid smoke. Pour bean mixture over chops. Cover and cook until pork is tender, 2 to 3 hours on low.

3. Transfer chops to serving platter, tent loosely with aluminum foil, and let rest for 5 minutes. Using large spoon, skim any white foam from surface of bean mixture. Transfer 1 cup cooked beans to bowl and mash with potato masher until smooth. Stir mashed beans, vinegar, and mustard into slow cooker and season with salt and pepper to taste. Serve.

Per serving: Cal 510; Fat 14g; Sat Fat 4g; Chol 115mg; Carb 41g; Protein 52g; Fiber 9g; Sodium 930mg * To reduce sodium level to 600mg, use low-sodium beans.

QUICK PREP TIP **TRIMMING BLADE-CUT PORK CHOPS**
Pork chops come from the loin of the pig and can be cut into blade chops, rib chops, center-cut chops, and sirloin chops. Cut from the shoulder end of the loin, blade chops may be the toughest choice, but they are also the best choice for long, slow braising where their intramuscular fat and connective tissue can break down and turn incredibly tender. While other cuts of chops may be leaner, we find blade chops to be essential for achieving moist and tender chops in the slow cooker—leaner chops become very dry when braised for hours. And like other cuts of meat, in moderation, blade chops can be an acceptable choice for healthy eating. That said, we still trim away any excess fat from the edges of the chops to help reduce fat and calories.

Smothered Pork Chops with Apples

Serves 4 • **Cooking Time** 2 to 3 hours on Low • **Slow Cooker Size** 5½ to 7 Quarts

☑ **WHY THIS RECIPE WORKS:** For a lighter yet still hearty version of smothered pork chops, we traded in the usual bacon and buttery gravy for Golden Delicious apples, which held their shape but became tender and saucy in the slow cooker. To deliver the best flavor, we sautéed the apples and onion until they were softened and caramelized, then created a thickened sauce with just a tablespoon of flour and a little bit of chicken broth. Worcestershire sauce tempered the sweetness of the apples and deepened the flavor of the sauce. To get the tender chops we wanted, ¾-inch blade-cut pork chops were crucial. While they contain a bit more fat than other center-cut chops, they are the only chops that can handle hours of braising in the slow cooker without drying out. We covered the chops with the apple mixture, and as the apples and onion released their juices as they cooked, they braised the chops, adding deep flavor.

4	**(8-ounce) bone-in blade-cut pork chops, ¾ inch thick, trimmed**
	Salt and pepper
2	**teaspoons canola oil**
2	**Golden Delicious apples, peeled, cored, and sliced ½ inch thick**
1	**onion, halved and sliced ¼ inch thick**
1	**tablespoon all-purpose flour**
2	**teaspoons minced fresh thyme or ½ teaspoon dried**
½	**cup chicken broth**
2	**tablespoons Worcestershire sauce**
2	**bay leaves**
2	**tablespoons minced fresh parsley**
2	**teaspoons cider vinegar**

1. Season chops with salt and pepper and nestle into bottom of slow cooker.

2. Heat oil in 12-inch skillet over medium heat until shimmering. Add apples and onion and cook until softened and well browned, about 10 minutes. Stir in flour and thyme and cook for 1 minute. Slowly whisk in broth, scraping up any browned bits and smoothing out any lumps. Stir in Worcestershire and bay leaves, then pour apple mixture over chops. Cover and cook until pork is tender, 2 to 3 hours on low.

3. Transfer chops to serving platter, tent loosely with aluminum foil, and let rest for 5 minutes. Using large spoon, skim any white foam from surface of apple mixture. Discard bay leaves. Stir in parsley and vinegar and season with salt and pepper to taste. Spoon apple mixture over chops and serve.

Per serving: Cal 380; Fat 14g; Sat Fat 4g; Chol 115mg; Carb 19g; Protein 43g; Fiber 3g; Sodium 450mg

---

QUICK PREP TIP
PREPARING APPLES FOR COOKING
After peeling apple, cut sides squarely away from core. Then slice or cut each piece as directed in recipe.

Provençal Pork Tenderloin with Ratatouille

Serves 4   •   **Cooking Time** 1 to 2 hours on Low   •   **Slow Cooker Size** 5½ to 7 Quarts

✔ **WHY THIS RECIPE WORKS:** For this simple braised pork tenderloin, we turned to Provence for inspiration, pairing this lean cut with a robust ratatouille. Traditionally, ratatouille is a labor of love, with many recipes demanding that each vegetable be cooked separately for the perfect texture. We found that the slow cooker eliminated much of this fussy preparation with just a little up-front prep. Broiling the eggplant, zucchini, and aromatics together before adding them to the slow cooker not only allowed us to use less oil but also ensured browned and flavorful vegetables with no excess water. The flavor of fresh tomatoes was far too muted after slow cooking, so we opted for a can of crushed tomatoes, which added the perfect combination of tomato pieces and flavorful sauce needed to braise our tenderloins. We stirred in a tablespoon of olive oil, along with peppery fresh basil, to brighten and enrich the finished dish. Because they are cooked gently and not browned, the tenderloins will be rosy throughout. Check the tenderloins' temperature after 1 hour of cooking and continue to monitor until they register 145 degrees. You will need an oval slow cooker for this recipe.

Vegetable oil spray
1   **pound eggplant, cut into ½-inch pieces**
1   **pound zucchini, cut into ½-inch pieces**
1   **onion, chopped**
3   **garlic cloves, minced**
1   **tablespoon tomato paste**
1   **teaspoon minced fresh thyme or ¼ teaspoon dried**
    Salt and pepper
1   **(28-ounce) can crushed tomatoes**
2   **(12-ounce) pork tenderloins, trimmed of all visible fat**
¼   **cup chopped fresh basil**
1   **tablespoon extra-virgin olive oil**

1. Adjust oven rack 6 inches from broiler element and heat broiler. Line rimmed baking sheet with aluminum foil and spray with oil spray. Toss eggplant, zucchini, onion, garlic, tomato paste, thyme, ¼ teaspoon salt, and ¼ teaspoon pepper together in bowl. Spread vegetable mixture evenly in prepared sheet and lightly spray with oil spray. Broil vegetables until softened and beginning to brown, 8 to 10 minutes, stirring twice during broiling; transfer to slow cooker. Stir in tomatoes.

2. Season tenderloins with salt and pepper and nestle into slow cooker, side by side, alternating thicker end to thinner end. Cover and cook until pork registers 145 degrees, 1 to 2 hours on low.

3. Transfer pork to carving board, tent loosely with aluminum foil, and let rest for 5 minutes. Using large spoon, skim any white foam from surface of ratatouille. Stir in basil and oil and season with salt and pepper to taste. Slice pork ¼ inch thick and serve.

Per serving: Cal 350; Fat 8g; Sat Fat 2g; Chol 110mg; Carb 28g; Protein 42g; Fiber 8g; Sodium 740mg *To reduce sodium level to 500mg, use no-salt-added tomatoes.

QUICK PREP TIP **CHOPPING BASIL**
Freshly chopped basil can quickly turn black through a process called oxidation. The change in color doesn't lessen its flavor; but is there a way to preserve the color appeal without sacrificing flavor? We tried several tricks we had come across to find out. Dropping basil into boiling water, then transferring it to ice water to stop the cooking and "fix" the color was too much trouble. Coating basil with oil before chopping it made it difficult to chop and barely helped. Coating just-chopped basil with oil did slow the color change, but it also made the basil a little oily. Our conclusion? The tricks aren't worth the fuss. For the best flavor and easiest prep, chop basil just before you need it.

Spiced Pork Tenderloin with Carrots and Radishes

Serves 4 • **Cooking Time** 1 to 2 hours on Low • **Slow Cooker Size** 5½ to 7 Quarts

✔ **WHY THIS RECIPE WORKS:** We wanted to make tender spice-rubbed pork tenderloins with a healthy and easy side dish—all in the slow cooker. Carrots and radishes were an appealingly fresh combination that paired well with the simple spice combination that we used. First, we jump-started the carrots in the microwave to ensure that they would cook through by the time our tenderloins were done. We decided not to parcook the radishes so that they would retain a slight crunch in the finished dish. Next, we seasoned the pork with fragrant cumin and paprika, giving the tenderloins a boost of flavor and appealing color. We found that microwaving the spices kept them from tasting harsh. Because they are cooked gently and not browned, the tenderloins will be rosy throughout. Check the tenderloins' temperature after 1 hour of cooking and continue to monitor until they register 145 degrees. You will need an oval slow cooker for this recipe.

1½ **pounds carrots, peeled and sliced ¼ inch thick on bias**
10 **radishes, trimmed and sliced ¼ inch thick**
¼ **cup chicken broth**
3 **tablespoons extra-virgin olive oil**
1 **teaspoon ground cumin**
1 **teaspoon paprika**
2 **(12-ounce) pork tenderloins, trimmed of all visible fat**
 Salt and pepper
2 **tablespoons lime juice**
2 **tablespoons minced fresh cilantro**
4 **teaspoons honey**
1 **teaspoon minced canned chipotle chile in adobo sauce**

1. Microwave carrots and ¼ cup water in covered bowl, stirring occasionally, until crisp-tender, about 8 minutes. Drain carrots and transfer to slow cooker. Stir in radishes and broth.

2. Microwave 1 teaspoon oil, cumin, and paprika in bowl until fragrant, about 30 seconds; let cool slightly. Rub tenderloins with spice mixture and season with salt and pepper. Nestle tenderloins into slow cooker, side by side, alternating thicker end to thinner end. Cover and cook until pork registers 145 degrees, 1 to 2 hours on low.

3. Transfer pork to carving board, tent loosely with aluminum foil, and let rest for 5 minutes.

4. Whisk remaining 8 teaspoons oil, lime juice, cilantro, honey, and chipotle together in bowl and season with salt and pepper to taste. Drain vegetable mixture and return to now-empty slow cooker. Stir in 2 tablespoons of dressing and season with salt and pepper to taste. Slice pork ¼ inch thick and serve with carrot mixture and remaining dressing.

Per serving: Cal 380; Fat 15g; Sat Fat 2.5g; Chol 110mg; Carb 23g; Protein 38g; Fiber 5g; Sodium 390mg

---

QUICK PREP TIP
PREPARING PORK TENDERLOIN
To remove sinewy silverskin, slip boning knife underneath silverskin, angle blade slightly upward, and use gentle back-and-forth motion to remove it from tenderloin. To ensure that tenderloins cook through evenly, nestle them into slow cooker side by side, alternating thicker end to thinner end.

Teriyaki Pork Tenderloin

Serves 4 • **Cooking Time** 1 to 2 hours on Low • **Slow Cooker Size** 4 to 7 Quarts

✓ **WHY THIS RECIPE WORKS:** Cooking a lean roast like pork tenderloin in a slow cooker is tricky because it can quickly turn overcooked and dry. We discovered that nestling two tenderloins side by side, alternating the narrow and thicker ends, helped to insulate the meat and prevented it from overcooking. Once we had the method in hand, we flavored the pork with a teriyaki glaze, made with equal parts sugar and low-sodium soy sauce and seasoned with fresh ginger, garlic, and mirin. To ensure a properly clingy glaze, we simply thickened the sauce with some cornstarch over medium heat, glazed the pork with the thickened sauce, and ran the pork under the broiler before serving. To prevent the pork from overcooking under the broiler, we remove it from the slow cooker just shy of 145 degrees. Because they are cooked gently and not browned, the tenderloins will be rosy throughout. Check the tenderloins' temperature after 1 hour of cooking and continue to monitor until they register 140 degrees. You will need an oval slow cooker for this recipe. Serve with rice.

⅓ cup low-sodium soy sauce
⅓ cup sugar
2 tablespoons mirin
½ teaspoon grated fresh ginger
1 garlic clove, minced
2 (12-ounce) pork tenderloins, trimmed of all visible fat
1½ teaspoons cornstarch
1 tablespoon water
2 scallions, sliced thin
1 teaspoon sesame seeds, toasted

1. Combine soy sauce, sugar, mirin, ginger, and garlic in slow cooker. Nestle pork into slow cooker, side by side, alternating thicker end to thinner end. Cover and cook until pork registers 140 degrees, 1 to 2 hours on low.

2. Adjust oven rack 6-inches from broiler element and heat broiler. Transfer pork to aluminum foil–lined rimmed baking sheet. Transfer cooking liquid to small saucepan and bring to simmer over medium heat. Whisk cornstarch and water together, then whisk into cooking liquid and simmer until thickened, 3 to 5 minutes.

3. Brush pork heavily with glaze and broil until spotty brown on top, about 5 minutes. Transfer pork to carving board, tent loosely with aluminum foil, and let rest for 5 minutes. Slice pork ¼ inch thick, drizzle with remaining glaze, and sprinkle with scallions and sesame seeds. Serve.

Per serving: Cal 290; Fat 4g; Sat Fat 1g; Chol 110mg; Carb 22g; Protein 37g; Fiber 0g; Sodium 800mg

---

ON THE SIDE SESAME SNAP PEAS
Heat 1 teaspoon canola oil in 12-inch nonstick skillet over medium-high heat until shimmering. Add 1 pound sugar snap peas, strings removed, and cook until lightly browned, about 2 minutes. Add ¼ cup water and ¼ teaspoon salt, cover, and cook until peas are bright green, about 2 minutes. Uncover and let water evaporate, 30 to 60 seconds. Push peas to sides of skillet. Add 1 teaspoon canola oil, 1 minced garlic clove, 1 tablespoon low-sodium soy sauce, 2 teaspoons sugar, and 1 teaspoon rice vinegar to center of skillet and cook, mashing mixture into skillet, until fragrant, about 30 seconds. Off heat, add 2 teaspoons toasted sesame seeds and ⅛ teaspoon sesame oil and toss to coat beans. Serves 4.

Per Serving: Cal 90; Fat 3.5g; Sat Fat 0g; Chol 0mg; Carb 12g; Protein 4g; Fiber 3g; Sodium 280mg

Pork Loin with Dried Fig Compote

Serves 8 • **Cooking Time** 2 to 3 hours on Low • **Slow Cooker Size** 5½ to 7 Quarts

WHY THIS RECIPE WORKS: Our goal was to pair a tender pork loin roast with a rich fruit compote in the slow cooker. To keep it simple and healthy, we used unsweetened applesauce as the base for our compote, then stirred in chopped dried figs. Minced shallot and balsamic vinegar added complexity and balanced the sweetness. The aromatics and sweet figs were flavorful enough that we could skip searing the pork loin, saving us both time and extra dirty dishes. As the pork cooked, the figs hydrated and thickened the compote, resulting in a rich, flavorful accompaniment that was low in fat and calories. To add herbaceous depth, we steeped a sprig of fresh rosemary in the compote while the pork rested and stirred in another dash of balsamic vinegar for brightness before serving. A wider, shorter pork loin roast (about 8 inches long) will fit in the slow cooker best. Check the temperature of the pork loin after 2 hours of cooking and continue to monitor until it registers 140 degrees. We found that leaving a ⅛-inch-thick layer of fat on top of the roast is ideal; if your roast has a thicker fat cap, trim it to be about ⅛ inch thick. You will need an oval slow cooker for this recipe.

1   **shallot, minced**

1   **teaspoon canola oil**

1   **cup unsweetened applesauce**

1   **cup dried figs, stemmed and chopped**

2   **tablespoons balsamic vinegar**

2   **bay leaves**
     Salt and pepper

1   **(3-pound) boneless pork loin roast, fat trimmed to ⅛ inch**

1   **teaspoon minced fresh thyme or ¼ teaspoon dried**

1   **sprig fresh rosemary**

1. Microwave shallot and oil in bowl until shallot is softened, about 1 minute; transfer to slow cooker. Stir in applesauce, figs, 1 tablespoon vinegar, bay leaves, and ¼ teaspoon salt. Season roast with thyme, salt, and pepper and nestle fat side up into slow cooker. Cover and cook until pork registers 140 degrees, 2 to 3 hours on low.

2. Transfer roast to carving board, tent loosely with aluminum foil, and let rest for 15 minutes. Stir rosemary sprig into compote and let steep for 10 minutes. Discard rosemary sprig and bay leaves. Stir in remaining 1 tablespoon vinegar and season with salt and pepper to taste. Slice pork ¼ inch thick and serve with compote.

Per serving: Cal 290; Fat 10g; Sat Fat 3.5g; Chol 85mg; Carb 17g; Protein 33g; Fiber 2g; Sodium 320mg

---

SMART SHOPPING PORK LOIN ROASTS

Buying the right pork loin will make a difference in these slow-cooker recipes. Look for a 3-pound pork loin roast that is wide and short (top) (about 8 inches long), and steer clear of those that are long and narrow (bottom). Narrow pork loins don't fit as easily into the slow cooker and are prone to overcooking because they cook through more quickly.

ALL ABOUT Slow-Cooker Steaks, Chops, and Roasts

Leaner cuts of meat like beef blade steaks, pork loin and pork tenderloin, and roast beef are notorious for turning tough and dry even when cooked traditionally, so we were at first reluctant to try our hand at making them in a slow cooker. But to our surprise, we found that the slow cooker is actually helpful when cooking these cuts since the low, moist heat cooks them gently to the proper doneness. Here are some important tips for cooking these cuts successfully in a slow cooker.

Trimming and Portioning

Beef and pork can be healthy as long as you trim away unwanted fat and are mindful of portion size. An untrimmed steak or beef roast can add up to 20 grams of fat and 180 calories to your meal. And by choosing a moderate 6 ounces of  protein per person (raw weight) instead of 8 or 12 ounces (as many traditional recipes call for), you can easily limit fat and calories and still have a satisfyingly ample yet still "healthy" portion size for dinner.

Monitor Lean Roasts

While well-marbled roasts can cook all day and still come out moist, leaner roasts like pork tenderloins, pork loins, and beef eye-round roasts need to cook for a limited amount of time or risk becoming dry and overcooked. To make sure these roasts remain moist, we cook them on low and use 1-hour time ranges. Start monitoring their temperature at the lower end of the time range and take them out of the slow cooker as soon as they reach  the desired temperature. After you make these roasts for the first time, you should have some idea of how long it takes to cook them properly in your slow cooker.

Pork Tenderloin	145 degrees
Pork Loin	140 degrees
Beef Eye-Round Roast	120–125 degrees (medium-rare) 130–135 degrees (medium)

Maximize Flavor—Even with Less Fat

Although fat certainly helps to add flavor, we found other ways to enhance our lean meats. To prevent our steaks, chops, and roasts from turning out bland, we often season them liberally with robust spice rubs and braise them in bases of wine, broth, whiskey, or even applesauce with plenty of aromatics. As the roasts cook, they are infused with the bold flavor of the seasonings and braising liquid. Another way to add flavor  with a minimum of fat is by browning roasts on the stovetop before adding them to the slow cooker, which we take advantage of in a few recipes where this made a big difference.

Add Vegetables

We found that it was relatively easy to incorporate vegetables, beans, or grains into the slow cooker so they could cook alongside our steaks or roasts, which is both convenient and healthy. Sometimes, as was the case with Roast Beef with Warm Garden Potato Salad (page 119), we added fresh vegetables to the slow cooker as the roast rested to cook through in a flash. Fresh and bright vinaigrettes brought an extra flavor punch to our sides with few calories and little fat.

Let It Rest

After cooking almost any piece of meat, it is crucial to allow it to rest. During this time, the proteins relax and reabsorb any accumulated meat juices and redistribute them throughout the meat, resulting in more juicy and tender cuts and less pooled drippings. For lean cuts of meat that are prone to drying out and turning tough, this resting time is especially important for ensuring that they stay moist and tender.

Pork Loin with Warm Spiced Chickpea Salad

Serves 8 • **Cooking Time** 2 to 3 hours on Low • **Slow Cooker Size** 5½ to 7 Quarts

✓ **WHY THIS RECIPE WORKS:** Inspired by the lively flavors of Moroccan cuisine, we set out to create a healthy and satisfying meal featuring moist pork and a warm-spiced salad with contrasting textures, straight from the slow cooker. For maximum flavor, we decided to sear the roast and use the rendered fat to bloom the spices. A combination of coriander, cumin, and cloves created an authentic and flavorful base for our side dish. Chickpeas, with their slightly nutty flavor and creamy texture, complemented the pork perfectly with the added benefit of being high in fiber and low in calories. We nestled the seared pork on top of the chickpeas to cook gently. Once the pork was done cooking, we let it rest while we finished our warm chickpea salad. We added dried apricots, roasted red peppers, and shallots at the end and allowed them to just warm through, keeping their flavors and textures distinct to balance the spice-infused chickpeas. A splash of vinegar and a generous sprinkling of chopped mint rounded out the salad with bright freshness. A wider, shorter pork loin roast (about 8 inches long) will fit in the slow cooker best. Check the temperature of the pork loin after 2 hours of cooking and continue to monitor until it registers 140 degrees. We found that leaving a ⅛-inch-thick layer of fat on top of the roast is ideal; if your roast has a thicker fat cap, trim it to be about ⅛ inch thick. You will need an oval slow cooker for this recipe.

1	**(3-pound) boneless pork loin roast, fat trimmed to ⅛ inch**
	Salt and pepper
2	**teaspoons canola oil**
2	**garlic cloves, minced**
1	**teaspoon ground coriander**
½	**teaspoon ground cumin**
¼	**teaspoon ground cloves**
½	**cup chicken broth**
3	**(14-ounce) cans chickpeas, rinsed**
½	**cup dried apricots, chopped**
½	**cup jarred roasted red peppers, rinsed, patted dry, and chopped**
1	**shallot, sliced thin**
1	**tablespoon white wine vinegar**
¼	**cup chopped fresh mint**

1. Pat roast dry with paper towels and season with salt and pepper. Heat oil in 12-inch skillet over medium-high heat until just smoking. Brown roast well on all sides, 7 to 10 minutes; transfer to plate. Add garlic, coriander, cumin, and cloves to now-empty skillet and cook over medium heat until fragrant, about 30 seconds. Slowly whisk in broth, scraping up any browned bits; transfer to slow cooker.

2. Stir chickpeas into slow cooker. Nestle roast fat side up into slow cooker. Cover and cook until pork registers 140 degrees, 2 to 3 hours on low.

3. Transfer roast to carving board, tent loosely with aluminum foil, and let rest for 15 minutes. Stir apricots, red peppers, shallot, and vinegar into chickpea mixture and let sit until heated through, about 5 minutes. Stir in mint and season with salt and pepper to taste. Slice pork ¼ inch thick and serve.

Per serving: Cal 350; Fat 11g; Sat Fat 3.5g; Chol 85mg; Carb 22g; Protein 37g; Fiber 4g; Sodium 530mg

---

SMART SHOPPING **ROASTED RED PEPPERS**

We tasted eight brands of roasted red peppers, both straight out of the jars and in roasted red pepper soup, to find the best one. Overall, tasters preferred firmer, smokier, sweeter-tasting peppers packed in simple brines made of salt and water. Peppers packed in brines that contained garlic, vinegar, olive oil, and grape must—characteristic of most of the European brands—rated second. Our winner? Tasters preferred the domestically produced **Dunbars Sweet Roasted Peppers**, which lists only red bell peppers, water, salt, and citric acid in its ingredient list.

Pork Loin with Fennel, Oranges, and Olives

Serves 8 • **Cooking Time** 2 to 3 hours on Low • **Slow Cooker Size** 5½ to 7 Quarts

✓ **WHY THIS RECIPE WORKS:** Fennel, oranges, and olives are a classic Italian combination that we wanted to accompany our tender pork loin roast. After quickly searing the roast to give it a deep color and more satisfying flavor, we sautéed the fennel in white wine until softened. We uncovered the skillet and caramelized the fennel before transferring it to the slow cooker, and then nestled the seared roast on top. While the roast rested, we stirred orange segments and chopped kalamata olives into the fennel. The bright citrus of the oranges and the brininess of the olives combined with the anise flavor of the fennel to create the perfect medley of Mediterranean flavors. A wider, shorter pork loin roast (about 8 inches long) will fit in the slow cooker best. Check the temperature of the pork loin after 2 hours of cooking and continue to monitor until it registers 140 degrees. We found that leaving a ⅛-inch-thick layer of fat on top of the roast is ideal; if your roast has a thicker fat cap, trim it to be about ⅛ inch thick. You will need an oval slow cooker for this recipe.

1 **(3-pound) boneless pork loin roast, fat trimmed to ⅛ inch**

1 **teaspoon herbes de Provence**
Salt and pepper

2 **teaspoons canola oil**

3 **fennel bulbs, stalks discarded, bulbs halved, cored, and sliced thin (9 cups)**

½ **cup dry white wine**

2 **garlic cloves, minced**

4 **oranges, plus 1 tablespoon grated orange zest**

½ **cup pitted kalamata olives, chopped**

2 **tablespoons minced fresh tarragon**

1. Pat roast dry with paper towels and season with herbes de Provence, salt, and pepper. Heat oil in 12-inch skillet over medium-high heat until just smoking. Brown roast well on all sides, 7 to 10 minutes; transfer to plate.

2. Add fennel and wine to now-empty skillet, cover, and cook, stirring occasionally, until fennel begins to soften, about 5 minutes. Uncover and continue to cook until fennel is dry and browned, about 5 minutes. Stir in garlic and cook until fragrant, about 30 seconds; transfer to slow cooker. Nestle roast fat side up into slow cooker. Cover and cook until pork registers 140 degrees, 2 to 3 hours on low.

3. Transfer roast to carving board, tent loosely with aluminum foil, and let rest for 15 minutes. Meanwhile, cut away peel and pith from oranges. Quarter oranges, then slice crosswise into ½-inch-thick pieces. Stir orange segments, orange zest, and olives into fennel mixture and let sit until heated through, about 5 minutes. Stir in tarragon and season with salt and pepper to taste. Slice pork ¼ inch thick and serve.

Per serving: Cal 320; Fat 12g; Sat Fat 3.5g; Chol 85mg; Carb 16g; Protein 34g; Fiber 4g; Sodium 410mg

---

QUICK PREP TIP
CUTTING CITRUS INTO PIECES
Slice off top and bottom of citrus, then cut away peel and pith using paring knife. Cut citrus into wedges as directed in recipe. Working with 2 wedges at a time, slice into ½-inch-thick pieces.

Roast Beef with Hearty Mushroom Gravy

Serves 8 • **Cooking Time** 1 to 2 hours on Low • **Slow Cooker Size** 5½ to 7 Quarts

✔️ **WHY THIS RECIPE WORKS:** The eye-round roast, an ultralean cut of beef, is perfectly suited to the low-and-slow heat of a slow cooker, which turns this otherwise tough cut as tender as prime rib with significantly less fat. After trimming all the fat from the roast, we seasoned it and quickly seared it in a nonstick skillet to create a flavorful crust. A small amount of butter, stirred into the gravy at the end, added a welcome richness without adding a lot of fat to the dish. Look for an eye-round roast that is uniformly shaped to ensure even cooking. Check the temperature of the roast after 1 hour of cooking and continue to monitor until it registers 120 to 125 degrees (for medium-rare). We prefer this roast cooked to medium-rare, but if you prefer to cook it to medium, cook the roast until it registers 130 to 135 degrees. You will need an oval slow cooker for this recipe.

1   **(3-pound) boneless eye-round roast, trimmed of all visible fat**
     Salt and pepper
1   **tablespoon canola oil**
8   **ounces cremini mushrooms, trimmed and sliced thin**
1   **onion, chopped fine**
2   **tablespoons tomato paste**
2   **tablespoons all-purpose flour**
1   **teaspoon minced fresh thyme or ¼ teaspoon dried**
⅛   **ounce dried porcini mushrooms, rinsed and minced**
1¼   **cups beef broth**
1   **tablespoon unsalted butter**
2   **tablespoons minced fresh parsley**

1. Pat roast dry with paper towels and season with salt and pepper. Heat 2 teaspoons oil in 12-inch nonstick skillet over medium-high heat until just smoking. Brown roast well on all sides, 7 to 10 minutes; transfer to plate.

3. Heat remaining 1 teaspoon oil in now-empty skillet over medium-high heat until shimmering. Add cremini mushrooms, onion, and tomato paste and cook until vegetables are softened, about 5 minutes. Stir in flour, thyme, and porcini mushrooms and cook for 1 minute. Slowly whisk in broth, scraping up any browned bits and smoothing out any lumps, and bring to boil; transfer to slow cooker. Nestle browned roast into slow cooker. Cover and cook until beef registers 120 to 125 degrees (for medium-rare), 1 to 2 hours on low.

4. Transfer roast to carving board, tent loosely with foil, and let rest for 15 minutes. Whisk butter, parsley, and any accumulated meat juices into gravy and season with salt and pepper to taste. Slice beef thinly against grain and serve.

Per serving: Cal 270; Fat 8g; Sat Fat 3g; Chol 105mg; Carb 5g; Protein 40g; Fiber 1g; Sodium 360mg

---

ON THE SIDE CREAMY MASHED POTATOES
Cover 3 pounds russet potatoes, peeled, sliced ½ inch thick, and rinsed well, with water and 1 tablespoon salt in Dutch oven. Bring to boil, then reduce to simmer and cook until tender, 15 to 20 minutes. Drain potatoes, wipe pot dry, then return potatoes to pot. Mash potatoes with potato masher until few small lumps remain. Fold in ¾ cup 2 percent low-fat milk, warmed, ⅔ cup low-fat sour cream, and 3 tablespoons melted butter. Season with salt and pepper to taste. Serves 8.

Per serving: Cal 210; Fat 6g; Sat Fat 3g; Chol 15mg; Carb 32g; Protein 5g; Fiber 2g; Sodium 105mg

Roast Beef with Warm Garden Potato Salad

Serves 8 • **Cooking Time** 1 to 2 hours on Low • **Slow Cooker Size** 5½ to 7 Quarts

✓ **WHY THIS RECIPE WORKS:** A juicy roast beef and potato dinner is always inviting and surprisingly well-suited to the slow cooker. We cooked the roast at a low temperature, giving it a moist, even doneness and rosy color from edge to center. The potatoes propped up the roast and ensured that the meat wasn't sitting in any cooking juices. We kept the green beans bright by briefly steaming them in the microwave. Look for potatoes measuring 1 to 2 inches in diameter; do not substitute full-size Yukon Gold potatoes or they will not cook through properly. Look for an eye-round roast that is uniformly shaped to ensure even cooking. Check the temperature of the roast after 1 hour of cooking and continue to monitor until it registers 120 to 125 degrees (for medium-rare). We prefer this roast cooked to medium-rare, but if you prefer to cook it to medium, cook the roast until it registers 130 to 135 degrees. You will need an oval slow cooker for this recipe.

2	pounds small Yukon Gold potatoes, unpeeled, quartered
1	(3-pound) boneless eye-round roast, trimmed of all visible fat
1½	teaspoons garlic powder
	Salt and pepper
2	tablespoons extra-virgin olive oil
2	pounds green beans, trimmed and cut into 1-inch lengths
¼	cup chopped fresh parsley
3	tablespoons white wine vinegar
1	shallot, minced
2	tablespoons Dijon mustard
2	tablespoons minced fresh chives

1. Microwave potatoes and ¼ cup water in covered bowl, stirring occasionally, until almost tender, about 15 minutes; transfer to slow cooker.

2. Pat roast dry with paper towels and season with garlic powder, salt, and pepper. Heat 2 teaspoons oil in 12-inch non-stick skillet over medium-high heat until just smoking. Brown roast well on all sides, 7 to 10 minutes. Place roast on top of potatoes in slow cooker. Cover and cook until beef registers 120 to 125 degrees (for medium-rare), 1 to 2 hours on low.

3. Transfer roast to carving board, tent loosely with foil, and let rest for 15 minutes. Meanwhile, microwave green beans and ¼ cup water in large covered bowl, stirring occasionally, until just tender, 6 to 8 minutes. Drain green beans and return to now-empty bowl. Drain potatoes and transfer to bowl with green beans.

4. Whisk remaining 4 teaspoons oil, parsley, vinegar, shallot, 2 tablespoons water, mustard, and chives together in small bowl. Pour dressing over green bean–potato mixture and gently toss to combine. Season with salt and pepper to taste. Slice meat thinly against grain and serve.

Per serving: Cal 360; Fat 9g; Sat Fat 2.5g; Chol 100mg; Carb 26g; Protein 43g; Fiber 4g; Sodium 350mg

---

QUICK PREP TIP TRIMMING GREEN BEANS QUICKLY
Instead of trimming the ends from one green bean at a time, line up the beans on a cutting board and trim all the ends with just one slice.

Asian-Style Pulled Pork Tacos with Pear and Cucumber Slaw

Serves 4 • **Cooking Time** 2 to 3 hours on Low • **Slow Cooker Size** 4 to 7 Quarts

✓ **WHY THIS RECIPE WORKS:** This incredibly easy and multidimensional recipe features tender shredded pork, flavorful sauce, and a crunchy pickled slaw. We found that we could make a sauce and season our pork all at once by combining hoisin, ginger, and Sriracha in the slow cooker. Boneless country-style pork ribs were a great choice for the slow cooker; after a few hours of braising, they were moist and extra-tender. We let the cooked pork rest briefly before shredding it and stirring it back into the sauce. To add freshness and crunch to our tacos, we made a quick pickled slaw while the meat cooked. A simple combination of Asian pears, carrots, and cucumber tossed with rice vinegar provided the perfect balance to our rich taco filling. A little bit more sesame oil and Sriracha in the slaw brought together the flavors of the dish while keeping it light and fresh.

2	Asian pears, peeled, quartered, cored, and sliced thin
2	carrots, peeled and cut into 2-inch-long matchsticks
1	cucumber, peeled, halved lengthwise, seeded, and sliced thin
¼	cup rice vinegar
1	onion, chopped fine
4	garlic cloves, minced
2	teaspoons toasted sesame oil
1	teaspoon grated fresh ginger
¼	cup hoisin sauce
¼	cup water
2	teaspoons Sriracha sauce
1½	pounds boneless country-style pork ribs, trimmed of all visible fat
	Salt and pepper
¼	cup fresh cilantro leaves
12	(6-inch) corn tortillas, warmed

1. Combine pears, carrots, cucumber, and vinegar in bowl; set aside until ready to serve.

2. Microwave onion, garlic, 1 teaspoon oil, and ginger in bowl, stirring occasionally, until onion is softened, about 5 minutes; transfer to slow cooker. Stir in hoisin, water, and 1 teaspoon Sriracha. Nestle pork into slow cooker, cover, and cook until pork is tender, 2 to 3 hours on low.

3. Transfer pork to carving board, let cool slightly, then shred into bite-size pieces using 2 forks, discarding excess fat. Stir shredded pork into sauce and season with salt and pepper to taste.

4. Add remaining 1 teaspoon oil, remaining 1 teaspoon Sriracha, and cilantro to pear and cucumber slaw and toss to combine. Season with salt and pepper to taste. Divide shredded pork among warm tortillas and top with slaw. Serve.

Per serving: Cal 520; Fat 15g; Sat Fat 4g; Chol 125mg; Carb 58g; Protein 40g; Fiber 7g; Sodium 740mg

---

QUICK PREP TIP WARMING TORTILLAS
Warming the tortillas up before serving is crucial for both their flavor and their texture. If your tortillas are very dry, pat each tortilla with a little water before warming them. Toast tortillas, 1 at a time, directly on cooking grate over medium gas flame until slightly charred around edges, about 30 seconds per side. Or toast tortillas, 1 at a time, in dry skillet over medium-high heat until softened and speckled brown, 20 to 30 seconds per side. Once warmed, immediately wrap tortillas in aluminum foil or clean dish towel to keep them warm and soft until serving time.

Beef and Broccoli "Stir-Fry"

Serves 4 • **Cooking Time** 7 to 8 hours on Low or 4 to 5 hours on High • **Slow Cooker Size** 4 to 7 Quarts

WHY THIS RECIPE WORKS: Normally, stir-fry includes splattering hot oil and hectic, last-minute ingredient additions that require lots of advance work. We found a way to simulate a stir-fry in the slow cooker for an easy, light, and mess-free dinner without piles of prep bowls and greasy pans. We chose boneless chuck roast because it contains a fair amount of connective tissue that breaks down and makes the meat meltingly tender after hours in the slow cooker (and since chuck roasts have chunks of visible fat, it's easy to remove the excess when cutting up the roast for braising). A combination of chicken broth and low-sodium soy sauce created the body of our "stir-fry" sauce, and instant tapioca gave it the perfect clingy consistency. Sesame oil and dry mustard added richness and depth, and we studded the sauce with ginger and red pepper flakes for two different dimensions of heat. A little extra sesame oil and soy sauce stirred in at the end reinforced the meaty, savory flavors of the sauce. At the same time, we stirred in a splash of acidic orange juice to brighten the dish and add a hint of balancing sweetness. To keep the broccoli bright and fresh, we waited until the end of cooking and briefly steamed it in the microwave before combining it with the tender chunks of beef. After trimming the beef, you should have 1½ pounds of usable meat. Serve with rice.

3	scallions, white parts minced, green parts sliced thin on bias
2	tablespoons grated fresh ginger
4	garlic cloves, minced
2	teaspoons toasted sesame oil
¼	teaspoon red pepper flakes
¼	teaspoon dry mustard
½	cup chicken broth
2	tablespoons low-sodium soy sauce, plus extra for seasoning
2	tablespoons packed brown sugar
1½	tablespoons instant tapioca
2	pounds boneless beef chuck-eye roast, trimmed of all visible fat and cut into 1½-inch pieces
1½	pounds broccoli florets, cut into 1-inch pieces
¼	cup orange juice

1. Microwave scallion whites, ginger, garlic, 1 teaspoon oil, pepper flakes, and mustard in bowl, stirring occasionally, until fragrant, about 1 minute; transfer to slow cooker. Stir in broth, 1 tablespoon soy sauce, sugar, and tapioca. Stir beef into slow cooker, cover, and cook until beef is tender, 7 to 8 hours on low or 4 to 5 hours on high.

2. Microwave broccoli and ¼ cup water in covered bowl, stirring occasionally, until tender, about 6 minutes. Drain broccoli, then stir into beef mixture along with orange juice, remaining 1 teaspoon oil, and remaining 1 tablespoon soy sauce. Let sit until heated through, about 5 minutes. Season with extra soy sauce to taste. Sprinkle with scallion greens and serve.

Per serving: Cal 360; Fat 10g; Sat Fat 3g; Chol 110mg; Carb 24g; Protein 44g; Fiber 6g; Sodium 510mg

---

ON THE SIDE OVEN-BAKED BROWN RICE
Adjust oven rack to middle position and heat oven to 375 degrees. Spread 1½ cups long- or short-grain brown rice in 8-inch square baking dish. Bring 2⅓ cups water, 2 teaspoons extra-virgin olive oil, and ¼ teaspoon salt to boil in covered saucepan; once boiling, immediately pour water mixture over rice. Cover baking dish tightly with doubled layer of aluminum foil and bake until rice is tender, about 1 hour. Remove baking dish from oven and uncover. Fluff rice with fork, then cover dish with clean dish towel; let rice sit for 5 minutes. Uncover and let rice sit for 5 minutes longer. Serves 4. (To double recipe, use 13 by 9-inch baking dish; bake as directed.)

Per serving: Cal 280; Fat 4.5g; Sat Fat 0.5g; Chol 0mg; Carb 54g; Protein 6g; Fiber 2g; Sodium 150mg

Shredded Beef Tacos

Serves 4 • **Cooking Time** 7 to 8 hours on Low or 4 to 5 hours on High • **Slow Cooker Size** 4 to 7 Quarts

✔ **WHY THIS RECIPE WORKS:** Classic shredded beef tacos are known for their robust meatiness but often rely on excessively fatty cuts of beef. In order to achieve moist, tender, and richly flavored beef tacos without going overboard on fat, we chose leaner chuck roast rather than our standard short ribs, which cut the fat content in half. Then we created a flavorful mixture of dried ancho chiles, chipotle chiles, tomato paste, and a hint of cinnamon. The different types of chiles created layers of heat without turning the sauce overly spicy. We bloomed the aromatics, including the dried chiles, with a small amount of oil in the microwave to bring out their full flavor and added them to the slow cooker with a little honey to balance the heat and water to evenly distribute the spices. Once the beef was pull-apart tender, we simply pureed the braising liquid into a rich, smooth sauce and tossed it with the shredded beef. The small amount of fat that remained contained the highest concentration of flavor—without it the sauce was flat and slightly bitter. To complement the warm spices of the beef, we topped our tacos with a cool and tangy cabbage slaw, which we kept light and simple by tossing with just a splash of lime juice. After trimming the beef, you should have 1½ pounds of usable meat.

½ **head napa cabbage, cored and sliced thin (6 cups)**

1 **carrot, peeled and shredded**

1 **jalapeño chile, stemmed, seeded, and sliced thin**

¼ **cup lime juice (2 limes), plus lime wedges for serving**

¼ **cup chopped fresh cilantro Salt and pepper**

½ **onion, chopped fine**

1 **ounce (2 to 3) dried ancho chiles, stemmed, seeded, and torn into 1-inch pieces**

3 **garlic cloves, minced**

1 **tablespoon tomato paste**

1 **teaspoon canola oil**

1 **teaspoon minced canned chipotle chile in adobo sauce**

½ **teaspoon ground cinnamon**

¾ **cup water, plus extra as needed**

1 **tablespoon honey**

2 **pounds boneless beef chuck-eye roast, trimmed of all visible fat and cut into 2-inch pieces**

12 **(6-inch) corn tortillas, warmed**

1. Combine cabbage, carrot, jalapeño, lime juice, cilantro, and ½ teaspoon salt in large bowl. Cover and refrigerate until ready to serve.

2. Microwave onion, anchos, garlic, tomato paste, oil, chipotle, and cinnamon in bowl, stirring occasionally, until onion is softened, about 5 minutes; transfer to slow cooker. Stir in water and honey. Season beef with salt and pepper and nestle into slow cooker. Cover and cook until beef is tender, 7 to 8 hours on low or 4 to 5 hours on high.

3. Transfer beef to bowl and let cool slightly. Shred into bite-size pieces using 2 forks, discarding excess fat.

4. Process cooking liquid in blender until smooth, about 1 minute. (Adjust sauce consistency with extra hot water as needed.) Season with salt and pepper to taste. Stir 1 cup sauce into shredded beef. Toss slaw to recombine. Divide shredded beef among warm tortillas and top with slaw. Serve with remaining sauce and lime wedges.

Per serving: Cal 490; Fat 11g; Sat Fat 3g; Chol 110mg; Carb 51g; Protein 44g; Fiber 7g; Sodium 660mg

SMART SHOPPING DRIED ANCHO CHILES
Ancho chiles, technically dried poblano peppers, are dark mahogany red, with wrinkly skin and deep, sweet, raisiny flavor. Their heat level is mild to medium. Just as dried fruit has a more concentrated taste than its fresh counterpart, chiles gain a more intense character when dried. For dried chiles with the best flavor, buy ones that are pliable and smell slightly fruity.

Fish and Shellfish

● **EASY PREP**

Poached Salmon with Caper Relish

Serves 4 • **Cooking Time** 1 to 2 hours on Low • **Slow Cooker Size** 5½ to 7 Quarts

✓ **WHY THIS RECIPE WORKS:** A slow cooker is the perfect vehicle for poaching salmon (and other fish) as it requires less monitoring than the classic stovetop method but can yield comparable results with less chance of overcooking. To ensure that the salmon cooked evenly, we came up with some tricks: We started by making a foil sling inside the slow cooker for easy removal and lined the foil with lemon slices. We rested the salmon on the lemon to keep it elevated for even cooking. To punch up the flavor of this mild dish, we paired the fish with a briny caper and herb relish, adding freshness and bright herbal notes. Use salmon fillets of similar thickness so that they cook at the same rate, or buy a 1½-pound salmon fillet and cut it into four equal pieces. Leave the skin on the salmon to keep the bottom of the fillets from becoming overcooked and ensure the fillets stay together when removed from the slow cooker. Check the salmon's temperature after 1 hour of cooking and continue to monitor until it registers 135 degrees. You will need an oval slow cooker for this recipe. For information on making a foil sling, see page 129.

1 lemon, sliced ¼ inch thick

2 tablespoons minced fresh parsley, stems reserved

2 tablespoons minced fresh tarragon, stems reserved

¼ cup dry white wine

4 (6-ounce) skin-on salmon fillets, 1 to 1½ inches thick
   Salt and pepper

1 shallot, minced

2 tablespoons capers, rinsed and minced

1 tablespoon honey

1 tablespoon cider vinegar

1 tablespoon extra-virgin olive oil

1. Fold sheet of aluminum foil into 12 by 9-inch sling; press widthwise into slow cooker. Arrange lemon slices in single layer in bottom of prepared slow cooker. Scatter parsley stems and tarragon stems over lemon. Pour wine into slow cooker, then add water until liquid level is even with lemon slices (about ¼ cup water). Season salmon with salt and pepper and place skin side down on top of lemon. Cover and cook until salmon is opaque throughout when checked with tip of paring knife and registers 135 degrees (for medium), 1 to 2 hours on low.

2. Meanwhile, combine minced parsley, minced tarragon, shallot, capers, honey, vinegar, and oil in bowl and season with salt and pepper to taste.

3. Using sling, transfer salmon to baking sheet. Gently lift and tilt fillets with spatula to remove parsley stems, tarragon stems, and lemon slices and transfer to plates; discard poaching liquid. Serve with relish.

Per serving (wild salmon): Cal 300; Fat 14g; Sat Fat 2g; Chol 95mg; Carb 6g; Protein 34g; Fiber 0g; Sodium 340mg

Per serving (farmed salmon): Cal 410; Fat 26g; Sat Fat 6g; Chol 95mg; Carb 6g; Protein 35g; Fiber 0g; Sodium 370mg

---

ON THE SIDE ROASTED BROCCOLI

Adjust oven rack to lowest position and heat oven to 500 degrees. Place aluminum foil–lined rimmed baking sheet in oven. Cut 2 pounds broccoli at juncture of crowns and stalks. Peel stalks and cut into ½-inch-thick planks about 3 inches long. Place crowns upside down and cut in half through central stalk, then cut each half into 3 or 4 wedges for 3- to 4-inch-diameter crown, or into 6 wedges for 4- to 5-inch-diameter crown. Toss with 1 tablespoon extra-virgin olive oil and ½ teaspoon sugar and season with salt and pepper. Carefully place broccoli on baking sheet and roast until tender, 14 to 16 minutes. Serves 4.

Per Serving: Cal 110; Fat 4.5g; Sat Fat 0.5g; Chol 0mg; Carb 16g; Protein 6g; Fiber 6g; Sodium 75mg

Poached Salmon with Tangerine Relish

Serves 4 • **Cooking Time** 1 to 2 hours on Low • **Slow Cooker Size** 5½ to 7 Quarts

✔ **WHY THIS RECIPE WORKS:** Poaching salmon in the slow cooker produces supremely silky results, and when the fish is paired with a quick citrus salsa, it makes a fresh and easy meal. Propping the fillets up on tangerine slices added bright flavor and helped the salmon steam evenly while the cilantro stems flavored the poaching liquid. For our relish we liked sweet tangerines with the salmon and added white wine vinegar for acidity and ginger for subtle heat. To solve the problem of getting the salmon out of the slow cooker, we used a simple foil sling. Use salmon fillets of similar thickness so that they cook at the same rate, or buy a 1½-pound salmon fillet and cut it into four equal pieces. Leave the skin on the salmon to keep the bottom of the fillets from becoming overcooked and ensure the fillets stay together when removed from the slow cooker. You can substitute oranges for the tangerines, if desired. Check the salmon's temperature after 1 hour of cooking and continue to monitor until it registers 135 degrees. You will need an oval slow cooker for this recipe. For information on making a foil sling, see page 129.

4   tangerines
2   tablespoons minced fresh
     cilantro, stems reserved
¼   cup dry white wine
4   (6-ounce) skin-on salmon fillets,
     1 to 1½ inches thick
     Salt and pepper
1   tablespoon white wine vinegar
1   tablespoon extra-virgin olive oil
2   teaspoons grated fresh ginger

1. Fold sheet of aluminum foil into 12 by 9-inch sling; press widthwise into slow cooker. Slice 1 tangerine ¼ inch thick and arrange slices in single layer in bottom of prepared slow cooker. Scatter cilantro stems over tangerine. Pour wine into slow cooker, then add water until liquid level is even with tangerine slices (about ¼ cup water). Season salmon with salt and pepper and place skin side down on top of tangerine. Cover and cook until salmon is opaque throughout when checked with tip of paring knife and registers 135 degrees, 1 to 2 hours on low.

2. Meanwhile, cut away peel and pith from remaining 3 tangerines. Cut tangerines into 8 wedges, then slice each wedge crosswise into ½-inch-thick pieces. Combine tangerine pieces, reserved juice, minced cilantro, vinegar, oil, and ginger in bowl and season with salt and pepper to taste.

3. Using sling, transfer salmon to baking sheet. Gently lift and tilt fillets with spatula to remove cilantro stems and tangerine slices and transfer to plates; discard poaching liquid. Serve with relish.

Per serving (wild salmon): Cal 310; Fat 15g; Sat Fat 2g; Chol 95mg; Carb 9g; Protein 34g; Fiber 1g; Sodium 220mg

Per serving (farmed salmon): Cal 420; Fat 27g; Sat Fat 6g; Chol 95mg; Carb 9g; Protein 35g; Fiber 1g; Sodium 250mg

SMART SHOPPING WILD VERSUS FARMED SALMON
In season, we've always preferred the more pronounced flavor of wild-caught salmon to that of farmed Atlantic salmon, traditionally the main farm-raised variety in this country. But with more wild and farmed species now available, we decided to reevaluate. We tasted three kinds of wild Pacific salmon and two farmed. While we love the stronger flavor of wild-caught fish, if you're going to spend the extra money, make sure it looks and smells fresh, and realize that high quality is available only from late spring through the end of summer.

ALL ABOUT Fish and Shellfish in the Slow Cooker

There are a lot of reasons to eat fish and shellfish if you are trying to eat healthy: They are a good source of high-quality protein; are typically low in calories, fat (particularly the saturated kind), and cholesterol; and provide valuable vitamins, minerals, and fatty acids. While overcooked fish and rubbery shellfish are all too common, the combination of the slow cooker's low temperature and mild heat is terrific for producing moist fish fillets and tender shrimp and scallops. Here are a few key points about successfully cooking fish and shellfish in the slow cooker.

Keep a Ruler and Thermometer Handy

Ensuring moist fish in the slow cooker starts at the fish counter where we grab 1 to 1½-inch-thick fillets and steaks, which can cook for a longer period of time without drying out. It is also important to choose fillets or steaks that are similar in size and thickness so that each piece will cook at the same rate. To further guarantee that the fish is properly cooked, we use the low setting and 1-hour time ranges

to reduce the opportunity for overcooking. Start monitoring the fish's temperature at the low end of the range until you have experience cooking it in your slow cooker.

Stir in Shrimp and Scallops at the End

Yes, you can cook shrimp and scallops in a slow cooker, but the key is to add them toward the end of the cooking time and let the moist heat of the slow cooker gently cook them through. For instance, we learned it takes just 20 minutes to cook shrimp in a slow cooker, so for a seafood stew or soup, we let the base of broth, vegetables, and aromatics simmer for several hours to soften the vegetables and meld flavors before we add the shrimp. For our slow-cooker shrimp boil, most of the ingredients cook all day, but again, the shrimp is stirred in last. Scallops take a little longer than shrimp to cook through in a slow cooker, but the same principle holds true; for Scallops with Creamy Braised Leeks (page 138), we use the majority of the slow-cooker time to braise the leeks in wine and cream, then add the scallops for the last 30 minutes.

Use a Sling When Poaching

To make it easy to remove delicate fish from the slow cooker after poaching, we often use a foil sling. To form a sling, fold a sheet of aluminum foil into a 12 by 9-inch rectangle and press it widthwise into the slow cooker. Before serving, use the ends of the sling as handles to lift the fish out of the slow cooker fully intact.

Poach with No Fat

Poaching is a naturally low-calorie, low-fat method for cooking fish, but it typically requires prepping a slew of ingredients for the poaching broth, only to dump out at the end of cooking, plus much of the fish's flavor leaches out into the liquid. Fortunately, in the slow cooker these problems can be easily solved using a shallow poaching technique: We simply rest the fish on top of a few citrus slices to keep it elevated for even cooking, and we use just enough liquid to gently steam, not simmer, the fish. Also, during our testing, we learned that adding wine to the poaching liquid helped to achieve perfectly cooked fish quickly at a lower temperature. This is because wine lowers water's boiling point and produces more vapor to cook the fillets.

Don't Try to Cook Clams or Mussels in a Slow Cooker

After much testing with clams and mussels, we learned that by the time they become hot enough for the shells to open up (and sometimes they don't open up), their tender meat is tough and inedible. In short, the slow cooker doesn't get hot enough fast enough to be able to safely cook clams or mussels.

Cod Peperonata

Serves 4 • **Cooking Time** 1 to 2 hours on Low • **Slow Cooker Size** 5½ to 7 Quarts

☑ **WHY THIS RECIPE WORKS:** This sweet, simple fish dish is found all over the Mediterranean and highlights the fresh flavors of peppers, onions, and tomatoes. For our slow-cooker version we prepared the classic bell pepper base and added garlic, thyme, paprika, and wine for a deeper flavor. Red and yellow peppers are the best choices because of their natural sweetness; tasters found green peppers to have a bitter, off-putting flavor. Thinly slicing the peppers and onions proved to be well worth the effort as they cooked down to a soft, velvety consistency while bigger slices still maintained some crunch and marred the smooth texture of the sauce. Once the sauce was prepared, we simply nestled the cod into the liquid and let the fish braise in the moist environment. Within 1 to 2 hours, the fish was cooked through—the result being a tender, moist, and very well-seasoned braised cod. We rounded out the peperonata with balsamic vinegar for a rich and slightly sweet finish. Use cod fillets of similar thickness so that they cook at the same rate. Halibut and haddock are good substitutes for the cod. Check the cod's temperature after 1 hour of cooking and continue to monitor until it registers 140 degrees. You will need an oval slow cooker for this recipe.

2	red or yellow bell peppers, stemmed, seeded, and sliced thin
1	onion, halved and sliced thin
2	tablespoons tomato paste
4	garlic cloves, minced
1	tablespoon paprika
5	teaspoons extra-virgin olive oil
2	teaspoons minced fresh thyme or ½ teaspoon dried
¼	teaspoon red pepper flakes
1	(14.5-ounce) can diced tomatoes, drained
¼	cup dry white wine
	Salt and pepper
4	(6-ounce) skinless cod fillets, 1 to 1½ inches thick
2	tablespoons coarsely chopped fresh basil
2	teaspoons balsamic vinegar

1. Microwave bell peppers, onion, tomato paste, garlic, paprika, 1 teaspoon oil, thyme, and pepper flakes in covered bowl, stirring occasionally, until vegetables are softened, 8 to 10 minutes; transfer to slow cooker.

2. Stir tomatoes, wine, ¼ teaspoon salt, and ¼ teaspoon pepper into slow cooker. Season cod with salt and pepper and nestle into slow cooker. Spoon portion of sauce over cod. Cover and cook until cod flakes apart when gently prodded with paring knife and registers 140 degrees, 1 to 2 hours on low.

3. Gently transfer cod to plates. Stir basil and vinegar into sauce and season with salt and pepper to taste. Spoon sauce over cod and drizzle each portion with 1 teaspoon oil before serving.

Per serving: Cal 270; Fat 7g; Sat Fat 1g; Chol 75mg; Carb 15g; Protein 33g; Fiber 4g; Sodium 640mg *To reduce sodium level to 390mg, use no-salt-added tomatoes.

QUICK PREP TIP
TUCKING THE TAIL
If you end up with a piece of fish with a thinner tail end, simply tuck the thinner end under before nestling it into the slow cooker so that it will cook at the same rate as the other pieces.

Coconut Cod with Edamame

Serves 4 • **Cooking Time** 1 to 2 hours on Low • **Slow Cooker Size** 5½ to 7 Quarts

✔ WHY THIS RECIPE WORKS: A nutty, Thai-inspired coconut sauce does wonders for lean, mildly flavored cod without requiring a lot of work. We combined coconut milk with fish sauce, ginger, garlic, and red pepper flakes for the slightest hint of heat. The bold sauce infused the fish with flavor as it poached in the slow cooker. While cooking, the cod rested on top of a bed of edamame to prevent the bottom of the fish from overcooking. The nutty edamame base gave our meal the additional benefit of a side dish that soaked up the rich sauce. To our creamy side dish we added bright fresh cilantro and rice vinegar to balance the sweetness of the coconut milk. Use cod fillets of similar thickness so that they cook at the same rate. Halibut and haddock are good substitutes for the cod. Check the cod's temperature after 1 hour of cooking and continue to monitor until it registers 140 degrees. You will need an oval slow cooker for this recipe. Serve with rice or couscous.

2	shallots, minced
4	garlic cloves, minced
1	tablespoon grated fresh ginger
1	teaspoon canola oil
⅛	teaspoon red pepper flakes
2	cups frozen edamame, thawed
½	cup canned light coconut milk
2	tablespoons fish sauce, plus extra for seasoning
4	(6-ounce) skinless cod fillets, 1 to 1½ inches thick
	Salt and pepper
¼	cup chopped fresh cilantro
2	teaspoons rice vinegar

1. Microwave shallots, garlic, ginger, oil, and pepper flakes in bowl, stirring occasionally, until shallots are softened, about 2 minutes; transfer to slow cooker. Stir in edamame, coconut milk, and fish sauce. Season cod with salt and pepper and nestle into slow cooker. Spoon portion of sauce over cod. Cover and cook until cod flakes apart when gently prodded with paring knife and registers 140 degrees, 1 to 2 hours on low.

2. Gently transfer cod to plates. Stir cilantro and vinegar into sauce and season with extra fish sauce to taste. Serve.

Per serving: Cal 300; Fat 8g; Sat Fat 2g; Chol 75mg; Carb 13g; Protein 42g; Fiber 5g; Sodium 600mg

---

ON THE SIDE **BULGUR PILAF WITH SHIITAKE MUSHROOMS AND SCALLIONS**
Heat 2 teaspoons canola oil in large saucepan over medium heat. Add 1 finely chopped onion, 8 ounces thinly sliced shiitake mushrooms, and ¼ teaspoon salt, cover, and cook until softened, about 5 minutes. Uncover and continue to cook until onion and mushrooms are dry and browned, about 5 minutes. Stir in 1 tablespoon grated fresh ginger and 2 minced garlic cloves and cook until fragrant, about 30 seconds. Stir in 1 cup rinsed medium-grain bulgur, 1½ cups chicken broth, and 1 teaspoon low-sodium soy sauce and bring to simmer. Reduce heat to low, cover, and simmer until bulgur is tender, 16 to 18 minutes. Off heat, cover saucepan with clean dish towel; let sit for 10 minutes. Add 2 thinly sliced scallions and fluff bulgur with fork. Season with salt and pepper to taste. Serves 4.

Per serving: Cal 180; Fat 3g; Sat Fat 0g; Chol 0mg; Carb 34g; Protein 7g; Fiber 8g; Sodium 390mg

Stuffed Sole with Creamy Tomato Sauce

Serves 4 • **Cooking Time** 1 to 2 hours on Low • **Slow Cooker Size** 5½ to 7 Quarts

✔ **WHY THIS RECIPE WORKS:** While it may seem implausible to create such a delicate dish in the slow cooker, we embraced the challenge. We poached the fish in white wine, which imparted subtle flavor. And by rolling the fillets into bundles with a moist spinach filling, we reduced the likelihood of overcooking. Be sure to squeeze the spinach dry thoroughly or the filling will be watery. Check the doneness of the sole after 1 hour of cooking and continue to monitor until it flakes apart when gently prodded with a paring knife. You will need an oval slow cooker for this recipe. For information on making a foil sling, see page 129.

2 lemons (1 sliced ¼ inch thick, plus ½ teaspoon grated lemon zest and 1 tablespoon juice)

¼ cup dry white wine

10 ounces frozen chopped spinach, thawed and squeezed dry

4 ounces (½ cup) part-skim ricotta cheese

¼ cup chopped fresh basil
   Pinch nutmeg
   Salt and pepper

8 (3-ounce) boneless, skinless sole fillets, ¼ to ½ inch thick

8 ounces cherry tomatoes

1 small shallot, peeled and quartered

1 tablespoon extra-virgin olive oil

1. Fold sheet of aluminum foil into 12 by 9-inch sling; press widthwise into slow cooker. Arrange lemon slices in single layer in bottom of prepared slow cooker. Pour wine into slow cooker, then add water until liquid level is even with lemon slices (about ¼ cup water). Combine spinach, ricotta, 2 tablespoons basil, lemon zest, nutmeg, ¼ teaspoon salt, and ¼ teaspoon pepper in bowl.

2. Season sole with salt and pepper and place skinned side up on cutting board. Mound filling evenly in center of fillets, fold tapered ends tightly over filling, then fold over thicker ends to make tidy bundles. Place bundles seam side down on top of lemon. Cover and cook until sole flakes apart when gently prodded with paring knife, 1 to 2 hours on low.

3. Meanwhile, process tomatoes, shallot, oil, and lemon juice in blender until smooth, 1 to 2 minutes. Strain sauce through fine-mesh strainer into bowl, pressing on solids to extract as much liquid as possible; discard solids. Season with salt and pepper to taste.

4. Using sling, transfer bundles to baking sheet. Gently lift and tilt bundles with spatula to remove lemon slices and transfer to plates; discard poaching liquid. Spoon sauce over bundles and sprinkle with remaining 2 tablespoons basil. Serve.

Per serving: Cal 230; Fat 10g; Sat Fat 2.5g; Chol 85mg; Carb 8g; Protein 27g; Fiber 2g; Sodium 960mg

QUICK PREP TIP
MAKING SOLE BUNDLES
Place sole skinned side up. Divide spinach mixture equally among fillets, mounding in middle of each. Fold tapered end of sole tightly over filling, then fold thicker end over top to make tidy bundle.

Swordfish with Papaya Salsa

Serves 4 • **Cooking Time** 1 to 2 hours on Low • **Slow Cooker Size** 5½ to 7 Quarts

✔**WHY THIS RECIPE WORKS:** Hearty swordfish steaks are a great option for gentle poaching in the slow cooker because the low heat renders their firm meat exceptionally moist and tender. To keep the bottoms of the steaks from overcooking and to add flavor to the poaching liquid, we propped the steaks up on lime slices and cilantro stems. A simple aluminum foil sling made it easier to remove the steaks from the slow cooker in one piece. A fresh papaya salsa of sweet fruit, hot jalapeño, bright cilantro, and tangy lime juice added complex, fresh flavors to this simple fish. If your papaya is underripe, season the salsa with sugar to taste. Use swordfish steaks of similar thickness so that they cook at the same rate. Check the swordfish's temperature after 1 hour of cooking and continue to monitor until it registers 140 degrees. You will need an oval slow cooker for this recipe. For information on making a foil sling, see page 129.

2	**limes (1 sliced ¼ inch thick, plus ½ teaspoon grated lime zest and 2 tablespoons juice)**
2	**tablespoons minced fresh cilantro, stems reserved**
¼	**cup dry white wine**
4	**(6-ounce) swordfish steaks, 1½ inches thick**
	Salt and pepper
1	**papaya, peeled, seeded, and cut into ½-inch pieces**
1	**jalapeño chile, stemmed, seeded, and minced**
1	**teaspoon extra-virgin olive oil**

1. Fold sheet of aluminum foil into 12 by 9-inch sling; press widthwise into slow cooker. Arrange lime slices in single layer in bottom of prepared slow cooker. Scatter cilantro stems over lime slices. Pour wine into slow cooker, then add water until liquid level is even with lime slices (about ¼ cup water). Season swordfish with salt and pepper and place on top of lime slices. Cover and cook until swordfish flakes apart when gently prodded with paring knife and registers 140 degrees, 1 to 2 hours on low.

2. Meanwhile, combine papaya, jalapeño, oil, and lime zest and juice in bowl. Season with salt and pepper to taste.

3. Using sling, transfer swordfish to baking sheet. Gently lift and tilt steaks with spatula to remove cilantro stems and lime slices and transfer to plates; discard poaching liquid. Serve with salsa.

Per serving: Cal 290; Fat 12g; Sat Fat 3g; Chol 110mg; Carb 11g; Protein 34g; Fiber 1g; Sodium 310mg

---

QUICK PREP TIP REVIVING TIRED HERBS
We rarely use an entire bunch of herbs at once. Inevitably, a few days later they look less than fresh, and we have to throw them out and start all over. Is there a way to revive tired herbs? With a little research, we found that soaking herbs in water restores the pressure of the cell contents against the cell wall, causing them to become firmer as the dehydrated cells plump up. So, to test the theory, we purposely let several bunches of parsley, cilantro, and mint sit in the refrigerator until they became limp, sorry-looking versions of their former selves, then we tried bringing the herbs back to life by soaking them in tepid and cold water. We found that trimming the stems, then soaking the herbs for 10 minutes in cold water perks them up better than soaking them in tepid water. These herbs had a fresher look and an improved texture.

Halibut with Warm Bean Salad

Serves 4 • **Cooking Time** 1 to 2 hours on Low • **Slow Cooker Size** 5½ to 7 Quarts

✓ **WHY THIS RECIPE WORKS:** For this healthy fish dinner, we gently cooked meaty halibut fillets on a bed of creamy white beans flavored by shallot, lemon zest, and bay leaves. In the short time it took the fish to cook through perfectly, the beans absorbed the flavors of the cooking liquid. After removing the fish from the slow cooker, we finished our side dish by draining the beans and tossing them with a zesty dressing and green beans (which we steamed in the microwave, leaving them tender and not too crunchy). The classic combination of honey and Dijon mustard thickened the dressing enough to coat the beans without having to use a lot of oil. The final addition of briny kalamata olives paired well with fresh tarragon, intensifying the overall flavor of our dish. Use halibut fillets of similar thickness so that they cook at the same rate. Cod and haddock are good substitutes for the halibut. Check the halibut's temperature after 1 hour of cooking and continue to monitor until it registers 140 degrees. You will need an oval slow cooker for this recipe.

1   **(15-ounce) can small white beans, rinsed**

1   **shallot, sliced thin**

2   **(2-inch) strips lemon zest plus 1 tablespoon juice**

2   **bay leaves**

4   **(6-ounce) skinless halibut fillets, 1 to 1½ inches thick**

4   **teaspoons extra-virgin olive oil**
Salt and pepper

8   **ounces green beans, trimmed and cut into 1-inch lengths**

2   **tablespoons chopped fresh tarragon**

1   **teaspoon Dijon mustard**

1   **teaspoon honey**

2   **tablespoons chopped pitted kalamata olives**

1. Stir white beans, ½ cup water, shallot, lemon zest, and bay leaves into slow cooker. Rub halibut with 2 teaspoons oil and season with salt and pepper. Nestle halibut into slow cooker, cover, and cook until halibut flakes apart when gently prodded with paring knife and registers 140 degrees, 1 to 2 hours on low.

2. Meanwhile, microwave green beans with 1 tablespoon water in covered bowl, stirring occasionally, until tender, 4 to 6 minutes. Drain green beans and return to now-empty bowl. Whisk remaining 2 teaspoons oil, lemon juice, tarragon, mustard, and honey together in separate bowl.

3. Gently remove halibut from slow cooker and transfer to plates. Discard lemon zest. Drain white bean mixture and transfer to bowl with green beans. Add dressing and olives and toss to combine. Season with salt and pepper to taste. Serve.

Per serving: Cal 330; Fat 11g; Sat Fat 1.5g; Chol 55mg; Carb 19g; Protein 41g; Fiber 5g; Sodium 640mg *To reduce sodium level to 460mg, use low-sodium beans.

SMART SHOPPING SHALLOTS
When shopping, avoid shallots packaged in cardboard and cellophane boxes, which prevent you from checking out each shallot. Instead, go for loose shallots or the ones packed in plastic netting. They should feel firm and heavy and have no soft spots. Since most of our recipes call for less than 3 table-spoons of minced shallot, in the test kitchen we use only medium shallots (which yield about 3 tablespoons minced) or small shal-lots (which yield 2 tablespoons or less). A medium shallot should be about 1½ to 2 inches wide.

California-Style Fish Tacos

Serves 4 • **Cooking Time** 1 to 2 hours on Low • **Slow Cooker Size** 5½ to 7 Quarts

✓**WHY THIS RECIPE WORKS:** Simple and fresh fish tacos combine tender fish, crisp sliced cabbage, and a tangy sauce. We wanted a recipe for fish tacos that offered the same great flavor that we could prepare in our slow cooker. To start, we chose mild but sturdy halibut fillets and coated them with a spice rub that we bloomed in the microwave. The fillets sat on a bed of sliced limes, and we added just enough water to steam the fish, ensuring that it would be moist and flaky. After trying a variety of dairy products for our sauce, we settled on a combination of two— light mayonnaise and low-fat sour cream—for tangy flavor and richness. Lime juice and chipotle chiles gave the sauce a subtle, smoky heat and tang. Cabbage salad mixed with fresh cilantro, scallions, and lime juice had a nice crunch and was the perfect finishing touch. Use halibut fillets of similar thickness so that they cook at the same rate. Cod and haddock are good substitutes for the halibut. Check the halibut's temperature after 1 hour of cooking and continue to monitor until it registers 140 degrees. You will need an oval slow cooker for this recipe. For information on making a foil sling, see page 129.

4	limes (1 sliced ¼ inch thick, plus 3 tablespoons juice and lime wedges for serving)
1	tablespoon extra-virgin olive oil
1	tablespoon minced canned chipotle chile in adobo sauce
½	teaspoon ground coriander
¼	teaspoon ground cumin
	Salt and pepper
4	(6-ounce) skinless halibut fillets, 1 to 1½ inches thick
½	small head green cabbage, cored and sliced thin (4 cups)
6	tablespoons minced fresh cilantro
3	scallions, sliced thin
¼	cup light mayonnaise
¼	cup low-fat sour cream
2	garlic cloves, minced
12	(6-inch) corn tortillas, warmed

1. Fold sheet of aluminum foil into 12 by 9-inch sling; press widthwise into slow cooker. Arrange lime slices in single layer in bottom of prepared slow cooker. Add water to slow cooker until liquid level is even with lime slices (about ½ cup water).

2. Microwave 2 teaspoons oil, 2 teaspoons chipotle, coriander, cumin, ½ teaspoon salt, and ¼ teaspoon pepper in bowl until fragrant, about 30 seconds; let cool slightly. Rub halibut with spice mixture, then place on top of lime slices. Cover and cook until halibut flakes apart when gently prodded with paring knife and registers 140 degrees, 1 to 2 hours on low.

3. Meanwhile, combine cabbage, ¼ cup cilantro, scallions, 2 tablespoons lime juice, remaining 1 teaspoon oil, and ¼ teaspoon salt in bowl. In separate bowl, combine mayonnaise, sour cream, garlic, remaining 1 tablespoon lime juice, remaining 1 teaspoon chipotle, and remaining 2 tablespoons cilantro. Season with salt and pepper to taste.

4. Using sling, transfer halibut to cutting board. Gently lift and tilt fillets with spatula to remove lime slices; discard poaching liquid. Cut each fillet into 3 equal pieces. Spread sauce evenly onto warm tortillas, top with fish and cabbage, and serve with lime wedges.

Per serving: Cal 480; Fat 15g; Sat Fat 2g; Chol 60mg; Carb 41g; Protein 40g; Fiber 5g; Sodium 540mg

---

SMART SHOPPING LIGHT MAYONNAISE
Mayonnaise is a big offender when it comes to fat and calories—not a shock given that it's made from egg yolks and vegetable oil, plus a few other ingredients—so we recommend using light mayo. But you can't use just any jar; brands vary widely in taste and fat content and the labeling can be confusing. In our taste tests, we found that **Hellmann's Light** worked best; it offered a creamy texture and good flavor comparable to that of the full-fat variety.

Scallops with Creamy Braised Leeks

Serves 4 • **Cooking Time** 2 to 3 hours on Low • **Slow Cooker Size** 4 to 7 Quarts

WHY THIS RECIPE WORKS: Taking inspiration from the French classic *coquilles St. Jacques*, we set out to create a lighter and more contemporary dish that paired briny, sweet scallops with a creamy sauce made primarily of leeks and white wine. Our main obstacle was finding the right dairy product to give our sauce richness and body. We tried a variety of lower-fat options, from milk to yogurt, but were unsuccessful; every sauce was too thin or bland. In order to get the rich sauce we were looking for, we settled on a small amount of cream enriched with Pecorino Romano cheese (it was well worth the extra calories). To further develop the flavor of our sauce, we cooked the leeks with the garlic, cream, and white wine until the leeks started to break down and sweeten the sauce. We then nestled the scallops into this hot leek mixture to poach for 30 minutes until tender. Topping it all with parsley at the end ensured a bright, fresh finish. We recommend buying "dry" scallops, which don't have chemical additives and taste better than "wet." Dry scallops will look ivory or pinkish; wet scallops are bright white.

1	pound leeks, white and light green parts only, halved lengthwise, sliced thin, and washed thoroughly
4	garlic cloves, minced
1	teaspoon extra-virgin olive oil
⅓	cup heavy cream
¼	cup dry white wine
1½	pounds large sea scallops, tendons removed
	Salt and pepper
¼	cup grated Pecorino Romano cheese
2	tablespoons minced fresh parsley

1. Microwave leeks, garlic, and oil in bowl, stirring occasionally, until leeks are softened, about 5 minutes; transfer to slow cooker. Stir in cream and wine. Cover and cook until leeks are tender but not mushy, 2 to 3 hours on low.

2. Season scallops with salt and pepper and nestle into slow cooker. Spoon portion of sauce over scallops. Cover and cook until sides of scallops are firm and centers are opaque, 30 to 40 minutes.

3. Transfer scallops to serving platter. Stir Pecorino into sauce and season with salt and pepper to taste. Pour sauce over scallops and sprinkle with parsley. Serve.

Per serving: Cal 260; Fat 11g; Sat Fat 6g; Chol 70mg; Carb 15g; Protein 23g; Fiber 1g; Sodium 880mg

QUICK PREP TIP
PREPPING SCALLOPS
The small, crescent-shaped muscle that is sometimes attached to the scallop will be incredibly tough when cooked. Use your fingers to peel this muscle away from the side of each scallop before cooking.

Shrimp and Cheesy Polenta

Serves 4 • **Cooking Time** 3 to 4 hours on Low • **Slow Cooker Size** 4 to 7 Quarts

WHY THIS RECIPE WORKS: This healthier spin on the Southern favorite shrimp and grits features rich-tasting polenta and tender shrimp infused with a hint of heat. The slow cooker is the perfect vehicle for cooking creamy polenta without the need to monitor the pot—the low, slow heat gently cooks the polenta, keeping it lump-free and creamy. We wanted a cheesy taste without using tons of cheese, so we added dry mustard powder, which enhanced the cheese flavor of the dish. To the mustard we added scallions, garlic, and chipotle to ensure that our polenta was anything but bland. We whisked in polenta with the water and milk and cooked it until tender, without stirring. It was done when most of the liquid had been absorbed, and we finished by stirring in low-fat cheddar for flavor. As for the shrimp, we simply nestled them into the polenta for just 20 minutes until cooked through. Be sure to use traditional polenta, not instant polenta.

3	scallions, white parts minced, green parts sliced thin on bias
1	tablespoon unsalted butter
2	garlic cloves, minced
1	teaspoon minced canned chipotle chile in adobo sauce
½	teaspoon dry mustard
4	cups water
1	cup coarse-ground polenta
½	cup whole milk
	Salt and pepper
4	ounces 50 percent light cheddar cheese, shredded (1 cup)
1	pound extra-large shrimp (21 to 25 per pound), peeled and deveined

1. Lightly spray inside of slow cooker with vegetable oil spray. Microwave scallion whites, butter, garlic, chipotle, and mustard in bowl, stirring occasionally, until scallions are softened, about 2 minutes; transfer to slow cooker. Whisk in water, polenta, milk, and ¼ teaspoon salt. Cover and cook until polenta is tender, 3 to 4 hours on low.

2. Stir cheddar into polenta until melted and season with salt and pepper to taste. Season shrimp with pepper and nestle into polenta. Cover and cook on high until shrimp are opaque throughout, about 20 minutes. Sprinkle with scallion greens and serve.

Per serving: Cal 320; Fat 10g; Sat Fat 6g; Chol 135mg; Carb 32g; Protein 24g; Fiber 2g; Sodium 820mg

---

SMART SHOPPING POLENTA

Buying polenta can be confusing. Not only are there several different types of polenta widely available at the market—traditional, instant, and precooked—but they all are simply labeled "polenta." Here's how to tell them apart. The real deal (left) is labeled as either "polenta" or "traditional polenta," and it is nothing more than a package of coarse-ground cornmeal with a very even grind and no small floury bits; it is often sold in clear bags so you can inspect it. Don't be tempted to buy coarse-grain cornmeal without the term "polenta" clearly listed on the package, as it often includes a portion of fine, floury bits that will make the

polenta taste gluey. Instant polenta (center) and precooked tubes of polenta (right) are parcooked convenience products that have short cooking times (much like instant rice). Precooked polenta is easy to spot thanks to its tubelike packaging. Instant polenta, on the other hand, can look just like traditional polenta at the store and is identifiable only by the word "instant" in its title (which can be slightly hidden, in our experience).

Shrimp Boil with Corn and Potatoes

Serves 6 • **Cooking Time** 6 to 7 hours on Low or 4 to 5 hours on High • **Slow Cooker Size** 5½ to 7 Quarts

✔ **WHY THIS RECIPE WORKS:** A classic South Carolina shrimp boil is made by simmering shrimp, smoked sausage, corn on the cob, and potatoes in a broth seasoned with Old Bay. We found out that this dish translated well to a slow cooker. In the warm and moist environment of the slow cooker, we were able to gently cook everything to achieve perfectly cooked meat, seafood, and vegetables. We began by microwaving sausage to render fat and bloom the spices. For the base, we replaced some of the cooking liquid (water in this case) with clam juice to reinforce the taste of the sea and amp up the flavor. We flavored the broth with enough Old Bay to infuse the vegetables with flavor without becoming salty and overwhelming. We used only enough liquid to barely cover the ingredients, but enough to concentrate the flavors so they weren't overpowering but also weren't watered down. We cooked the sausage, potatoes, and corn until the potatoes were tender, then added the shrimp. This ensured intact potatoes, plump corn, and nicely cooked sausage and shrimp. Fresh corn on the cob is important to the success of this dish; do not substitute frozen corn on the cob. Use small red potatoes measuring 1 to 2 inches in diameter.

8	ounces andouille sausage, cut into 1-inch lengths
2	ribs celery, cut into 2-inch lengths
2	tablespoons tomato paste
4	teaspoons Old Bay seasoning
¼	teaspoon red pepper flakes
1½	pounds small red potatoes, unpeeled, halved
1	(8-ounce) bottle clam juice
3	ears corn, husks and silk removed, halved
3	bay leaves
1½	pounds extra-large shrimp (21 to 25 per pound), peeled, deveined, and tails removed

1. Microwave andouille, celery, tomato paste, Old Bay, and pepper flakes in bowl, stirring occasionally, until celery is softened, about 5 minutes; transfer to slow cooker. Stir in 4 cups water, potatoes, clam juice, corn, and bay leaves. Cover and cook until potatoes are tender, 6 to 7 hours on low or 4 to 5 hours on high.

2. Stir shrimp into slow cooker, cover, and cook on high until opaque throughout, about 20 minutes. Strain shrimp boil and discard bay leaves. Serve.

Per serving: Cal 270; Fat 8g; Sat Fat 2g; Chol 130mg; Carb 29g; Protein 23g; Fiber 3g; Sodium 820mg

---

SMART SHOPPING ANDOUILLE
Traditional andouille (pronounced "an-DOO-ee") sausage from Louisiana is made from ground pork, salt, and garlic seasoned with plenty of black pepper, then slowly smoked over pecan wood and sugarcane for up to 14 hours. Used in a wide range of Louisiana dishes, such as gumbo, jambalaya, and red beans and rice, it bolsters any dish with intense smoky, spicy, and earthy flavor. We tasted four brands in search of the right combination of smokiness and heat with a traditionally chewy but dry texture. Not surprisingly, a sausage straight from Louisiana, **Jacob's World Famous Andouille**, won the contest with the smokiest and spiciest flavors in the lineup.

Pasta

● **EASY PREP**   ● **VEGETARIAN**

Spaghetti with Cherry Tomato Sauce

Serves 6 • **Cooking Time** 7 to 8 hours on Low or 4 to 5 hours on High • **Slow Cooker Size** 4 to 7 Quarts

✓ **WHY THIS RECIPE WORKS:** For a fresh tomato sauce any time of the year, we turned to cherry tomatoes, which are reliably sweet even in the dead of winter. What we love about this recipe is how easy it is to assemble, plus it's naturally healthy, as slow-cooked cherry tomatoes, when combined with lots of fresh herbs, need little embellishment. First, we simply microwaved the aromatics—onion, garlic, and oregano—with tomato paste and a little oil until softened and added them to the slow cooker along with more than 2 pounds of halved cherry tomatoes. In the slow cooker, the tomatoes collapsed and softened, becoming even sweeter and more flavorful as they absorbed some of the flavor of the aromatics. To ensure that our sauce had the right texture, we added a little tapioca. Still, the sauce wasn't quite thick enough, which wasn't surprising given that the slow cooker allows for almost no evaporation, so at the end of the cooking time we simply mashed the tomatoes a little with a potato masher. Soy sauce provided depth and cut the acidity of the tomatoes without being noticeable. To finish, we added olive oil for richness and a dose of fresh basil and parsley for freshness.

1	onion, chopped fine
6	tablespoons tomato paste
6	garlic cloves, minced
1	tablespoon extra-virgin olive oil
1	tablespoon minced fresh oregano or 1 teaspoon dried
2½	pounds cherry tomatoes, halved
2	tablespoons instant tapioca
1	tablespoon low-sodium soy sauce
	Salt and pepper
¼	cup chopped fresh basil
¼	cup chopped fresh parsley
1	pound whole-wheat spaghetti

1. Microwave onion, tomato paste, garlic, 1 teaspoon oil, and oregano in bowl, stirring occasionally, until onion is softened, about 5 minutes; transfer to slow cooker. Stir in tomatoes, tapioca, soy sauce, ½ teaspoon salt, and ½ teaspoon pepper. Cover and cook until tomatoes are very soft and beginning to disintegrate, 7 to 8 hours on low or 4 to 5 hours on high.

2. Using potato masher, mash tomato mixture until mostly smooth. Stir in basil, parsley, and remaining 2 teaspoons oil.

3. Bring 4 quarts water to boil in large pot. Add pasta and 1 tablespoon salt and cook, stirring often, until al dente. Reserve ½ cup cooking water, then drain pasta and return it to pot. Add sauce to pasta and toss to combine. Season with salt and pepper to taste and adjust consistency with reserved cooking water as needed. Serve.

Per serving: Cal 340; Fat 5g; Sat Fat 0g; Chol 0mg; Carb 64g; Protein 12g; Fiber 12g; Sodium 520mg

---

SMART SHOPPING TOMATO PASTE
Tomato paste is naturally full of glutamates, which stimulate tastebuds just as salt and sugar do, and it brings out subtle flavors and savory notes, even in recipes in which tomato flavor isn't at the forefront. In our slow-cooker recipes, we made maximum use of tomato paste since the long cooking time tends to dull flavors. To find the best tomato paste, we gathered 10 top-selling brands and sampled each one uncooked, cooked plain, and in marinara sauce. **Goya Tomato Paste** earned top marks in both the uncooked and cooked tastings, and it came in second in our marinara test. Tasters praised it for being "rich, bold, and complex" and found it offered a "bright, robust tomato flavor."

Spaghetti with Garden Vegetable Marinara

Serves 6 • **Cooking Time** 7 to 8 hours on Low or 4 to 5 hours on High • **Slow Cooker Size** 4 to 7 Quarts

✔ **WHY THIS RECIPE WORKS:** For a slow-cooker marinara sauce packed with vegetables and a consistently fresh taste, we turned to canned tomatoes and built a robust sauce that included carrots and zucchini. We started by microwaving the carrots along with traditional aromatics—onion, tomato paste, garlic, oregano, and red pepper flakes—for a deeply flavorful backbone; dried porcini along with a little soy sauce provided welcome meaty depth without adding fat. Getting the texture right was more of a challenge. We found that a combination of crushed tomatoes and canned tomato sauce gave the sauce a perfect chunky texture and heartiness. We finished the sauce by adding the zucchini at the end, as it needed only a quick stint in the slow cooker to completely cook through; otherwise it turned mushy and lackluster during the long cooking time. Stirring in the basil right before serving gave this healthy sauce a final punch of garden freshness.

1 **onion, chopped fine**

3 **carrots, peeled, quartered lengthwise, and sliced ¼ inch thick**

¼ **ounce dried porcini mushrooms, rinsed and minced**

2 **tablespoons tomato paste**

2 **tablespoons extra-virgin olive oil**

4 **garlic cloves, minced**

1 **tablespoon minced fresh oregano or 1 teaspoon dried Pinch red pepper flakes**

1 **(28-ounce) can crushed tomatoes**

1 **(15-ounce) can tomato sauce**

2 **tablespoons low-sodium soy sauce Salt and pepper**

1 **bay leaf**

1 **zucchini, quartered lengthwise and sliced ¼ inch thick**

¼ **cup chopped fresh basil**

1 **pound whole-wheat spaghetti**

1. Microwave onion, carrots, mushrooms, tomato paste, 1 teaspoon oil, garlic, oregano, and pepper flakes in bowl, stirring occasionally, until vegetables are softened, about 5 minutes; transfer to slow cooker. Stir in tomatoes, tomato sauce, soy sauce, ½ teaspoon salt, and bay leaf. Cover and cook until sauce is deeply flavored, 7 to 8 hours on low or 4 to 5 hours on high.

2. Discard bay leaf. Stir in zucchini, cover, and cook on high until tender, 20 to 30 minutes. Stir in basil and remaining 5 teaspoons oil.

3. Bring 4 quarts water to boil in large pot. Add pasta and 1 tablespoon salt and cook, stirring often, until al dente. Reserve ½ cup cooking water, then drain pasta and return it to pot. Add sauce and toss to combine. Season with salt and pepper to taste and adjust consistency with reserved cooking water as needed. Serve.

Per serving: Cal 390; Fat 7g; Sat Fat 0.5g; Chol 0mg; Carb 69g; Protein 15g; Fiber 14g; Sodium 1220mg *To reduce sodium level to 610mg, use no-salt-added tomatoes.

SMART SHOPPING EXTRA-VIRGIN OLIVE OIL
Extra-virgin olive oil has a uniquely fruity flavor that makes it a great choice for making vinaigrettes and pestos or stirring into pasta sauces at the end of cooking for an extra flavor boost. However, the available options can be overwhelming. Many things can impact the quality and flavor of olive oil, but the type of olives, the time of harvesting (earlier means greener, more peppery; later, more golden and mild), and the method of processing are the most important factors. The best-quality oil comes from olives picked at their peak and processed as soon as possible, without heat or chemicals (which can coax more oil from the olives but at the expense of flavor). Our favorite oils were produced from a blend of olives and, thus, were well rounded. Our top pick is **Columela Extra-Virgin Olive Oil** from Spain.

Linguine with Mushroom Bolognese

Serves 6 • **Cooking Time** 7 to 8 hours on Low or 4 to 5 hours on High • **Slow Cooker Size** 4 to 7 Quarts

✓ **WHY THIS RECIPE WORKS:** For a vegetarian take on classic Bolognese with long-cooked flavor, we turned to mushrooms, deciding on cremini for their firm texture and savory flavor. To keep things simple, we used the food processor to chop the mushrooms and the vegetables. Since the mushrooms take on more flavor when browned and because there is no opportunity for evaporation in a slow cooker, we sautéed them and the other vegetables in a skillet to drive off excess moisture and build flavor. We first tried tomato puree as the tomato base for our sauce, but we found it was a little too thick; the mushrooms required more liquid to cook in. We discovered that processing whole peeled tomatoes gave us the extra liquid we needed while keeping the fresh tomato flavor. Finishing this hearty sauce with a little heavy cream helped smooth out any sharpness and gave it a nice creaminess, and parsley and lemon juice brightened it up.

2 pounds cremini mushrooms, trimmed and quartered
1 onion, chopped coarse
1 carrot, peeled and chopped coarse
1 (28-ounce) can whole peeled tomatoes
2 teaspoons extra-virgin olive oil
½ ounce dried porcini mushrooms, rinsed and minced
2 tablespoons tomato paste
3 garlic cloves, minced
1 tablespoon minced fresh oregano or 1 teaspoon dried
½ cup dry red wine
Salt and pepper
1 teaspoon sugar
1 bay leaf
2 tablespoons chopped fresh parsley
¼ cup heavy cream
1 tablespoon lemon juice
1 pound whole-wheat linguine

1. Working in batches, pulse cremini mushrooms in food processor until pieces are no larger than ½ inch, 5 to 7 pulses; transfer to large bowl. Pulse onion and carrot in now-empty processor until finely chopped, 5 to 7 pulses; transfer to bowl with mushrooms. Pulse tomatoes and their juice in again-empty processor until almost smooth, 6 to 8 pulses; set aside separately.

2. Heat oil in 12-inch skillet over medium heat until shimmering. Add processed vegetables and porcini mushrooms, cover, and cook until softened, about 5 minutes. Uncover and continue to cook until vegetables are dry and browned, 12 to 14 minutes. Stir in tomato paste, garlic, and oregano and cook until fragrant, about 1 minute. Stir in wine, scraping up any browned bits, and simmer until nearly evaporated, about 3 minutes; transfer to slow cooker.

3. Stir processed tomatoes, 1 teaspoon salt, sugar, ½ teaspoon pepper, and bay leaf into slow cooker. Cover and cook until sauce is deeply flavored, 7 to 8 hours on low or 4 to 5 hours on high.

4. Discard bay leaf. Stir in parsley, cream, and lemon juice.

5. Bring 4 quarts water to boil in large pot. Add pasta and 1 tablespoon salt and cook, stirring often, until al dente. Reserve ½ cup cooking water, then drain pasta and return it to pot. Add sauce to pasta and toss to combine. Season with salt and pepper to taste and adjust consistency with reserved cooking water as needed. Serve.

Per serving: Cal 400; Fat 8g; Sat Fat 2.5g; Chol 15mg; Carb 65g; Protein 15g; Fiber 11g; Sodium 790mg *To reduce sodium level to 650mg, use no-salt-added tomatoes.

Rigatoni alla Norma

Serves 6 • **Cooking Time** 2 to 3 hours on Low • **Slow Cooker Size:** 4 to 7 Quarts

WHY THIS RECIPE WORKS: Rigatoni alla Norma is a pasta dish with a gutsy tomato sauce studded with chunks of eggplant. What is challenging when trying to keep this dish on the healthy side is cooking the eggplant without using copious amounts of oil. We tried adding the eggplant to the slow cooker without parcooking it, but we ended up with mushy, flavorless chunks of eggplant floating in our sauce. We found that a quick stint under the broiler after a toss with our aromatics was all it took to rid the eggplant of moisture and add flavor. To build the base for our sauce, we started with crushed tomatoes and added tomato sauce, which gave the sauce the right clingy consistency. For a spicy backbone, we included a generous amount of red pepper flakes. Anchovy fillets provided deep, savory flavor without unwanted fishiness. Fresh basil and olive oil added at the end rounded out the flavor of this easy sauce, and shards of ricotta salata, a slightly aged ricotta, added a salty tang. If you can't find ricotta salata, you can substitute feta or Pecorino Romano.

Vegetable oil spray
3 pounds eggplant, cut into 1-inch pieces
6 garlic cloves, minced
1½ tablespoons tomato paste
1 tablespoon sugar
1 (28-ounce) can crushed tomatoes
1 (15-ounce) can tomato sauce
6 anchovy fillets, rinsed and minced
Salt and pepper
¼ teaspoon red pepper flakes
1 pound whole-wheat rigatoni
¼ cup chopped fresh basil
2 tablespoons extra-virgin olive oil
3 ounces ricotta salata, shredded (¾ cup)

1. Adjust oven rack 6 inches from broiler element and heat broiler. Line rimmed baking sheet with aluminum foil and spray with oil spray. Toss eggplant, garlic, tomato paste, and sugar together in bowl. Spread eggplant mixture evenly in prepared sheet and lightly spray with oil spray. Broil eggplant until softened and beginning to brown, 10 to 12 minutes, rotating sheet halfway through broiling; transfer to slow cooker. Stir in tomatoes, tomato sauce, anchovies, ¼ teaspoon salt, ¼ teaspoon pepper, and pepper flakes. Cover and cook until flavors meld and eggplant is tender, 2 to 3 hours on low.

2. Bring 4 quarts water to boil in large pot. Add pasta and 1 tablespoon salt and cook, stirring often, until al dente. Reserve ½ cup cooking water, then drain pasta and return it to pot. Add sauce, basil, and oil and toss to combine. Season with salt and pepper to taste and adjust consistency with reserved cooking water as needed. Sprinkle with ricotta salata and serve.

Per serving: Cal 480; Fat 11g; Sat Fat 3g; Chol 15mg; Carb 78g; Protein 18g; Fiber 18g; Sodium 1290mg *To reduce sodium level to 690mg, use no-salt-added tomatoes.

SMART SHOPPING ANCHOVY FILLETS VERSUS PASTE
Since most recipes call for only a small number of anchovies, we wondered whether a tube of anchovy paste might be a more convenient option. Made from pulverized anchovies, vinegar, salt, and water, anchovy paste promises all the flavor of oil-packed anchovies without the mess. We tested the paste and jarred or canned anchovies side by side in recipes calling for an anchovy or two. Tasters found little difference, though a few astute tasters felt that the paste had a "saltier" and "slightly more fishy" flavor. You can substitute ¼ teaspoon of the paste for each fillet. However, when a recipe calls for more than a couple of anchovies, stick with jarred or canned, as the paste's more intense flavor will be overwhelming. Our favorite brand of canned anchovies is **Ortiz Oil-Packed Anchovies**.

Spaghetti with Artichokes and Olives

Serves 6 • **Cooking Time** 1 to 2 hours on Low • **Slow Cooker Size** 4 to 7 Quarts

✓ **WHY THIS RECIPE WORKS:** For a pasta sauce that was a little bit out of the ordinary, we set out to pair delicate artichokes with garlic, olives, and capers in a sauce that was just creamy enough to coat the pasta. To start, we turned to frozen artichokes, which have a far fresher flavor than canned or jarred and are more convenient than fresh. To infuse them with flavor, we simply added them to the slow cooker along with vegetable broth, whose sweetness was welcome here, and a hefty dose of aromatics. Shallots and six cloves of garlic ensured that the base of this sauce was anything but dull; thyme added earthiness, and lemon juice and zest kept things bright. We needed something to make the sauce clingy and cohesive, but pouring in lots of cream was a nonstarter for our healthy sauce, and tapioca simply made it gummy. We found that a little cream microwaved along with some cornstarch rounded out this sauce perfectly without adding lots of fat.

18	ounces frozen artichoke hearts, thawed, patted dry, and halved lengthwise
1½	cups vegetable broth
2	shallots, halved and sliced thin
6	garlic cloves, minced
1	tablespoon grated lemon zest plus 2 tablespoons juice
2	teaspoons minced fresh thyme or ½ teaspoon dried
	Salt and pepper
⅛	teaspoon red pepper flakes
½	cup heavy cream
2	teaspoons cornstarch
½	cup pitted kalamata olives, halved
¼	cup chopped fresh basil
¼	cup chopped fresh parsley
1	tablespoon capers, rinsed
1	pound whole-wheat spaghetti

1. Combine artichokes, broth, shallots, garlic, lemon zest and juice, thyme, ½ teaspoon salt, ¼ teaspoon pepper, and pepper flakes in slow cooker. Cover and cook until heated through and flavors meld, 1 to 2 hours on low.

2. Whisk cream and cornstarch together in bowl. Microwave at 50 percent power, whisking occasionally, until thickened and steaming, about 3 minutes. Stir thickened cream, olives, basil, parsley, and capers into sauce. Season with salt and pepper to taste.

3. Bring 4 quarts water to boil in large pot. Add pasta and 1 tablespoon salt and cook, stirring often, until al dente. Reserve ½ cup cooking water, then drain pasta and return it to pot. Add sauce and toss to combine. Season with salt and pepper to taste and adjust consistency with reserved cooking water as needed. Serve.

Per serving: Cal 510; Fat 13g; Sat Fat 5g; Chol 25mg; Carb 86g; Protein 16g; Fiber 19g; Sodium 770mg *To reduce sodium level to 610mg, use low-sodium broth.

QUICK PREP TIP KEEPING HERBS FRESH LONGER
To get the most out of fresh herbs, we start by gently rinsing and drying them before loosely rolling them in a few sheets of paper towels. Then we put the roll of herbs in a zipper-lock bag and place it in the crisper drawer of our refrigerator. (Note that basil should not be washed until you are ready to use it.) Stored in this manner, the herbs stay fresh and ready to use for up to a week.

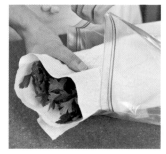

Spaghetti with Braised Kale and Chickpeas

Serves 6 • **Cooking Time** 5 to 6 hours on Low or 3 to 4 hours on High • **Slow Cooker Size** 5½ to 7 Quarts

✓ **WHY THIS RECIPE WORKS:** Classic pasta sauces that marry hearty greens and beans usually rely on lots of oil and often cream to make the dish cohesive and rich tasting, but we were after a healthier version, one we could make in a slow cooker. Tackling it head-on, we started by adding just a little bacon to the mix, which infused the sauce with smoky undertones; to keep things easy, we microwaved it along with the aromatics, which included a hefty dose of garlic and pungent minced rosemary. As for the chickpeas, whose nutty flavor paired well with the earthy kale, we found that pureeing half of them in the blender with some of the broth gave the sauce body that would otherwise have come from cream. The kale was added raw to the slow cooker along with the bacon mixture, the pureed and whole beans, and the remaining chicken broth. At the end of the cooking time, we had a flavorful, brothy pasta sauce that needed just lemon zest and juice for brightening and Parmesan cheese for added richness.

1	onion, chopped fine
2	slices bacon, chopped fine
6	garlic cloves, minced
2	teaspoons minced fresh rosemary or ½ teaspoon dried
¼	teaspoon red pepper flakes
2	(14-ounce) cans chickpeas, rinsed
2¼	cups chicken broth
1	pound kale, stemmed and cut into 1-inch pieces
	Salt and pepper
1	pound whole-wheat spaghetti
2	ounces Parmesan cheese, finely grated (1 cup), plus extra for serving
1	tablespoon grated lemon zest plus 1 teaspoon juice

1. Lightly spray inside of slow cooker with vegetable oil spray. Microwave onion, bacon, garlic, rosemary, and pepper flakes in bowl, stirring occasionally, until onion is softened, about 5 minutes; transfer to slow cooker.

2. Process half of chickpeas and 1 cup broth in blender until smooth, about 30 seconds; transfer to slow cooker. Stir in remaining chickpeas, remaining 1¼ cups broth, kale, and ½ teaspoon pepper. Cover and cook until kale is tender, 5 to 6 hours on low or 3 to 4 hours on high.

3. Bring 4 quarts water to boil in large pot. Add pasta and 1 tablespoon salt and cook, stirring often, until al dente. Reserve ½ cup cooking water, then drain pasta and return it to pot. Add sauce, Parmesan, and lemon zest and juice and toss to combine. Season with salt and pepper to taste and adjust consistency with reserved cooking water as needed. Serve with extra Parmesan.

Per serving: Cal 440; Fat 10g; Sat Fat 2.5g; Chol 15mg; Carb 67g; Protein 22g; Fiber 12g; Sodium 750mg *To reduce sodium level to 420mg, use unsalted broth and low-sodium chickpeas.

QUICK PREP TIP **COOKING WITH WHOLE-WHEAT PASTA**

Whole-wheat pasta delivers up to three times more dietary fiber than traditional white pasta, so it is a great choice for pairing with the healthy sauces in this chapter (although they will work equally well with white pastas). However, if you are new to cooking with whole-wheat pasta, there are a few things to keep in mind. First, unlike traditional white pasta, which generally comes in 1-pound boxes or sleeves, whole-wheat is sometimes sold in odd amounts, such as 14.5 ounces. So, it's worth double-checking the box to make sure you are buying the right amount of pasta. Second, everyone knows when white pasta is done—it's tender, or what we refer to as "al dente"—but because of whole-wheat pasta's composition, its texture is slightly firmer when it's fully cooked. Keep this in mind and aim for a slightly firmer bite than you would with white pasta.

Penne with Butternut Squash and Sage

Serves 6 • **Cooking Time** 4 to 5 hours on Low or 3 to 4 hours on High • **Slow Cooker Size** 4 to 7 Quarts

✔ **WHY THIS RECIPE WORKS:** Pasta paired with butternut squash and a sage-infused butter sauce is always a winner, but all too often this dish loses its focus with too much butter overwhelming the delicate nuttiness of the squash. We were hoping to create a lighter and more brothy version of this sauce in the slow cooker. To start, we got out a skillet to create our base, sautéing onion in butter, then adding the aromatics. Once the aromatics were softened, we added flour to the pan and cooked it briefly to eliminate any raw flavor; then we deglazed the pan with broth and wine, making sure to scrape up any browned bits on the bottom of the pan. To this flavorful base we added more broth and the squash; as it simmered in the slow cooker, the mixture became super-flavorful, making the perfect delicate sauce for the pasta. At the end of the cooking time we added spinach, which gave the dish a bright green color and healthy kick; a little Parmesan added even more flavor and creaminess, and additional sage gave the sauce a fresh herbal boost.

4	**tablespoons unsalted butter**
1	**onion, chopped fine**
2	**garlic cloves, minced**
3	**tablespoons minced fresh sage**
¼	**teaspoon red pepper flakes**
3	**tablespoons all-purpose flour**
2½	**cups vegetable broth**
¼	**cup dry white wine**
1½	**pounds butternut squash, peeled, seeded, and cut into ½-inch pieces (4 cups)**
	Salt and pepper
1	**pound whole-wheat penne**
3	**ounces (3 cups) baby spinach**
2	**ounces Parmesan cheese, finely grated (1 cup), plus extra for serving**

1. Melt butter in 12-inch skillet over medium heat. Add onion and cook until softened and lightly browned, 5 to 7 minutes. Stir in garlic, 1½ tablespoons sage, and pepper flakes and cook until fragrant, about 30 seconds. Stir in flour and cook for 1 minute. Slowly whisk in 1 cup broth and wine, scraping up any browned bits and smoothing out any lumps; transfer to slow cooker.

2. Stir remaining 1½ cups broth, squash, ¾ teaspoon salt, and ¼ teaspoon pepper into slow cooker. Cover and cook until squash is tender, 4 to 5 hours on low or 3 to 4 hours on high.

3. Bring 4 quarts water to boil in large pot. Add pasta and 1 tablespoon salt and cook, stirring often, until al dente. Reserve ½ cup cooking water, then drain pasta and return it to pot. Add sauce, spinach, Parmesan, and remaining 1½ tablespoons sage and toss until spinach is slightly wilted. Season with salt and pepper to taste and adjust consistency with reserved cooking water as needed. Serve with extra Parmesan.

Per serving: Cal 430; Fat 12g; Sat Fat 6g; Chol 25mg; Carb 66g; Protein 15g; Fiber 11g; Sodium 900mg *To reduce sodium level to 640mg, use low-sodium broth.

QUICK PREP TIP GRATING HARD CHEESE
When grating Parmesan and other hard cheeses, we use a rasp-style grater because it produces lighter, fluffier shreds of cheese that melt seamlessly into pasta dishes and sauces.

Weeknight Meat Sauce with Rigatoni

Serves 6 • **Cooking Time** 6 to 7 hours on Low or 4 to 5 hours on High • **Slow Cooker Size** 4 to 7 Quarts

✓ **WHY THIS RECIPE WORKS:** This meat sauce has all of the flavor you would expect from a traditional long-simmered, full-fat version. With leaner 93 percent lean ground beef as our starting point, we found in early tests that if we simply added it to the slow cooker without parcooking it, we were left with mushy, mealy meat. We tried microwaving it, but the sauce just didn't taste rich enough, so we got out a skillet and browned the aromatics and a little tomato paste; deglazing the pan with wine ensured we captured all the flavorful browned bits. We then added the beef, cooking it just a few minutes before adding it to the slow cooker. Tomato puree gave this sauce good body, and a can of diced tomatoes gave it an appealing chunky texture that we liked. And while soy sauce may seem like an odd addition to a beefy pasta sauce, we found that just 2 tablespoons added a noticeable depth of meaty flavor that would ordinarily come from building the sauce on the stovetop.

1	tablespoon extra-virgin olive oil
1	large onion, chopped fine
	Salt and pepper
6	garlic cloves, minced
1	tablespoon minced fresh oregano or 1 teaspoon dried
	Pinch red pepper flakes
¼	cup tomato paste
⅓	cup white wine
1	pound 93 percent lean ground beef
1	(28-ounce) can tomato puree
1	(14.5-ounce) can diced tomatoes
2	tablespoons low-sodium soy sauce
1	pound whole-wheat rigatoni
	Sugar
¼	cup chopped fresh basil

1. Heat oil in 12-inch skillet over medium heat until shimmering. Add onion and ½ teaspoon salt and cook until softened and lightly browned, 8 to 10 minutes. Stir in garlic, oregano, and pepper flakes and cook until fragrant, about 30 seconds. Stir in tomato paste and cook until lightly browned, about 1 minute. Stir in wine and let simmer for 1 minute. Stir in beef and cook, breaking up meat with wooden spoon, until no longer pink, about 5 minutes; transfer to slow cooker.

2. Stir tomato puree, tomatoes, and soy sauce into slow cooker. Cover and cook until sauce has thickened and beef is tender, 6 to 7 hours on low or 4 to 5 hours on high.

3. Bring 4 quarts water to boil in large pot. Add pasta and 1 tablespoon salt and cook, stirring often, until al dente. Reserve ½ cup cooking water, then drain pasta and return it to pot. Season sauce with salt, pepper, and sugar to taste, add to pasta with basil, and toss to combine. Adjust consistency with reserved cooking water as needed. Serve.

Per serving: Cal 480; Fat 10g; Sat Fat 2.5g; Chol 50mg; Carb 69g; Protein 29g; Fiber 12g; Sodium 850mg *To reduce sodium level to 650mg, use no-salt-added-tomatoes.

SMART SHOPPING TOMATO PUREE
Tomato puree, like tomato sauce, is cooked and strained to remove the tomato seeds, making it much smoother and thicker than other canned tomato products. But tomato puree has a slightly thicker consistency than tomato sauce, which makes it especially useful in our slow-cooker sauces—it helps us achieve the consistency of a stovetop sauce without the benefit of the reduction that comes with a long simmer in an uncovered pot or skillet. Our favorite brand is **Muir Glen Organic Tomato Puree**, which offers a nice, thick consistency and tomatoey flavor.

Classic Meatballs and Marinara with Spaghetti

Serves 6 • **Cooking Time** 4 to 5 hours on Low • **Slow Cooker Size** 5½ to 7 Quarts

✓ **WHY THIS RECIPE WORKS:** Adapting this traditional Italian classic for a slow cooker and making it healthy presented several challenges. We had to make the meatballs healthier, yet tasty, and with a consistency that would hold up in the slow cooker. Swapping the traditional meatball mix for leaner ground turkey was our first step. To bind the meatballs, we used a mixture of panko, grated Parmesan, and milk, which eliminated the need to bind them with an egg. To keep our meatballs from falling apart in the slow cooker, we parcooked them in the microwave first. Using crushed tomatoes in combination with tomato sauce and paste gave the sauce full-bodied tomato flavor and kept the consistency just right: a little chunky, yet thick enough to coat the pasta. Be sure to use 93 percent lean ground turkey, not ground turkey breast (also labeled 99 percent fat free), or else the meatballs will be dry.

1	**pound 93 percent lean ground turkey**
½	**cup panko bread crumbs**
1	**ounce Parmesan cheese, grated (½ cup)**
¼	**cup whole milk**
¼	**cup minced fresh parsley**
6	**garlic cloves, minced**
2	**teaspoons dried oregano**
	Salt and pepper
1	**(28-ounce) can crushed tomatoes**
1	**(15-ounce) can tomato sauce**
2	**tablespoons tomato paste**
2	**tablespoons low-sodium soy sauce**
2	**teaspoons sugar**
	Pinch red pepper flakes
1	**pound whole-wheat spaghetti**
¼	**cup chopped fresh basil**

1. Using hands, mix together ground turkey, panko, Parmesan, milk, parsley, one-third of garlic, 1½ teaspoons oregano, and ½ teaspoon pepper in bowl until uniform. Pinch off and roll mixture into twelve 2-tablespoon-size meatballs and arrange on large plate. Microwave meatballs until firm, about 5 minutes.

2. Combine tomatoes, tomato sauce, tomato paste, soy sauce, sugar, pepper flakes, ½ teaspoon salt, ½ teaspoon pepper, remaining garlic, and remaining ½ teaspoon oregano in slow cooker. Transfer microwaved meatballs and any accumulated juices to slow cooker. Cover and cook until meatballs are tender, 4 to 5 hours on low.

3. Bring 4 quarts water to boil in large pot. Add pasta and 1 tablespoon salt and cook, stirring often, until al dente. Reserve ½ cup cooking water, then drain pasta and return it to pot. Add several large spoonfuls of sauce (without meatballs) to pasta and toss to combine. Season with salt and pepper to taste and adjust consistency with reserved cooking water as needed. Divide pasta among individual serving bowls and top with meatballs and remaining sauce. Sprinkle with basil and serve.

Per serving: Cal 480; Fat 8g; Sat Fat 2g; Chol 50mg; Carb 70g; Protein 31g; Fiber 12g; Sodium 1340mg *To reduce sodium level to 730mg, use no-salt-added tomatoes.

ON THE SIDE CLASSIC GREEN SALAD
Whisk 2 tablespoons extra-virgin olive oil, 1 tablespoon vinegar (red wine, white wine, or champagne), 1 tablespoon water, 1 teaspoon Dijon mustard, ⅛ teaspoon salt, and pinch pepper together in large bowl. Add 10 cups lightly packed mesclun greens and toss to coat. Season with salt and pepper to taste. Serves 6.

Per serving: Cal 50; Fat 4.5g; Sat Fat 0.5g; Chol 0mg; Carb 0g; Protein 0g; Fiber 0g; Sodium 70mg

Spaghetti with Meatballs Florentine

Serves 6 • **Cooking Time** 4 to 5 hours on Low • **Slow Cooker Size** 4 to 7 Quarts

✓ **WHY THIS RECIPE WORKS:** This healthy twist on classic spaghetti and meatballs features tender, lean meatballs made ultraflavorful with a mixture of spinach, garlic, and Parmesan and a robust marinara to which we also added fresh spinach. Rather than add raw meatballs to the sauce in the slow cooker, we gave them a quick spin in the microwave first to help them firm up. For our marinara, we needed three tomato products to achieve the right balance of flavor and texture: chunky crushed tomatoes, smooth tomato sauce, and rich tomato paste. Stirring in more spinach at the end kept it bright and created a colorful, healthy, and delicious sauce to accompany our modern take on classic meatballs.

1   **pound 93 percent lean ground beef**
5   **ounces (5 cups) baby spinach (1 cup chopped)**
½   **cup panko bread crumbs**
¼   **cup whole milk**
¼   **cup grated Parmesan cheese**
6   **garlic cloves, minced**
    Salt and pepper
½   **teaspoon red pepper flakes**
1   **(28-ounce) can crushed tomatoes**
1   **(15-ounce) can tomato sauce**
2   **tablespoons tomato paste**
2   **tablespoons low-sodium soy sauce**
2   **teaspoons sugar**
1   **pound whole-wheat spaghetti**
¼   **cup chopped fresh basil**

1. Using hands, mix together ground beef, chopped spinach, panko, milk, Parmesan, one-third of garlic, ¼ teaspoon salt, and ¼ teaspoon pepper flakes in bowl until uniform. Pinch off and roll mixture into twelve 2-tablespoon-size meatballs and arrange on large plate. Microwave meatballs until firm, about 5 minutes.

2. Combine tomatoes, tomato sauce, tomato paste, soy sauce, sugar, ¼ teaspoon salt, remaining garlic, and remaining ¼ teaspoon pepper flakes in slow cooker. Transfer microwaved meatballs and any accumulated juices to slow cooker. Cover and cook until meatballs are tender, 4 to 5 hours on low.

3. Bring 4 quarts water to boil in large pot. Add pasta and 1 tablespoon salt and cook, stirring often, until al dente. Reserve ½ cup cooking water, then drain pasta and return it to pot. Add several large spoonfuls of sauce (without meatballs) and remaining 4 cups spinach to pasta and toss until spinach is slightly wilted. Season with salt and pepper to taste and adjust consistency with reserved cooking water as needed.

4. Divide pasta among individual serving bowls and top with meatballs and remaining sauce. Sprinkle with basil and serve.

Per serving: Cal 490; Fat 8g; Sat Fat 2.5g; Chol 50mg; Carb 72g; Protein 32g; Fiber 13g; Sodium 1430mg *To reduce sodium level to 980mg, use no-salt-added tomatoes.

SMART SHOPPING WHOLE-WHEAT SPAGHETTI

We recently sampled 18 brands of whole-wheat spaghetti, including a few multigrain brands as well, tasting them with olive oil and with sauces. Two were whole-grain imposters, with refined wheat as their first ingredient. Most 100 percent whole-wheat and 100 percent whole-grain pastas fell to the bottom of the rankings, with "mushy" or "doughy" textures and "sour," "fishy" flavors. However, one boasted a good chewy and firm texture, making it our top pick. **Bionaturae Organic 100% Whole Wheat Spaghetti** was praised for its "earthy," "wheaty," "nutty" flavor and "pleasantly chewy," "firm" texture. Three things put this spaghetti ahead of the rest: It's custom milled for good flavor, extruded through a bronze, not Teflon, die to build gluten in the dough, and slowly dried for a sturdier texture.

Beef Ragu with Rigatoni

Serves 6 • **Cooking Time** 9 to 10 hours on Low or 6 to 7 hours on High • **Slow Cooker Size** 4 to 7 Quarts

✔ **WHY THIS RECIPE WORKS:** This super-simple ragu can simmer for the entire day in the slow cooker without your watchful eye. In our quest for an effortless yet full-flavored sauce that would be on the healthy side, we began by searching for the best cut of meat. We wanted a cut that could withstand the long cooking time and would become meltingly tender. It was hard to beat economical and beefy-tasting chuck roast, which can easily be made leaner by removing excess visible fat. Onion and garlic provided aromatic notes, and the pairing of tomato paste and tomato puree gave the sauce the necessary consistency and bold tomato flavor that complemented the rich beef perfectly. Three different herbs added their earthy charm to the sauce, amping up its depth of flavor: oregano, rosemary, and a bay leaf. As a finishing touch, a splash of red wine vinegar brightened up this hearty pasta dinner. After trimming the beef, you should have 1½ pounds of usable meat.

1   **onion, chopped fine**
2   **tablespoons tomato paste**
3   **garlic cloves, minced**
1½   **teaspoons minced fresh oregano**
     or ½ teaspoon dried
1   **teaspoon minced fresh rosemary**
     or ¼ teaspoon dried
1   **teaspoon extra-virgin olive oil**
1   **(28-ounce) can tomato puree**
2   **tablespoons low-sodium**
     soy sauce
     Salt and pepper
1   **bay leaf**
2   **pounds boneless beef chuck-eye**
     roast, trimmed of all visible fat
     and cut into 2-inch pieces
1   **tablespoon red wine vinegar**
1   **pound whole-wheat rigatoni**

1. Microwave onion, tomato paste, garlic, oregano, rosemary, and oil in bowl, stirring occasionally, until onion is softened, about 5 minutes; transfer to slow cooker. Stir in tomato puree, soy sauce, ½ teaspoon salt, ½ teaspoon pepper, and bay leaf, then stir in beef. Cover and cook until beef is tender, 9 to 10 hours on low or 6 to 7 hours on high.

2. Discard bay leaf. Break beef into about 1-inch pieces with tongs. Stir in vinegar.

3. Bring 4 quarts water to boil in large pot. Add pasta and 1 tablespoon salt and cook, stirring often, until al dente. Reserve ½ cup cooking water, then drain pasta and return it to pot. Add sauce to pasta and toss to combine. Season with salt and pepper to taste and adjust consistency with reserved cooking water as needed. Serve.

Per serving: Cal 470; Fat 8g; Sat Fat 2g; Chol 75mg; Carb 63g; Protein 37g; Fiber 11g; Sodium 660mg *To reduce sodium level to 630mg, use no-salt-added tomatoes.

ON THE SIDE ARUGULA AND FENNEL SALAD WITH SHAVED PARMESAN
Whisk 2 tablespoons extra-virgin olive oil, 2 tablespoons lemon juice, 1 tablespoon water, 1 teaspoon Dijon mustard, ½ teaspoon minced fresh thyme, 1 small minced garlic clove, ⅛ teaspoon salt, and pinch pepper together in large bowl. Add 6 cups lightly packed baby arugula and 1 thinly sliced fennel bulb and toss to coat. Season with salt and pepper to taste. Garnish with ¼ cup shaved Parmesan cheese. Serves 6.

Per serving: Cal 70; Fat 6g; Sat Fat 1g; Chol 0mg; Carb 5g; Protein 2g; Fiber 2g; Sodium 140mg

Linguine with Sausage and Fennel

Serves 6 • **Cooking Time** 4 to 5 hours on Low or 3 to 4 hours on High • **Slow Cooker Size** 4 to 7 Quarts

✔ **WHY THIS RECIPE WORKS:** We set out to create a hearty yet healthy creamy meat sauce in the slow cooker that married the rich flavor of sausage with aromatic fennel. We decided on turkey sausage, as it is leaner than other options but still has great flavor. In order to maximize this flavor, we got out the skillet to brown the meat, which provided welcome savory and rich undertones. Keeping things streamlined, we moved on to cook the carrots and fennel in the leftover fat of the sausage, which enhanced their already-bold flavors. To make sure we got every last drop of that flavor, we sprinkled flour into the pan and stirred it around with the vegetables. This also helped thicken our sauce. Deglazing with a little broth and white wine allowed us to scrape up any flavorful browned bits in the pan before we added everything to the slow cooker. Finishing the sauce with just a quarter cup of cream added extra richness while keeping it relatively lean. Minced fresh tarragon and orange zest and juice complemented the flavors of the sausage and fennel and added a fresh note.

1   teaspoon extra-virgin olive oil
1   pound hot or sweet Italian turkey sausage, casings removed
2   fennel bulbs, ¼ cup fronds minced, stalks discarded, bulbs halved, cored, and sliced ¼ inch thick
2   carrots, peeled, quartered lengthwise, and sliced ¼ inch thick
4   garlic cloves, minced
    Pinch red pepper flakes
⅓   cup all-purpose flour
3   cups chicken broth
¼   cup dry white wine
1   bay leaf
¼   cup heavy cream
1   tablespoon grated orange zest plus 1½ tablespoons juice
1   tablespoon minced fresh tarragon
    Salt and pepper
1   pound whole-wheat linguine

1. Heat oil in Dutch oven over medium heat until shimmering. Add sausage and cook, breaking up meat with wooden spoon, until no longer pink, about 5 minutes. Stir in fennel and carrots and cook until vegetables are softened and lightly browned, 8 to 10 minutes. Stir in garlic and pepper flakes and cook until fragrant, about 30 seconds. Stir in flour and cook for 1 minute. Slowly stir in 1 cup broth and wine, scraping up any browned bits and smoothing out any lumps; transfer to slow cooker.

2. Stir remaining 2 cups broth and bay leaf into slow cooker. Cover and cook until sausage is tender, 4 to 5 hours on low or 3 to 4 hours on high.

3. Discard bay leaf. Stir in cream, orange zest and juice, tarragon, and reserved fennel fronds. Season with salt and pepper to taste.

4. Bring 4 quarts water to boil in large pot. Add pasta and 1 tablespoon salt and cook, stirring often, until al dente. Reserve ½ cup cooking water, then drain pasta and return it to pot. Add sauce to pasta and toss to combine. Season with salt and pepper to taste and adjust consistency with reserved cooking water as needed. Serve.

Per serving: Cal 430; Fat 11g; Sat Fat 3.5g; Chol 45mg; Carb 62g; Protein 22g; Fiber 11g; Sodium 790mg *To reduce sodium level to 600mg, use unsalted broth.

SMART SHOPPING WHITE WINE FOR COOKING
When a recipe calls for dry white wine, it's tempting to grab whatever open bottle is in the fridge. We have found that only Sauvignon Blanc consistently boils down to a "clean" yet sufficiently acidic flavor that meshes nicely with a variety of ingredients in savory recipes. Vermouth can be an acceptable substitute in certain recipes. Never buy supermarket cooking wine, which has added sodium and a vinegary flavor.

Penne with Chicken and Broccolini

Serves 6 • **Cooking Time** 3 to 4 hours on Low • **Slow Cooker Size** 4 to 7 Quarts

✓ WHY THIS RECIPE WORKS: With its enticing combination of moist chicken, fresh broccolini, and sweet red bell pepper, this rich sauce pairs perfectly with whole-wheat penne. We chose bone-in chicken breasts, which stayed moist throughout the cooking time and also added a deep chicken flavor to the sauce. To build the base, we microwaved the aromatics—onion and garlic—along with oregano, red pepper flakes, and a little olive oil. Then we added the chicken broth and the chicken. For a little more depth and brightness, we added a splash of white wine. And to thicken the sauce enough to coat the pasta properly, we simply added a little tapioca at the outset. As this flavorful base simmered with the chicken, it took on a deep, complex flavor. Once the chicken was tender, we removed it from the slow cooker, let it rest briefly, then shredded it into bite-size pieces. Meanwhile, we microwaved the broccolini and then added it and some grated Parmesan to the sauce along with the chicken for a bright, fresh, and healthy pasta dinner.

1	onion, chopped fine
6	garlic cloves, minced
2	tablespoons extra-virgin olive oil
1	tablespoon minced fresh oregano or 1 teaspoon dried
¼	teaspoon red pepper flakes
2	cups chicken broth
1	red bell pepper, stemmed, seeded, and cut into ½-inch pieces
¼	cup dry white wine
2	tablespoons instant tapioca
	Salt and pepper
2	(12-ounce) bone-in split chicken breasts, skin removed, trimmed of all visible fat
12	ounces broccolini, trimmed and cut into 1-inch pieces
2	ounces Parmesan cheese, finely grated (1 cup), plus extra for serving
1	pound whole-wheat penne

1. Microwave onion, garlic, 1 teaspoon oil, oregano, and pepper flakes in bowl, stirring occasionally, until onion is softened, about 5 minutes; transfer to slow cooker. Stir in broth, bell pepper, wine, tapioca, and ½ teaspoon salt. Nestle chicken into slow cooker, cover, and cook until chicken is tender, 3 to 4 hours on low.

2. Transfer chicken to carving board, let cool slightly, then shred into bite-size pieces using 2 forks; discard bones.

3. Microwave broccolini and 1 tablespoon water in covered bowl, stirring occasionally, until tender, about 5 minutes. Drain broccolini, then stir into sauce along with shredded chicken, Parmesan, and remaining 5 teaspoons oil. Let sit until heated through, about 5 minutes.

4. Bring 4 quarts water to boil in large pot. Add pasta and 1 tablespoon salt and cook, stirring often, until al dente. Reserve ½ cup cooking water, then drain pasta and return it to pot. Add sauce and toss to combine. Season with salt and pepper to taste and adjust consistency with reserved cooking water as needed. Serve with extra Parmesan.

Per serving: Cal 470; Fat 11g; Sat Fat 2.5g; Chol 55mg; Carb 57g; Protein 33g; Fiber 9g; Sodium 730mg *To reduce sodium level to 610mg, use unsalted broth.

SMART SHOPPING BROCCOLINI
Broccolini is a hybrid of Chinese kale and broccoli. It is typically sold in bunches like asparagus, and it can be prepared similarly. Its flavor is "slightly mineral" and "sweet, like a cross between spinach and asparagus." Unlike broccoli, which has large florets, broccolini consists mostly of stems and stalks. When prepping broccolini, first trim off and discard the thicker stalk ends, usually the bottom 2 inches of each stalk. Then cut the remaining stems and florets as desired.

Penne with Chicken and Mushroom Sauce

Serves 6 • **Cooking Time** 3 to 4 hours on Low • **Slow Cooker Size** 4 to 7 Quarts

WHY THIS RECIPE WORKS: Inspired by the classic flavors of chicken cacciatore, a savory Italian braise that includes mushrooms, tomatoes, onions, and herbs, we set out to create a hearty pasta sauce that would pair perfectly with whole-wheat pasta. We didn't skimp on the mushrooms and settled on two bold types to ensure a hearty sauce: cremini and porcini. Microwaving the cremini with our aromatics—onion, garlic, and tomato paste—was an easy way to bloom the aromatics and soften the mushrooms before adding them to the slow cooker. For the base of our sauce, we chose crushed tomatoes, which allowed the earthiness of the mushrooms to shine through, and a little soy sauce for deep meaty notes. Bone-in chicken breasts gave the sauce richness, and they were moist enough to shred easily by the end of the cooking time. Finally, a sprinkling of minced parsley, stirred in just before serving, contributed a hit of freshness.

1	pound cremini mushrooms, trimmed and sliced ¼ inch thick
1	onion, halved and sliced thin
2	tablespoons tomato paste
6	garlic cloves, minced
1	tablespoon extra-virgin olive oil
¼	ounce dried porcini mushrooms, rinsed and minced
1	(28-ounce) can crushed tomatoes
1	tablespoon low-sodium soy sauce
	Salt and pepper
2	(12-ounce) bone-in split chicken breasts, skin removed, trimmed of all visible fat
1	pound whole-wheat penne
¼	cup chopped fresh parsley

1. Microwave cremini mushrooms, onion, tomato paste, garlic, 1 teaspoon oil, and porcini mushrooms in covered bowl, stirring occasionally, until vegetables are softened, about 10 minutes; transfer to slow cooker. Stir in tomatoes, soy sauce, ½ teaspoon salt, and ½ teaspoon pepper. Nestle chicken into slow cooker, cover, and cook until chicken is tender, 3 to 4 hours on low.

2. Transfer chicken to carving board, let cool slightly, then shred into bite-size pieces using 2 forks; discard bones. Stir shredded chicken into sauce and let sit until heated through, about 5 minutes.

3. Bring 4 quarts water to boil in large pot. Add pasta and 1 tablespoon salt and cook, stirring often, until al dente. Reserve ½ cup cooking water, then drain pasta and return it to pot. Add sauce and parsley and toss to combine. Season with salt and pepper to taste and adjust consistency with reserved cooking water as needed. Serve.

Per serving: Cal 430; Fat 6g; Sat Fat 1g; Chol 45mg; Carb 63g; Protein 30g; Fiber 11g; Sodium 720mg *To reduce sodium level to 560mg, use no-salt-added tomatoes.

SMART SHOPPING CRUSHED TOMATOES
The coarse consistency of crushed tomatoes provided great body and flavor for our Penne with Chicken and Mushroom Sauce as well as many of our other slow-cooker pasta sauces, though we often combined it with other types of canned tomatoes to achieve the right consistency. We prefer chunky and fresh-tasting **Tuttorosso Crushed Tomatoes in Thick Puree with Basil**. Muir Glen Organic Crushed Tomatoes with Basil came in a close second in our testing.

Shrimp Fra Diavolo with Linguine

Serves 6 • **Cooking Time** 7 to 8 hours on Low or 4 to 5 hours on High • **Slow Cooker Size** 4 to 7 Quarts

✓ **WHY THIS RECIPE WORKS:** Shrimp Fra Diavolo, a restaurant favorite, at first glance seems like an unlikely candidate for a slow-cooker recipe, but in truth it works exceedingly well. Fra Diavolo (which translates to "brother devil" in Italian) is simply a super-spicy tomato sauce that is often paired with seafood. To create a tomato sauce with a definite kick, we gave traditional aromatics a boost with a heaping amount of garlic and red pepper flakes. We achieved fresh tomato flavor with a combination of crushed and diced tomatoes. White wine instead of red kept the sauce bright and light, and soy sauce added depth without being noticeable. Over the long cooking time the flavors melded into a robust sauce. Because shrimp need only a brief moment to cook through, tossing them in right at the end allowed them to poach in the flavorful base in the time it took the pasta to cook on the stovetop. Parsley's earthiness finished off this garlicky and spicy sauce studded with sweet, plump shrimp.

1	onion, chopped fine
6	garlic cloves, minced
2	tablespoons tomato paste
4	teaspoons extra-virgin olive oil
1	tablespoon minced fresh oregano or 1 teaspoon dried
½	teaspoon red pepper flakes
1	(28-ounce) can crushed tomatoes
1	(14.5-ounce) can diced tomatoes, drained
¼	cup dry white wine
2	tablespoons low-sodium soy sauce
2	teaspoons sugar
	Salt and pepper
1½	pounds extra-large shrimp (21 to 25 per pound), peeled, deveined, and tails removed
¼	cup chopped fresh parsley
1	pound whole-wheat linguine

1. Microwave onion, garlic, tomato paste, 1 teaspoon oil, oregano, and pepper flakes in bowl, stirring occasionally, until onion is softened, about 5 minutes; transfer to slow cooker. Stir in crushed tomatoes, diced tomatoes, wine, soy sauce, sugar, and ½ teaspoon pepper. Cover and cook until sauce is deeply flavored, 7 to 8 hours on low or 4 to 5 hours on high.

2. Stir shrimp into sauce, cover, and cook on high until opaque throughout, about 20 minutes. Stir in parsley and remaining 1 tablespoon oil and season with salt and pepper to taste.

3. Bring 4 quarts water to boil in large pot. Add pasta and 1 tablespoon salt and cook, stirring often, until al dente. Reserve ½ cup cooking water, then drain pasta and return it to pot. Add sauce and toss to combine. Season with salt and pepper to taste and adjust consistency with reserved cooking water as needed. Serve.

Per serving: Cal 420; Fat 6g; Sat Fat 0.5g; Chol 105mg; Carb 65g; Protein 24g; Fiber 12g; Sodium 1130mg *To reduce sodium level to 850mg, use no-salt-added tomatoes.

ON THE SIDE BROCCOLI RABE WITH BALSAMIC VINAIGRETTE
Stir 2 pounds broccoli rabe, trimmed and cut into 1-inch pieces, into large pot of salted boiling water. Cook until wilted and tender, 2 to 3 minutes. Drain. Submerge broccoli rabe in bowl of cold water, drain, and pat dry. Whisk together 2 tablespoons extra-virgin olive oil, 2 tablespoons balsamic vinegar, 1 tablespoon honey, 1 minced shallot, and ¼ teaspoon dry mustard in large bowl. Season with salt and pepper to taste. Add broccoli rabe and toss to combine. Serves 6.

Per serving: Cal 110; Fat 4.5g; Sat Fat 0.5g; Chol 0mg; Carb 12g; Protein 6g; Fiber 0g; Sodium 140mg

Casseroles

● **EASY PREP**   ● **VEGETARIAN**

Chicken Pot Pie

Serves 8 • **Cooking Time** 3 to 5 hours on Low • **Slow Cooker Size** 4 to 7 Quarts

✔ **WHY THIS RECIPE WORKS:** With its buttery, flaky topping and tender chicken and vegetables coated in a velvety sauce, chicken pot pie is a sure crowd-pleaser. But a single serving can pack in over 30 grams of fat. To lighten this family-friendly classic (and reengineer it for the slow cooker), we had to cut back on the fat in both the topping and the filling. A combination of mushrooms, carrots, and onion formed the base of our filling, which we bound with a flour-thickened sauce. Adding a bit of tomato paste and soy sauce to the filling helped ramp up its flavor even further, and finishing it with a small amount of heavy cream provided the right amount of richness. We then brightened the filling with peas at the end. Moving on to the topping, we knew high-calorie pie dough and biscuits were out. We had to get creative, as our ideal topping needed to be quick and easy to prepare but provide a nice crunch. A crumble topping was the perfect finish for our pot pie, as it could be mixed quickly in a bowl and baked until crisp in just 15 minutes.

1 tablespoon unsalted butter, plus 4 tablespoons melted

8 ounces cremini mushrooms, trimmed and sliced thin

4 carrots, peeled, halved lengthwise, and sliced ¼ inch thick

1 onion, chopped fine

2 tablespoons tomato paste

1 teaspoon minced fresh thyme or ¼ teaspoon dried

1¾ cups (8¾ ounces) plus ⅓ cup all-purpose flour

2½ cups chicken broth, plus extra as needed

1 tablespoon low-sodium soy sauce
Salt and pepper

3 (12-ounce) bone-in split chicken breasts, skin removed, trimmed of all visible fat

1 ounce Parmesan cheese, grated fine (½ cup)

1½ teaspoons baking powder

½ teaspoon baking soda

⅔ cup buttermilk

1 cup frozen peas, thawed

¼ cup heavy cream

1. Melt 1 tablespoon butter in 12-inch skillet over medium heat. Add mushrooms, carrots, and onion and cook until softened and lightly browned, about 8 minutes. Stir in tomato paste and thyme and cook until fragrant, about 1 minute. Stir in ⅓ cup flour and cook for 1 minute. Slowly stir in broth, soy sauce, and ½ teaspoon salt, scraping up any browned bits and smoothing out any lumps; transfer to slow cooker. Season chicken with salt and pepper and nestle into slow cooker. Cover and cook until chicken is tender, 3 to 5 hours on low.

2. Meanwhile, adjust oven rack to upper-middle position and heat oven to 450 degrees. Whisk remaining 1¾ cups flour, Parmesan, baking powder, baking soda, ¼ teaspoon salt, and ½ teaspoon pepper together in large bowl. In separate bowl, whisk buttermilk and remaining 4 tablespoons melted butter together. Add buttermilk mixture to flour mixture and gently stir until just combined and no pockets of flour remain (do not overmix). Crumble mixture into irregularly shaped pieces ranging from ½ to ¾ inch each and spread evenly on parchment paper–lined rimmed baking sheet. Bake until fragrant and golden brown, about 15 minutes, rotating sheet halfway through baking. Let crumble topping cool on sheet.

3. Transfer chicken to carving board, let cool slightly, then shred into bite-size pieces using 2 forks; discard bones. Stir shredded chicken, peas, and cream into filling and let sit until heated through, about 5 minutes. (Adjust filling consistency with extra hot broth as needed.) Season with salt and pepper to taste. Top individual portions with crumble topping before serving.

Per serving: Cal 360; Fat 13g; Sat Fat 7g; Chol 85mg; Carb 33g; Protein 27g; Fiber 3g; Sodium 920mg *To reduce sodium level to 800mg, use unsalted broth.

Hearty Beef and Vegetable Pot Pie

Serves 8 • **Cooking Time** 5 to 7 hours on Low or 3 to 5 hours on High • **Slow Cooker Size** 4 to 7 Quarts

✓ **WHY THIS RECIPE WORKS:** To make our healthy version of beef pot pie in a slow cooker with all the nuances of a slow-simmered beef stew, we limited the amount of beef (using beef chuck roast, which we've found to be the best cut for stews) and added a significant amount of vegetables. To deepen the meaty flavor of our vegetable-rich pie, we made sure to brown half of the beef to develop a nice fond before softening our vegetables. Tomato paste, garlic, and thyme enhanced the savory notes of the beef, and flour helped thicken the filling; we deglazed the pan with wine and a little of the broth to capture all of the flavorful browned bits on the bottom of the Dutch oven. Though puff pastry is not your standard low-fat fare, we found that one sheet provided the perfect flaky, buttery topping without increasing the fat significantly. After trimming the beef, you should have 2¼ pounds of usable meat. To thaw frozen puff pasty, allow it to sit either in the refrigerator for 24 hours or on the counter for 30 minutes to 1 hour.

3	pounds boneless beef chuck-eye roast, trimmed of all visible fat and cut into 1-inch pieces
1	teaspoon canola oil
12	ounces portobello mushroom caps, gills removed, caps halved and sliced ¼ inch thick
12	ounces turnips, peeled and cut into ½-inch pieces
4	carrots, peeled, halved lengthwise, and sliced ½ inch thick
2	tablespoons tomato paste
4	garlic cloves, minced
2	teaspoons minced fresh thyme or ½ teaspoon dried
½	cup all-purpose flour
½	cup dry red wine
3	cups beef broth, plus extra as needed
2	cups frozen pearl onions
2	tablespoons low-sodium soy sauce
	Salt and pepper
1	(9½ by 9-inch) sheet puff pastry, thawed
1½	cups frozen peas, thawed
1	sprig fresh rosemary
¼	cup chopped fresh parsley

1. Pat beef dry with paper towels. Heat oil in Dutch oven over medium-high heat until just smoking. Brown half of beef on all sides, about 8 minutes; transfer to slow cooker along with remaining beef.

2. Add mushrooms, turnips, and carrots to fat left in pot, cover, and cook until softened, about 5 minutes. Uncover and continue to cook until vegetables are dry and browned, about 5 minutes. Stir in tomato paste, garlic, and thyme and cook until fragrant, about 1 minute. Stir in flour and cook for 1 minute. Slowly stir in wine, scraping up any browned bits, and simmer until almost completely evaporated, about 2 minutes. Stir in 1 cup broth, smoothing out any lumps; transfer to slow cooker.

3. Stir remaining 2 cups broth, onions, soy sauce, and ¾ teaspoon salt into slow cooker. Cover and cook until beef is tender, 5 to 7 hours on low or 3 to 5 hours on high.

4. Meanwhile, adjust oven rack to middle position and heat oven to 400 degrees. Roll puff pastry into 14 by 10-inch rectangle on lightly floured counter. Using sharp knife, cut pastry in half lengthwise, then into quarters widthwise to create 8 pieces. Transfer pieces to parchment paper–lined baking sheet and bake until puffed and lightly browned, about 15 minutes, rotating sheet halfway through baking. Let cool on sheet.

5. Stir peas and rosemary sprig into slow cooker and let steep for 10 minutes. Discard rosemary sprig. (Adjust filling consistency with extra hot broth as needed.) Stir in parsley and season with salt and pepper to taste. Top each individual portion with pastry pieces before serving.

Per serving: Cal 410; Fat 14g; Sat Fat 6g; Chol 85mg; Carb 33g; Protein 36g; Fiber 5g; Sodium 830mg *To reduce sodium level to 670mg, use low-sodium broth.

ALL ABOUT Casseroles in the Slow Cooker

Instead of heavy, calorie-rich dishes topped with fatty cheese and crumbs, we turned to the slow cooker for hearty but healthy casseroles. While not every successful casserole follows the same hard-and-fast rules, there are a few general guidelines to keep in mind. Here's what you should know.

Prepare Your Slow Cooker

Most slow cookers have a hotter side (typically the back side, opposite the side with the controls) that can cause dense casseroles like baked ziti to burn. To solve this problem we lined the slow-cooker insert with an aluminum foil collar. For recipes that we wanted to lift out of the insert intact, like Spanish Tortilla with Roasted Red Peppers (page 232), we first lined the slow cooker with a foil collar, then lined it completely with foil.

To make a foil collar: Fold sheets of heavy-duty aluminum foil until you have a six-layered foil rectangle that measures roughly 16 inches long by 4 inches wide. (Depending on the width of the foil, you will need either two or three sheets of foil.) Then press the collar into the back side of the slow-cooker insert; the food will help hold the collar in place during cooking.

To make a foil liner: Line the slow-cooker insert with a foil collar, then fit two large sheets of heavy-duty foil in the slow cooker, perpendicular to one another, with the extra foil hanging over the edges. Before serving, these overhanging edges can be used as handles to pull the food out of the slow cooker fully intact and transfer it to a platter for serving.

Use Cheese Smartly

Many casseroles in this book wouldn't be complete without some cheese to boost flavor. Low-fat options like light cheddar gave our fillings the richness we wanted but became waxy when used as toppings, so we folded the cheese into the filling instead. For a cheesy finish we often chose to use a full-fat cheese (with the exception of mozzarella where part-skim worked fine), or a hard cheese like Parmesan or Asiago, or a soft cheese naturally low in fat like *queso fresco* or feta. This technique worked perfectly in recipes like our Farro and Wild Mushroom Gratin (page 176), where the shredded cheese was saved for the topping of the casserole, giving each bite a savory and rich flavor.

Drive Off Excess Moisture

In the moist environment of a slow cooker, there is no opportunity to drive off moisture as there is in an oven, so excess moisture in the form of sauce or liquid that has leached out of vegetables can cause havoc when it comes to casseroles that need cohesiveness. In addition to controlling the amount and thickness of our sauces and fillings, in some cases we also found it important to precook vegetables in order to drive out moisture.

Don't Overcook Slow-Cooker Casseroles

Our casseroles have relatively short cooking times; otherwise, we ended up with mushy pasta, bland vegetables, and dry meat. You'll find a range of cooking times for casseroles; be sure to follow our guidance on the times and settings for vibrant flavors and properly cooked casseroles.

Pasta: Raw or Cooked?

When making slow-cooker casseroles with pasta, how you handle the pasta makes a huge difference in the success of the dish. For baked ziti, raw or partially cooked pasta did not work, but toasting it with oil in the microwave did, and it prevented the pasta from becoming bloated. We found that microwaving the pasta at 50 percent power, and stirring it occasionally, gently toasted the pasta; note that only a portion will look toasted and blistered.

Rustic Pork and White Bean Casserole

Serves 6 • **Cooking Time** 2 to 4 hours on Low • **Slow Cooker Size** 4 to 7 Quarts

✔ **WHY THIS RECIPE WORKS:** Inspired by the French classic cassoulet, we set out to create a healthy casserole in our slow cooker packed with vegetables and smoky pork flavor. For the meat we turned to easy-prep and lean boneless country-style pork ribs, cutting them into 1-inch pieces before adding them to the slow cooker. For smoky flavor, bacon was an easy choice, and we microwaved it along with the aromatics and vegetables. For the broth base, we liked a combination of crushed tomatoes and white wine. To ensure that everything was perfectly cooked, we microwaved chopped onions, carrots, and parsnips with plenty of garlic, as well as tomato paste for richness and body. To thicken the casserole, we mashed 1 can of beans to a paste before adding them to the slow cooker. The other can of beans was left whole and simmered along with the vegetables and the aromatics. The finishing touch to our rustic casserole was crusty toasted croutons made from a small baguette; chopped fresh oregano tossed with the croutons along with a little olive oil added a welcome peppery taste.

8	ounces parsnips, peeled and cut into ½-inch pieces
4	carrots, peeled and cut into ½-inch pieces
2	onions, chopped fine
2	slices bacon, chopped fine
3	tablespoons tomato paste
6	garlic cloves, minced
2	(15-ounce) cans cannellini beans, rinsed
1	cup canned crushed tomatoes
¼	cup dry white wine
3	tablespoons minced fresh oregano
	Salt and pepper
1½	pounds boneless country-style pork ribs, trimmed of all visible fat and cut into 1-inch pieces
1	(12-inch) baguette, cut into ½-inch pieces
2	tablespoons extra-virgin olive oil

1. Lightly spray inside of slow cooker with vegetable oil spray. Microwave parsnips, carrots, onions, bacon, tomato paste, and garlic in covered bowl until vegetables are softened, 8 to 10 minutes; transfer to slow cooker.

2. Mash half of beans in bowl with potato masher until smooth; transfer to slow cooker. Stir in remaining beans, tomatoes, wine, 1 tablespoon oregano, and ½ teaspoon salt, then stir in pork. Cover and cook until pork is tender, 2 to 4 hours on low.

3. Meanwhile, adjust oven rack to middle position and heat oven to 450 degrees. Arrange bread in single layer on rimmed baking sheet and bake until browned and crisp, about 10 minutes, stirring halfway through baking. Toss croutons with oil and remaining 2 tablespoons oregano and season with salt and pepper to taste.

4. Season filling with salt and pepper to taste. Top individual portions with croutons before serving.

Per serving: Cal 540; Fat 16g; Sat Fat 4.5g; Chol 90mg; Carb 62g; Protein 38g; Fiber 11g; Sodium 1030mg *To reduce sodium level to 760mg, use low-sodium beans and no-salt-added tomatoes.

ON THE SIDE GREEN BEAN AND BLACK OLIVE SALAD
Bring 2½ quarts water to boil in large saucepan. Add 1½ pounds trimmed green beans and 1 tablespoon salt and cook until bright green and tender, about 5 minutes. Drain beans, rinse under cold water until cool, and drain well again; transfer to large bowl. Toss with ¼ cup chopped pitted black olives, 2 tablespoons chopped fresh basil, 1 tablespoon olive oil, 1 tablespoon lemon juice, and 1 minced garlic clove. Season with salt and pepper to taste. Serves 6.

Per serving: Cal 70; Fat 4g; Sat Fat 0.5g; Chol 0mg; Carb 9g; Protein 2g; Fiber 3g; Sodium 180mg

Mexican Lasagna

Serves 6 • **Cooking Time** 1 to 2 hours on Low • **Slow Cooker Size** 5½ to 7 Quarts

☑ **WHY THIS RECIPE WORKS:** Mexican lasagna blends the meaty, cheesy layers of Italian lasagna with sweet red bell peppers, beans, and corn tortillas. We opted to use lean ground turkey, which offered a hearty texture and subtle meaty flavor while also keeping our dish on the lighter side. After browning the turkey and aromatics (which proved to be a vital step in developing flavor), we added tomato sauce and paste and let it reduce to get rid of excess moisture which made the casserole soggy. Because we found that low-fat cheddar turned waxy when layered into the lasagna alone, we opted to include it in the filling instead. With the addition of beans and low-fat cheddar cheese we had a rich and flavorful filling. A light coating of vegetable oil spray prevented the corn tortillas from becoming soggy when covered with sauce in the slow cooker. Be sure to use 93 percent lean ground turkey, not ground turkey breast (also labeled 99 percent fat free). For information on making a foil collar, see page 169. You will need an oval slow cooker for this recipe. Serve with salsa, diced avocado, plain Greek yogurt, and lime wedges.

1	teaspoon canola oil
2	red bell peppers, stemmed, seeded, and cut into ½-inch pieces
1	onion, chopped fine
4	garlic cloves, minced
2	teaspoons minced canned chipotle chile in adobo sauce
2	teaspoons chili powder
1	teaspoon ground cumin
1½	pounds 93 percent lean ground turkey
1	(28-ounce) can tomato sauce
⅓	cup tomato paste
1	(15-ounce) can black beans, rinsed
2	ounces 50 percent light cheddar cheese, shredded (½ cup)
½	cup chopped fresh cilantro
	Salt and pepper
	Vegetable oil spray
9	(6-inch) corn tortillas

1. Heat oil in Dutch oven over medium heat until shimmering. Add bell peppers and onion and cook until softened, about 8 minutes. Stir in garlic, chipotle, chili powder, and cumin and cook until fragrant, about 30 seconds. Add turkey and cook, breaking up meat with wooden spoon, until no longer pink, 5 to 8 minutes.

2. Add tomato sauce and tomato paste and bring to simmer. Reduce heat to medium-low and cook, stirring occasionally, until thickened, 8 to 10 minutes. Off heat, stir in beans, cheddar, ¼ cup cilantro, and ¼ teaspoon salt. Season with salt and pepper to taste.

3. Line slow cooker with aluminum foil collar and lightly spray with oil spray. Spray both sides of tortillas with oil spray. Stack tortillas, wrap in damp dish towel, and place on plate; microwave until warm and pliable, about 1 minute.

4. Spread one-third of turkey mixture in bottom of prepared slow cooker. Arrange 3 tortillas in single layer on top, tearing tortillas as needed; repeat layering 2 more times. Cover and cook until casserole is heated through, 1 to 2 hours on low.

5. Remove foil collar. Sprinkle with remaining ¼ cup cilantro. Serve.

Per serving: Cal 380; Fat 12g; Sat Fat 3.5g; Chol 70mg; Carb 39g; Protein 32g; Fiber 8g; Sodium 1210mg *To reduce sodium level to 510mg, use no-salt-added tomato sauce and low-sodium beans.

Vegetable Enchiladas with Squash and Beans

Serves 4 • **Cooking Time** About 1 hour on Low • **Slow Cooker Size** 5½ to 7 Quarts

✓ **WHY THIS RECIPE WORKS:** What makes enchiladas so irresistible is all the melted cheese and a heavy rich sauce—which is exactly what makes them bad for you. For our healthy slow-cooker take on this classic, we were determined to make it as rich and flavorful as the original, minus all the fat. The first thing we had to do was cut back on the cheese. We chose *queso fresco* for our filling and topping instead of cheddar or Monterey Jack, as we were able to use more cheese without loading up the dish with tons of fat. For the rest of our filling, we liked summer squash and pinto beans, but they were too soggy. In order to fix this, we sautéed the squash to rid it of excess moisture before combining it with the pinto beans. For a deeply flavored sauce, we got out the skillet and sautéed the aromatics along with tomato paste and chipotle chile. For the right consistency, we thickened it by making a roux and deglazing the pan with broth. When forming our enchiladas, simply rolling the filling in cold tortillas didn't cut it as the enchiladas broke and tore. Heating the tortillas in the microwave helped to make them pliable. You will need an oval slow cooker for this recipe. Serve with salsa, diced avocado, plain Greek yogurt, shredded lettuce, and lime wedges.

2	teaspoons extra-virgin olive oil
4	scallions, white and green parts separated and sliced thin
⅓	cup tomato paste
4	garlic cloves, minced
1	tablespoon minced canned chipotle chile in adobo sauce
1	teaspoon ground cumin
1	tablespoon all-purpose flour
2½	cups vegetable broth
	Salt and pepper
1	(15-ounce) can pinto beans, rinsed
1	summer squash (8 ounces), cut into ¼-inch pieces
5	ounces queso fresco, crumbled (1¼ cups)
1	tablespoon lime juice
8	(6-inch) corn tortillas

1. Heat 1 teaspoon oil in 12-inch nonstick skillet over medium heat until shimmering. Add scallion whites and cook until softened, about 2 minutes. Stir in tomato paste, garlic, chipotle, and cumin and cook until fragrant, about 1 minute. Stir in flour and cook for 1 minute. Slowly whisk in broth, smoothing out any lumps. Bring to simmer and cook until sauce is thickened and measures 2 cups, about 5 minutes. Season with salt and pepper to taste; transfer to bowl. Wipe skillet clean.

2. Mash half of beans in bowl with potato masher until smooth. Heat remaining 1 teaspoon oil in now-empty skillet over medium heat until shimmering. Add squash and cook until softened, about 5 minutes. Off heat, stir in ½ cup sauce, mashed beans, ½ cup queso fresco, lime juice, and remaining whole beans. Season with salt and pepper to taste.

3. Lightly spray inside of slow cooker with vegetable oil spray. Spread ½ cup sauce in bottom of slow cooker. Stack tortillas, wrap in damp dish towel, and place on plate; microwave until warm and pliable, about 1 minute.

4. Working with 1 warm tortilla at a time, spread ⅓ cup filling across center of tortilla, roll tortilla tightly around filling, and place side by side in prepared slow cooker, seam side down. Pour ½ cup sauce evenly over enchiladas. Cover and cook until enchiladas are heated through, about 1 hour on low.

5. Pour remaining ½ cup sauce over enchiladas and sprinkle with remaining ¾ cup queso fresco; let sit until heated through, about 5 minutes. Sprinkle with scallion greens and serve.

Per serving: Cal 320; Fat 8g; Sat Fat 2.5g; Chol 10mg; Carb 50g; Protein 14g; Fiber 8g; Sodium 870mg *To reduce sodium level to 480mg, use low-sodium broth.

Turkish-Style Eggplant Casserole

Serves 4 • **Cooking Time** 3 to 4 hours on Low or 2 to 3 hours on High • **Slow Cooker Size** 5½ to 7 Quarts

✔ **WHY THIS RECIPE WORKS:** Earthy and versatile, eggplant pairs well with traditional Turkish spices, namely, paprika, cumin, cayenne pepper, and cinnamon. We paired eggplant, which we rubbed with a spice mixture and broiled before adding it to the slow cooker to cook off extra moisture and keep the slices firm, with bulgur, a popular grain of the region that cooks perfectly in the steamy environment of the slow cooker. An herb-yogurt sauce added a welcome richness and tang to this spiced dish. When shopping, don't confuse bulgur with cracked wheat, which has a much longer cooking time and will not work in this recipe. You will need an oval slow cooker for this recipe.

	Vegetable oil spray
2	teaspoons paprika
1½	teaspoons ground cumin
	Salt and pepper
⅛	teaspoon cayenne pepper
⅛	teaspoon ground cinnamon
1½	pounds eggplant, sliced into ½-inch-thick rounds
1	onion, chopped fine
2	tablespoons extra-virgin olive oil
4	garlic cloves, minced
1	tablespoon tomato paste
1	cup medium-grind bulgur, rinsed
1	cup plus 2 tablespoons water
4	tomatoes, cored and sliced ½ inch thick
1	cup 2 percent Greek yogurt
¼	cup chopped fresh parsley
2	tablespoons chopped fresh mint

1. Adjust oven rack 6 inches from broiler element and heat broiler. Line rimmed baking sheet with aluminum foil and spray with oil spray. Combine paprika, cumin, ¾ teaspoon salt, cayenne, and cinnamon in bowl. Arrange eggplant in single layer in prepared sheet, lightly spray with oil spray, and season with half of spice mixture. Flip eggplant, lightly spray with oil spray, and season with remaining spice mixture. Broil eggplant until softened and beginning to brown, 10 to 12 minutes, flipping eggplant halfway through broiling.

2. Lightly spray inside of slow cooker with oil spray. Microwave onion, 1 teaspoon oil, garlic, and tomato paste in bowl, stirring occasionally, until onion is softened, about 5 minutes; transfer to slow cooker. Stir in bulgur, 1 cup water, and ¾ teaspoon salt. Shingle alternating slices of eggplant and tomatoes into 3 tightly fitting rows on top of bulgur mixture. Cover and cook until eggplant and bulgur are tender and all water is absorbed, 3 to 4 hours on low or 2 to 3 hours on high.

3. Combine yogurt, parsley, mint, and remaining 2 tablespoons water in bowl. Season with salt and pepper to taste. Drizzle casserole with remaining 5 teaspoons oil and serve with yogurt sauce.

Per serving: Cal 320; Fat 11g; Sat Fat 2g; Chol 5mg; Carb 48g; Protein 12g; Fiber 13g; Sodium 950mg

---

QUICK PREP TIP **ASSEMBLING TURKISH-STYLE EGGPLANT CASSEROLE**
After combining bulgur mixture in slow cooker, shingle alternating slices of eggplant and tomatoes into 3 tightly fitting rows on top. Vegetable rows may overlap slightly.

Farro and Wild Mushroom Gratin

Serves 4 • **Cooking Time** 3 to 4 hours on Low or 2 to 3 hours on High • **Slow Cooker Size** 4 to 7 Quarts

✔ **WHY THIS RECIPE WORKS:** We love the sweet, nutty flavor and chewy bite of farro. While this hulled whole-wheat kernel has been popular in Italy for centuries, it has only recently gained popularity in the United States for its health benefits as well as its flavor and texture. We set out to create a rich and creamy version using the slow cooker, with a risotto-like texture without the fuss. Farro typically takes twice as long to cook as Arborio rice but does not require the stirring or excess amount of fat to achieve the same creamy texture. Instead of sautéing our farro, we began by microwaving it along with the aromatics before stirring in a combination of hot broth, water, and wine to jump-start the cooking. For flavor, we loved the rich earthiness of shiitake, cremini, and meaty porcini mushrooms along with the velvety farro. We finished by sprinkling Gruyère over the casserole for a melted topping, and parsley for fresh flavor. Do not substitute pearl, quick-cooking, or presteamed farro for the whole farro in this recipe; you may need to read the ingredient list on the package carefully to determine if the farro is presteamed. For an accurate measurement of boiling water, bring a full kettle of water to a boil and then measure out the desired amount.

1	cup whole farro
1	onion, chopped fine
½	ounce dried porcini mushrooms, rinsed and minced
3	garlic cloves, minced
2	teaspoons minced fresh thyme or ½ teaspoon dried
1	teaspoon canola oil
8	ounces shiitake mushrooms, stemmed and halved if small or quartered if large
8	ounces cremini mushrooms, trimmed and sliced thin
1½	cups boiling water
1	cup vegetable broth
⅓	cup dry white wine
	Salt and pepper
4	ounces Gruyère cheese, shredded (1 cup)
¼	cup chopped fresh parsley

1. Lightly spray inside of slow cooker with vegetable oil spray. Microwave farro, onion, porcini mushrooms, garlic, thyme, and oil in bowl, stirring occasionally, until onion is softened, about 5 minutes; transfer to slow cooker. Stir in shiitake mushrooms, cremini mushrooms, 1 cup boiling water, broth, wine, and ¾ teaspoon salt. Cover and cook until farro is tender, 3 to 4 hours on low or 2 to 3 hours on high.

2. Stir ½ cup Gruyère and remaining ½ cup boiling water into farro until mixture is creamy. Season with salt and pepper to taste. Sprinkle with remaining ½ cup Gruyère, cover, and cook on high until cheese is melted, about 5 minutes. Sprinkle with parsley and serve.

Per serving: Cal 380; Fat 13g; Sat Fat 6g; Chol 30mg; Carb 47g; Protein 18g; Fiber 6g; Sodium 740mg *To reduce sodium level to 580mg, use low-sodium broth.

QUICK PREP TIP **STORING MUSHROOMS**
Curious about the best way to store mushrooms once you get them home from the market, we pitted several storing methods against each other over a five-day period to see what worked and what didn't. Among the things we tried were leaving them in their original box and covering them with plastic wrap or a damp paper towel, wrapping them in aluminum foil, storing them in a paper bag, storing them in a paper bag cut with air holes, storing them in an airtight zipper-lock bag, and simply leaving them uncovered. The winning method turned out to be either the original packaging (if purchased in a tray wrapped in plastic) or a simple paper bag (if purchased loose). The other methods were flat-out losers and turned the mushrooms either slimy or dried out in just a couple of days.

Thai Tofu and Rice Casserole

Serves 4 • **Cooking Time** 3 to 4 hours on High • **Slow Cooker Size** 4 to 7 Quarts

✓ **WHY THIS RECIPE WORKS:** For a hearty vegetarian casserole from the slow cooker we paired tofu with coconut-and-miso-infused brown rice and earthy shiitake mushrooms. The key to the success of this dish was the liquid-to-rice ratio. We knew rice would be a challenge in the slow cooker, as we needed enough liquid for the rice to absorb but not so much that the casserole was watered down. In the end, 1½ cups of water plus 1½ cups of light coconut milk to 1 cup of short-grain brown rice (its texture was consistently the best in the slow cooker) was just right. Brown rice needs a head start with boiling water, which we infused with umami-rich miso for its salty flavor and subtle sweetness. To take our healthy rice casserole to the next level we decided to infuse it with Thai flavors. Ginger was added for its subtle heat and its complement to the sweeter coconut milk. For additional savory notes we added a leek, garlic, and red pepper flakes. You can substitute firm tofu here if desired; avoid silken, soft, or medium-firm tofu as these varieties will break down while cooking. Do not substitute long-grain brown rice for short-grain rice. For an accurate measurement of boiling water, bring a full kettle of water to a boil and then measure out the desired amount.

14	ounces extra-firm tofu, cut into ½-inch pieces
1	leek, white and light green parts only, halved lengthwise, sliced thin, and washed thoroughly
1	cup short-grain brown rice
2	teaspoons grated fresh ginger
2	garlic cloves, minced
1	teaspoon canola oil
¼	teaspoon red pepper flakes
1½	cups boiling water
3	tablespoons white miso
1½	cups canned light coconut milk
12	ounces shiitake mushrooms, stemmed and halved if small or quartered if large
¾	teaspoon salt
¼	cup minced fresh cilantro

1. Spread tofu on paper towel–lined baking sheet and let drain for 20 minutes. Microwave leek, rice, ginger, garlic, oil, and pepper flakes in bowl, stirring occasionally, until leek is softened, about 5 minutes.

2. Lightly spray inside of slow cooker with vegetable oil spray. Whisk boiling water and miso together in slow cooker until miso is fully dissolved. Gently stir in coconut milk, mushrooms, salt, drained tofu, and leek mixture. Cover and cook until rice is tender, 3 to 4 hours on high.

3. Turn slow cooker off and let casserole rest, covered, until fully set, about 20 minutes. Sprinkle with cilantro and serve.

Per serving: Cal 400; Fat 14g; Sat Fat 5g; Chol 0mg; Carb 53g; Protein 16g; Fiber 4g; Sodium 820mg

---

SMART SHOPPING **TOFU**
Tofu is made from the curds of soy milk. Although freshly made tofu is common across the Pacific, in the United States tofu is typically sold in refrigerated blocks packed in water. A good food choice for health-conscious eaters, tofu is high in protein as well as iron, calcium, and one of the omega-3 fatty acids. It is also relatively low in fat and calories and is cholesterol-free. Tofu is available in a variety of textures, including silken, soft, medium-firm, firm, and extra-firm. We prefer to use extra-firm in our slow-cooker dishes because it holds its shape well when cooked for an extended period of time. Tofu is perishable and should be kept well chilled. If you want to keep an opened package of tofu fresh for several days, cover the tofu with fresh water in an airtight container and store it in the refrigerator, changing the water daily. Any hint of sourness means the tofu is past its prime (we prefer to use it within a few days of opening).

Quinoa, Sweet Potato, and Corn Casserole

Serves 4 • **Cooking Time** 3 to 4 hours on Low or 2 to 3 hours on High • **Slow Cooker Size** 4 to 7 Quarts

WHY THIS RECIPE WORKS: This fresh casserole pairs quinoa with sweet red bell peppers, earthy sweet potatoes, and corn. To build a flavorful base we started by microwaving the sweet potatoes with shallot, garlic, chili powder, and oregano, which complemented the nutty flavor of the quinoa. Red bell peppers offered brightness and acidity, along with corn—we opted for the frozen variety for convenience and consistent flavor year-round. We found quinoa to be well suited to the slow cooker, where the flavors could meld over time and become creamy for a richer-tasting dish. We topped our casserole with cilantro for more color and avocado for its buttery and creamy texture. We like the convenience of prewashed quinoa; rinsing removes the quinoa's bitter protective coating (called saponin). If you buy unwashed quinoa (or if you are unsure if it's washed), rinse it before cooking.

1 **pound sweet potatoes, peeled and cut into ½-inch pieces**

2 **shallots, minced**

4 **teaspoons chili powder**

3 **garlic cloves, minced**

2 **teaspoons minced fresh oregano or ½ teaspoon dried**

1 **teaspoon canola oil**

2 **cups vegetable broth**

1 **cup prewashed quinoa**

2 **red bell peppers, stemmed, seeded, and cut into ½-inch pieces**

 Salt and pepper

1 **cup frozen corn, thawed**

1 **avocado, halved, pitted, and cut into ½-inch pieces**

2 **tablespoons minced fresh cilantro**

 Lime wedges

1. Lightly spray inside of slow cooker with vegetable oil spray. Microwave potatoes, shallots, chili powder, garlic, oregano, and oil in covered bowl, stirring occasionally, until vegetables are softened, 6 to 8 minutes; transfer to slow cooker. Stir in broth, quinoa, bell peppers, and 1 teaspoon salt. Cover and cook until potatoes and quinoa are tender, 3 to 4 hours on low or 2 to 3 hours on high.

2. Turn slow cooker off. Top casserole with corn, cover, and let casserole rest until fully set, about 10 minutes. Sprinkle with avocado and cilantro and serve with lime wedges.

Per serving: Cal 410; Fat 13g; Sat Fat 1.5g; Chol 0mg; Carb 67g; Protein 11g; Fiber 12g; Sodium 1060mg *To reduce sodium level to 750mg, use low-sodium broth.

QUICK PREP TIP
CUTTING UP AN AVOCADO
Cut avodado in half around pit, lodge edge of knife blade into pit, and twist to remove, then use wooden spoon to remove pit from blade. Make ½-inch crosshatch incisions in avocado flesh with knife, cutting down to skin. Then gently scoop out pieces with spoon.

Spring Polenta Casserole

Serves 4 • **Cooking Time** 3 to 4 hours on Low • **Slow Cooker Size** 4 to 7 Quarts

✔ WHY THIS RECIPE WORKS: Mildly flavored and very easy to prepare, polenta makes a great backdrop for a healthy casserole. This firm-textured casserole combines rich and hearty polenta and garden-fresh vegetables for a vegetarian entrée you wouldn't expect to make in a slow cooker. We began with the polenta and decided to use a combination of water and milk to boost its richness. To flavor the polenta we added a minced shallot for its intense but mildly sweet onion flavor and thinly sliced white mushrooms for a subtle earthiness. We microwaved them briefly before adding them to the slow cooker, where they softened and cooked perfectly in the same amount of time as the polenta. At the end of the cooking time we topped the casserole with thin asparagus cut on the bias and halved cherry tomatoes for a fresh and bright flavor. For richness, we also added a cup of grated Parmesan as the finishing touch. After an additional 20 to 30 minutes, our casserole was fully formed and ready to serve. Be sure to use traditional polenta, not instant polenta. You will need an oval slow cooker for this recipe.

8   ounces white mushrooms, trimmed and sliced thin
1   shallot, minced
1   teaspoon canola oil
3   cups water, plus extra as needed
1   cup polenta
½   cup whole milk
      Salt and pepper
8   ounces thin asparagus, trimmed and cut on bias into ½-inch lengths
8   ounces cherry tomatoes, halved
2   ounces Parmesan cheese, grated (1 cup)

1. Lightly spray inside of slow cooker with vegetable oil spray. Microwave mushrooms, shallot, and oil in bowl, stirring occasionally, until vegetables are softened, about 5 minutes; transfer to slow cooker. Stir in water, polenta, milk, 1 teaspoon salt, and ¼ teaspoon pepper. Cover and cook until polenta is tender, 3 to 4 hours on low.

2. Top polenta with asparagus and tomatoes, then sprinkle with Parmesan. Cover and cook on high until vegetables are tender and cheese is melted, 20 to 30 minutes. Serve.

Per serving: Cal 270; Fat 7g; Sat Fat 3g; Chol 15mg; Carb 37g; Protein 13g; Fiber 4g; Sodium 860mg

---

QUICK PREP TIP
PREPARING ASPARAGUS SPEARS
Remove 1 stalk of asparagus from bunch and bend it at thicker end until it snaps. With broken asparagus as guide, trim tough ends from remaining asparagus, using chef's knife.

Savory Bread Pudding with Fennel and Spinach

Serves 6 • **Cooking Time** 4 to 5 hours on Low • **Slow Cooker Size** 5½ to 7 Quarts

✔ **WHY THIS RECIPE WORKS:** A savory bread pudding makes a great brunch dish or even a light dinner. Usually, though, it requires some advance planning since the key is an overnight stay in the fridge, which allows the bread to soak up the custard before the casserole goes into the oven. Using the slow cooker eliminates this step and makes it even easier to make bread pudding, as the slow, gentle cooking time allows the bread to fully absorb the liquid without drying out or burning. We had to soak the bread in the custard for only 10 minutes before adding it to the slow cooker. To lighten this dish, we began by using only egg whites. While lean, this variation was disappointingly watery. Replacing the traditional heavy cream with skim milk did nothing to help thicken and bind the pudding. We settled on a combination of whole eggs and 2 percent milk, which provided the best results, keeping the custard just thick enough. For our bread, we tried several varieties but preferred French bread for its strong crumb and neutral flavor. To round out the flavors of this bread pudding, we liked the sweet anise flavor of fennel, in combination with hearty chopped spinach and tangy feta cheese—which is naturally low in fat. We prefer the softer crust of French or Italian bread here; avoid using rustic loaves with thick crusts, if possible. Don't let this bread pudding cook longer than 5 hours or it will become dried out and rubbery. For information on making a foil collar, see page 169. You will need an oval slow cooker for this recipe.

1¾	**cups 2 percent low-fat milk**
6	**large eggs**
¼	**cup dry white wine**
	Salt and pepper
6	**ounces French or Italian bread, cut into ½-inch pieces (5 cups)**
1	**fennel bulb, stalks discarded, bulb halved, cored, and sliced thin**
2	**teaspoons minced fresh thyme or ½ teaspoon dried**
1	**garlic clove, minced**
1	**teaspoon canola oil**
10	**ounces frozen chopped spinach, thawed and squeezed dry**
4	**ounces feta cheese, crumbled (1 cup)**

1. Whisk milk, eggs, wine, ¾ teaspoon salt, and ¼ teaspoon pepper together in large bowl. Stir in bread and let sit, pressing on bread occasionally, until custard is mostly absorbed, about 10 minutes.

2. Line slow cooker with aluminum foil collar and lightly spray with vegetable oil spray. Microwave fennel, thyme, garlic, and oil in bowl, stirring occasionally, until vegetables are softened, about 5 minutes. Fold fennel mixture, spinach, and ½ cup feta into soaked bread mixture; transfer to prepared slow cooker. Cover and cook until center is set, 4 to 5 hours on low.

3. Turn slow cooker off and remove foil collar. Sprinkle bread pudding with remaining ½ cup feta. Cover and let bread pudding cool for 20 minutes before serving.

Per serving: Cal 280; Fat 12g; Sat Fat 5g; Chol 210mg; Carb 24g; Protein 16g; Fiber 3g; Sodium 890mg

---

QUICK PREP TIP EGG SIZES
If you do not have large eggs on hand, substitutions are possible. See the chart for help in making accurate calculations. For half of an egg, whisk the yolk and white together, measure, and then divide in half.

LARGE		JUMBO	EXTRA-LARGE	MEDIUM
1	=	1	1	1
2	=	1½	2	2
3	=	2½	2½	3½
4	=	3	3½	4½
5	=	4	4	6
6	=	5	5	7

Easy Baked Ziti

Serves 4 • **Cooking Time** 2 to 3 hours on High • **Slow Cooker Size** 5½ to 7 Quarts

✔ **WHY THIS RECIPE WORKS:** Baked ziti usually requires multiple steps, from cooking the pasta, making a sauce, to layering in the cheese, and then a stint in the oven. Our goal was to simplify the process by making this classic dish in a slow cooker. But getting tender pasta and gooey melted cheese from the slow cooker requires a few tricks. First there is the issue of the pasta: Precooked pasta turned mushy and raw pasta didn't fare well either. Instead, we microwaved raw ziti with a little oil before putting it into the slow cooker. We then jump-started the cooking process by adding boiling water to the pasta in the slow cooker before adding the sauce. For the sauce, we tried a variety of canned tomato products, but it was a combination of crushed tomatoes and tomato paste that provided the right depth of flavor along with the aromatics. The last obstacle was the cheese. We wanted to keep this dish low-fat, but fat-free cheese turned rubbery and hard in the slow cooker. The better solution was to use full-fat ricotta and part-skim mozzarella somewhat sparingly. We dolloped on a small amount of each and cooked for an additional 5 minutes. For an accurate measurement of boiling water, bring a full kettle of water to a boil and then measure out the desired amount. For information on making a foil collar, see page 169. You will need an oval slow cooker for this recipe.

8	ounces (2½ cups) ziti
1	teaspoon extra-virgin olive oil
1½	cups boiling water
1	(28-ounce) can crushed tomatoes
1½	tablespoons tomato paste
4	garlic cloves, minced
2	teaspoons minced fresh oregano or ½ teaspoon dried
	Salt and pepper
¼	teaspoon red pepper flakes
4	ounces (½ cup) whole-milk ricotta cheese
3	ounces part-skim mozzarella, shredded (¾ cup)
½	cup chopped fresh basil

1. Line slow cooker with aluminum foil collar and lightly spray with vegetable oil spray. Microwave ziti and oil in bowl at 50 percent power, stirring occasionally, until some pasta pieces look toasted and blistered, 3 to 5 minutes. Transfer hot pasta to prepared slow cooker and immediately stir in boiling water (pasta will sizzle). Stir in crushed tomatoes, tomato paste, garlic, oregano, ½ teaspoon salt, and pepper flakes until evenly combined. Cover and cook until pasta is tender, 2 to 3 hours on high.

2. Remove foil collar. Gently stir pasta, adding hot water as needed to loosen sauce consistency, and season with salt and pepper to taste. Dollop spoonfuls of ricotta on casserole and sprinkle with mozzarella. Cover and cook on high until cheese is melted, about 5 minutes. Sprinkle with basil and serve.

Per serving: Cal 410; Fat 11g; Sat Fat 4.5g; Chol 25mg; Carb 60g; Protein 20g; Fiber 6g; Sodium 920mg *To reduce sodium level to 390mg, use no-salt-added tomatoes.

QUICK PREP TIP **TOASTING PASTA**
Toasting raw pasta with oil in the microwave prevents the pasta from becoming bloated. We find that microwaving the pasta at 50 percent power and stirring it occasionally gently toasts the pasta. However, if you have a weaker microwave, you may need to toast your pasta for a longer period than we've specified in the recipe. If your microwave does not have a power level button, you can toast the pasta on high power for half the amount of time given in the recipe, stirring the pasta more frequently.

Lemony Orzo with Zucchini and Arugula

Serves 4 • **Cooking Time** 1 to 2 hours on High • **Slow Cooker Size** 4 to 7 Quarts

WHY THIS RECIPE WORKS: For an alternative to a classic pasta casserole, we turned to orzo, which pairs well with delicate vegetables and works perfectly in the slow cooker because it cooks best with very little stirring (overmanipulating the orzo causes it to release its starch and become sticky). Toasting the orzo in the microwave before adding it to the slow cooker was the key to an outstanding casserole with tender, not gummy, orzo. Chicken broth formed a solid cooking base for our casserole, and we heated it in the micro-wave to jump-start the cooking. We narrowed down our list of vegetables to zucchini and arugula; onion and garlic added aromatic depth and sweetness. Grated Asiago cheese stirred in at the end made the orzo extra-creamy, arugula added a peppery taste, and lemon zest and juice added brightness that balanced the creamy flavors. A sprinkling of more Asiago cheese to finish was the perfect topping for a healthy cheesy casserole. You will need an oval slow cooker for this recipe.

2½	**cups chicken broth, plus extra as needed**
1	**cup orzo**
1	**onion, chopped fine**
4	**garlic cloves, minced**
1	**teaspoon extra-virgin olive oil**
⅛	**teaspoon red pepper flakes**
1	**pound zucchini, quartered lengthwise and sliced ½ inch thick**
	Salt and pepper
3	**ounces Asiago cheese, grated (¾ cup)**
2	**ounces (2 cups) baby arugula**
1	**teaspoon grated lemon zest plus 1 tablespoon juice**

1. Lightly spray inside of slow cooker with vegetable oil spray. Microwave broth in bowl until steaming, about 3 minutes. In separate bowl, microwave orzo, onion, garlic, oil, and pepper flakes, stirring occasionally, until orzo is lightly toasted, 5 to 7 minutes. Transfer orzo mixture to slow cooker and immedi-ately stir in hot broth, zucchini, and ¼ teaspoon salt. Cover and cook until orzo and zucchini are tender, 1 to 2 hours on high.

2. Gently stir ½ cup Asiago into slow cooker until cheese is melted and orzo is creamy. (Adjust orzo consistency with extra hot broth as needed.) Stir in arugula and lemon zest and juice. Sprinkle casserole with remaining ¼ cup Asiago, cover, and cook on high until cheese is melted and arugula is slightly wilted, about 5 minutes. Serve.

Per serving: Cal 310; Fat 10g; Sat Fat 4.5g; Chol 20mg; Carb 42g; Protein 15g; Fiber 4g; Sodium 690mg *To reduce sodium level to 450mg, use unsalted broth.

SMART SHOPPING ARUGULA

While it is sold in the salad section of almost every grocery store, arugula should not be relegated to a life constantly coated in dressing. That's because its delicate, dark leaves and peppery bite also make it perfect for wilting into soups, stews, and casseroles in a similar way to spinach or Swiss chard. Mature arugula is sold in bunches, usually with roots attached. It can bruise easily and can be very sandy, so wash it thoroughly in several changes of water, gently dry it in a salad spinner, and store it directly in the spinner. Baby arugula requires less attention as it commonly comes prewashed in cellophane bags or plastic containers. For the longest shelf life, store baby arugula in its original container.

Cooking for Two

● EASY PREP   ● VEGETARIAN

French Onion Soup

Serves 2 • **Cooking Time** 8 to 9 hours on Low or 5 to 6 hours on High • **Slow Cooker Size** 4 to 7 Quarts

WHY THIS RECIPE WORKS: This soup is so rich and flavorful and so packed with sweet caramelized onions, no one would ever guess that it was made in a slow cooker. The secret? For the deeply browned flavor that usually comes only with fussy stovetop browning, we microwaved the onions to soften them before adding them to the slow cooker. Given the moist heat of the slow cooker, we had to be inventive in order to infuse the soup with as much concentrated flavor as possible. A small amount of apple butter contributed to the soup's rich, silken texture and complemented the browned sweetness of the onions. For meaty flavor without adding any beef bones or broth, we turned to soy sauce and dried porcini mushrooms, which delivered plenty of umami while keeping the soup vegetarian. We stirred boiling water into the well-browned onions at the end to fill out our soup. Just a few small slices of baguette topped with melted Gruyère were enough to provide the quintessential topping for our soup without going overboard on fat and calories. Check the onions at the beginning of the time range and continue to monitor until they are properly browned; the onions can go from caramelized to burnt very quickly if left too long in a slow cooker. For an accurate measurement of boiling water, bring a full kettle of water to a boil and then measure out the desired amount.

2	onions, halved and sliced ¼ inch thick
⅛	ounce dried porcini mushrooms, rinsed and minced
1	tablespoon unsalted butter
1	teaspoon minced fresh thyme or ¼ teaspoon dried
1½	tablespoons all-purpose flour
3	tablespoons apple butter
2	tablespoons dry sherry
1	tablespoon low-sodium soy sauce
1½	cups boiling water
	Salt and pepper
4	(½-inch-thick) slices baguette
1	ounce Gruyère cheese, shredded (¼ cup)

1. Lightly spray inside of slow cooker with vegetable oil spray. Microwave onions, mushrooms, butter, and thyme in bowl, stirring occasionally, until onions are softened, about 5 minutes; transfer to slow cooker. Whisk flour, apple butter, sherry, and soy sauce together in bowl until smooth, then stir into slow cooker. Cover and cook until onions are softened and deep golden brown, 8 to 9 hours on low or 5 to 6 hours on high.

2. Stir boiling water into slow cooker. Let soup sit until heated through, about 5 minutes. Season with salt and pepper to taste.

3. Just before serving, adjust oven rack 6 inches from broiler element and heat broiler. Place baguette slices on baking sheet and broil until golden brown and crisp on both sides, about 2 minutes per side. Sprinkle Gruyère on toasted bread and continue to broil until cheese is melted, about 2 minutes. Portion soup into individual bowls and top with toasted bread.

Per serving: Cal 440; Fat 13g; Sat Fat 7g; Chol 30mg; Carb 65g; Protein 14g; Fiber 6g; Sodium 800mg

---

QUICK PREP TIP NO-TEARS ONION SLICING
When an onion is cut, the cells that are damaged in the process release sulfuric compounds as well as various enzymes that mix to form a new compound that evaporates in the air and irritates the eyes, causing us to cry. Of all the suggested ways to lessen this teary effect, we've found the best options are to protect the eyes by covering them with goggles or contact lenses, or to introduce a flame (from a candle or gas burner) near the cut onions. The flame changes the activity of the compound that causes the tearing, and contact lenses and goggles simply form a physical barrier that the compound cannot penetrate. So if you want to keep tears at bay when handling onions, light a candle or gas burner or put on some ski goggles.

Chicken and Garden Vegetable Soup

Serves 2 • **Cooking Time** 2 to 3 hours on Low • **Slow Cooker Size** 4 to 7 Quarts

✓ WHY THIS RECIPE WORKS: Creating anything garden fresh in a slow cooker is a tall order, but we beat the odds by developing a recipe for a bright, lively-tasting chicken and vegetable soup. We found that the trick was adding the vegetables in stages. Onion, garlic, and carrot went in at the start so their flavors would deepen and meld into a richly flavored broth. We stirred in yellow squash and peas at the end of cooking so that they would turn tender but not mushy and dull-tasting. For a finishing touch of bright, herbal flavor, we stirred in fresh parsley just before serving. To ensure that our soup was hearty and filling but also healthy, we chose a bone-in split chicken breast. Although breast meat is lean, the bones helped protect the meat so it retained its moisture during cooking. We simply discarded the bones after cooking, shredded the meat, and stirred it back into our soup, giving us juicy, flavorful bites of chicken to complement the soup's fresh vegetable flavor.

1   **teaspoon extra-virgin olive oil**
1   **onion, chopped fine**
1   **carrot, peeled and sliced ¼ inch thick**
1   **tablespoon tomato paste**
2   **garlic cloves, minced**
1   **teaspoon minced fresh thyme or ¼ teaspoon dried**
2   **cups chicken broth**
1   **bay leaf**
     Salt and pepper
1   **(12-ounce) bone-in split chicken breast, skin removed, trimmed of all visible fat**
1   **small yellow summer squash, quartered lengthwise and sliced ¼ inch thick**
½   **cup frozen peas, thawed**
1   **tablespoon chopped fresh parsley**

1. Heat oil in 12-inch skillet over medium heat until shimmering. Add onion and carrot and cook until vegetables are softened, about 5 minutes. Stir in tomato paste, garlic, and thyme and cook until fragrant, about 30 seconds. Stir in 1 cup broth, scraping up any browned bits; transfer to slow cooker.

2. Stir remaining 1 cup broth, bay leaf, and ¼ teaspoon salt into slow cooker. Nestle chicken into slow cooker, cover, and cook until chicken is tender, 2 to 3 hours on low.

3. Transfer chicken to carving board, let cool slightly, then shred into bite-size pieces using 2 forks; discard bones. Discard bay leaf. Stir summer squash into soup, cover, and cook on high until tender, about 20 minutes.

4. Stir in shredded chicken and peas and let sit until heated through, about 5 minutes. Stir in parsley and season with salt and pepper to taste. Serve.

Per serving: Cal 260; Fat 6g; Sat Fat 1g; Chol 70mg; Carb 21g; Protein 32g; Fiber 5g; Sodium 1020mg *To reduce sodium level to 570mg, use unsalted broth.

SMART SHOPPING FROZEN PEAS
Individually frozen right after being shucked from the pod, frozen peas are often sweeter and fresher-tasting than the "fresh" peas that may have spent days in storage. We've seen two varieties in the freezer aisle: regular frozen peas and bags labeled "petite peas" (also called "petit pois" or "baby sweet peas"). We tasted each type with butter, and tasters unanimously favored the smaller peas for their sweeter flavor and creamier texture. Regular peas had tougher skins and mealier interiors. Since both varieties are the same price, we're going with the petite peas from now on.

Asian Beef and Vegetable Soup

Serves 2 • **Cooking Time** 5 to 6 hours on Low or 3 to 4 hours on High • **Slow Cooker Size** 4 to 7 Quarts

✔ WHY THIS RECIPE WORKS: To make a healthy and delicious Asian-style beef soup in the slow cooker, we wanted to add lots of flavor without difficult techniques and hard-to-find ingredients. Spicy ginger and aromatic onion and garlic lent bold flavor, and a hint of sesame oil and dried shiitake mushrooms added depth and richness. Chicken broth won out over beef broth in this soup because it let our aromatic flavors shine through. We chose boneless blade steaks instead of a larger chuck roast because the steaks are easy to buy in small quantities—perfect when cooking for two. They are also relatively lean and still turn meltingly tender in the slow cooker. For a final pop of color and texture, we stirred in snow peas at the end of cooking, microwaving them just beforehand to ensure that they maintained their healthy brightness and crisp texture. Finishing the soup with soy sauce and a little extra ginger helped boost the flavors, and sliced scallions added a burst of freshness.

1	onion, chopped fine
3	garlic cloves, minced
1	tablespoon tomato paste
1	tablespoon grated fresh ginger
1	teaspoon toasted sesame oil
1	cup chicken broth
½	cup water
1	carrot, peeled and sliced ¼ inch thick
¼	ounce dried shiitake mushrooms, rinsed and minced
2	(6-ounce) beef blade steaks, ¾ to 1 inch thick, trimmed of all visible fat and cut into 1-inch pieces
6	ounces sugar snap peas, strings removed, cut into 1-inch pieces
2	scallions, sliced thin
1	tablespoon low-sodium soy sauce, plus extra for seasoning Salt and pepper

1. Microwave onion, garlic, tomato paste, 2 teaspoons ginger, and oil in bowl, stirring occasionally, until onion is softened, about 5 minutes; transfer to slow cooker. Stir in broth, water, carrot, and mushrooms, then stir in beef. Cover and cook until beef is tender, 5 to 6 hours on low or 3 to 4 hours on high.

2. Microwave snap peas with 1 tablespoon water in covered bowl, stirring occasionally, until tender, about 3 minutes. Drain snap peas, then stir into soup along with scallions, soy sauce, and remaining 1 teaspoon ginger. Season with salt, pepper, and extra soy sauce to taste. Serve.

Per serving: Cal 330; Fat 12g; Sat Fat 4.5g; Chol 100mg; Carb 24g; Protein 36g; Fiber 6g; Sodium 740mg *To reduce sodium level to 550mg, use unsalted broth.

QUICK PREP TIP
TRIMMING SNAP PEAS
Using paring knife and your thumb, snip off tip of pea and pull along flat side of pod to remove string at same time.

Hearty Turkey Stew with Squash and Spinach

Serves 2 • **Cooking Time** 3 to 4 hours on Low • **Slow Cooker Size** 4 to 7 Quarts

✔️ **WHY THIS RECIPE WORKS:** For a twist on classic chicken stew, we turned to meaty turkey thighs, pairing them with earthy butternut squash and baby spinach. Garlic, thyme, and red pepper flakes added complex depth of flavor and worked nicely with the mellow taste and silky texture of the butternut squash. We gave the aromatics a jump start in the microwave before adding them to the slow cooker to bloom the seasonings and soften the onion. Delicate baby spinach added freshness and needed to cook for just a few minutes at the end to warm through and wilt into the stew. The amount of spinach may seem like a lot at first, but the leaves wilt down substantially. A sprinkling of grated Parmesan cheese is a must here—its nutty and salty flavor enhances the other flavors in the stew. You can substitute an equal amount of bone-in chicken thighs for the turkey.

1 onion, chopped fine

3 garlic cloves, minced

1 tablespoon tomato paste

1 teaspoon extra-virgin olive oil

1 teaspoon minced fresh thyme or ¼ teaspoon dried

⅛ teaspoon red pepper flakes

1 pound butternut squash, peeled, seeded, and cut into ½-inch pieces (3 cups)

2 cups chicken broth, plus extra as needed

2 teaspoons instant tapioca

1 bay leaf

Salt and pepper

1 pound bone-in turkey thighs, skin removed, trimmed of all visible fat

2 ounces (2 cups) baby spinach

¼ cup grated Parmesan cheese

1. Lightly spray inside of slow cooker with vegetable oil spray. Microwave onion, garlic, tomato paste, oil, thyme, and pepper flakes in bowl, stirring occasionally, until onion is softened, about 5 minutes; transfer to slow cooker. Stir in squash, broth, tapioca, bay leaf, and ¼ teaspoon salt. Nestle turkey into slow cooker, cover, and cook until turkey is tender, 3 to 4 hours on low.

2. Transfer turkey to carving board and let cool slightly. Cut turkey into 1-inch pieces; discard bones. Discard bay leaf.

3. Stir turkey and spinach into stew and let sit until spinach is slightly wilted, about 5 minutes. (Adjust stew consistency with extra hot broth as needed.) Season with salt and pepper to taste. Sprinkle each portion with 2 tablespoons Parmesan before serving.

Per serving: Cal 350; Fat 9g; Sat Fat 2.5g; Chol 100mg; Carb 38g; Protein 36g; Fiber 7g; Sodium 1190mg *To reduce sodium level to 810mg, use unsalted broth.

QUICK PREP TIP SPRAYING YOUR SLOW COOKER

When cooking a smaller amount of food in the slow cooker, as with our scaled-down recipes for two, more evaporation can occur, causing some dishes to stick to the sides of the slow-cooker insert and burn. To avoid this, be sure to spray the sides of the slow-cooker insert with vegetable oil spray before adding any food. (The small amount of oil adds a negligible amount of fat to the recipes.) This not only prevents your dishes from burning but also makes serving and cleanup easier.

Sweet Potato and Mango Curry with Snap Peas

Serves 2 • **Cooking Time** 4 to 5 hours on Low or 3 to 4 hours on High • **Slow Cooker Size** 4 to 7 Quarts

✔ **WHY THIS RECIPE WORKS:** To create a healthy vegetarian curry that was easy to make for two, we chose sweet potato, snap peas, and mango—produce that's easy to buy in small quantities—to pack in both nutrition and Indian flavors. To ensure that all the components cooked evenly, we simmered only the sweet potato in the slow cooker, in a curry- and ginger-studded broth, until it was perfectly tender. Mashing a portion of the sweet potato gave the curry more substantial body. We microwaved the snap peas until they were just crisp-tender, then stirred them into the cooked potato along with chopped fresh mango. Coconut milk was a must for a silky texture, and we eliminated some fat by choosing light coconut milk, preserving its flavor by stirring it in at the end of cooking. To finish our curry with an extra pop of flavor, we stirred in more grated ginger and fresh cilantro. Serve with rice.

1	**tablespoon grated fresh ginger**
2	**garlic cloves, minced**
2	**teaspoons curry powder**
2	**teaspoons tomato paste**
1	**teaspoon canola oil**
1	**sweet potato, peeled and cut into ¾-inch pieces**
1	**cup vegetable broth, plus extra as needed**
	Salt and pepper
6	**ounces sugar snap peas, strings removed, cut into 1-inch pieces**
½	**cup canned light coconut milk**
1	**mango, peeled, pitted, and cut into ½-inch pieces**
2	**tablespoons minced fresh cilantro**

1. Lightly spray inside of slow cooker with vegetable oil spray. Microwave 2 teaspoons ginger, garlic, curry powder, tomato paste, and oil in bowl, stirring occasionally, until fragrant, about 1 minute; transfer to slow cooker. Stir in potato, broth, and ¼ teaspoon salt. Cover and cook until potato is tender, 4 to 5 hours on low or 3 to 4 hours on high.

2. Transfer half of cooked potato to bowl and mash with potato masher until smooth. Microwave snap peas and coconut milk in covered bowl, stirring occasionally, until snap peas are tender, about 4 minutes; stir into curry. Stir in mashed potato, mango, and remaining 1 teaspoon ginger. Let sit until heated through, about 5 minutes. (Adjust curry consistency with extra hot broth as needed.) Stir in cilantro and season with salt and pepper to taste. Serve.

Per serving: Cal 250; Fat 8g; Sat Fat 4g; Chol 0mg; Carb 41g; Protein 4g; Fiber 6g; Sodium 760mg *To reduce sodium level to 450mg, use low-sodium broth.

ON THE SIDE SIMPLE WHITE RICE

Heat 1 teaspoon oil in small saucepan over medium heat until shimmering. Stir in ¾ cup rinsed long-grain white rice and cook until edges of grains begin to turn translucent, about 2 minutes. Stir in 1¼ cups water and ¼ teaspoon salt and bring to boil. Reduce heat to low, cover, and simmer until all liquid is absorbed, 18 to 22 minutes. Remove saucepan from heat. Remove lid, place clean dish towel over saucepan, then replace lid. Let rice sit for 10 minutes, then gently fluff with fork. Serves 2.

Per serving: Cal 250; Fat 2.5g; Sat Fat 0g; Chol 0mg; Carb 52g; Protein 5g; Fiber 0g; Sodium 300mg

Spicy Chipotle Chicken Chili

Serves 2 • **Cooking Time** 2 to 3 hours on Low • **Slow Cooker Size** 4 to 7 Quarts

✓**WHY THIS RECIPE WORKS:** This hearty south-of-the-border chili features a spicy broth with bites of tender shredded chicken and chickpeas. We started by microwaving onion, garlic, and tomato paste plus chili powder and canned chipotle chiles—dried, smoked jalapeños in a chile sauce—for the smoky flavors of our chili. We stirred this mixture into the slow cooker along with chicken broth to make a delicious spicy broth. As the chicken gently cooked in this flavorful liquid, it was slowly infused with the broth's bold flavor. Creamy canned chickpeas were an easy addition to bulk up the chili, and we mashed a portion of the beans after cooking to thicken it. Frozen corn, another easy addition, lent a pop of color and a nice textural contrast when stirred in at the end to just heat through. Bright, herbaceous cilantro, stirred in just before serving, added freshness and balance to our spicy, healthy chili. Serve with your favorite chili garnishes.

1	onion, chopped fine
1	teaspoon canola oil
1	teaspoon minced canned chipotle chile in adobo sauce
1	garlic clove, minced
1	teaspoon tomato paste
½	teaspoon chili powder
1½	cups chicken broth
1	(14-ounce) can chickpeas, rinsed
	Salt and pepper
1	(12-ounce) bone-in split chicken breast, skin removed, trimmed of all visible fat
1	cup frozen corn, thawed
2	tablespoons minced fresh cilantro

1. Lightly spray inside of slow cooker with vegetable oil spray. Microwave onion, oil, chipotle, garlic, tomato paste, and chili powder in bowl, stirring occasionally, until onion is softened, about 5 minutes; transfer to slow cooker. Stir in broth, chickpeas, and ¼ teaspoon salt. Nestle chicken into slow cooker, cover, and cook until chicken is tender, 2 to 3 hours on low.

2. Transfer chicken to carving board, let cool slightly, then shred into bite-size pieces using 2 forks; discard bones.

3. Transfer 1 cup cooked chickpeas to bowl and mash with potato masher until mostly smooth. Stir shredded chicken, mashed chickpeas, and corn into chili and let sit until heated through, about 5 minutes. Stir in cilantro and season with salt and pepper to taste. Serve.

Per serving: Cal 390; Fat 9g; Sat Fat 1g; Chol 70mg; Carb 43g; Protein 35g; Fiber 7g; Sodium 1150mg *To reduce sodium level to 680mg, use unsalted broth and low-sodium beans.

SMART SHOPPING CILANTRO

Cilantro, the fresh leaves and stems of the coriander plant, is a love-it-or-loathe-it herb. It finds the love in Southeast Asian and Latin cuisines, where it's a core ingredient. The flavorful stems can be chopped and used along with the leaves. Because cooking attenuates the flavor, we almost always add cilantro at the end of cooking. Store it like basil with its stems in water, or wrapped in damp paper towels and placed in a plastic bag in the crisper drawer of your refrigerator.

Hearty Vegetarian Chili

Serves 2 • **Cooking Time** 9 to 10 hours on Low or 6 to 7 hours on High • **Slow Cooker Size** 4 to 7 Quarts

✓ WHY THIS RECIPE WORKS: Vegetarian chilis often rely on a mix of beans and vegetables for heartiness, but this combination failed to deliver the meaty depth we were looking for. We wanted a robust chili that was as rich, savory, and deeply satisfying as any meat chili out there, and significantly healthier. We started with dried navy beans, which turned tender and creamy with the long simmer; a combination of chipotle chili in adobo sauce, chili powder, and cumin delivered a subtle heat and warm spice notes. We ramped up the intensity and depth of our chili with soy sauce, dried porcini, and tomato paste, which gave a meaty flavor to our dish. To up the depth of the chili, we tried adding a variety of ingredients, such as rice, nuts, and seeds, but only bulgur provided the textural dimension our chili had been missing, plus it was light on prep. After a quick soak in boiling water, it needed just 10 minutes in the slow cooker to fully soften and absorb the rich flavors. When shopping, don't confuse bulgur with cracked wheat, which has a much longer cooking time and will not work in this recipe. For an accurate measurement of boiling water, bring a full kettle of water to a boil and then measure out the desired amount. Serve with your favorite chili garnishes.

1 onion, chopped fine

2 tablespoons tomato paste

1 tablespoon minced fresh oregano or 1 teaspoon dried

2 teaspoons chili powder

1 teaspoon canola oil

1 teaspoon minced canned chipotle chile in adobo sauce

1 teaspoon ground cumin

¾ cup dried navy beans, picked over and rinsed

1 tablespoon low-sodium soy sauce

¼ ounce dried porcini mushrooms, rinsed and minced

Salt and pepper

¼ cup medium-grind bulgur, rinsed

2 tablespoons minced fresh cilantro

1. Lightly spray inside of slow cooker with vegetable oil spray. Microwave onion, tomato paste, oregano, chili powder, oil, chipotle, and cumin in bowl, stirring occasionally, until onion is softened, about 5 minutes; transfer to slow cooker. Stir in 3 cups water, beans, soy sauce, mushrooms, and ¼ teaspoon salt. Cover and cook until beans are tender, 9 to 10 hours on low or 6 to 7 hours on high.

2. Meanwhile, combine bulgur and 1 cup boiling water in bowl, cover, and let sit until bulgur is softened, about 10 minutes; drain bulgur.

3. Stir softened bulgur into chili, cover, and cook on high until tender, 5 to 10 minutes. (Adjust chili consistency with extra hot water as needed.) Stir in cilantro and season with salt and pepper to taste. Serve.

Per serving: Cal 400; Fat 5g; Sat Fat 0.5g; Chol 0mg; Carb 71g; Protein 21g; Fiber 24g; Sodium 750mg

---

SMART SHOPPING DRIED MUSHROOMS
Like fresh fruits and vegetables, dried mushrooms can vary dramatically in quality from package to package and brand to brand. Always inspect the mushrooms before you buy. Avoid those with small holes, which indicate that the mushroom was perhaps home to pinworms. Instead, look for large, smooth mushrooms, free of worm holes, dust, and grit.

Pesto Chicken with Fennel and Tomato Couscous

Serves 2 • **Cooking Time** 1 to 2 hours on Low • **Slow Cooker Size** 4 to 7 Quarts

✔**WHY THIS RECIPE WORKS:** For a simple, healthy chicken dinner for two with fresh Italian flavors, we combined bone-in chicken breasts with pesto, fennel, and fresh cherry tomatoes. Just 2 tablespoons of prepared basil pesto gave us plenty of bright flavor without adding a lot of fat and kept the tops of the breasts moist as they gently simmered in a simple braising liquid of chicken broth, softened fennel, and garlic. Once the chicken was cooked, we used the flavorful braising liquid, enriched with the chicken's juices and the nutty fennel, to cook couscous for a quick and easy side dish. After 10 minutes, we stirred quartered cherry tomatoes and chopped basil into the couscous before serving for a pop of freshness. Be sure to use regular (or fine-grain) couscous; large-grain couscous, often labeled "Israeli-style," takes much longer to cook and won't work in this recipe. Check the chicken's temperature after 1 hour of cooking and continue to monitor until it registers 160 degrees.

1 **small fennel bulb, stalks discarded, bulb halved, cored, and sliced thin**
1 **teaspoon extra-virgin olive oil**
1 **garlic clove, minced**
½ **cup chicken broth, plus extra as needed**
2 **(12-ounce) bone-in split chicken breasts, skin removed, trimmed of all visible fat**
2 **tablespoons prepared basil pesto**
½ **cup couscous**
1 **tablespoon lemon juice**
1 **tablespoon water**
4 **ounces cherry tomatoes, quartered**
1 **tablespoon chopped fresh basil**
 Salt and pepper

1. Lightly spray inside of slow cooker with vegetable oil spray. Microwave fennel, oil, and garlic in bowl, stirring occasionally, until fennel is softened, about 5 minutes; transfer to slow cooker. Stir in broth. Rub chicken with 1 tablespoon pesto and nestle into slow cooker. Cover and cook until chicken registers 160 degrees, 1 to 2 hours on low.

2. Transfer chicken to plate and tent loosely with aluminum foil. Strain cooking liquid into liquid measuring cup, reserving solids. Reserve ½ cup strained cooking liquid and discard remaining liquid; or add extra hot broth as needed to measure ½ cup. Stir reserved liquid, reserved solids, and couscous into now-empty slow cooker, cover, and cook on high until couscous is tender, about 10 minutes.

3. Meanwhile, whisk lemon juice, water, and remaining 1 tablespoon pesto together in small bowl. Add tomatoes and basil to cooked couscous and fluff with fork to combine. Season with salt and pepper to taste. Serve chicken with couscous and pesto sauce.

Per serving: Cal 550; Fat 16g; Sat Fat 3.5g; Chol 155mg; Carb 42g; Protein 56g; Fiber 5g; Sodium 310mg

---

SMART SHOPPING **BROTH ALTERNATIVES**
When you cook for two, you know the frustration of recipes calling for just half a cup of broth. Luckily, there are a few handy alternatives—bouillon and broth concentrates—that make it easy to use smaller amounts and avoid waste. These dehydrated and concentrated forms of chicken and beef broth are shelf-stable and cost-effective (because you're not paying for the water) and last for up to two years once opened. We particularly like **Better Than Bouillon Chicken Base**, which costs just $5.99 for a jar that makes 38 cups of broth.

Braised Chicken Thighs with Garlicky Spinach

Serves 2 • **Cooking Time** 3 to 4 hours on Low • **Slow Cooker Size** 4 to 7 Quarts

✔ **WHY THIS RECIPE WORKS:** A specialty from the Catalonian region of Spain, sautéed spinach with garlic, raisins, and pine nuts is a simple yet satisfying combination of flavors and textures. To create a complete meal in the slow cooker inspired by this traditional tapas dish, we braised chicken thighs in an aromatic mixture of onion, garlic, and sweet paprika with a bit of tomato paste for depth. We then used the flavorful braising liquid to wilt the spinach and meld all of the flavors. Quick-cooking, delicate spinach may not seem like a good match for the slow cooker, but by adding it for just 15 minutes at the end of cooking, we had perfectly crisp-tender spinach without all of the oil typically needed for sautéing. We placed the cooked thighs on top of the spinach as the leaves cooked, which both kept the chicken warm and moist and weighed down the spinach so it stayed submerged in the liquid. A splash of lemon juice added bright acidity to the spinach and balanced the rich, tender chicken thighs perfectly.

1	onion, chopped fine
4	garlic cloves, sliced thin
2	teaspoons tomato paste
1	teaspoon canola oil
½	teaspoon paprika
⅛	teaspoon red pepper flakes
¼	cup water
4	(6-ounce) bone-in chicken thighs, skin removed, trimmed of all visible fat
	Salt and pepper
12	ounces (12 cups) baby spinach
¼	cup golden raisins
1	tablespoon lemon juice, plus lemon wedges for serving
1	tablespoon toasted pine nuts

1. Lightly spray inside of slow cooker with vegetable oil spray. Microwave onion, garlic, tomato paste, oil, paprika, and pepper flakes in bowl, stirring occasionally, until onion is softened, about 5 minutes; transfer to slow cooker. Stir in water. Season chicken with salt and pepper, place in slow cooker, and turn to coat with onion mixture. Cover and cook until chicken is tender, 3 to 4 hours on low.

2. Transfer chicken to plate. Stir spinach into slow cooker, 1 handful at a time, until slightly wilted. Stir in raisins, then nestle chicken into spinach with any accumulated juices. Cover and cook on high until spinach is fully wilted and tender, about 20 minutes.

3. Transfer chicken to plates. Stir lemon juice and pine nuts into spinach and season with salt and pepper to taste. Serve chicken and spinach with lemon wedges.

Per serving: Cal 480; Fat 15g; Sat Fat 2.5g; Chol 195mg; Carb 44g; Protein 46g; Fiber 11g; Sodium 650mg

---

SMART SHOPPING GARLIC SUBSTITUTES

When garlic is a predominant flavor in a recipe, nothing comes close to fresh. However, garlic substitutes have a long shelf life and require no prep, so in recipes that call for only a clove or two, the convenience may be worth a little loss in flavor. Both granulated garlic and garlic powder are made from garlic cloves that are dehydrated and ground; dehydrated minced garlic is minced while fresh, then dehydrated and packaged, but it must be reconstituted before use. We prefer garlic powder; substitute ¼ teaspoon for every clove of fresh garlic.

Braised Steaks with Horseradish Smashed Potatoes

Serves 2 • **Cooking Time** 8 to 9 hours on Low or 5 to 6 hours on High • **Slow Cooker Size** 4 to 7 Quarts

✓ WHY THIS RECIPE WORKS: We wanted a hearty steak-and-potatoes dinner that required minimal prep and wasn't overloaded with fat. Since blade steaks braise nicely in the slow cooker and are easy to buy in pairs, they were a natural choice. We braised the steaks in a mix of onions, garlic, and tomato paste until they were nearly fall-apart tender. To keep the potatoes separate from the steaks, we used our successful technique of wrapping the potatoes in a cheesecloth bundle, allowing them to steam atop the steaks without inhibiting the meat's doneness. Once they were fully cooked, we smashed the potatoes with a small amount of milk for richness. Spicy horseradish added a kick to the potatoes that paired perfectly with the steaks, and fresh chives added herbal freshness. Buy refrigerated prepared horseradish, not the shelf-stable kind, which contains preservatives and additives. For information on making a cheesecloth bundle, see page 102.

1	onion, chopped fine
4	teaspoons tomato paste
3	garlic cloves, minced
1	teaspoon canola oil
1	cup beef broth
2	(6-ounce) beef blade steaks, ¾ to 1 inch thick, trimmed of all visible fat
	Salt and pepper
1	pound red potatoes, unpeeled, cut into 1-inch pieces
⅓	cup warm milk, plus extra as needed
1	tablespoon prepared horseradish
1	tablespoon minced fresh chives

1. Lightly spray inside of slow cooker with vegetable oil spray. Microwave onion, tomato paste, garlic, and oil in bowl, stirring occasionally, until onion is softened, about 5 minutes; transfer to slow cooker. Stir in broth. Season steaks with salt and pepper and nestle into slow cooker. Loosely tie potatoes in cheesecloth bundle; lay bundle on top of steaks. Cover and cook until beef is tender, 8 to 9 hours on low or 5 to 6 hours on high.

2. Transfer potatoes to large bowl. Transfer steaks to serving platter, tent loosely with aluminum foil, and let rest for 5 minutes.

3. Meanwhile, break potatoes into large chunks with rubber spatula. Fold in warm milk, horseradish, and chives until incorporated and only small chunks of potato remain. (Adjust consistency of potatoes with extra warm milk as needed.) Season with salt and pepper to taste. Season sauce with salt and pepper to taste, drizzle over steaks, and serve with potatoes.

Per serving: Cal 450; Fat 14g; Sat Fat 5g; Chol 100mg; Carb 48g; Protein 37g; Fiber 6g; Sodium 700mg *To reduce sodium level to 490mg, use low-sodium broth.

SMART SHOPPING PREPARED HORSERADISH
Bottled prepared horseradish, which is made with grated horseradish root and vinegar, can taste strikingly different depending on where it is displayed in the store. Shelf-stable products are full of additives and have a far weaker flavor than those found in the refrigerator aisle. We definitely prefer the refrigerated variety, and after a test kitchen tasting, highest marks were given to those with fine (versus coarse) texture and sinus-clearing heat. Our favorite was **Boar's Head All-Natural Horseradish**. Make sure that you don't buy a creamy horseradish sauce, which will add unwanted fat and calories.

Braised Pork Chops with Cranberry-Orange Compote

Serves 2 • **Cooking Time** 2 to 3 hours on Low • **Slow Cooker Size** 4 to 7 Quarts

✔ **WHY THIS RECIPE WORKS:** To keep a pair of pork chops from drying out in the slow cooker, we chose blade-cut pork chops, which provided a balance of dark and light meat, and the moderate amount of fat kept the chops tender throughout braising while also keeping this dish in healthy territory. But even with this cut, we had to limit the chops' exposure to the heat and found it best to stick to the low setting on the slow cooker. We paired this flavorful cut with a simple compote-style sauce made with unsweetened applesauce as its base. Dried cranberries and orange juice flavored the sauce, and shallot and Dijon mustard added depth. A splash of cider vinegar before serving punched up the flavor of our sauce, which paired perfectly with the rich pork chops.

1	shallot, minced
1	teaspoon canola oil
¾	teaspoon minced fresh thyme or ⅛ teaspoon dried
½	cup unsweetened applesauce
⅓	cup dried cranberries
⅓	cup orange juice
2	teaspoons Dijon mustard
2	(8-ounce) bone-in blade-cut pork chops, ¾ inch thick, trimmed
	Salt and pepper
1	teaspoon cider vinegar

1. Lightly spray inside of slow cooker with vegetable oil spray. Microwave shallot, oil, and thyme in bowl until shallot is softened, about 2 minutes; transfer to slow cooker. Stir in applesauce, cranberries, orange juice, and mustard. Season chops with salt and pepper and nestle into slow cooker. Cover and cook until pork is tender, 2 to 3 hours on low.

2. Transfer chops to serving platter, tent loosely with aluminum foil, and let rest for 5 minutes. Using large spoon, skim any white foam from surface of sauce. Stir in vinegar and season with salt and pepper to taste. Spoon sauce over chops and serve.

Per serving: Cal 340; Fat 11g; Sat Fat 3g; Chol 75mg; Carb 32g; Protein 28g; Fiber 2g; Sodium 360mg

---

ON THE SIDE BUTTERMILK MASHED POTATOES
Cover 1 pound Yukon Gold potatoes, peeled and sliced ½ inch thick, with water in medium saucepan and add 1 tablespoon salt. Bring to boil, then reduce to simmer and cook until tender, 12 to 15 minutes. Drain potatoes, wipe pot dry, then return potatoes to pot. Mash potatoes with potato masher until few small lumps remain. Fold in ⅓ cup buttermilk and 1 tablespoon melted butter. Season with salt and pepper to taste. Serves 2.

Per serving: Cal 260; Fat 6g; Sat Fat 3.5g; Chol 15mg; Carb 42g; Protein 7g; Fiber 3g; Sodium 350mg

Pork Tenderloin with Spiced Bulgur Salad

Serves 2 • **Cooking Time** 1 to 2 hours on Low • **Slow Cooker Size** 4 to 7 Quarts

✓ **WHY THIS RECIPE WORKS:** Bulgur, a staple in Middle Eastern cooking, is high in fiber and protein, yet low in fat and calories, making it a particularly healthy choice to accompany a lean pork tenderloin. We seasoned the pork with warm spices and cooked it in the slow cooker along with the bulgur until both were perfectly tender, the gentle cooking environment preserving the pork's moisture. To transform the bulgur into a satisfying side dish, we stirred in tart pomegranate seeds, fresh mint, and tangy feta cheese. When shopping, don't confuse bulgur with cracked wheat, which has a much longer cooking time and will not work in this recipe. Because it is cooked gently and not browned, the tenderloin will be rosy throughout. Check the tenderloin's temperature after about 1 hour of cooking and continue to monitor until it registers 145 degrees. You will need an oval slow cooker for this recipe.

1	**shallot, minced**
1	**tablespoon extra-virgin olive oil**
1	**garlic clove, minced**
1	**cup chicken broth**
½	**cup medium-grind bulgur, rinsed**
¼	**teaspoon ground cinnamon**
	Pinch cayenne pepper
1	**(12-ounce) pork tenderloin,** **trimmed of all visible fat**
	Salt and pepper
¼	**cup pomegranate seeds**
1	**ounce feta cheese,** **crumbled (¼ cup)**
2	**tablespoons chopped fresh mint**
1	**tablespoon lemon juice**
2	**teaspoons molasses**
1	**teaspoon honey**

1. Lightly spray inside of slow cooker with vegetable oil spray. Microwave shallot, 1 teaspoon oil, and garlic in bowl until fragrant, about 30 seconds; transfer to slow cooker. Stir in broth and bulgur.

2. Microwave 1 teaspoon oil, cinnamon, cayenne in bowl until fragrant, about 30 seconds; let cool slightly. Rub tenderloin with spice mixture and season with salt and pepper. Nestle tenderloin into slow cooker, cover, and cook until pork registers 145 degrees, 1 to 2 hours on low.

3. Transfer pork to carving board, brushing any bulgur that sticks to pork back into slow cooker. Tent tenderloin loosely with aluminum foil and let rest for 5 minutes.

4. Drain bulgur mixture, if necessary, and return to now-empty slow cooker. Add pomegranate seeds, feta, and mint to bulgur mixture and fluff with fork to combine. Season with salt and pepper to taste. Whisk lemon juice, molasses, honey, and remaining 1 teaspoon oil together in bowl. Slice pork ¼ inch thick. Serve pork with bulgur salad and dressing.

Per serving: Cal 490; Fat 16g; Sat Fat 4.5g; Chol 125mg; Carb 44g; Protein 45g; Fiber 8g; Sodium 630mg *To reduce sodium level to 440mg, use unsalted broth.

QUICK PREP TIP RELEASING POMEGRANATE SEEDS
The hundreds of small, sparkling crimson kernels inside a pomegranate are tart, slightly crunchy, and completely edible—seed and all. To release the kernels with less mess (the juice stains), halve the pomegranate and submerge it in a bowl of water. As you gently pull it apart, the seeds will sink, separating from the bitter pith and membrane that hold them.

Poached Salmon with Creamy Cucumber-Dill Salad

Serves 2 • **Cooking Time** About 1 hour on Low • **Slow Cooker Size** 4 to 7 Quarts

✓**WHY THIS RECIPE WORKS:** Rather than poach our salmon on the stovetop where we'd have to carefully monitor the heat level, we took advantage of the walk-away convenience of the slow cooker. To prevent the bottom of our salmon from overcooking, we rested our fillets on lemon slices and dill stems, then added a small amount of wine and water to the slow cooker to create a moist cooking environment. For a fresh and light side dish, we mixed together a simple cucumber salad dressed with Greek yogurt, dill, and lemon juice. Use salmon fillets of similar thickness so that they cook at the same rate. Leave the skin on the salmon to keep the bottom of the fillets from becoming overcooked and ensure the fillets stay together when removed from the slow cooker. Check the salmon's temperature after 45 minutes of cooking and continue to monitor until it registers 135 degrees. For information on making a foil sling, see page 129.

1   **lemon, sliced ¼ inch thick, plus 1 tablespoon juice**

2   **tablespoons minced fresh dill, stems reserved**

¼   **cup dry white wine**

2   **(6-ounce) skin-on salmon fillets, 1 to 1½ inches thick**
    Salt and pepper

¼   **cup 2 percent Greek yogurt**

1   **cucumber, peeled, halved lengthwise, seeded, and sliced thin**

1. Fold sheet of aluminum foil into 12 by 9-inch sling; press widthwise into slow cooker. Arrange lemon slices in single layer in bottom of prepared slow cooker. Scatter dill stems over lemon. Pour wine into slow cooker, then add water until liquid level is even with lemon slices (about ¼ cup water). Season salmon with salt and pepper and place skin side down on top of lemon. Cover and cook until salmon is opaque throughout when checked with tip of paring knife and registers 135 degrees (for medium), about 1 hour on low.

2. Meanwhile, whisk yogurt, lemon juice, and minced dill together in medium bowl. Stir in cucumber and season with salt and pepper to taste.

3. Using sling, transfer salmon to baking sheet. Gently lift and tilt fillets with spatula to remove dill stems and lemon slices and transfer to plates; discard poaching liquid. Serve with salad.

Per serving (wild salmon): Cal 270; Fat 12g; Sat Fat 2g; Chol 95mg; Carb 4g; Protein 37g; Fiber 1g; Sodium 230mg

Per serving (farmed salmon): Cal 390; Fat 24g; Sat Fat 6g; Chol 95mg; Carb 4g; Protein 38g; Fiber 1g; Sodium 260mg

QUICK PREP TIP
SEEDING A CUCUMBER
Peel and halve cucumber lengthwise. Run small spoon inside each cucumber half to scoop out seeds and surrounding liquid.

Vegetable Enchiladas with Poblanos and Beans

Serves 2 • **Cooking Time** About 1 hour on Low • **Slow Cooker Size** 4 to 7 Quarts

✔ **WHY THIS RECIPE WORKS:** Preparing enchiladas can be a labor-intensive endeavor, but it doesn't have to be. We streamlined this dish and turned it into a meatless weeknight meal. First, we chose a hearty filling and bold flavors that work well in the slow cooker. Nutrient-rich beans were a given for bulk and protein. Zucchini, corn, and tomatoes were all in the running, but poblano chiles won over tasters with their noticeable but mild kick. For the best texture and flavor, we decided to sauté the poblanos with aromatics and a robust selection of spices—chili powder, cumin, and coriander—before mixing them with the beans. To keep this dish light and fresh-tasting, we chose tomatillo salsa over heavier red enchilada sauce and included a small amount of Monterey Jack cheese for the filling and melted cheese topping. Once filled, we placed the enchiladas seam side down in the slow cooker and nestled them tightly together to ensure that they wouldn't fall apart during cooking. Jarred tomatillo salsa is also called "salsa verde."

1	cup canned black beans, rinsed
1	teaspoon canola oil
1	poblano chile, stemmed, seeded, and chopped
1	onion, chopped fine
2	garlic cloves, minced
½	teaspoon chili powder
¼	teaspoon ground cumin
⅛	teaspoon ground coriander
1	cup jarred tomatillo salsa
2	ounces Monterey Jack cheese, shredded (½ cup)
	Salt and pepper
4	(6-inch) corn tortillas

1. Mash ½ cup beans in bowl with potato masher until smooth. Heat oil in 12-inch nonstick skillet over medium heat until shimmering. Add poblano and onion and cook until softened and lightly browned, 8 to 10 minutes. Stir in garlic, chili powder, cumin, and coriander and cook until fragrant, about 30 seconds. Off heat, stir in mashed beans, ¼ cup tomatillo salsa, ¼ cup Monterey Jack, and remaining ½ cup whole beans. Season with salt and pepper to taste.

2. Lightly spray inside of slow cooker with vegetable oil spray. Spread ¼ cup tomatillo salsa in bottom of slow cooker. Stack tortillas, wrap in damp dish towel, and place on plate; microwave until warm and pliable, about 1 minute.

3. Working with 1 warm tortilla at a time, spread ⅓ cup filling across center of tortilla, roll tortilla tightly around filling, and place side by side in prepared slow cooker, seam side down. Pour remaining ½ cup tomatillo salsa over enchiladas, covering tortillas completely, then sprinkle remaining ¼ cup Monterey Jack across center of enchiladas. Cover and cook until enchiladas are heated through, about 1 hour on low. Serve.

Per serving: Cal 410; Fat 15g; Sat Fat 5g; Chol 30mg; Carb 55g; Protein 17g; Fiber 12g; Sodium 1090mg *To reduce sodium level to 950mg, use low-sodium beans.

ON THE SIDE CLASSIC GUACAMOLE
Mash 1 pitted and peeled avocado in medium bowl with potato masher (or fork) until mostly smooth. Fold in 3 tablespoons minced fresh cilantro, 1 thinly sliced scallion, ½ minced jalapeño chile, ¼ teaspoon grated lime zest plus 1 tablespoon juice, and 1 small minced garlic clove. Season with salt and pepper to taste. Makes ¾ cup. (Recipe can be doubled.)

Per serving: Cal 45; Fat 3.5g; Sat Fat 0.5g; Chol 0mg; Carb 3g; Protein 1g; Fiber 2g; Sodium 0mg

Stuffed Acorn Squash

Serves 2 • **Cooking Time** 2 to 3 hours on High • **Slow Cooker Size** 4 to 7 Quarts

✓**WHY THIS RECIPE WORKS:** Quinoa, often called a "superfood" because of its exceptional nutritional profile, has an appealing texture and nutty flavor. For a healthier version of stuffed acorn squash, quinoa was a natural choice over the typical couscous-based fillings in many recipes. To keep prep simple, we wanted to cook the quinoa in the microwave with our aromatics. We found that this worked well as long as we let the quinoa sit undisturbed for a few minutes after cooking to fully absorb the water. Shallot, garlic, and thyme added savory notes, and a small amount of goat cheese added a pleasant tang and richness as it bound the stuffing together. Dried cranberries complemented the nutty flavor of the quinoa and added a pop of color to the mixture. Once filled, we placed the squash halves in the slow cooker with a small amount of water to help them steam, and in just a couple of hours we had perfectly tender squash. A sprinkling of toasted pecans added a welcome crunch, and minced tarragon brought an herbal freshness that completed this flavorful and healthy dish. We like the convenience of prewashed quinoa; rinsing removes the quinoa's bitter protective coating (called saponin). If you buy unwashed quinoa (or if you are unsure if it's washed), rinse it before cooking.

⅓ **cup prewashed quinoa**

1 **shallot, minced**

2 **garlic cloves, minced**

1 **teaspoon minced fresh thyme or ¼ teaspoon dried**
Salt and pepper

2 **ounces goat cheese, crumbled (½ cup)**

⅓ **cup dried cranberries**

1 **small acorn squash (1 pound), halved pole to pole and seeded**

2 **tablespoons chopped pecans, toasted**

1 **tablespoon minced fresh tarragon**

1. Microwave 1 cup water, quinoa, shallot, garlic, thyme, and ¼ teaspoon salt in large bowl, stirring occasionally, until almost all water is absorbed, 7 to 10 minutes. Cover quinoa and let sit until remaining water has been absorbed, about 10 minutes. Fluff quinoa with fork, then gently fold in goat cheese and cranberries.

2. Pour ½ cup water into slow cooker. Season squash with salt and pepper. Mound quinoa mixture into squash and pack lightly with spoon. Transfer squash to slow cooker, cover, and cook until squash is tender, 2 to 3 hours on high.

3. Using tongs, transfer squash halves to plates and sprinkle with pecans and tarragon. Serve.

Per serving: Cal 400; Fat 13g; Sat Fat 5g; Chol 15mg; Carb 63g; Protein 12g; Fiber 8g; Sodium 410mg

---

SMART SHOPPING GOAT CHEESE
Goat cheese boasts an assertive, tangy flavor and a creamy-yet-crumbly texture that works well in many dishes, from salads and appetizers to pastas and pizza. To find the best one, we tasted nine brands plain and baked, rating them on flavor, texture, and tanginess. Our favorite goat cheese is **Laura Chenel's Chèvre Fresh Chèvre Log**, which tasters found to be "rich-tasting" with a "grassy" and "tangy" finish. It was "smooth" and "creamy" both unheated and baked, and it kept its "lemony, bright flavor."

Creamy Farro with Swiss Chard

Serves 2 • **Cooking Time** 3 to 4 hours on Low or 2 to 3 hours on High • **Slow Cooker Size** 4 to 7 Quarts

✔ **WHY THIS RECIPE WORKS:** A healthy whole-grain staple in Italian cooking, farro is a hearty grain that lends itself particularly well to the slow cooker. For extra nutty flavor, we briefly toasted the grains in the microwave. Sweet, earthy carrots paired well with the nutty farro and required only the simplest of aromatics—onion, garlic, and fresh thyme—to round out the flavors. Thoroughly stirring the cooked farro with some additional hot water helped to release starches in the grains that gave the dish a pleasant creaminess. To balance the sweet, nutty flavors and boost nutrition, we added slightly bitter Swiss chard to the mix. Since it required minimal cooking time, we stirred in the chard near the end of cooking so that it would turn just tender but retain its brightness. Do not substitute pearl, quick-cooking, or presteamed farro for the whole farro in this recipe; you may need to read the ingredient list on the package carefully to determine if the farro is presteamed. For an accurate measurement of boiling water, bring a full kettle of water to a boil and then measure out the desired amount.

½ cup whole farro
1 onion, chopped fine
1 tablespoon extra-virgin olive oil
1 garlic clove, minced
½ teaspoon minced fresh thyme or ⅛ teaspoon dried
3 carrots, peeled, quartered lengthwise, and sliced ¼ inch thick
1 cup vegetable broth
Salt and pepper
¼ cup grated Parmesan cheese
½–1 cup boiling water
8 ounces Swiss chard, stemmed and cut into 1-inch pieces

1. Lightly spray inside of slow cooker with vegetable oil spray. Microwave farro, onion, 1 teaspoon oil, garlic, and thyme in bowl, stirring occasionally, until onion is softened, about 5 minutes; transfer to slow cooker. Stir in carrots, broth, and ¼ teaspoon salt. Cover and cook until farro is tender, 3 to 4 hours on low or 2 to 3 hours on high.

2. Stir Parmesan and ½ cup boiling water into farro until mixture is creamy but still somewhat thin. If farro is stiff and thick, add remaining water as needed, ¼ cup at a time, until mixture is thinned. Stir in Swiss chard, one handful at a time, until slightly wilted. Cover and cook on high until chard is softened, about 20 minutes. (Adjust farro consistency with extra boiling water as needed.) Season with salt and pepper to taste. Drizzle each portion with 1 teaspoon oil before serving.

Per serving: Cal 360; Fat 12g; Sat Fat 2g; Chol 5mg; Carb 57g; Protein 12g; Fiber 9g; Sodium 980mg *To reduce sodium level to 670mg, use low-sodium broth.

QUICK PREP TIP STORING PARMESAN CHEESE
After conducting a number of tests to find the best storage method for Parmesan wedges, we found that the best way to preserve their flavor and texture is to wrap them in parchment paper, then aluminum foil. However, if you're hanging onto just a small piece of cheese, tossing it into a zipper-lock bag works almost as well; just be sure to squeeze out as much air as possible before fastening the seal. Note that these methods also work for Pecorino Romano.

Warm Southwestern Lentil and Bean Salad

Serves 2 • **Cooking Time** 4 to 5 hours on Low or 3 to 4 hours on High • **Slow Cooker Size** 4 to 7 Quarts

✔ **WHY THIS RECIPE WORKS:** The most important step in making a lentil salad is perfecting the cooking of the lentils so they maintain their shape and firm-tender bite. Often, the best way to perfectly cook lentils is in the oven, which heats them gently and uniformly. We found that the slow cooker acted a lot like an oven in this instance, cooking the lentils without any hands-on monitoring. Adding a little salt and lime juice to the cooking liquid (we used vegetable broth) gave us lentils that were firm yet creamy. Once we had perfectly cooked lentils, all we had left to do was to pair the healthy legumes with boldly flavored ingredients. We chose spicy chipotle chile in adobo sauce and earthy oregano and enhanced the Southwestern flavors at the end by adding corn, tomatoes, lime juice, and *queso fresco*. To make this dish even heartier, we added canned pinto beans to the slow cooker along with the lentils. Fresh cilantro leaves and crunchy pepitas added brightness and crunch to our hearty vegetarian entrée salad. We prefer French green lentils, or *lentilles du Puy*, for this recipe, but it will work with any type of lentil except red or yellow. You can serve this dish over mixed greens if desired.

1 cup vegetable broth

1 cup canned pinto beans, rinsed

⅔ cup lentils, picked over and rinsed

3 tablespoons lime juice (2 limes)

2 garlic cloves, minced

1½ teaspoons minced canned chipotle chile in adobo sauce

1 teaspoon minced fresh oregano or ¼ teaspoon dried
 Salt and pepper

6 ounces cherry tomatoes, halved

½ cup frozen corn, thawed

1 shallot, sliced thin

2 teaspoons extra-virgin olive oil

½ cup cilantro leaves

1 ounce queso fresco, crumbled (¼ cup)

1 tablespoon raw pepitas, toasted

1. Lightly spray inside of slow cooker with vegetable oil spray. Combine broth, beans, lentils, 1 tablespoon lime juice, garlic, chipotle, oregano, and ½ teaspoon salt in slow cooker. Cover and cook until lentils are tender, 4 to 5 hours on low or 3 to 4 hours on high.

2. Gently stir tomatoes, corn, shallot, oil, and remaining 2 tablespoons lime juice into lentils. Season with salt and pepper to taste. Sprinkle with cilantro, queso fresco, and pepitas. Serve.

Per serving: Cal 500; Fat 12g; Sat Fat 2g; Chol 5mg; Carb 78g; Protein 26g; Fiber 18g; Sodium 1250mg *To reduce sodium level to 800mg, use low-sodium broth and low-sodium beans.

SMART SHOPPING PEPITAS
Hulled pumpkin seed kernels, also known as pepitas, are actually one of the most flavorful seeds out there that are also high in important nutrients. They are high in manganese, magnesium, iron, copper, vitamin K, and zinc, as well as being a good source of protein (a quarter cup contains about 8 to 9 grams). When toasted (which is how we like them best), they have a nutty, slightly sweet flavor that makes them the perfect addition to many dishes. They add a wonderful textural crunch to salads, such as our Warm Southwestern Lentil and Bean Salad, or sprinkled over your favorite fall soup—think Creamy Butternut Squash and Apple Soup (page 32). A handful sprinkled over yogurt is also a big winner.

Vegetable Mains and Sides

● EASY PREP   ● VEGETARIAN

Mediterranean Braised Green Beans

Serves 6 • **Cooking Time** 7 to 8 hours on Low or 4 to 5 hours on High • **Slow Cooker Size** 5½ to 7 Quarts

☑ WHY THIS RECIPE WORKS: Slowly braising green beans with the bold flavors of the Mediterranean turns them meltingly tender and infuses them with big taste. Instead of using canned tomatoes, which made this dish too watery, we used tomato paste to provide deep flavor and minimize the amount of liquid. Thinly sliced onion and garlic and oregano gave the dish an aromatic backbone. For subtle heat, we included a small amount of red pepper flakes. Microwaving our aromatics briefly worked to jump-start their cooking and made for a more complex flavor. We added briny capers at the end of cooking rather than the beginning, which made them stand out among the beans and provided a salty kick. The dish needed a little added richness to meld all the ingredients at the end, so we simply added a tablespoon of olive oil.

1	onion, halved and sliced thin
4	teaspoons extra-virgin olive oil
3	garlic cloves, sliced thin
	Salt and pepper
2	teaspoons minced fresh oregano or ½ teaspoon dried
⅛	teaspoon red pepper flakes
½	cup water
⅓	cup tomato paste
2	pounds green beans, trimmed
2	tablespoons capers, rinsed and minced
1	tablespoon minced fresh parsley

1. Microwave onion, 1 teaspoon oil, garlic, ¾ teaspoon salt, oregano, and pepper flakes in bowl, stirring occasionally, until onion is softened, about 5 minutes; transfer to slow cooker. Stir in water and tomato paste, then stir in beans. Cover and cook until beans are tender, 7 to 8 hours on low or 4 to 5 hours on high.

2. Stir in remaining 1 tablespoon oil, capers, and parsley. Season with salt and pepper to taste. Serve. (Green beans can be held on warm or low setting for up to 2 hours.)

Per serving: Cal 90; Fat 3.5g; Sat Fat 0.5g; Chol 0mg; Carb 15g; Protein 3g; Fiber 5g; Sodium 490mg

SMART SHOPPING CAPERS
An ideal caper has the perfect balance of saltiness, sweetness, acidity, and crunch. These sun-dried, pickled flower buds have a strong flavor that develops as they are cured, either immersed in a salty brine or packed in salt. From previous tastings we knew we preferred the compact size and slight crunch of tiny nonpareil capers, so we tasted six nationally available supermarket brands, evaluating them on their sharpness, saltiness, and overall appeal. The winner, **Reese Non-Pareil Capers**, had a bold, salty flavor that tasters loved.

Sesame-Ginger Braised Green Beans

Serves 6 • **Cooking Time** 7 to 8 hours on Low or 4 to 5 hours on High • **Slow Cooker Size** 5½ to 7 Quarts

✓**WHY THIS RECIPE WORKS:** Asian-style green beans are a classic and healthy vegetable side; we moved them to the slow cooker to turn them into a hands-off dish that could braise all day. Cooking just half of the ginger and sesame oil with the green beans infused the beans with flavor, and stirring in a fresh portion of each once the beans were tender preserved their vibrant taste. A mixture of aromatics, hoisin, and a tablespoon of water created a sauce with the perfect consistency for coating the green beans as they gently simmered and soaked up flavor. Finally, sprinkling the beans with toasted sesame seeds and thinly sliced scallions provided the finishing touch for this easy vegetable side.

1	onion, chopped fine
2	teaspoons toasted sesame oil
2	teaspoons grated fresh ginger
2	garlic cloves, minced
⅓	cup hoisin sauce
1	tablespoon water
2	pounds green beans, trimmed
	Salt and pepper
2	scallions, sliced thin
1	teaspoon sesame seeds, toasted

1. Microwave onion, 1 teaspoon oil, 1 teaspoon ginger, and garlic in bowl, stirring occasionally, until onion is softened, about 5 minutes; transfer to slow cooker. Stir in hoisin and water, then stir in beans. Cover and cook until beans are tender, 7 to 8 hours on low or 4 to 5 hours on high.

2. Stir in remaining 1 teaspoon oil and remaining 1 teaspoon ginger. Season with salt and pepper to taste. (Green beans can be held on warm or low setting for up to 2 hours.) Sprinkle with scallions and sesame seeds before serving.

Per serving: Cal 90; Fat 2g; Sat Fat 0g; Chol 0mg; Carb 20g; Protein 3g; Fiber 4g; Sodium 490mg

---

SMART SHOPPING SESAME OIL
Raw sesame oil, which is very mild and light in color, is used mostly for cooking, while toasted sesame oil, which has a deep amber color, is primarily used for seasoning because of its intense flavor. For the biggest hit of flavor, we prefer to use toasted sesame oil. Just a little of this oil will give dishes a deep, nutty flavor—but too much will be overpowering.

Beet and Wheat Berry Salad with Arugula and Apples

Serves 6 • **Cooking Time** 10 to 11 hours on Low or 7 to 8 hours on High • **Slow Cooker Size** 5½ to 7 Quarts

✔ **WHY THIS RECIPE WORKS:** This hearty vegetarian entrée features nutty wheat berries, earthy beets, crisp apples, and fresh arugula, all tied together at the end with a lively vinaigrette and fresh goat cheese. The flavor of wheat berries works especially well in salads and pairs nicely with the sweet and rich beets. Even better, the wheat berries can be slowly simmered alongside the beets, which we wrapped in foil to keep the cooking even and the deep color from bleeding into the grain. Minced garlic and thyme, added right to the slow cooker, provided an aromatic backbone. Once the wheat berries were tender, we drained them and dressed them with a simple red wine vinaigrette. Baby arugula and Granny Smith apples rounded out our salad with their bitter and sweet-tart notes, and crumbled goat cheese provided a creamy, tangy counterpoint to the wheat berries and beets. To ensure even cooking, we recommend using beets that are similar in size—roughly 3 inches in diameter. Once fully cooked, the wheat berries will still retain a pleasingly chewy texture.

1 **cup wheat berries**
2 **garlic cloves, minced**
2 **teaspoons minced fresh thyme or ½ teaspoon dried**
   Salt and pepper
1 **pound beets, trimmed**
3 **tablespoons extra-virgin olive oil**
3 **tablespoons red wine vinegar**
   Pinch sugar
4 **ounces (4 cups) baby arugula**
1 **Granny Smith apple, peeled, cored, halved, and cut into ¼-inch-thick wedges**
4 **ounces goat cheese, crumbled (1 cup)**

1. Combine 5 cups water, wheat berries, garlic, thyme, and ½ teaspoon salt in slow cooker. Wrap beets individually in aluminum foil and place in slow cooker. Cover and cook until wheat berries and beets are tender, 10 to 11 hours on low or 7 to 8 hours on high.

2. Transfer beets to cutting board, open foil, and let cool. Rub off beet skins with paper towels and cut beets into ½-inch-thick wedges.

3. Drain wheat berries and return to now-empty slow cooker. Whisk oil, vinegar, ½ teaspoon salt, pinch pepper, and sugar together in bowl; stir into wheat berries. Gently fold in beets, arugula, and apple and season with salt and pepper to taste. Sprinkle with goat cheese and serve.

Per serving: Cal 280; Fat 12g; Sat Fat 4g; Chol 10mg; Carb 35g; Protein 9g; Fiber 7g; Sodium 430mg

---

QUICK PREP TIP REMOVING BEET SKINS
Once beets are cooled completely, cradle each beet in your hand with several layers of paper towels, then gently rub off skin.

Beets with Oranges and Walnuts

Serves 4 • **Cooking Time** 6 to 7 hours on Low or 4 to 5 hours on High • **Slow Cooker Size** 4 to 7 Quarts

✔ **WHY THIS RECIPE WORKS:** For a vegetable side with enticing colors, flavors, and textures, we used tangy oranges, vibrant beets, hearty walnuts, and a balanced vinaigrette. To ensure even cooking, we recommend using beets that are similar in size—roughly 3 inches in diameter.

1½ **pounds beets, trimmed**
2 **oranges**
¼ **cup white wine vinegar**
1½ **tablespoons extra-virgin olive oil**
1 **tablespoon honey**
   Salt and pepper
¼ **cup walnuts, toasted and chopped coarse**
2 **tablespoons minced fresh chives**

1. Wrap beets individually in aluminum foil and place in slow cooker. Add ½ cup water, cover, and cook until beets are tender, 6 to 7 hours on low or 4 to 5 hours on high.

2. Transfer beets to cutting board, open foil, and let cool; discard cooking liquid. Rub off beet skins with paper towels and cut beets into ½-inch-thick wedges.

3. Cut away peel and pith from oranges. Quarter oranges and slice crosswise into ½-inch-thick pieces. Whisk vinegar, oil, and honey together in large bowl. Add beets and orange pieces and toss to coat. Season with salt and pepper to taste. Sprinkle with walnuts and chives and serve.

Per serving: Cal 210; Fat 10g; Sat Fat 1g; Chol 0mg; Carb 29g; Protein 4g; Fiber 7g; Sodium 135mg

---

Beets with Pepitas and Queso Fresco

Serves 4 • **Cooking Time** 6 to 7 hours on Low or 4 to 5 hours on High • **Slow Cooker Size** 4 to 7 Quarts

✔ **WHY THIS RECIPE WORKS:** Crumbled *queso fresco*, toasted pepitas, and fresh cilantro turn this slow-cooked vegetable side into an impressive restaurant-style dish. To ensure even cooking, we recommend using beets that are similar in size—roughly 3 inches in diameter.

1½ **pounds beets, trimmed**
1½ **tablespoons extra-virgin olive oil**
1 **tablespoon honey**
2 **teaspoons grated lime zest plus 3 tablespoons juice**
½ **teaspoon minced canned chipotle chile in adobo sauce**
   Salt and pepper
1½ **ounces queso fresco, crumbled (⅓ cup)**
¼ **cup fresh cilantro leaves**
2 **tablespoons pepitas, toasted**

1. Wrap beets individually in aluminum foil and place in slow cooker. Add ½ cup water, cover, and cook until beets are tender, 6 to 7 hours on low or 4 to 5 hours on high.

2. Transfer beets to cutting board, open foil, and let cool; discard cooking liquid. Rub off beet skins with paper towels and cut beets into ½-inch-thick wedges.

3. Whisk oil, honey, lime zest and juice, and chipotle together in large bowl. Add beets and toss to coat. Season with salt and pepper to taste. Sprinkle with queso fresco, cilantro, and pepitas and serve.

Per serving: Cal 180; Fat 8g; Sat Fat 1.5g; Chol 5mg; Carb 23g; Protein 5g; Fiber 5g; Sodium 150mg

Braised Red Cabbage with Fennel and Orange

Serves 6 • **Cooking Time** 5 to 6 hours on Low or 3 to 4 hours on High • **Slow Cooker Size** 5½ to 7 Quarts

VEGETARIAN

✓ **WHY THIS RECIPE WORKS:** For a fresh take on braised cabbage, we added fennel to this slow-cooker version of the classic. The slow cooker, with its enclosed heat environment, is perfect for braising cabbage while trapping the enticing aromas of the fennel. However, adding the vegetables directly to the slow cooker left them too crunchy for our liking. To get the texture just right, we precooked the cabbage along with the fennel in the microwave to soften them slightly. For a braising liquid that would add another flavor dimension to this dish, we selected sweet and tangy orange juice, enhancing it with spices and herbs such as fennel seeds, bay leaves, and thyme. A bit of sugar rounded out the sweetness, and vinegar perked up the flavors and added balance.

1	head red cabbage (2 pounds), cored and shredded
2	fennel bulbs, 2 tablespoons fronds minced, stalks discarded, bulbs halved, cored, and sliced ½ inch thick
1	onion, chopped fine
2	teaspoons canola oil
	Salt and pepper
1	cup orange juice (2 oranges)
2	tablespoons packed light brown sugar, plus extra as needed
2	sprigs fresh thyme
½	teaspoon fennel seeds
3	bay leaves
2	tablespoons white wine vinegar, plus extra as needed

1. Microwave cabbage, fennel slices, onion, oil, and ½ teaspoon salt in covered bowl, stirring occasionally, until vegetables are softened, 15 to 20 minutes. Drain cabbage mixture and transfer to slow cooker. Stir in orange juice, 1 tablespoon sugar, thyme sprigs, fennel seeds, and bay leaves. Cover and cook until cabbage is tender, 5 to 6 hours on low or 3 to 4 hours on high.

2. Discard thyme sprigs and bay leaves. Stir in vinegar and remaining 1 tablespoon sugar. Season with salt, pepper, extra sugar, and extra vinegar to taste. (Cabbage can be held on warm or low setting for up to 2 hours.) Sprinkle with fennel fronds before serving.

Per serving: Cal 130; Fat 2g; Sat Fat 0g; Chol 0mg; Carb 28g; Protein 4g; Fiber 6g; Sodium 280mg

---

QUICK PREP TIP SHREDDING CABBAGE
Cut cabbage into quarters, then trim and discard hard core. Separate cabbage into small stacks of leaves that flatten when pressed and slice into ¼-inch-thick strips.

Glazed Carrots with Peas and Mint

Serves 6 • **Cooking Time** 5 to 6 hours on Low or 3 to 4 hours on High • **Slow Cooker Size** 4 to 7 Quarts

✓ **WHY THIS RECIPE WORKS:** Cooking our glazed carrots in the slow cooker gave us a family-friendly and fuss-free side dish. Once tender, the carrots were simply drained and returned to the slow cooker along with peas, honey, ginger, lemon zest and juice, and butter to heat through and make a quick glaze. Mint provided a fresh, herbaceous note to this appealing side.

2½	**pounds carrots, peeled and sliced on bias ¼ inch thick**
	Salt and pepper
2	**tablespoons honey**
2	**teaspoons grated fresh ginger**
2	**teaspoons grated lemon zest plus 2 tablespoons juice**
1	**cup frozen peas, thawed**
1	**tablespoon unsalted butter**
2	**teaspoons minced fresh mint**

1. Combine carrots, ¾ cup water, and ¼ teaspoon salt in slow cooker. Press 16 by 12-inch sheet of parchment paper firmly onto carrots, folding down edges as needed. Cover and cook until carrots are tender, 5 to 6 hours on low or 3 to 4 hours on high.

2. Discard parchment. Drain carrots and return to now-empty slow cooker. Whisk honey, ginger, and lemon zest and juice together in bowl. Stir honey mixture, peas, and butter into slow cooker and let sit until heated through, about 5 minutes. Stir in mint and season with salt and pepper to taste. Serve. (Carrots can be held on warm or low setting for up to 2 hours; loosen glaze with hot water as needed.)

Per serving: Cal 120; Fat 2g; Sat Fat 1g; Chol 5mg; Carb 25g; Protein 3g; Fiber 6g; Sodium 160mg

---

Simple Glazed Root Vegetables

Serves 6 • **Cooking Time** 5 to 6 hours on Low or 3 to 4 hours on High • **Slow Cooker Size** 4 to 7 Quarts

✓ **WHY THIS RECIPE WORKS:** Roasted root vegetables make an appealing side dish for roast chicken or meat, but tying up your oven isn't always practical. Using the slow cooker frees up your oven, and the vegetables cook evenly in the moderate heat. Once the vegetables were tender, we simply drained them and tossed them with a bit of orange marmalade, a pat of butter, fresh parsley, and lemon juice to create a quick glaze.

1	**pound parsnips, peeled and cut into 1-inch pieces**
1	**pound rutabaga, peeled and cut into 1-inch pieces**
1	**celery root (14 ounces), peeled and cut into 1-inch pieces**
	Salt and pepper
3	**tablespoons orange marmalade**
1	**tablespoon unsalted butter**
2	**teaspoons minced fresh parsley**
2	**teaspoons lemon juice**

1. Combine parsnips, rutabaga, celery root, ¾ cup water, and ½ teaspoon salt in slow cooker. Press 16 by 12-inch sheet of parchment paper firmly onto vegetables, folding down edges as needed. Cover and cook until vegetables are tender, 5 to 6 hours on low or 3 to 4 hours on high.

2. Discard parchment. Drain vegetables and return to now-empty slow cooker. Stir in marmalade, butter, parsley, and lemon juice. Season with salt and pepper to taste. Serve. (Vegetables can be held on warm or low setting for up to 2 hours; loosen glaze with hot water as needed.)

Per serving: Cal 140; Fat 2.5g; Sat Fat 1.5g; Chol 5mg; Carb 30g; Protein 3g; Fiber 6g; Sodium 180mg

Creamed Corn

Serves 6 • **Cooking Time** 3 to 4 hours on Low • **Slow Cooker Size** 4 to 7 Quarts

✓**WHY THIS RECIPE WORKS:** Once you taste our healthy slow-cooker version of creamed corn—with its deep flavor, creamy texture, and simple ingredient list—you'll never go back to using the canned alternative. To get the best in both texture and flavor, we used a combination of whole kernels cut from the cobs and grated corn. The kernels became tender yet maintained a slight bite owing to the gentle cooking environment of the slow cooker, and the grated corn contributed just the right thickness. A combination of evaporated milk and cornstarch gave us the thickening power and heat stability of a heavier dairy product, such as cream, while keeping the recipe low in fat. A single slice of bacon, discarded after cooking, imparted a rich and smoky quality to the finished corn without too many additional calories. Don't forget to scrape the cobs with the back of a knife to collect the flavorful corn pulp and "milk" for extra body before discarding them.

4	ears corn, husks and silk removed
1	shallot, minced
2	tablespoons unsalted butter
1	garlic clove, minced
	Pinch cayenne pepper
1	(12-ounce) can 2 percent low-fat evaporated milk
2	tablespoons cornstarch
1	slice bacon
2	sprigs fresh thyme
	Salt and pepper

1. Cut kernels from 3 ears corn into bowl, reserving cobs. Grate remaining 1 ear corn over large holes of box grater into bowl, reserving cob. Using back of butter knife, firmly scrape pulp and milk from cobs into bowl. Add corn to slow cooker; discard cobs.

2. Microwave shallot, butter, garlic, and cayenne in bowl, stirring occasionally, until shallot is softened, about 2 minutes; transfer to slow cooker. Stir in evaporated milk, cornstarch, bacon, thyme sprigs, ½ teaspoon salt, and ⅛ teaspoon pepper. Cover and cook until corn is tender, 3 to 4 hours on low.

3. Discard bacon and thyme sprigs. Whisk corn mixture to recombine and let rest until fully set, about 15 minutes. Season with salt and pepper to taste and serve.

Per serving: Cal 170; Fat 8g; Sat Fat 3g; Chol 20mg; Carb 20g; Protein 7g; Fiber 1g; Sodium 290mg

---

QUICK PREP TIP PREPARING FRESH CORN
First cut kernels off 3 ears corn using paring knife, standing cobs upright inside large bowl to help catch any flying kernels. Second, grate 1 more ear corn over large holes of box grater into bowl. Third, use back of butter knife to scrape corn milk from spent cobs; this natural cornstarch helps thicken corn mixture.

Cauliflower with Lemon-Caper Dressing

Serves 4 • **Cooking Time** 2 to 3 hours on Low • **Slow Cooker Size** 5½ to 7 Quarts

☑ **WHY THIS RECIPE WORKS:** With its tightly bound florets and thick stalks, cauliflower is hearty enough for the slow cooker and makes a perfectly tender vegetable side without risk of overcooking. A bright dressing put a fresh Mediterranean spin on this healthy side. You will need an oval slow cooker for this recipe.

- 4 **garlic cloves, lightly crushed and peeled**
- 2 **sprigs fresh thyme**
- **Salt and pepper**
- ⅛ **teaspoon red pepper flakes**
- 1 **head cauliflower (2 pounds)**
- 2 **tablespoons extra-virgin olive oil**
- 2 **teaspoons grated lemon zest plus 1 tablespoon juice**
- 2 **teaspoons capers, rinsed**
- 1 **tablespoon minced fresh parsley**

1. Combine 1 cup water, garlic, thyme sprigs, ½ teaspoon salt, and pepper flakes in slow cooker. Trim outer leaves of cauliflower and cut stem flush with bottom of head. Cut head into 8 equal wedges, keeping core and florets intact. Place wedges cut side down in slow cooker (wedges may overlap). Cover and cook until cauliflower is tender, 2 to 3 hours on low.

2. Whisk oil, lemon zest and juice, capers, and parsley together in large bowl; season with salt and pepper to taste. Using slotted spoon, transfer cauliflower to bowl, brushing away any garlic or thyme sprigs that stick to cauliflower; discard cooking liquid. Gently toss cauliflower to coat with dressing. Serve.

Per serving: Cal 120; Fat 8g; Sat Fat 1g; Chol 0mg; Carb 12g; Protein 4g; Fiber 5g; Sodium 250mg

---

Fennel with Orange-Tarragon Dressing

Serves 4 • **Cooking Time** 8 to 9 hours on Low or 5 to 6 hours on High • **Slow Cooker Size** 5½ to 7 Quarts

☑ **WHY THIS RECIPE WORKS:** Garlic, juniper berries, and thyme provide seasoning for this tender braised fennel which makes an unusual and appealing side dish enhanced with a flavorful dressing. Don't core the fennel bulb before cutting it into wedges; the core will help hold the layers of fennel together during cooking. You will need an oval slow cooker for this recipe.

- 2 **garlic cloves, lightly crushed and peeled**
- 2 **sprigs fresh thyme**
- 1 **teaspoon juniper berries (optional)**
- **Salt and pepper**
- 2 **fennel bulbs, stalks discarded, halved, each half cut into 4 wedges**
- 2 **tablespoons extra-virgin olive oil**
- 2 **teaspoons grated orange zest plus 1 tablespoon juice**
- 1 **teaspoon minced fresh tarragon**

1. Combine 1 cup water, garlic, thyme sprigs, juniper berries, if using, and ½ teaspoon salt in slow cooker. Place fennel wedges cut side down in slow cooker. Cover and cook until fennel is tender, 8 to 9 hours on low or 5 to 6 hours on high.

2. Whisk oil, orange zest and juice, and tarragon together in large bowl; season with salt and pepper to taste. Using slotted spoon, transfer fennel to bowl, brushing away any garlic, thyme sprigs, or juniper berries that stick to fennel; discard cooking liquid. Gently toss fennel to coat with dressing. Serve.

Per serving: Cal 100; Fat 7g; Sat Fat 1g; Chol 0mg; Carb 9g; Protein 2g; Fiber 4g; Sodium 210mg

Sweet-and-Sour Braised Swiss Chard

Serves 4 • **Cooking Time** 1 to 2 hours on Low • **Slow Cooker Size** 5½ to 7 Quarts

☑ **WHY THIS RECIPE WORKS:** Using the slow cooker to prepare Swiss chard was a no-brainer—the low heat helped to turn the chard tender and mellowed its assertive flavor. To infuse our slow-cooked greens with flavor, we started by microwaving the stems with oil and aromatics since the stems take longer to cook than the leaves. For a bright and lively flavor, we added sweet-tart fig preserves along with the chard leaves. To brighten the flavors at the end, a hefty dose of balsamic vinegar was key, and a mere tablespoon of butter added richness. Toasted pine nuts added even more flavor and rustic appeal. Spraying the slow cooker with vegetable oil spray prevents the leafy greens from sticking to the side of the slow cooker and burning. You can substitute apricot preserves for the fig preserves, if desired.

2	pounds Swiss chard, stems chopped fine, leaves sliced into 1-inch-wide strips
2	teaspoons minced fresh thyme or ½ teaspoon dried
1	teaspoon canola oil
1	garlic clove, minced
	Salt and pepper
⅛	teaspoon red pepper flakes
¼	cup fig preserves
2	tablespoons balsamic vinegar
1	tablespoon unsalted butter
2	tablespoons pine nuts, toasted

1. Lightly spray inside of slow cooker with vegetable oil spray. Microwave chard stems, thyme, oil, garlic, ¼ teaspoon salt, and pepper flakes in bowl, stirring occasionally, until stems are softened, about 5 minutes; transfer to slow cooker. Stir in preserves, then stir in chard leaves. Cover and cook until chard is tender, 1 to 2 hours on low.

2. Stir in vinegar and butter and season with salt and pepper to taste. (Swiss chard can be held on warm or low setting for up to 2 hours.) Stir in pine nuts before serving.

Per serving: Cal 160; Fat 8g; Sat Fat 2g; Chol 10mg; Carb 22g; Protein 5g; Fiber 4g; Sodium 650mg

---

SMART SHOPPING BALSAMIC VINEGAR
We were curious about the differences among the various brands of balsamic vinegar found at the supermarket, so we bought a bunch of them (ranging from $5 to $20) and pitted them against one another in a taste test. Right off the bat, we found that the sweetness and viscosity of the vinegars made a difference. A good balsamic vinegar must be sweet and thick, but it should also offer a bit of acidity. In the end, one supermarket vinegar—**Lucini Gran Riserva Balsamico**—impressed us with its nice balance of sweet and tangy.

Braised Swiss Chard with Shiitakes and Peanuts

Serves 4 • **Cooking Time** 1 to 2 hours on Low • **Slow Cooker Size** 5½ to 7 Quarts

✔ **WHY THIS RECIPE WORKS:** For an Asian take on braised Swiss chard, we turned to toasted sesame oil, a hefty dose of grated fresh ginger, and minced garlic as our aromatic base. And for heartiness we added shiitake mushrooms, braising them along with the chard. Once the chard was perfectly tender, we stirred in rice vinegar and some additional ginger, keeping the flavors fresh and vibrant. A small amount of butter added some needed richness but minimal calories. Spraying the slow cooker with vegetable oil spray prevents the chard leaves from sticking to the side of the slow cooker and burning.

2	pounds Swiss chard, stems chopped fine, leaves sliced into 1-inch-wide strips
4	ounces shiitake mushrooms, stemmed and sliced ¼ inch thick
3	garlic cloves, minced
2	teaspoons grated fresh ginger
2	teaspoons toasted sesame oil
	Salt and pepper
⅛	teaspoon red pepper flakes
1	tablespoon rice vinegar
1	tablespoon unsalted butter
1	teaspoon sugar
2	tablespoons chopped peanuts
2	scallions, sliced thin

1. Lightly spray inside of slow cooker with vegetable oil spray. Microwave chard stems, mushrooms, garlic, 1 teaspoon ginger, 1 teaspoon oil, ¼ teaspoon salt, and pepper flakes in bowl, stirring occasionally, until vegetables are softened, about 5 minutes; transfer to slow cooker. Stir in chard leaves, cover, and cook until chard is tender, 1 to 2 hours on low.

2. Stir in vinegar, butter, sugar, remaining 1 teaspoon ginger, and remaining 1 teaspoon oil and season with salt and pepper to taste. (Swiss chard can be held on warm or low setting for up to 2 hours.) Sprinkle with peanuts and scallions before serving.

Per serving: Cal 130; Fat 8g; Sat Fat 2.5g; Chol 10mg; Carb 13g; Protein 6g; Fiber 4g; Sodium 630mg

---

QUICK PREP TIP KEEPING SCALLIONS FRESH
Too often, scallions go limp after just a few days in the fridge. We found that if we stand them in an inch of water in a tall container (covering them loosely with a zipper-lock bag and refreshing the water every three days), our scallions last for well over a week with very little loss in quality.

Stuffed Spiced Eggplants with Tomatoes and Pine Nuts

Serves 4 • **Cooking Time** 5 to 6 hours on Low • **Slow Cooker Size** 5½ to 7 Quarts

✓ WHY THIS RECIPE WORKS: When cooked, eggplants turn rich and creamy, losing the bitterness they have when raw. Italian eggplants, which are slightly smaller than the ubiquitous globe eggplants, are the ideal size and shape for stuffing when halved, and two of them fit easily in a slow cooker. Inspired by the flavors of Turkey, where stuffed eggplant is a way of life, we created a simple stuffing with canned diced tomatoes, Pecorino Romano, pine nuts, and aromatics including onion, garlic, oregano, and cinnamon. We simply nestled the halved eggplants cut side down in this fragrant mixture and let them cook until tender. After removing the eggplants from the slow cooker, we gently pushed the soft flesh to the sides to create a cavity, which we filled with the aromatic tomato mixture left behind in the slow cooker. Topped with extra cheese, pine nuts, and fresh chopped parsley, these eggplants look beautiful and are far easier to make than most traditional versions. Be sure to buy eggplants that are no more than 10 ounces; larger eggplants will not fit properly in your slow cooker. You may need to trim off the eggplant stems to help them fit. You will need an oval slow cooker for this recipe.

1 onion, chopped fine

1 tablespoon extra-virgin olive oil

3 garlic cloves, minced

2 teaspoons minced fresh oregano
   or ½ teaspoon dried

¼ teaspoon ground cinnamon

⅛ teaspoon cayenne pepper

1 (14.5-ounce) can diced
   tomatoes, drained

2 ounces Pecorino Romano
   cheese, grated (1 cup)

¼ cup pine nuts, toasted

1 tablespoon red wine vinegar
   Salt and pepper

2 (10-ounce) Italian eggplants,
   halved lengthwise

2 tablespoons minced fresh
   parsley

1. Microwave onion, 1 teaspoon oil, garlic, oregano, cinnamon, and cayenne in bowl, stirring occasionally, until onion is softened, about 5 minutes; transfer to slow cooker. Stir in tomatoes, ¾ cup Pecorino, pine nuts, vinegar, and ¼ teaspoon salt. Season eggplant halves with salt and pepper and nestle cut side down into slow cooker (eggplants may overlap slightly). Cover and cook until eggplants are tender, 5 to 6 hours on low.

2. Transfer eggplant halves cut side up to serving platter. Using 2 forks, gently push eggplant flesh to sides of each half to make room for filling. Stir remaining 2 teaspoons oil into tomato mixture and season with salt and pepper to taste. Mound tomato mixture evenly into eggplants and sprinkle with parsley and remaining ¼ cup Pecorino. Serve.

Per serving: Cal 210; Fat 13g; Sat Fat 3.5g; Chol 10mg; Carb 17g; Protein 7g; Fiber 6g; Sodium 710mg *To reduce sodium level to 180mg, use no-salt-added tomatoes.

QUICK PREP TIP
PREPARING EGGPLANT
Using 2 forks, gently push flesh to sides of each eggplant half to make room in center for filling.

Garlicky Braised Greens

Serves 4 • **Cooking Time** 7 to 8 hours on Low or 4 to 5 hours on High • **Slow Cooker Size** 5½ to 7 Quarts

✓ WHY THIS RECIPE WORKS: Hearty greens such as kale and collards are among the healthiest foods you can eat, and cooking them in the slow cooker is a convenient and hands-off approach that makes preparing these superfoods easy and foolproof. However, because these greens shrink so much as they cook, we were initially challenged to fit enough for four servings in the slow cooker. When raw, kale and collard greens are stiff, but when cooked, they become soft and tender. By microwaving half of the greens before combining them with the rest of the greens and the other ingredients, we were able to fit a full 2 pounds of greens into the slow cooker. Since greens can be drab and bland without much seasoning, we turned to garlic and red pepper flakes for a spicy kick. The spicy greens fared well with tasters, but they still had a bitterness that permeated the dish. Just a tablespoon of butter helped to mellow them, and a teaspoon of red wine vinegar provided just enough acidity for a bright finish. Spraying the slow cooker with vegetable oil spray prevents the leafy greens from sticking to the side of the slow cooker and burning.

4	garlic cloves, minced
1	teaspoon canola oil
¼	teaspoon red pepper flakes
1½	cups chicken broth
	Salt and pepper
2	pounds kale, stemmed and sliced into 1-inch-wide strips
1	tablespoon unsalted butter
1	teaspoon red wine vinegar

1. Lightly spray inside of slow cooker with vegetable oil spray. Microwave garlic, oil, and pepper flakes in bowl, stirring occasionally, until fragrant, about 30 seconds; transfer to slow cooker. Stir in broth and ½ teaspoon salt.

2. Microwave half of kale in covered bowl until slightly wilted, about 5 minutes; transfer to slow cooker. Stir in remaining kale, cover, and cook until kale is tender, 7 to 8 hours on low or 4 to 5 hours on high.

3. Stir in butter and vinegar and season with salt and pepper to taste. Serve. (Braised greens can be held on warm or low setting for up to 2 hours.)

Per serving: Cal 110; Fat 6g; Sat Fat 2g; Chol 10mg; Carb 11g; Protein 7g; Fiber 4g; Sodium 530mg

---

SMART SHOPPING PREPEELED VERSUS FRESH GARLIC

Many supermarkets carry jars or deli containers of prepeeled garlic cloves, but how do they compare to fresh garlic bought by the head? We tasted both kinds of garlic in various recipes, both raw and cooked, and, in all cases, results were mixed. However, we did notice a difference in shelf life: A whole head of garlic stored in a cool, dry place will last for at least a few weeks, while prepeeled garlic in a jar (which must be kept refrigerated) lasts for only about two weeks before turning yellowish and developing an overly pungent aroma, even if kept unopened in its original packaging. (In fact, in several instances we found containers of garlic that had started to develop this odor and color on the supermarket shelf.) But if you go through a lot of garlic, prepeeled cloves can be a fine alternative. Just make sure they look firm and white and have a matte finish when you purchase them.

Smoky Braised Greens with Black-Eyed Peas

Serves 4 • **Cooking Time** 7 to 8 hours on Low or 4 to 5 hours on High • **Slow Cooker Size** 5½ to 7 Quarts

VEGETARIAN

☑ **WHY THIS RECIPE WORKS:** Kale is often paired with black-eyed peas in Southern cooking. For our slow-cooker version of this dish, we used canned peas with our greens to create a hearty dish without a lot of extra hassle. Generally, this combo of kale and peas features smoky pork, but to keep things healthy, we opted to used smoked paprika instead, which gave our greens and peas surprising meaty depth and complexity. For a final touch before serving, we added a small amount of butter and sherry vinegar to tie together the flavors of the greens and black-eyed peas. Spraying the slow cooker with vegetable oil spray prevents the leafy greens from sticking to the side of the slow cooker and burning.

1	onion, chopped fine
3	garlic cloves, minced
2	teaspoons minced fresh thyme or ½ teaspoon dried
1½	teaspoons smoked paprika
1	teaspoon canola oil
1	(15-ounce) can black-eyed peas, rinsed
1½	cups water
	Salt and pepper
2	pounds kale, stemmed and sliced into 1-inch-wide strips
1	tablespoon unsalted butter
2	teaspoons sherry vinegar, plus extra for seasoning

1. Lightly spray inside of slow cooker with vegetable oil spray. Microwave onion, garlic, thyme, paprika, and oil in bowl, stirring occasionally, until onion is softened, about 5 minutes; transfer to slow cooker. Stir in peas, water, and ¼ teaspoon salt.

2. Microwave half of kale in covered bowl until slightly wilted, about 5 minutes; transfer to slow cooker. Stir in remaining kale, cover, and cook until kale is tender, 7 to 8 hours on low or 4 to 5 hours on high.

3. Stir in butter and vinegar and season with salt, pepper, and extra vinegar to taste. Serve. (Braised greens can be held on warm or low setting for up to 2 hours.)

Per serving: Cal 170; Fat 6g; Sat Fat 2g; Chol 10mg; Carb 24g; Protein 9g; Fiber 8g; Sodium 400mg

---

SMART SHOPPING SHERRY VINEGAR
Sherry vinegar is a great addition to any pantry because it has a lively, complex flavor, and a little of it can brighten up just about any soup, salad, or side dish. Unlike the complex and slightly sweet balsamic vinegar that Italian cooking favors, sherry vinegar, made from the Spanish fortified wine for which it is named, is smoother and a bit more potent. Sherry vinegar works well in sauces paired with hearty meats or in any dish where a bright and lively finishing touch would be welcome.

Mustard Green and Sweet Potato Tacos

Serves 4 • **Cooking Time** 3 to 4 hours on Low or 2 to 3 hours on High • **Slow Cooker Size** 4 to 7 Quarts

✓ **WHY THIS RECIPE WORKS:** It's easy to get stuck in a rut when cooking vegetables, but we found that stuffing soft tacos with superfoods like mustard greens and sweet potatoes made even the most carnivorous among us excited to eat veggies. In order for the sweet potatoes to be a manageable size for folding into a taco, we cut them into ½-inch pieces. But these small pieces cooked quickly and lost their shape, so we wrapped the starchy tubers in foil to help tame the heat of the slow cooker and keep them from falling apart. The tender vegetables needed a crunchy counterpoint, so we put together some quickly pickled radishes. A quick soak in a mixture of lime juice, salt, and sugar was all it took for the radishes to absorb the flavorful liquid and tame their bite. Make sure to assemble the pickled radishes just before finishing the tacos, or they'll lose their crunch. You can substitute an equal amount of Swiss chard for the mustard greens, if desired. For information on making a foil packet, see page 51. Spraying the slow cooker with vegetable oil spray prevents the mustard greens from sticking to the side of the slow cooker and burning.

1	onion, chopped fine
2	tablespoons minced fresh oregano or 2 teaspoons dried
4	teaspoons extra-virgin olive oil
4	garlic cloves, minced
1	teaspoon ground cumin
1	teaspoon ground coriander
	Salt and pepper
1½	pounds mustard greens, stemmed and cut into 1-inch pieces
1	pound sweet potatoes, peeled and cut into ½-inch pieces
2	teaspoons hot sauce
5	radishes, trimmed and sliced thin
1	shallot, halved and sliced thin
¼	cup lime juice (2 limes)
1	teaspoon sugar
12	(6-inch) corn tortillas, warmed
3	ounces queso fresco, crumbled (¾ cup)

1. Lightly spray inside of slow cooker with vegetable oil spray. Microwave onion, oregano, 1 teaspoon oil, garlic, cumin, and coriander in bowl, stirring occasionally, until onion is softened, about 5 minutes; transfer to slow cooker. Stir in ½ cup water and ¾ teaspoon salt, then stir in mustard greens. Season sweet potatoes with salt and pepper and wrap in foil packet; lay packet on top of greens. Cover and cook until greens and potatoes are tender, 3 to 4 hours on low or 2 to 3 hours on high.

2. Transfer foil packet to plate. Drain mustard green mixture and return to now-empty slow cooker. Carefully open foil packet (watch for steam) and gently fold potatoes into greens along with hot sauce and remaining 1 tablespoon oil. Season with salt and pepper to taste.

3. Combine radishes, shallot, lime juice, sugar, and ⅛ teaspoon salt in bowl. Divide mustard green–potato mixture among warm tortillas and top with radishes and queso fresco. Serve.

Per serving: Cal 380; Fat 10g; Sat Fat 2g; Chol 5mg; Carb 65g; Protein 11g; Fiber 11g; Sodium 570mg

---

ON THE SIDE CILANTRO RICE
Process 3 cups chicken broth and 1½ cups fresh cilantro leaves in blender or food processor until mostly smooth, about 15 seconds. Heat 2 teaspoons oil in small saucepan over medium heat until shimmering. Stir in 1½ cups rinsed long-grain white rice and cook until edges of grains begin to turn translucent, about 2 minutes. Stir in cilantro mixture and ½ teaspoon salt and bring to boil. Reduce heat to low, cover, and simmer until all liquid is absorbed, 18 to 22 minutes. Remove saucepan from heat. Remove lid, place clean dish towel over saucepan, then replace lid. Let rice sit for 10 minutes, then gently fluff with fork. Serves 4.

Per serving: Cal 260; Fat 2.5g; Sat Fat 0g; Chol 0mg; Carb 53g; Protein 8g; Fiber 0g; Sodium 680mg *To reduce sodium level to 390mg, use unsalted broth.

Red Flannel Hash with Poached Eggs

Serves 4 • **Cooking Time** 5 to 6 hours on Low or 3 to 4 hours on High • **Slow Cooker Size** 5½ to 7 Quarts

✔**WHY THIS RECIPE WORKS:** Hash is traditionally a heavy breakfast dish, complete with overflowing portions, salty chunks of meat, and a high fat content. For a healthier but still hearty hash, we took out the meat altogether and increased the amount of vegetables. Red beets cooked perfectly along with potatoes and provided a ruby hue, which is where this dish gets its name. To give our vegetables that real hash texture, we mashed a portion of them and stirred in just a quarter cup of cream after cooking. Dimpling the finished hash with the back of a spoon provided the perfect nests to hold eggs as they slowly cooked to perfection. To avoid staining your hands, hold beets in layers of paper towels while peeling them with a vegetable peeler. For information on making a foil collar, see page 169. You will need an oval slow cooker for this recipe.

2	**pounds russet potatoes, peeled and cut into ½-inch pieces**
12	**ounces beets, peeled and cut into ½-inch pieces**
½	**onion, chopped fine**
2	**garlic cloves, minced**
2	**teaspoons minced fresh thyme or ½ teaspoon dried**
1	**teaspoon canola oil**
1	**teaspoon paprika**
½	**cup chicken broth**
	Salt and pepper
¼	**cup heavy cream**
4	**large eggs**
2	**scallions, sliced thin**

1. Line slow cooker with aluminum foil collar and lightly spray with vegetable oil spray. Add potatoes and beets to slow cooker. Microwave onion, garlic, thyme, oil, and paprika in medium bowl, stirring occasionally, until onion is softened, about 3 minutes. Combine broth and 1 teaspoon salt. Stir broth mixture into vegetables, cover, and cook until vegetables are tender, 5 to 6 hours on low or 3 to 4 hours on high.

2. Remove foil collar. Transfer 2 cups cooked vegetables to bowl, mash smooth with potato masher, then return to slow cooker. Fold in cream until well combined and smooth hash into even layer.

3. Make 4 shallow divots (about 2½ inches wide) in hash using back of spoon. Working with 1 egg at a time, crack egg into small bowl, then gently pour into divot and season with salt and pepper. Cover and cook on high until whites are just beginning to set but still have some movement when slow cooker is gently shaken, 20 to 30 minutes.

4. Turn slow cooker off and let hash and eggs sit, covered, for 5 minutes. Sprinkle with scallions and serve.

Per serving: Cal 350; Fat 12g; Sat Fat 5g; Chol 205mg; Carb 48g; Protein 13g; Fiber 6g; Sodium 800mg *To reduce sodium level to 750mg, use unsalted broth.

QUICK PREP TIP POACHING THE EGGS
Using back of large spoon, make 4 large divots in surface of hash, about 2½ inches wide and 1½ inches deep. Crack 1 egg into small bowl, then gently pour into divot. Repeat with remaining eggs and cook as directed.

Spanish Tortilla with Roasted Red Peppers

Serves 8 • **Cooking Time** 3 to 4 hours on Low • **Slow Cooker Size** 5½ to 7 Quarts

☑ **WHY THIS RECIPE WORKS:** Often a Spanish tortilla is made by slow-cooking potatoes and onions and then adding beaten eggs to form a velvety cake somewhat like a frittata, with deep potato flavor. Served with a garlicky aïoli, it makes a great tapas dish when sliced into small squares or a hearty brunch or dinner when cut into wedges. Although it's traditionally cooked in large amounts of olive oil, we found that using just 2 tablespoons allowed us to keep the heart-healthy fat and bring great flavor to the dish, all while keeping the calorie count low. To pump up the flavors and pack the slow cooker with even more veggies, we added peas and red bell pepper to the mix, along with a hefty dose of minced garlic and fresh oregano. To ensure that the potatoes were perfectly cooked, we sliced them thin and gave them a quick spin in the microwave before adding them to the slow cooker. Placing a foil collar and liner in the slow cooker before assembling the tortilla prevented overbrowning and made the tortilla easy to remove and serve. In a pinch, Yukon Gold potatoes can be substituted for the russets. For information on making a foil collar and foil liner, see page 169. You will need an oval slow cooker for this recipe. Serve with Garlic Aïoli.

2	pounds russet potatoes, peeled, quartered lengthwise, and sliced ⅛ inch thick
2	onions, chopped fine
1	red bell pepper, stemmed, seeded, and cut into ½-inch pieces
2	tablespoons extra-virgin olive oil
6	garlic cloves, minced
1	tablespoon minced fresh oregano or 1 teaspoon dried
¼	teaspoon red pepper flakes
1	cup frozen peas
12	large eggs
1	teaspoon salt
½	teaspoon pepper

1. Line slow cooker with aluminum foil collar, then line with foil liner and lightly coat with vegetable oil spray. Microwave potatoes, onions, bell pepper, oil, garlic, oregano, and pepper flakes in large covered bowl, stirring occasionally, until potatoes are nearly tender, about 9 minutes. Stir in peas, then transfer potato mixture to slow cooker.

2. Whisk eggs, salt, and pepper together in bowl, then pour mixture evenly over potatoes. Gently press potatoes into egg mixture. Cover and cook until center of tortilla is just set, 3 to 4 hours on low.

3. Turn slow cooker off and let tortilla rest, covered, until fully set, about 20 minutes. Using liner, transfer tortilla to serving platter and serve.

Per serving: Cal 250; Fat 11g; Sat Fat 3g; Chol 280mg; Carb 26g; Protein 13g; Fiber 3g; Sodium 400mg

---

ON THE SIDE GARLIC AÏOLI
Combine ¼ cup light mayonnaise, ¼ cup plain whole-milk yogurt, 1 tablespoon extra-virgin olive oil, 2 minced garlic cloves, ½ teaspoon lemon juice, and ¼ teaspoon salt in bowl. Makes about ½ cup.

Per 1-tablespoon serving: Cal 40; Fat 4g; Sat Fat 0.5g; Chol 0mg; Carb 1g; Protein 0g; Fiber 0g; Sodium 140mg

Mashed Potatoes and Root Vegetables

Serves 6 • **Cooking Time** 6 to 7 hours on Low or 4 to 5 hours on High • **Slow Cooker Size** 4 to 7 Quarts

✓ WHY THIS RECIPE WORKS: For a change from classic mashed potatoes, we decided to incorporate other root vegetables, choosing celery root for its refreshing herbal and slightly anise-like flavor and parsnips for the sweetness and richness they bring to the table, especially when mashed or pureed. Since russets, with their high starch content, are perfect for mashing, turning creamy and smooth with a buttery richness, they were our starting point for the potatoes. We found that slicing the vegetables worked best as they cooked more evenly than chunks; spraying the top layer of the vegetables with vegetable oil spray kept them from discoloring during the long cooking time. To ensure even cooking, we added water for a steamy environment, then trapped the steam by laying a sheet of parchment paper on top of the vegetables. Once tender, we mashed them right in the slow cooker and folded in low-fat milk and just 4 tablespoons of melted butter for rich-tasting but not fat-laden mashed root vegetables. This recipe can easily be doubled in a 5½- to 7-quart slow cooker.

1	pound russet potatoes, peeled and sliced ¼ inch thick
8	ounces parsnips, peeled and sliced ¼ inch thick
½	celery root (7 ounces), peeled, halved, and sliced ¼ inch thick
½	cup water
	Salt and pepper
	Vegetable oil spray
⅓	cup 2 percent low-fat milk, warmed, plus extra as needed
4	tablespoons unsalted butter, melted

1. Combine potatoes, parsnips, celery root, water, and ¾ teaspoon salt in slow cooker. Spray top layer of vegetables with oil spray. Press 16 by 12-inch sheet of parchment paper firmly onto vegetables, folding down edges as needed. Cover and cook until vegetables are tender, 6 to 7 hours on low or 4 to 5 hours on high.

2. Discard parchment. Mash root vegetables with potato masher until smooth. Fold in milk and melted butter and season with salt and pepper to taste. Serve. (Mashed potatoes and root vegetables can be held on warm or low setting for up to 2 hours; loosen with extra warm milk as needed before serving.)

Per serving: Cal 170; Fat 8g; Sat Fat 5g; Chol 20mg; Carb 23g; Protein 3g; Fiber 3g; Sodium 340mg

---

QUICK PREP TIP ADDING A PARCHMENT SHIELD
We find that pressing a sheet of parchment paper on top of some vegetable and rice dishes helps to trap steam and promote even cooking. To create a parchment cover in the slow cooker, press a 16 by 12-inch sheet of parchment paper firmly onto vegetables or rice, folding down edges as needed.

Mashed Sweet Potatoes

Serves 6 • **Cooking Time** 5 to 6 hours on Low or 3 to 4 hours on High • **Slow Cooker Size** 4 to 7 Quarts

✔ **WHY THIS RECIPE WORKS:** Smooth and velvety with a buttery finish, these slow-cooker mashed sweet potatoes will keep you coming back for more. Pressing a piece of parchment on top of the potatoes results in even cooking, without any dry edges.

2	pounds sweet potatoes, peeled and sliced ¼ inch thick
½	cup water, plus extra as needed
1	teaspoon sugar
	Salt and pepper
2	sprigs fresh thyme
	Vegetable oil spray
6	tablespoons half-and-half, warmed
1	tablespoon unsalted butter, melted

1. Combine potatoes, water, sugar, ¾ teaspoon salt, and thyme sprigs in slow cooker. Spray top layer of potatoes with oil spray. Press 16 by 12-inch sheet of parchment paper firmly onto potatoes, folding down edges as needed. Cover and cook until potatoes are tender, 5 to 6 hours on low or 3 to 4 hours on high.

2. Discard parchment and thyme sprigs. Mash potatoes with potato masher until smooth. Fold in half-and-half and melted butter and season with salt and pepper to taste. Serve. (Mashed potatoes can be held on warm or low setting for up to 2 hours; loosen with hot water as needed before serving.)

Per serving: Cal 140; Fat 4g; Sat Fat 2.5g; Chol 10mg; Carb 25g; Protein 2g; Fiber 4g; Sodium 370mg

Indian-Spiced Mashed Butternut Squash

Serves 6 • **Cooking Time** 5 to 6 hours on Low or 3 to 4 hours on High • **Slow Cooker Size** 4 to 7 Quarts

✔ **WHY THIS RECIPE WORKS:** For a unique approach to mashed squash, we turned to an Indian flavor profile for inspiration. Garam masala, golden raisins, and toasted cashews transformed ordinary and mild-tasting butternut squash into an exciting side dish.

2	pounds butternut squash, peeled, halved lengthwise, seeded, and sliced ¼ inch thick
½	cup water, plus extra as needed
2	teaspoons packed brown sugar
	Salt and pepper
½	teaspoon garam masala
	Vegetable oil spray
6	tablespoons half-and-half, warmed
¼	cup golden raisins
¼	cup roasted cashews, chopped
1	tablespoon unsalted butter, melted

1. Combine squash, water, sugar, ¾ teaspoon salt, and garam masala in slow cooker. Spray top layer of squash with oil spray. Press 16 by 12-inch sheet of parchment paper firmly onto squash, folding down edges as needed. Cover and cook until squash is tender, 5 to 6 hours on low or 3 to 4 hours on high.

2. Discard parchment. Mash squash with potato masher until smooth. Fold in half-and-half, raisins, cashews, and melted butter. Season with salt and pepper to taste. Serve. (Mashed squash can be held on warm or low setting for up to 2 hours; loosen with hot water as needed before serving.)

Per serving: Cal 160; Fat 7g; Sat Fat 3g; Chol 10mg; Carb 24g; Protein 3g; Fiber 3g; Sodium 310mg

Olive Oil Mashed Potatoes

Serves 6 • **Cooking Time** 5 to 6 hours on Low or 3 to 4 hours on High • **Slow Cooker Size** 4 to 7 Quarts

✔ **WHY THIS RECIPE WORKS:** Traditional mashed potatoes are not particularly healthy given how much butter is required to achieve the right texture. Switching to olive oil not only made our mashed potatoes heart healthy but gave them a luxuriously smooth texture and an earthy flavor all their own. A sheet of parchment paper trapped the steam to ensure even cooking. This recipe can easily be doubled in a 5½- to 7-quart slow cooker.

2 **pounds russet potatoes, peeled and sliced ¼ inch thick**

1 **cup water, plus extra as needed**

3 **garlic cloves, lightly crushed and peeled**

Salt and pepper

Vegetable oil spray

3 **tablespoons extra-virgin olive oil**

2 **teaspoons lemon juice**

1. Combine potatoes, water, garlic, and 1 teaspoon salt in slow cooker. Spray top layer of potatoes with oil spray. Press 16 by 12-inch sheet of parchment paper firmly onto potatoes, folding down edges as needed. Cover and cook until potatoes are tender, 5 to 6 hours on low or 3 to 4 hours on high.

2. Discard parchment. Mash potatoes with potato masher until smooth. Fold in olive oil and lemon juice and season with salt and pepper to taste. Serve. (Mashed potatoes can be held on warm or low setting for up to 2 hours; loosen with hot water as needed before serving.)

Per serving: Cal 170; Fat 7g; Sat Fat 1g; Chol 0mg; Carb 25g; Protein 3g; Fiber 2g; Sodium 400mg

---

Buttermilk Smashed Red Potatoes

Serves 6 • **Cooking Time** 5 to 6 hours on Low or 3 to 4 hours on High • **Slow Cooker Size** 4 to 7 Quarts

✔ **WHY THIS RECIPE WORKS:** For our lower-fat smashed potato recipe, we turned to buttermilk, which is naturally low-fat, and a little sour cream. Use small red potatoes measuring 2 inches in diameter. This recipe can easily be doubled in a 5½- to 7-quart slow cooker, but you will need to increase the cooking time by 1 hour.

2 **pounds small red potatoes, halved**

3 **tablespoons extra-virgin olive oil**

3 **garlic cloves, lightly crushed and peeled**

2 **teaspoons minced fresh thyme or ½ teaspoon dried**

Salt and pepper

⅔ **cup buttermilk**

¼ **cup low-fat sour cream**

2 **tablespoons minced fresh chives**

1. Combine potatoes, oil, garlic, thyme, 1 teaspoon salt, and ¼ teaspoon pepper in slow cooker. Press 16 by 12-inch sheet of parchment paper firmly onto potatoes, folding down edges as needed. Cover and cook until potatoes are tender, 5 to 6 hours on low or 3 to 4 hours on high.

2. Discard parchment. Add buttermilk and sour cream to potatoes and, using potato masher, mash until combined and chunks of potatoes remain. Fold in chives and season with salt and pepper to taste. Serve. (Smashed potatoes can be held on warm or low setting for up to 2 hours; loosen with hot water as needed before serving.)

Per serving: Cal 200; Fat 8g; Sat Fat 1g; Chol 5mg; Carb 26g; Protein 4g; Fiber 3g; Sodium 450mg

Herbed Fingerling Potatoes with Lemon

Serves 6 • **Cooking Time** 5 to 6 hours on Low or 3 to 4 hours on High • **Slow Cooker Size** 4 to 7 Quarts

✓ **WHY THIS RECIPE WORKS:** Widely available at farm stands and now at many grocery stores too, fingerling potatoes are a nice alternative to standard white or red potatoes. They are creamy and dense and feel somehow special because of their small, narrow shape. So for a super-easy and attractive side dish, we turned to fingerlings, which require no prep work and turn perfectly tender in the slow cooker. Although they are traditionally roasted because boiling them dilutes their flavor and turns them mushy, we found that we could add them to the slow cooker without any liquid whatsoever, just some olive oil, garlic, and scallions for flavor, and they retained their delicate sweetness without a hint of mushiness. Unlike some other slow-cooker potato dishes, there was also no need to cover them with a sheet of parchment paper so they would cook through properly. Before serving, we simply added chopped fresh parsley and lemon zest and juice for bright color and flavor. Use fingerling potatoes measuring approximately 3 inches long and 1 inch in diameter. This recipe can easily be doubled in a 5½- to 7-quart slow cooker, but you will need to increase the cooking time by 1 hour.

2	**pounds fingerling potatoes**
4	**teaspoons extra-virgin olive oil**
2	**scallions, white parts minced, green parts sliced thin**
3	**garlic cloves, minced**
	Salt and pepper
1	**tablespoon chopped fresh parsley**
1	**teaspoon lemon zest plus 1 tablespoon juice**

1. Combine potatoes, 1 teaspoon oil, scallion whites, garlic, 1 teaspoon salt, and ¼ teaspoon pepper in slow cooker. Cover and cook until potatoes are tender, 5 to 6 on low or 3 to 4 hours on high.

2. Stir in parsley, lemon zest and juice, scallion greens, and remaining 1 tablespoon oil; season with salt and pepper to taste. Serve. (Potatoes can be held on warm or low setting for up to 2 hours.)

Per serving: Cal 160; Fat 3g; Sat Fat 0g; Chol 0mg; Carb 28g; Protein 4g; Fiber 2g; Sodium 400mg

---

SMART SHOPPING FINGERLING POTATOES
Potatoes generally fall into three groups: high-, medium-, and low-starch. The amount of starch can drastically affect a potato's cooking properties. The fingerling potatoes called for in this recipe are medium-starch potatoes, as are Yukon Golds, which are thus a fine substitute. However, we like the unique visual appeal of the fingerlings' oblong shape and small size. If substituting Yukon Gold potatoes, use small potatoes measuring 1 to 2 inches in diameter.

Braised Sweet Potatoes with Cilantro-Lime Dressing

Serves 4 • **Cooking Time** 3 to 4 hours on Low or 2 to 3 hours on High • **Slow Cooker Size** 5½ to 7 Quarts

WHY THIS RECIPE WORKS: Sweet potatoes are highly nutritious, so it's good to have lots of recipes that use them in your repertoire. They are also very mild in flavor, so they take well to many widely different approaches in terms of seasonings. They are perfect for slow cooking since they are dense and take a while to cook. Here, we chose to cook the sweet potatoes in a braising liquid infused with lemon grass, star anise, and ginger, which gave this superfood super flavor. After the sweet potatoes were tender, we tossed the aromatic and tender potato chunks with a fresh cilantro and lime vinaigrette, which provided a bright and spicy contrast and herbaceous note to the sweet potatoes. You will need an oval slow cooker for this recipe.

1   **lemon grass stalk, trimmed to bottom 6 inches and bruised with back of knife**

2   **star anise pods**

1   **tablespoon grated fresh ginger Salt and pepper**

2   **pounds sweet potatoes, peeled and sliced ½ inch thick**

1   **tablespoon chopped fresh cilantro**

1   **tablespoon packed brown sugar**

1   **tablespoon toasted sesame oil**

1   **teaspoon grated lime zest plus 4 teaspoons juice**

¼   **teaspoon fish sauce Pinch cayenne**

1. Combine 1 cup water, lemon grass, star anise, 2 teaspoons ginger, and ½ teaspoon salt in slow cooker. Nestle potatoes into slow cooker, cover, and cook until potatoes are tender, 3 to 4 hours on low or 2 to 3 hours on high.

2. Using slotted spoon, transfer potatoes to serving platter. Brush away any lemon grass or star anise that sticks to potatoes and discard cooking liquid. Whisk cilantro, sugar, oil, lime zest and juice, fish sauce, cayenne, and remaining 1 teaspoon ginger together in bowl; season with salt and pepper to taste. Drizzle dressing over potatoes and serve.

Per serving: Cal 220; Fat 3.5g; Sat Fat 0.5g; Chol 0mg; Carb 44g; Protein 4g; Fiber 7g; Sodium 280mg

SMART SHOPPING STAR ANISE
As the name suggests, these pods are star-shaped and they taste like anise. The warm, licorice-like flavor of star anise works well in foods both sweet and savory. It's an essential element of five-spice powder. Try flavoring sugar syrup with whole pods and drizzling the syrup over citrus fruits.

Braised Butternut Squash with Pecans and Cranberries

Serves 4 • **Cooking Time** 4 to 5 hours on Low or 3 to 4 hours on High • **Slow Cooker Size** 5½ to 7 Quarts

✔ **WHY THIS RECIPE WORKS:** Cooking this popular winter squash in a slow cooker makes for a wonderful everyday vegetable, but slow-cooked butternut squash is also right at home as a healthy side for a holiday dinner table, freeing up valuable oven space. We found that a small amount of liquid in the bottom of the slow cooker, plus a couple of aromatics, was all it took to deeply flavor and perfectly steam butternut squash. Pecans and dried cranberries dressed up the squash, and a quick vinaigrette tied the elements of this vegetable side together. You will need an oval slow cooker for this recipe.

1 cup chicken broth
2 garlic cloves, lightly crushed and peeled
2 sprigs fresh thyme
½ teaspoon black peppercorns
Salt and pepper
2 pounds butternut squash, peeled, halved lengthwise, seeded, and sliced 1 inch thick
2 tablespoons extra-virgin olive oil
1 teaspoon grated lemon zest plus 2 teaspoons juice
¼ cup pecans, toasted and chopped coarse
¼ cup dried cranberries
1 tablespoon minced fresh parsley

1. Combine broth, garlic, thyme sprigs, peppercorns, and ¼ teaspoon salt in slow cooker. Nestle squash into slow cooker, cover, and cook until squash is tender, 4 to 5 hours on low or 3 to 4 hours on high.

2. Using slotted spoon, transfer squash to serving platter. Brush away any garlic, thyme sprigs, or peppercorns that stick to squash and discard cooking liquid. Whisk oil and lemon zest and juice together in bowl; season with salt and pepper to taste. Drizzle dressing over squash and sprinkle with pecans, cranberries, and parsley. Serve.

Per serving: Cal 210; Fat 12g; Sat Fat 1.5g; Chol 0mg; Carb 27g; Protein 3g; Fiber 4g; Sodium 190mg

---

SMART SHOPPING PARSLEY
You've probably noticed that your neighborhood grocer offers two different varieties of this recognizable herb (though there are actually more than 30 varieties out there): curly-leaf and flat-leaf (also called Italian). Curly-leaf parsley is more popular, but in the test kitchen flat-leaf is by far the favorite. We find flat-leaf to have a sweet, bright flavor that's much preferable to the bitter, grassy tones of curly-leaf parsley. Flat-leaf parsley is also much more fragrant than its curly cousin.

Thai-Style Braised Butternut Squash with Tofu

Serves 4 • **Cooking Time** 3 to 4 hours on Low or 2 to 3 hours on High • **Slow Cooker Size** 4 to 7 Quarts

✓ **WHY THIS RECIPE WORKS:** For this easy-to-make main dish, we braised tofu and chunks of butternut squash in a highly aromatic liquid base. Making sure this braising medium was loaded with flavor was key since tofu tends to absorb liquid as it cooks. We turned to a trio of aromatics (onion, ginger, and garlic) along with Thai red curry paste and bloomed it all in the microwave to meld the flavors. A small amount of fish sauce enhanced the Southeast Asian flavors. At the end of the cooking time, we took this dish to the next level by adding light coconut milk, lime juice, and cilantro. You can substitute firm tofu here if desired; avoid silken, soft, or medium-firm tofu as these varieties will break down while cooking. Serve with rice.

1	onion, chopped fine
3	tablespoons Thai red curry paste
2	tablespoons grated fresh ginger
4	garlic cloves, minced
1	teaspoon canola oil
2	pounds butternut squash, peeled, seeded, and cut into 1-inch pieces
14	ounces extra-firm tofu, cut into ¾-inch pieces
1	cup water
2	teaspoons fish sauce, plus extra for seasoning
2	teaspoons instant tapioca
1	red bell pepper, stemmed, seeded, and cut into ¼-inch-wide strips
1	cup canned light coconut milk
1	tablespoon lime juice, plus extra for seasoning
⅓	cup fresh cilantro leaves
3	tablespoons chopped peanuts

1. Microwave onion, curry paste, 1 tablespoon ginger, garlic, and oil in bowl, stirring occasionally, until onion is softened, about 5 minutes; transfer to slow cooker. Stir in squash, tofu, water, fish sauce, and tapioca. Cover and cook until squash is tender, 3 to 4 hours on low or 2 to 3 hours on high.

2. Stir bell pepper into slow cooker, cover, and cook on high until tender, about 10 minutes. Stir in coconut milk, lime juice, and remaining 1 tablespoon ginger and let sit until heated through, about 5 minutes. Season with salt, pepper, extra fish sauce, and extra lime juice to taste. Sprinkle individual portions with cilantro and peanuts before serving

Per serving: Cal 320; Fat 14g; Sat Fat 4g; Chol 0mg; Carb 40g; Protein 14g; Fiber 8g; Sodium 570mg

---

QUICK PREP TIP

CUTTING BUTTERNUT SQUASH

Peel away tough outer skin using vegetable peeler, then trim off top and bottom of squash. Slice squash in half widthwise, separating solid, narrow neck piece from hollow, rounded bottom. Slice solid neck piece lengthwise into evenly sized planks, then cut into pieces as directed. Slice bottom piece in half, remove seeds with spoon, then cut into pieces as directed.

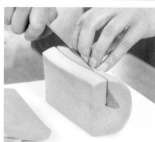

Maple-Orange Glazed Acorn Squash

Serves 4 • **Cooking Time** 3 to 4 hours on Low or 2 to 3 hours on High • **Slow Cooker Size** 5½ to 7 Quarts

WHY THIS RECIPE WORKS: A quintessential fall vegetable, acorn squash takes forever to roast and often emerges dry and a bit grainy. In the slow cooker, however, it turns tender easily without overcooking or drying out. And as an added bonus, you can perfume it with warm spices as it cooks. Here we created a cooking base made up of water, orange juice, cloves, and cinnamon and placed the squash cut side down in this flavorful mixture. And since we think a glaze greatly enhances acorn squash, we made a quick one in the microwave by combining maple syrup with coriander, cayenne pepper, and orange zest. This lively glaze elevated the humble slow-cooked vegetable, and toasted hazelnuts provided great crunch and flavor. Don't be tempted to substitute imitation maple syrup—it will be too sweet. You will need an oval slow cooker for this recipe.

2	teaspoons grated orange zest plus ½ cup juice
5	cloves
1	cinnamon stick
2	(1-pound) acorn squashes, quartered pole to pole and seeded
	Salt and pepper
¼	cup maple syrup
⅛	teaspoon ground coriander
	Pinch cayenne pepper
¼	cup hazelnuts, toasted, skinned, and chopped coarse
1	tablespoon chopped fresh parsley

1. Combine 1 cup water, orange juice, cloves, and cinnamon in slow cooker. Season squash with salt and pepper and shingle, cut side down, in slow cooker. Cover and cook until squash is tender, 3 to 4 hours on low or 2 to 3 hours on high.

2. Using tongs, transfer squash to serving platter. Brush away any cloves that stick to squash and discard cooking liquid and cinnamon stick. Microwave maple syrup, coriander, cayenne, and orange zest in bowl, stirring occasionally, until heated through, about 1 minute; season with salt and pepper to taste. Drizzle glaze over squash and sprinkle with hazelnuts and parsley. Serve.

Per serving: Cal 190; Fat 4.5g; Sat Fat 0g; Chol 0mg; Carb 38g; Protein 3g; Fiber 4g; Sodium 160mg

SMART SHOPPING MAPLE SYRUP
The syrup options these days can be daunting. There are the imitation pancake syrups like Mrs. Butterworth's and Log Cabin (basically high-fructose corn syrup laced with maple flavoring), and there's real maple syrup, which is sold as grade A (in light, medium, and dark amber) and darker grade B, often called "cooking syrup." Tasters unanimously panned the imitation stuff. Among the real syrups, they preferred dark with intense maple flavor to the delicate, pricey grade A light amber. The favorite was **Maple Grove Farms Pure Maple Syrup**, a grade A dark amber, but our runner-up, Highland Sugarworks, a grade B syrup, is great for those looking for even bolder maple flavor.

Rice, Grains, and Beans

● EASY PREP   ● VEGETARIAN

Brown Rice with Parmesan and Herbs

Serves 6 • **Cooking Time** 1 to 2 hours on High • **Slow Cooker Size** 5½ to 7 Quarts

✔ **WHY THIS RECIPE WORKS:** It's true that brown rice takes longer to cook and can be trickier than white rice to cook evenly. We wondered if the steady, gentle heat of the slow cooker would take the challenge out of cooking brown rice. After some experiments that resulted in burnt rice and undercooked grains, we learned that brown rice needs a head start with boiling water in the slow cooker, but that it can indeed emerge with light and fluffy grains every time. Cooking on high was best, and we laid a piece of parchment paper over the rice to protect the grains on top from drying out as the water was absorbed. For an accurate measurement of boiling water, bring a full kettle of water to a boil and then measure out the desired amount.

3   cups boiling water
2   cups long-grain brown rice, rinsed
1   tablespoon unsalted butter
    Salt and pepper
2   ounces Parmesan cheese, grated (1 cup)
½   cup chopped fresh basil, dill, or parsley
2   teaspoons lemon juice

1. Lightly spray inside of slow cooker with vegetable oil spray. Combine boiling water, rice, butter, ½ teaspoon salt, and ½ teaspoon pepper in slow cooker. Gently press 16 by 12-inch sheet of parchment paper onto surface of water, folding down edges as needed. Cover and cook until rice is tender and all water is absorbed, 1 to 2 hours on high.

2. Discard parchment. Fluff rice with fork, then gently fold in Parmesan, basil, lemon juice, and ¼ teaspoon pepper. Season with salt and pepper to taste. Serve.

Per serving: Cal 290; Fat 7g; Sat Fat 3g; Chol 10mg; Carb 48g; Protein 9g; Fiber 2g; Sodium 370mg

---

Brown Rice with Peas, Feta, and Mint

Serves 6 • **Cooking Time** 1 to 2 hours on High • **Slow Cooker Size** 5½ to 7 Quarts

✔ **WHY THIS RECIPE WORKS:** For a fresh and easy variation on slow-cooked brown rice, we stirred in frozen peas and chopped mint. Crumbled feta provided a tangy counterpoint to the nutty brown rice. For an accurate measurement of boiling water, bring a full kettle of water to a boil and then measure out the desired amount.

3   cups boiling water
2   cups long-grain brown rice, rinsed
1   tablespoon unsalted butter
    Salt and pepper
1   cup frozen peas, thawed
2   ounces feta cheese, crumbled (½ cup)
¼   cup chopped fresh mint
2   teaspoons lemon juice

1. Lightly spray inside of slow cooker with vegetable oil spray. Combine boiling water, rice, butter, and ½ teaspoon salt in slow cooker. Gently press 16 by 12-inch sheet of parchment paper onto surface of water, folding down edges as needed. Cover and cook until rice is tender and all water is absorbed, 1 to 2 hours on high.

2. Discard parchment. Fluff rice with fork, then gently fold in peas, feta, mint, and lemon juice. Season with salt and pepper to taste. Serve.

Per serving: Cal 290; Fat 6g; Sat Fat 3g; Chol 15mg; Carb 51g; Protein 8g; Fiber 3g; Sodium 310mg

Middle Eastern Basmati Rice Pilaf

Serves 6 • **Cooking Time** 1 to 2 hours on High • **Slow Cooker Size** 5½ to 7 Quarts

✔ **WHY THIS RECIPE WORKS:** For an easy, aromatic side dish that's big on flavor but not on fat, we paired basmati rice with warm spices, dried currants, and crunchy toasted almonds. To give the rice a pilaf-like texture, we briefly "toasted" it in the microwave along with our aromatics. This helped keep the grains separate during cooking. Then we poured boiling water over the grains, which helped to ensure even cooking. As with brown rice, we found that basmati cooked best on high, and we laid a piece of parchment paper over the mixture to prevent the grains on top from drying out as the water was absorbed. For an accurate measurement of boiling water, bring a full kettle of water to a boil and then measure out the desired amount.

2	cups basmati rice, rinsed
1	tablespoon extra-virgin olive oil
2	garlic cloves, minced
½	teaspoon ground turmeric
¼	teaspoon ground cinnamon
3	cups boiling water
⅓	cup dried currants
	Salt and pepper
¼	cup sliced almonds, toasted

1. Lightly spray inside of slow cooker with vegetable oil spray. Microwave rice, oil, garlic, turmeric, and cinnamon in bowl, stirring occasionally, until rice is lightly toasted and fragrant, about 2 minutes; transfer to slow cooker. Stir in boiling water, currants, and ½ teaspoon salt. Gently press 16 by 12-inch sheet of parchment paper onto surface of water, folding down edges as needed. Cover and cook until rice is tender and all water is absorbed, 1 to 2 hours on high.

2. Fluff rice with fork, then fold in almonds. Season with salt and pepper to taste. Serve.

Per serving: Cal 270; Fat 4.5g; Sat Fat 0.5g; Chol 0mg; Carb 54g; Protein 5g; Fiber 1g; Sodium 200mg

---

SMART SHOPPING BASMATI RICE

Prized for its nutty flavor and perfume-like aroma, basmati rice is eaten worldwide in pilafs and biryanis and as an accompaniment to curries. Choosing among the multitude of boxes, bags, and burlap sacks available today on supermarket shelves can be confusing. To find a truly great grain, we steamed seven brands, five from India and two domestic options. Matched against Indian imports, domestic brands Lundberg and Della suffered. They were less aromatic and the grains didn't elongate as much. Their overall texture was mushy, too. While all of the imported brands were acceptable, tasters overwhelmingly chose the longest sample—**Tilda Pure Basmati Rice**—as their favorite. It was praised for its "beautiful long grains," "slightly nutty" flavor, and especially "strong aroma."

Wild Rice Pilaf with Cranberries and Pecans

Serves 8 • **Cooking Time** 1 to 2 hours on High • **Slow Cooker Size** 5½ to 7 Quarts

✔ **WHY THIS RECIPE WORKS:** For a healthy, hands-off side dish that could feed a crowd, we chose wild rice because it is higher in protein than most other whole grains and is a good source of fiber, vitamins, and minerals. Since wild rice can easily go from tough to pasty, it was crucial to find the ratio of liquid to rice that would give our slow-cooker wild rice pilaf the right texture. After several tests, we found that 2½ cups chicken broth to 1½ cups wild rice produced rice that was evenly cooked, not wet or mushy. In pinning down the cooking time for our wild rice recipe, we also discovered that heating the broth improved the texture of the rice and resulted in evenly cooked grains. To keep this dish simple yet flavorful, we stirred in dried cranberries, which plumped nicely as the rice cooked, and their sweetness provided a good counterpoint to the nutty rice. A handful of toasted pecans and a sprinkling of fresh parsley added texture and color without much fuss, so this dish could go from slow cooker to table in no time. Do not use quick-cooking or presteamed wild rice in this recipe; you may need to read the ingredient list on the package carefully to determine if the wild rice is presteamed. To make this dish vegetarian, substitute vegetable broth for the chicken broth.

2½ cups chicken broth
1 onion, chopped fine
1 tablespoon extra-virgin olive oil
1½ teaspoons minced fresh thyme or ¼ teaspoon dried
1½ cups wild rice, picked over and rinsed
⅔ cup dried cranberries
Salt and pepper
2 bay leaves
½ cup pecans, toasted and chopped coarse
2 tablespoons minced fresh parsley

1. Lightly spray inside of slow cooker with vegetable oil spray. Microwave broth in bowl until steaming, about 3 minutes. In separate bowl, microwave onion, oil, and thyme, stirring occasionally, until onion is softened, about 5 minutes; transfer to slow cooker. Stir in hot broth, rice, cranberries, ½ teaspoon salt, and bay leaves. Gently press 16 by 12-inch sheet of parchment paper onto surface of water, folding down edges as needed. Cover and cook until rice is tender and all broth is absorbed, 1 to 2 hours on high.

2. Discard parchment and bay leaves. Fluff rice with fork, then gently fold in pecans and parsley. Season with salt and pepper to taste. Serve.

Per serving: Cal 220; Fat 7g; Sat Fat 0.5g; Chol 0mg; Carb 35g; Protein 6g; Fiber 3g; Sodium 310mg

---

SMART SHOPPING WILD RICE
Although it's usually stocked in the supermarket with long-grain, brown, and basmati, wild rice is actually an aquatic grass. (Wild rice is native to North America, growing naturally in lakes, but it is also cultivated in man-made paddies in Minnesota, California, and Canada.) When we tasted five brands both plain and in a soup, textural differences stood out the most; our top three, including our winner, cooked up springy and firm, while the other two blew out. What accounted for the difference? Processing. To create a shelf-stable product, manufacturers heat the grains, which gelatinizes their starches and drives out moisture, according to one of two methods: parching (the traditional approach) or parboiling. To parch, manufacturers load batches of rice into cylinders, which spin over a fire—an inexact process that produces "crumbly," "less toothsome" results. Parboiling, a newer method, steams the grains in a controlled pressurized environment. The upshot: more uniform and complete gelatinization, which translates into rice that cooks more evenly. In the end our favorite product, **Goose Valley Wild Rice**, benefited from the parboiling method: It retained a "bouncy pop" and the grains had a "crunchy exterior yet were tender inside." An added boon: Its flavor was "woodsy" and "pecan-y."

Farro Primavera

Serves 4 • **Cooking Time** 3 to 4 hours on Low or 2 to 3 hours on High • **Slow Cooker Size** 4 to 7 Quarts

✔ **WHY THIS RECIPE WORKS:** For a healthier take on pasta primavera we swapped pasta for whole-grain farro and nixed cream in favor of flavorful, nutty Parmesan cheese. Since most of the vegetables we had in mind, except leeks, would go into the slow cooker at the end to ensure bright colors and fresh flavors, the point of using a slow cooker was the hands-off approach to perfectly cooked farro. We found that briefly toasting the farro in the microwave before adding it to the slow cooker guaranteed that the grains cooked evenly. Since it was important to mellow the potent allium flavor of the leeks, we gave them a head start in the microwave along with the farro. Once the farro was tender, we stirred in some boiling water to help steam asparagus in the last few minutes of cooking. Peas rounded out the spring vegetables for our primavera, and a generous portion of Parmesan cheese and a little drizzle of extra-virgin olive oil turned our dish creamy and rich-tasting without adding a lot of extra fat. Do not substitute pearl, quick-cooking, or presteamed farro for the whole farro in this recipe; you may need to read the ingredient list on the package carefully to determine if the farro is presteamed. For an accurate measurement of boiling water, bring a full kettle of water to a boil and then measure out the desired amount.

2	cups vegetable broth
1	leek, white and light green parts only, halved lengthwise, sliced thin, and washed thoroughly
1	cup whole farro
1	tablespoon extra-virgin olive oil
2	garlic cloves, minced
1	teaspoon minced fresh thyme or ¼ teaspoon dried
	Salt and pepper
2	ounces Parmesan cheese, grated (1 cup), plus extra for serving
½–1	cup boiling water, plus extra as needed
1	pound thin asparagus, trimmed and cut into 1-inch lengths
1	cup frozen peas, thawed

1. Lightly spray inside of slow cooker with vegetable oil spray. Microwave broth in bowl until steaming, about 3 minutes. In separate bowl, microwave leek, farro, 1 teaspoon oil, garlic, and thyme, stirring occasionally, until leek is softened, about 5 minutes; transfer to slow cooker. Stir in hot broth and ½ teaspoon salt. Cover and cook until farro is tender, 3 to 4 hours on low or 2 to 3 hours on high.

2. Stir Parmesan and ½ cup boiling water into farro until mixture is creamy but still somewhat thin. If farro is stiff and thick, add remaining water as needed, ¼ cup at a time, until mixture is thinned. Stir in asparagus, cover, and cook on high until tender, about 20 minutes. Stir in peas and remaining 2 teaspoons oil and let sit until heated through, about 5 minutes. (Adjust farro consistency with extra boiling water as needed.) Season with salt and pepper to taste. Serve with extra Parmesan.

Per serving: Cal 340; Fat 10g; Sat Fat 2.5g; Chol 10mg; Carb 49g; Protein 16g; Fiber 8g; Sodium 780mg *To reduce sodium level to 470mg, use low-sodium broth.

ON THE SIDE SPINACH SALAD WITH SHERRY VINAIGRETTE
Whisk 2 tablespoons extra-virgin olive oil, 1 tablespoon sherry vinegar, ½ minced shallot, ½ teaspoon Dijon mustard, ¼ teaspoon salt, and pinch pepper together in large bowl. Add 6 cups baby spinach and 1 small red bell pepper, stemmed, seeded, and cut into ½-inch pieces, and toss to coat. Serves 4.

Per serving: Cal 90; Fat 7g; Sat Fat 1g; Chol 0mg; Carb 7g; Protein 1g; Fiber 3g; Sodium 230mg

Farro Risotto with Carrots and Goat Cheese

Serves 4 • **Cooking Time** 3 to 4 hours on Low or 2 to 3 hours on High • **Slow Cooker Size** 4 to 7 Quarts

✓ **WHY THIS RECIPE WORKS:** Risotto usually demands a cook's attention from start to finish, which is why this hands-off slow-cooker version is so appealing. Instead of traditional Arborio rice, we chose nutrient-rich farro and added healthy, colorful carrots. Finely grating the carrots allowed them to overcook slightly and "melt" into the farro to help create a creamy base. When the farro was tender, we stirred in handfuls of bright, fresh baby spinach. To keep the farro from becoming dry and sticky, we added an extra half-cup of boiling water to help wilt the spinach. A little bit of tangy goat cheese was the perfect finishing touch to give our risotto rich flavor and an ultracreamy texture. Do not substitute pearl, quick-cooking, or presteamed farro for the whole farro in this recipe; you may need to read the ingredient list on the package carefully to determine if the farro is presteamed. Use the small holes of a box grater to grate the carrots. For an accurate measurement of boiling water, bring a full kettle of water to a boil and then measure out the desired amount.

2	cups vegetable broth
1	cup whole farro
1	onion, chopped fine
1	tablespoon unsalted butter
2	garlic cloves, minced
¼	cup dry white wine
3	carrots, peeled and finely grated
	Salt and pepper
4	ounces goat cheese, crumbled (1 cup)
¼–¾	cup boiling water, plus extra as needed
4	ounces (4 cups) baby spinach

1. Lightly spray inside of slow cooker with vegetable oil spray. Microwave broth in bowl until steaming, about 3 minutes. In separate bowl, microwave farro, onion, butter, and garlic, stirring occasionally, until onion is softened, about 5 minutes; transfer to slow cooker. Stir in hot broth, wine, carrots, and ½ teaspoon salt. Cover and cook until farro is tender, 3 to 4 hours on low or 2 to 3 hours on high.

2. Stir goat cheese and ¼ cup boiling water into farro until mixture is creamy but still somewhat thin. If farro is stiff and thick, add remaining water as needed, ¼ cup at a time, until mixture is thinned. Stir in spinach, 1 handful at a time, until slightly wilted. Cover and cook on high until spinach is softened, about 15 minutes. (Adjust risotto consistency with extra boiling water as needed.) Season with salt and pepper to taste. Serve.

Per serving: Cal 340; Fat 11g; Sat Fat 6g; Chol 20mg; Carb 50g; Protein 13g; Fiber 8g; Sodium 880mg *To reduce sodium level to 570mg, use low-sodium broth.

SMART SHOPPING **YELLOW VERSUS WHITE ONIONS**
In our recipes, unless otherwise specified, we always use yellow onions, the kind that come in 5-pound bags at the supermarket. But wondering if there was any difference between these onions and white onions (color aside, of course), we decided to hold a blind taste test to find out. We tried them raw in pico de gallo, cooked in a simple tomato sauce, and caramelized. More than half a dozen tasters could not tell the difference between the two types; the others tasted only minor variations in sweetness and pungency. Our conclusion? Since we go through onions quickly, we find it easiest to buy a big bag of yellow onions, but you can use white and yellow onions interchangeably in any recipe calling for "onions."

Herbed Barley Pilaf

Serves 6 • **Cooking Time** 2 to 3 hours on High • **Slow Cooker Size** 4 to 7 Quarts

✔ **WHY THIS RECIPE WORKS:** Barley is a nutritious, high-fiber cereal grain with a nutty flavor similar to that of brown rice. For any everyday barley pilaf, we started by briefly toasting the grains in the microwave before adding them to the slow cooker, which ensured that they stayed separate and cooked evenly, giving us fluffy barley pilaf while maintaining the pleasant chew for which barley is known. Do not substitute hulled, hull-less, quick-cooking, or presteamed barley for the pearl barley in this recipe; you may need to read the ingredient list on the package carefully to determine if the barley is presteamed.

1½ **cups pearl barley, rinsed**
1 **onion, chopped fine**
1 **tablespoon extra-virgin olive oil**
2 **garlic cloves, minced**
1 **teaspoon minced fresh thyme or ¼ teaspoon dried**
3½ **cups chicken broth**
  Salt and pepper
¼ **cup chopped fresh basil, dill, or parsley**

1. Lightly spray inside of slow cooker with vegetable oil spray. Microwave barley, onion, 1 teaspoon oil, garlic, and thyme in bowl, stirring occasionally, until onion is softened, about 5 minutes; transfer to slow cooker. Stir in broth and ½ teaspoon salt. Cover and cook until barley is tender and all broth is absorbed, 2 to 3 hours on high.

2. Fluff barley with fork, then gently fold in basil and remaining 2 teaspoons oil. Season with salt and pepper to taste. Serve.

Per serving: Cal 230; Fat 3.5g; Sat Fat 0g; Chol 0mg; Carb 42g; Protein 8g; Fiber 9g; Sodium 500mg

---

Spiced Barley Pilaf with Dates and Parsley

Serves 6 • **Cooking Time** 2 to 3 hours on High • **Slow Cooker Size** 4 to 7 Quarts

✔ **WHY THIS RECIPE WORKS:** For a distinctive variation on our easy Herbed Barley Pilaf, we added a potent blend of Indian-inspired spices—ginger, cinnamon, and cardamom—plus dates for sweetness. Do not substitute hulled, hull-less, quick-cooking, or presteamed barley for the pearl barley in this recipe; you may need to read the ingredient list on the package carefully to determine if the barley is presteamed.

1½ **cups pearl barley, rinsed**
1 **onion, chopped fine**
1 **tablespoon extra-virgin olive oil**
2 **teaspoons grated fresh ginger**
⅛ **teaspoon ground cinnamon**
⅛ **teaspoon ground cardamom**
3½ **cups chicken broth**
  Salt and pepper
3 **ounces dates, chopped (½ cup)**
⅓ **cup chopped fresh parsley**
2 **teaspoons lemon juice**

1. Lightly spray inside of slow cooker with vegetable oil spray. Microwave barley, onion, 1 teaspoon oil, ginger, cinnamon, and cardamom in bowl, stirring occasionally, until onion is softened, about 5 minutes; transfer to slow cooker. Stir in broth and ½ teaspoon salt. Cover and cook until barley is tender and all broth is absorbed, 2 to 3 hours on high.

2. Fluff barley with fork, then gently fold in dates, parsley, lemon juice, and remaining 2 teaspoons oil. Season with salt and pepper to taste. Serve.

Per serving: Cal 270; Fat 3.5g; Sat Fat 0g; Chol 0mg; Carb 54g; Protein 8g; Fiber 10g; Sodium 500mg

Warm Summer Barley Salad

Serves 4 • **Cooking Time** 2 to 3 hours on High • **Slow Cooker Size** 4 to 7 Quarts

☑ **WHY THIS RECIPE WORKS:** To showcase the appealingly nutty taste of barley, we kept the flavors simple—just lemon and coriander—and constructed a salad pairing it with piles of fresh veggies and a light yogurt-herb dressing. We started with pearl barley, which is widely available in supermarkets and has a more pleasant pilaf-like texture when cooked than hulled barley, which still has the outer bran attached. To get perfectly cooked barley, we needed to find the right liquid-to-barley ratio for the slow cooker. After a few tests, we found that 2¼ cups water to 1 cup barley produced barley that was cooked through once all the water had been absorbed, while leaving the texture still on the soft side. Reducing the amount of liquid wasn't an option because it resulted in unevenly cooked barley. To maintain a bit of the grains' toothsome structure and ensure even cooking, we briefly toasted the barley in the microwave before adding it to the slow cooker. Do not substitute hulled, hull-less, quick-cooking, or presteamed barley for the pearl barley in this recipe; you may need to read the ingredient list on the package carefully to determine if the barley is presteamed. You can substitute zucchini for the summer squashes, if desired.

1	cup pearl barley, rinsed
2	tablespoons extra-virgin olive oil
1	teaspoon ground coriander
2¼	cups water
1	tablespoon grated lemon zest plus 1 tablespoon juice
	Salt and pepper
2	summer squashes
⅓	cup plain low-fat yogurt
2	tablespoons minced fresh chives
1	small garlic clove, minced
10	ounces cherry tomatoes, halved
½	cup fresh parsley leaves

1. Lightly spray inside of slow cooker with vegetable oil spray. Microwave barley, 1 teaspoon oil, and coriander in bowl, stirring occasionally, until barley is lightly toasted and fragrant, about 3 minutes; transfer to slow cooker. Stir in water, 2 teaspoons lemon zest, and ½ teaspoon salt. Cover and cook until barley is tender and all water is absorbed, 2 to 3 hours on high.

2. Using vegetable peeler or mandoline, shave squashes lengthwise into very thin ribbons. Whisk yogurt, chives, garlic, lemon juice, ¼ teaspoon salt, ¼ teaspoon pepper, remaining 5 teaspoons oil, and remaining 1 teaspoon lemon zest together in bowl. Fluff barley with fork, then gently fold in dressing, squash ribbons, tomatoes, and parsley. Season with salt and pepper to taste. Serve.

Per serving: Cal 300; Fat 9g; Sat Fat 1.5g; Chol 0mg; Carb 48g; Protein 8g; Fiber 11g; Sodium 470mg

---

QUICK PREP TIP MAKING SQUASH RIBBONS
Using vegetable peeler or mandoline, shave summer squash or zucchini lengthwise into very thin ribbons.

Creamy Parmesan-Rosemary Polenta

Serves 6 • **Cooking Time** 3 to 4 hours on Low • **Slow Cooker Size** 4 to 7 Quarts

WHY THIS RECIPE WORKS: Many polenta recipes deliver rich creaminess by piling on hefty amounts of cheese and butter. Not wanting to sacrifice creaminess or texture, we focused on getting the polenta perfectly tender. Remarkably, thanks to the gentle heat of the slow cooker (this recipe works best on low), our typical ratio of liquid to polenta worked just fine. Instead of using all water and stirring in lots of butter at the end, we added 1 cup of whole milk up front. This helped to deliver a rich, creamy texture with substantially less fat and calories. We finished the dish by steeping a sprig of rosemary in the polenta to infuse herbal flavor without adding bits of herbs to disturb the smooth texture of the dish. Just a cup of nutty Parmesan and a pat of butter stirred in at the end gave the polenta richness and flavor while keeping the dish light. Be sure to use traditional polenta, not instant polenta.

3 **cups water, plus extra as needed**

1 **cup whole milk**

1 **cup polenta**

2 **garlic cloves, minced**

   Salt and pepper

1 **sprig fresh rosemary**

2 **ounces Parmesan cheese, grated (1 cup)**

2 **tablespoons unsalted butter**

1. Lightly spray inside of slow cooker with vegetable oil spray. Whisk water, milk, polenta, garlic, and 1 teaspoon salt together in slow cooker. Cover and cook until polenta is tender, 3 to 4 hours on low.

2. Nestle rosemary sprig into polenta, cover, and let steep for 10 minutes. Discard rosemary sprig. Stir in Parmesan and butter and season with salt and pepper to taste. Serve. (Polenta can be held on warm or low setting for up to 2 hours before serving; loosen with extra hot water as needed.)

Per serving: Cal 190; Fat 8g; Sat Fat 4.5g; Chol 20mg; Carb 20g; Protein 7g; Fiber 1g; Sodium 580mg

---

SMART SHOPPING PARMESAN CHEESE

Genuine Italian Parmigiano-Reggiano cheese offers a buttery, nutty taste and crystal-line crunch. Produced for the past 800 years in northern Italy using traditional methods, this hard cow's-milk cheese has a distinctive flavor, but it comes at a steep price. Our top-rated brand, chosen from a lineup of supermarket cheeses, is **Boar's Head Parmigiano-Reggiano**; this Italian import costs about $18 per pound, and our tasters say it offers a "good crunch" and "nice tangy, nutty" flavor. For a more affordable option, they also liked **BelGioioso Parmesan**, which costs about half as much.

Creamy Mushroom Polenta

Serves 6 • **Cooking Time** 3 to 4 hours on Low • **Slow Cooker Size** 4 to 7 Quarts

WHY THIS RECIPE WORKS: Creamy polenta makes a great foil for stews and is also nice served alongside roasted meats or fish. This slightly dressed-up version incorporates simple white mushrooms that are thinly sliced. Since mushrooms can act like little sponges, we found that we needed additional water—3½ cups—to maintain the creamy texture of the polenta. A cup of whole milk ensured a rich-tasting dish without the need to add cheese or lots of butter. A sprinkling of chives stirred in at the end accented the woodsy flavor of the mushrooms. Be sure to use traditional polenta, not instant polenta.

1	**pound white mushrooms, trimmed and sliced thin**
3½	**cups water, plus extra as needed**
1	**cup whole milk**
1	**cup polenta**
2	**garlic cloves, minced**
	Salt and pepper
2	**tablespoons unsalted butter**
2	**tablespoons minced fresh chives**

1. Lightly spray inside of slow cooker with vegetable oil spray. Microwave mushrooms in covered bowl, stirring occasionally, until softened, about 10 minutes. Drain mushrooms and transfer to slow cooker. Stir in water, milk, polenta, garlic, and 1 teaspoon salt. Cover and cook until polenta is tender, 3 to 4 hours on low.

2. Stir butter and chives into polenta and season with salt and pepper to taste. Serve. (Polenta can be held on warm or low setting for up to 2 hours before serving; loosen with extra hot water as needed.)

Per serving: Cal 170; Fat 6g; Sat Fat 3g; Chol 15mg; Carb 23g; Protein 5g; Fiber 1g; Sodium 410mg

---

QUICK PREP TIP MUSHROOMS: WASH OR BRUSH?
Culinary wisdom holds that raw mushrooms must never touch water, lest they soak up the liquid and become soggy. Many sources call for cleaning dirty mushrooms with a soft bristled brush or a damp cloth. These fussy techniques may be worth the effort if you plan to eat the mushrooms raw, but we wondered whether mushrooms destined for the sauté pan could be simply rinsed and patted dry. To test this, we submerged 6 ounces of white mushrooms in a bowl of water for 5 minutes. We drained and weighed the mushrooms and found that they had soaked up only ¼ ounce (about 1½ teaspoons) of water, not nearly enough to affect their texture. So when we plan to cook mushrooms, we don't bother with the brush. Instead, we place the mushrooms in a salad spinner, rinse the dirt and grit away with cold water, and spin to remove excess moisture.

No-Fuss Quinoa with Lemon

Serves 6 • **Cooking Time** 3 to 4 hours on Low or 2 to 3 hours on High • **Slow Cooker Size** 4 to 7 Quarts

✔ **WHY THIS RECIPE WORKS:** We love quinoa for its nutty taste and ease of preparation. To keep the grains separate and fluffy during cooking, we toasted them in the microwave before adding the quinoa to the slow cooker. We dressed the quinoa simply with lemon and parsley to make a universally appealing side dish. We like the convenience of prewashed quinoa; rinsing removes the quinoa's bitter protective coating (called saponin). If you buy unwashed quinoa (or if you are unsure if it's washed), rinse it before cooking.

1½	**cups prewashed quinoa**
1	**onion, chopped fine**
1	**tablespoon extra-virgin olive oil**
1¾	**cups water**
2	**(2-inch) strips lemon zest plus 1 tablespoon juice**
	Salt and pepper
2	**tablespoons minced fresh parsley**

1. Lightly spray inside of slow cooker with vegetable oil spray. Microwave quinoa, onion, and 1 teaspoon oil in bowl, stirring occasionally, until onion is softened, about 5 minutes; transfer to slow cooker. Stir in water, lemon zest, and 1 teaspoon salt. Cover and cook until quinoa is tender and all water is absorbed, 3 to 4 hours on low or 2 to 3 hours on high.

2. Discard lemon zest. Fluff quinoa with fork, then gently fold in lemon juice, parsley, and remaining 2 teaspoons oil. Season with salt and pepper to taste. Serve.

Per serving: Cal 190; Fat 5g; Sat Fat 0.5g; Chol 0mg; Carb 30g; Protein 6g; Fiber 4g; Sodium 390mg

---

No-Fuss Quinoa with Corn and Jalapeños

Serves 6 • **Cooking Time** 3 to 4 hours on Low or 2 to 3 hours on High • **Slow Cooker Size** 4 to 7 Quarts

✔ **WHY THIS RECIPE WORKS:** For this quinoa side dish we turned to Southwestern flavors, adding jalapeños, lime, and corn. We like the convenience of prewashed quinoa; rinsing removes the quinoa's bitter protective coating (called saponin). If you buy unwashed quinoa (or if you are unsure if it's washed), rinse it before cooking.

1½	**cups prewashed quinoa**
1	**onion, chopped fine**
2	**jalapeño chiles, stemmed, seeded, and minced**
1	**tablespoon extra-virgin olive oil**
1¾	**cups water**
	Salt and pepper
1	**cup frozen corn, thawed**
⅓	**cup minced fresh cilantro**
2	**tablespoons lime juice**

1. Lightly spray inside of slow cooker with vegetable oil spray. Microwave quinoa, onion, jalapeños, and 1 teaspoon oil in bowl, stirring occasionally, until vegetables are softened, about 5 minutes; transfer to slow cooker. Stir in water and 1 teaspoon salt. Cover and cook until quinoa is tender and all water is absorbed, 3 to 4 hours on low or 2 to 3 hours on high.

2. Fluff quinoa with fork, then gently fold in corn, cilantro, lime juice, and remaining 2 teaspoons oil and let sit until heated through, about 5 minutes. Season with salt and pepper to taste. Serve.

Per serving: Cal 220; Fat 6g; Sat Fat 0.5g; Chol 0mg; Carb 35g; Protein 7g; Fiber 4g; Sodium 390mg

Greek Quinoa and Vegetable Lettuce Cups

Serves 4 • **Cooking Time** 3 to 4 hours on Low or 2 to 3 hours on High • **Slow Cooker Size** 4 to 7 Quarts

✔ **WHY THIS RECIPE WORKS:** Lettuce cups—like tortillas—are great vessels for all sorts of fillings. For a healthy filling that could be made in the slow cooker, we turned to quinoa and paired it with fresh vegetables and an herbaceous yogurt dressing. Since we wanted a cohesive quinoa mixture that was easy to scoop into the lettuce cups, we skipped the step of toasting the quinoa in the microwave. Putting the raw quinoa into the slow cooker gave it a softer, more cohesive texture. Our creamy yogurt dressing, flavored with tangy feta cheese and fresh mint, also helped to bind the quinoa mixture. Tomatoes and cucumber added healthy bulk to the mix, and shallot added a welcome bite. We tossed the quinoa and vegetables with part of the bold, flavorful dressing and reserved the rest to drizzle on once we scooped our salad into the lettuce cups. We like the convenience of prewashed quinoa; rinsing removes the quinoa's bitter protective coating (called saponin). If you buy unwashed quinoa (or if you are unsure if it's washed), rinse it before cooking.

1½	**cups vegetable broth**
1	**cup prewashed quinoa**
1	**tablespoon minced fresh oregano or 1 teaspoon dried**
2	**garlic cloves, minced**
⅔	**cup plain low-fat yogurt**
2	**ounces feta cheese, crumbled (½ cup)**
¼	**cup minced fresh mint**
2	**tablespoons red wine vinegar**
1	**tablespoon extra-virgin olive oil**
	Salt and pepper
2	**tomatoes, cored, seeded, and chopped**
1	**cucumber, peeled, halved lengthwise, seeded, and cut into ¼-inch pieces**
1	**small shallot, halved and sliced thin**
2	**heads Bibb lettuce (8 ounces each), leaves separated**

1. Lightly spray inside of slow cooker with vegetable oil spray. Combine broth, quinoa, oregano, and garlic in slow cooker. Cover and cook until quinoa is tender and all broth is absorbed, 3 to 4 hours on low or 2 to 3 hours on high.

2. Combine yogurt, feta, 2 tablespoons mint, vinegar, oil, ½ teaspoon salt, and ¼ teaspoon pepper in bowl, breaking up any large chunks of feta. Fluff quinoa with fork, then gently fold in ½ cup dressing, tomatoes, cucumber, shallot, and remaining 2 tablespoons mint. Season with salt and pepper to taste. Spoon quinoa mixture into lettuce leaves. Serve with remaining dressing.

Per serving: Cal 300; Fat 11g; Sat Fat 3.5g; Chol 15mg; Carb 38g; Protein 12g; Fiber 5g; Sodium 740mg *To reduce sodium level to 510mg, use low-sodium broth.

QUICK PREP TIP
SEEDING A TOMATO
Tomato seeds have great flavor, but in some dishes like our lettuce cups they can be distracting. To seed tomato, first cut it in half through equator, then use your finger to pull out seeds and gel that surrounds them.

Quinoa, Black Bean, and Mango Salad

Serves 4 • **Cooking Time** 3 to 4 hours on Low or 2 to 3 hours on High • **Slow Cooker Size** 4 to 7 Quarts

✓ WHY THIS RECIPE WORKS: Quinoa salad is a great option for a healthy vegetarian meal, and quinoa is also easy to cook in the slow cooker. We wanted to make this salad hearty enough for a main course while keeping it light and fresh tasting. To ensure perfectly cooked, fluffy grains, we "toasted" the quinoa briefly in the microwave before adding it to the slow cooker. Canned black beans were an easy and nutritional addition, and fresh mango and bell pepper stirred in before serving lent the salad heartiness, texture, and color. A simple splash of lime juice balanced the sweetness of the mango and brightened all the fresh flavors of this dish. Whole cilantro leaves and scallions added herbaceous notes, and sliced avocado topped off this salad with rich creaminess. We like the convenience of prewashed quinoa; rinsing removes the quinoa's bitter protective coating (called saponin). If you buy unwashed quinoa (or if you are unsure if it's washed), rinse it before cooking. For a heartier salad, you can serve this dish over mixed greens with diced avocado.

1½ cups prewashed quinoa
1 jalapeño chile, stemmed, seeded, and minced
2 tablespoons extra-virgin olive oil
1 garlic clove, minced
1 teaspoon ground cumin
1 teaspoon ground coriander
1¾ cups water
1 (15-ounce) can black beans, rinsed
   Salt and pepper
¼ cup lime juice (2 limes)
2 red bell peppers, stemmed, seeded, and chopped
1 mango, peeled, pitted, and cut into ¼-inch pieces
⅓ cup fresh cilantro leaves
3 scallions, sliced thin

1. Lightly spray inside of slow cooker with vegetable oil spray. Microwave quinoa, jalapeño, 1 teaspoon oil, garlic, cumin, and coriander in bowl, stirring occasionally, until quinoa is lightly toasted and fragrant, about 3 minutes; transfer to slow cooker. Stir in water, beans, and 1 teaspoon salt. Cover and cook until quinoa is tender and all water is absorbed, 3 to 4 hours on low or 2 to 3 hours on high.

2. Whisk lime juice and remaining 5 teaspoons oil together in bowl. Fluff quinoa with fork, then gently fold in dressing, bell peppers, mango, cilantro, and scallions. Season with salt and pepper to taste. Serve.

Per serving: Cal 410; Fat 12g; Sat Fat 1.5g; Chol 0mg; Carb 66g; Protein 13g; Fiber 10g; Sodium 840mg *To reduce sodium level to 740mg, use low-sodium beans.

QUICK PREP TIP CUTTING UP A MANGO
After cutting thin slice from 1 end of mango, rest mango on trimmed bottom and cut off skin in thin strips, top to bottom. Then, cut down along each side of flat pit to remove flesh, and trim any remaining flesh off sides of pit. Once fruit is removed from pit, it can be chopped or sliced as directed in recipe.

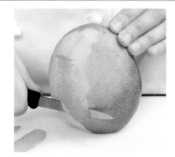

Warm Lentil Salad with Radishes and Mint

Serves 4 • **Cooking Time** 4 to 5 hours on Low or 3 to 4 hours on High • **Slow Cooker Size** 4 to 7 Quarts

WHY THIS RECIPE WORKS: Lentils may be small but they pack big nutritional value. They're low in calories but high in dietary fiber, both soluble and insoluble, as well as vitamins and minerals such as folate and magnesium. To deliver a healthy and tasty side dish starring lentils, we chose *lentilles du Puy* for their earthy, complex flavor and firm yet tender texture. These legumes hold their shape well when cooked, making them perfect for our warm lentil salad. With a ratio of 2½ cups broth to 1 cup lentils, we were able to produce perfectly cooked lentils in the slow cooker. We flavored the lentils simply with garlic, thyme, and paprika and stirred in sliced radishes and chopped mint to bring crunch and bright freshness to our salad before serving. We prefer French green lentils, or lentilles du Puy, for this recipe, but it will work with any type of lentil except red or yellow. For a heartier salad, you can serve this dish over mixed greens.

1	tablespoon extra-virgin olive oil
2	garlic cloves, minced
1½	teaspoons minced fresh thyme or ¼ teaspoon dried
1	teaspoon paprika
2½	cups vegetable broth
1	cup lentils, picked over and rinsed
2½	tablespoons red wine vinegar
	Salt and pepper
6	radishes, trimmed, halved, and sliced thin
¼	cup chopped fresh mint
1	shallot, halved and sliced thin

1. Microwave 1 teaspoon oil, garlic, thyme, and paprika in bowl, stirring occasionally, until fragrant, about 30 seconds; transfer to slow cooker. Stir in broth, lentils, 1 tablespoon vinegar, and ¼ teaspoon salt. Cover and cook until lentils are tender, 4 to 5 hours on low or 3 to 4 hours on high.

2. Stir in radishes, mint, shallot, remaining 2 teaspoons oil, and remaining 1½ tablespoons vinegar. Season with salt and pepper to taste. Serve.

Per serving: Cal 210; Fat 4.5g; Sat Fat 0.5g; Chol 0mg; Carb 32g; Protein 11g; Fiber 8g; Sodium 640mg *To reduce sodium level to 250mg, use low-sodium broth.

SMART SHOPPING RED WINE VINEGAR
The number of red wine vinegars has exploded in the past decade. To find the best, tasters sampled 10 brands plain, in a vinaigrette, and in pickled onions. For an everyday option, our winner, **Laurent du Clos Red Wine Vinegar**, is hard to beat. At 35 cents per ounce, it's not the least expensive brand we tried, but the price is reasonable for a vinegar that doesn't compromise on flavor.

Rustic Braised Lentils with Eggplant

Serves 4 • **Cooking Time** 7 to 9 hours on Low or 4 to 6 hours on High • **Slow Cooker Size** 4 to 7 Quarts

WHY THIS RECIPE WORKS: For a hearty, healthy vegetarian main dish, we paired French green lentils, *lentilles du Puy*, with eggplant and created a braised dish overflowing with flavor. We first broiled the eggplant with our aromatics to deepen its flavor and ensure that the eggplant cooked evenly and didn't turn mushy in the slow cooker. Then we combined it with cherry tomatoes that broke down and created a fresh tomato sauce to envelop the eggplant and lentils. We found it important to put the lentils and broth in the bottom of the slow cooker so that the lentils cooked thoroughly and evenly. We then layered the broiled eggplant and fresh tomatoes on top of the lentils and stirred it all together at the end of cooking. A sprinkling of crumbled feta cheese, parsley, and a drizzle of extra-virgin olive oil completed this healthy dish with rich, bright freshness. We prefer French green lentils for this recipe, but it will work with any type of lentil except red or yellow.

VEGETARIAN

Vegetable oil spray

2 pounds eggplant, cut into 1-inch pieces

1 onion, chopped fine

1 tablespoon tomato paste

2 garlic cloves, minced

2 teaspoons minced fresh thyme or ½ teaspoon dried
  Salt and pepper

2 cups vegetable broth

1 cup lentils, picked over and rinsed

2 tablespoons red wine vinegar

10 ounces cherry tomatoes, halved

4 teaspoons extra-virgin olive oil

2 ounces feta cheese, crumbled (½ cup)

¼ cup minced fresh parsley

1. Adjust oven rack 6 inches from broiler element and heat broiler. Line rimmed baking sheet with aluminum foil and spray with oil spray. Toss eggplant, onion, tomato paste, garlic, thyme, and ½ teaspoon salt together in bowl. Spread eggplant mixture evenly in prepared sheet and lightly spray with oil spray. Broil eggplant until softened and beginning to brown, 10 to 12 minutes, rotating sheet halfway through broiling.

2. Combine broth, lentils, and 1 tablespoon vinegar in slow cooker. Spread eggplant mixture and tomatoes on top of lentils. Cover and cook until lentils are tender, 7 to 9 hours on low or 4 to 6 hours on high.

3. Stir in oil and remaining 1 tablespoon vinegar. Season with salt and pepper to taste. Sprinkle with feta and parsley and serve.

Per serving: Cal 340; Fat 11g; Sat Fat 3g; Chol 15mg; Carb 50g; Protein 16g; Fiber 15g; Sodium 850mg *To reduce sodium level to 540mg, use low-sodium broth.

SMART SHOPPING FETA CHEESE

In 2005, the European Union ruled that only cheese produced in Greece from at least 70 percent sheep's milk can rightfully bear the label "feta." Here in the United States, where these stipulations don't apply, imitators abound. We tasted five brands, both imports and domestic. Tasters preferred the "barnyard" taste of the sheep's- and goat's-milk imports, giving **Mt. Vikos Traditional Feta**, which hails from the mother country, the top spot. Keep feta submerged in the brine in which it was packed. When stored properly, feta can keep for up to three months, though it will become considerably saltier and more pungent over time.

Southwestern-Style Black Beans and Bulgur

Serves 6 • **Cooking Time** 9 to 11 hours on Low or 6 to 8 hours on High • **Slow Cooker Size** 4 to 7 Quarts

✔ **WHY THIS RECIPE WORKS:** The low-and-slow heat of the slow cooker is ideal for cooking beans, and we wanted an easy dinner starring the protein-rich superfood black beans. To ensure perfectly cooked beans, we submerged them in 6 cups of liquid—half vegetable broth for flavor, and half water to control sodium content. We infused our beans and cooking liquid with bold flavors using garlic, cumin, and chili powder. Once the beans were perfectly tender, we stirred in bulgur for another healthful, fiber-rich element. In the slow cooker, bulgur readily absorbed the extra cooking liquid and all of its rich flavors. To add freshness and textural variety to the dish, we made a red pepper salsa with whole fresh cilantro leaves, scallions, lime juice, and just a little bit of oil. The brightness of the salsa, along with a sprinkling of smooth *queso fresco*, perfectly complemented the warm beans and bulgur for a hearty and healthy vegetarian dinner. When shopping, don't confuse bulgur with cracked wheat, which has a much longer cooking time and will not work in this recipe.

1	onion, chopped fine
2	tablespoons extra-virgin olive oil
4	garlic cloves, minced
1	tablespoon ground cumin
2	teaspoons chili powder
3	cups vegetable broth
3	cups water
1	pound (2½ cups) dried black beans, picked over and rinsed
	Salt and pepper
1	cup medium-grind bulgur, rinsed
2	red bell peppers, stemmed, seeded, and chopped fine
½	cup fresh cilantro leaves
3	scallions, sliced thin
¼	cup lime juice (2 limes)
4	ounces queso fresco, crumbled (1 cup)

1. Microwave onion, 2 teaspoons oil, garlic, cumin, and chili powder in bowl, stirring occasionally, until onion is softened, about 5 minutes; transfer to slow cooker. Stir in broth, water, beans, and 1 teaspoon salt. Cover and cook until beans are tender, 9 to 11 hours on low or 6 to 8 hours on high.

2. Stir bulgur into beans, cover, and cook on high until bulgur is tender and most of liquid is absorbed, 20 to 30 minutes.

3. Combine bell peppers, cilantro, scallions, 2 tablespoons lime juice, ¼ teaspoon salt, and remaining 4 teaspoons oil in bowl. Stir remaining 2 tablespoons lime juice into bean mixture and season with salt and pepper to taste. Top individual portions with pepper salsa and queso fresco before serving.

Per serving: Cal 440; Fat 7g; Sat Fat 1.5g; Chol 5mg; Carb 74g; Protein 21g; Fiber 13g; Sodium 930mg *To reduce sodium level to 620mg, use low-sodium broth.

SMART SHOPPING DRIED BLACK BEANS
Though canned beans are incredibly convenient, for dishes in which the beans truly take center stage, we prefer the flavor and texture provided by dried beans. To find the best dried black beans, we sampled three brands cooked plain and in a recipe for black beans and rice. Surprisingly, the single mail-order variety, a pricey heirloom bean, became mushy, but the beans from the two national supermarket brands were perfectly creamy. Our favorite was **Goya Dried Black Beans**, which offered "nutty," "buttery" bean flavor and a reliably uniform texture.

Boston Baked Beans

Serves 6 • **Cooking Time** 9 to 11 hours on Low or 6 to 8 hours on High • **Slow Cooker Size** 4 to 7 Quarts

✔ **WHY THIS RECIPE WORKS:** The deep, sweet-and-smoky flavor of Boston baked beans is often the result of high-sugar, high-fat ingredients such as ketchup and salt pork. We knew that the low, slow cooking of the slow cooker is particularly well suited to cooking beans without presoaking, so we knew the trick would be reducing the fat and sugar without sacrificing flavor or texture. To get the beans to cook evenly, we needed a full 6 cups of water in the slow cooker. Once we had evenly tender beans, we drained the mixture, reserving a cup of the cooking liquid to stir back into the beans and create a perfectly saucy consistency. Next, we focused on building flavor. Just two slices of bacon added to the slow cooker infused our beans with smoky, savory depth, without adding a lot of excess fat since we removed them before serving. We experimented with scaling back traditional ingredients such as molasses and brown sugar to see what quantities were actually necessary. We found that the molasses was crucial for flavor and texture, so cutting back wasn't an option. Instead, we were able to reduce the amount of brown sugar, keeping just a little for its caramel background notes. To brighten things up at the end of cooking, spicy brown mustard and a splash of cider vinegar went in, along with more molasses to round out the acidity. Don't use robust or blackstrap molasses, which will become bitter tasting in the slow cooker.

1 **onion, chopped fine**

2 **slices bacon**

6 **cups water, plus extra as needed**

1 **pound (2½ cups) dried navy beans, picked over and rinsed**

5 **tablespoons molasses**
   Salt and pepper

2 **tablespoons packed dark brown sugar**

1 **tablespoon brown mustard**

1 **tablespoon cider vinegar**

1. Microwave onion and bacon in bowl, stirring occasionally, until onion is softened, about 5 minutes; transfer to slow cooker. Stir in water, beans, 2 tablespoons molasses, and 1 teaspoon salt. Cover and cook until beans are tender, 9 to 11 hours on low or 6 to 8 hours on high.

2. Discard bacon. Drain beans, reserving 1 cup cooking liquid. Return beans to now-empty slow cooker and stir in reserved cooking liquid, sugar, mustard, vinegar, and remaining 3 tablespoons molasses. Season with salt and pepper to taste. Serve. (Beans can be held on warm or low setting for up to 2 hours; loosen with extra hot water as needed before serving.)

Per serving: Cal 360; Fat 5g; Sat Fat 1.5g; Chol 5mg; Carb 63g; Protein 18g; Fiber 19g; Sodium 430mg

---

SMART SHOPPING BACON

Premium bacon can cost double or triple the price of ordinary bacon. Is it worth it? To find out, we bought six artisanal mail-order bacons and two high-end grocery store bacons. We were amazed to find that two of the four highest-rated bacons were supermarket brands. **Applegate Farms Uncured Sunday Bacon** and **Farmland/Carando Apple Cider Cured Bacon, Applewood Smoked** were a step up from the usual mass-produced bacon, straddling the gap between artisanal and more mainstream supermarket styles. Although these bacons didn't receive quite the raves of the two top-ranked premium bacons, tasters praised them both for good meaty flavor and mild smokiness—plus they were far more convenient than ordering bacon by mail.

Mexican-Style Beans

Serves 6 • **Cooking Time** 9 to 11 hours on Low or 6 to 8 hours on High • **Slow Cooker Size** 4 to 7 Quarts

✔ **WHY THIS RECIPE WORKS:** To deliver flavorful, robust Mexican-style beans from the slow cooker, and keep our side dish light, we needed to amp up the aromatics and spices. Since the beans required a full 6 cups of liquid to cook evenly in the slow cooker, we knew that we would need to drain away some of that cooking liquid. To ensure that our beans remained full of flavor, we boosted the amount of garlic, oregano, and chili powder. Instead of fatty sausage or bacon, we added smoky chipotle chiles in adobo, and we exchanged 1 cup of water for beer to give our beans an extra dimension of flavor. When we stirred 1 cup of reserved cooking liquid back into the tender beans, we created a sauce that was rich and bold. A little bit of brown sugar rounded things out, and a hit of fresh lime juice and cilantro added brightness at the end. We prefer a dark Mexican beer, such as Negra Modelo, but any lager or ale will work in this recipe.

1　onion, chopped fine

4　garlic cloves, minced

1　tablespoon minced fresh oregano or 1 teaspoon dried

1　tablespoon extra-virgin olive oil

1　tablespoon chili powder

2　teaspoons minced canned chipotle chile in adobo sauce

5　cups water, plus extra as needed

1　pound (2½ cups) dried pinto beans, picked over and rinsed

1　cup beer
　　Salt and pepper

2　tablespoons minced fresh cilantro

1　tablespoon packed brown sugar

1　tablespoon lime juice, plus extra for seasoning

1. Microwave onion, garlic, oregano, 1 teaspoon oil, chili powder, and chipotle in bowl, stirring occasionally, until onion is softened, about 5 minutes; transfer to slow cooker. Stir in water, beans, beer, and 1 teaspoon salt. Cover and cook until beans are tender, 9 to 11 hours on low or 6 to 8 hours on high.

2. Drain beans, reserving 1 cup cooking liquid. Return beans to now-empty slow cooker and stir in reserved cooking liquid, cilantro, sugar, lime juice, and remaining 2 teaspoons oil. Season with salt, pepper, and extra lime juice to taste. Serve. (Beans can be held on warm or low setting for up to 2 hours; loosen with extra hot water as needed before serving.)

Per serving: Cal 320; Fat 2.5g; Sat Fat 0g; Chol 0mg; Carb 54g; Protein 16g; Fiber 19g; Sodium 350mg

---

QUICK PREP TIP STORING CITRUS

Unlike bananas or peaches, which ripen at room temperature, citrus fruits stop ripening the moment they are picked, thus beginning a slow and steady decline in texture and flavor. To improve their shelf life, commercially grown citrus are buffed with a thin layer of food-safe wax that prevents moisture from escaping through the fruits' porous rind. To test how well the wax coating works, we bought lemons, limes, and oranges and stored half in the refrigerator and half at room temperature. The fruit that was refrigerated remained firm and juicy for about three weeks, while citrus that was left at room temperature began to discolor and dehydrate in as little as five days. Ultimately, the only downside to storing citrus in the fridge is that it's more difficult to squeeze juice from a cold citrus fruit. To make life easier, let your citrus sit at room temperature for about 15 minutes before juicing.

Braised White Beans with Olive Oil and Sage

Serves 6 • **Cooking Time** 9 to 11 hours on Low or 6 to 8 hours on High • **Slow Cooker Size** 4 to 7 Quarts

✓ WHY THIS RECIPE WORKS: Perfect alongside pork, chicken, or fish, these slow-cooked beans deliver rich flavor and a creamy, tender texture. The beans themselves—we found that small white beans worked well here—required no prep, other than being picked over and rinsed. To ensure that the beans took on robust flavor during their long stint in the slow cooker, we simmered them with onion, a hefty amount of garlic, and a little sage. Once the beans were perfectly cooked, we drained the mixture and reserved a cup of the flavorful cooking liquid to stir back into the beans. We then mashed a portion of the beans to thicken the sauce and enhance the creamy consistency of the dish. Since beans are so low in fat and high in fiber, we knew we could dress them up with some good-quality olive oil without breaking our fat and calorie budgets. Extra fresh sage stirred in at the end enhanced the earthy, herbaceous flavors.

1	onion, chopped fine
5	garlic cloves, minced
2	tablespoons extra-virgin olive oil
2	teaspoons minced fresh sage
3	cups vegetable broth
3	cups water
1	pound (2½ cups) dried small white beans, picked over and rinsed
	Salt and pepper

1. Microwave onion, garlic, 1 teaspoon oil, and 1 teaspoon sage in bowl, stirring occasionally, until onion is softened, about 5 minutes; transfer to slow cooker. Stir in broth, water, beans, and 1 teaspoon salt. Cover and cook until beans are tender, 9 to 11 hours on low or 6 to 8 hours on high.

2. Drain beans, reserving 1 cup cooking liquid. Return one-third of beans to now-empty slow cooker and mash with potato masher until smooth. Stir in reserved cooking liquid, remaining beans, remaining 5 teaspoons oil, and remaining 1 teaspoon sage. Season with salt and pepper to taste. Serve.

Per serving: Cal 310; Fat 6g; Sat Fat 1g; Chol 0mg; Carb 51g; Protein 16g; Fiber 19g; Sodium 550mg

---

SMART SHOPPING DRIED BEANS

When shopping for beans, it is imperative to select "fresh" dried beans. Buy those that are uniform in size and have a smooth exterior. When dried beans are fully hydrated and cooked, they should be plump with a taut skin and have creamy insides; spent beans will have wrinkled skins and a dry, almost gritty texture. Uncooked beans should be stored in a cool, dry place in a sealed plastic or glass container. Though dried beans can be stored for up to one year, it is best to use them within a month or two of purchase.

Smoky Braised Chickpeas

Serves 6 • **Cooking Time** 9 to 11 hours on Low or 6 to 8 hours on High • **Slow Cooker Size** 4 to 7 Quarts

 **WHY THIS RECIPE WORKS:** Chickpeas are prized for their high fiber content as well as for being an excellent source of minerals and protein. But they also have a great buttery texture, and they easily soak up the flavors of other ingredients they're cooked with, making them ideal for cooking in a flavor-packed broth over a long, slow stint in the slow cooker. We infused vegetable broth with distinctive sweet smoked paprika and a sliced red onion for flavor and texture. Once our chickpeas were perfectly tender and creamy, we drained away all but a cup of the cooking liquid, using what we reserved to create a simple, smoky sauce. Mashing a portion of the beans enhanced the creamy consistency of the dish without adding any extra fat, and citrusy cilantro added brightness and a simple, colorful finish.

1   **red onion, halved and sliced thin**
1   **tablespoon extra-virgin olive oil**
1   **tablespoon smoked paprika**
3   **cups vegetable broth**
3   **cups water**
1   **pound (2½ cups) dried chickpeas, picked over and rinsed**
     Salt and pepper
¼   **cup chopped fresh cilantro**

1. Microwave onion, 1 teaspoon oil, and paprika in bowl, stirring occasionally, until onion is softened, about 5 minutes; transfer to slow cooker. Stir in broth, water, chickpeas, and 1 teaspoon salt. Cover and cook until chickpeas are tender, 9 to 11 hours on low or 6 to 8 hours on high.

2. Drain chickpeas, reserving 1 cup cooking liquid. Return one-third of chickpeas to now-empty slow cooker and mash with potato masher until smooth. Stir in reserved cooking liquid, cilantro, remaining chickpeas, and remaining 2 teaspoons oil. Season with salt and pepper to taste. Serve.

Per serving: Cal 310; Fat 7g; Sat Fat 0g; Chol 0mg; Carb 49g; Protein 15g; Fiber 14g; Sodium 560mg

---

SMART SHOPPING PAPRIKA
"Paprika" is a generic term for a spice made from ground dried red peppers that is available in several forms. Sweet paprika (also called "Hungarian paprika," or simply "paprika") is the most common. Typically made from a combination of mild red peppers, it is prized more for its deep scarlet hue than for its very subtle flavor. Smoked paprika, a Spanish favorite, is produced by drying sweet or hot peppers over smoldering oak embers. We don't recommend using this variety for all paprika applications; it is best for seasoning grilled meats or adding a smoky aroma to boldly flavored dishes such as our braised chickpeas. Hot paprika, most often used in chilis, curries, and stews, can range from slightly spicy to punishingly assertive. Although hot paprika shouldn't be substituted for sweet paprika in cooking, sweet paprika can be substituted for hot by adding cayenne pepper.

Desserts

● **EASY PREP**

Chocolate Snack Cake

Serves 6 • **Cooking Time** 1 to 2 hours on High • **Slow Cooker Size** 5½ to 7 Quarts

✔ **WHY THIS RECIPE WORKS:** By creating a supersteamy environment in the slow cooker, we were able to easily turn out a moist, tender, and low-fat chocolate cake. As we did with many of our slow-cooker cakes, we added water to the slow cooker and then elevated the pan on an aluminum foil rack. To lower the fat, we reduced the amount of chocolate, then reinforced the flavor with a little instant espresso powder. Sour cream allowed us to eliminate a lot of the butter and eggs without affecting flavor or moisture. You will need a 6-inch springform pan for this recipe, or you can substitute a 6-inch round cake pan. For an accurate measurement of boiling water, bring a full kettle of water to a boil and then measure out the desired amount.

1½	ounces unsweetened chocolate, chopped fine
3	tablespoons unsweetened cocoa powder
3	tablespoons unsalted butter, cut into 3 pieces
¼	teaspoon instant espresso powder
¼	cup boiling water
½	cup (2½ ounces) all-purpose flour
½	teaspoon salt
½	teaspoon baking soda
⅛	teaspoon baking powder
½	cup packed (3½ ounces) light brown sugar
¼	cup sour cream
1	large egg, room temperature
½	teaspoon vanilla extract
	Confectioners' sugar

1. Add ½ inch water (about 2 cups) to slow cooker and place aluminum foil rack in bottom. Grease 6-inch springform pan and line with parchment paper.

2. Combine chocolate, cocoa, butter, and espresso powder in large bowl. Pour water over mixture, cover, and let sit until chocolate and butter are melted, 3 to 5 minutes. Whisk mixture until smooth; let cool slightly. In separate bowl, whisk flour, salt, baking soda, and baking powder together. Whisk brown sugar, sour cream, egg, and vanilla into cooled chocolate mixture until well combined. Stir in flour mixture until just incorporated.

3. Scrape batter into prepared pan and smooth top. Gently tap pan on counter to release air bubbles. Set pan on rack in prepared slow cooker, cover, and cook until toothpick inserted in center comes out with few moist crumbs attached, 1 to 2 hours on high.

4. Let cake cool in pan on wire rack for 10 minutes. Run small knife around edge of cake, then remove sides of pan. Remove cake from pan bottom, discarding parchment, and let cool completely on rack, 1 to 2 hours. Transfer to serving platter and dust with confectioners' sugar. Serve.

Per serving: Cal 230; Fat 12g; Sat Fat 7g; Chol 50mg; Carb 30g; Protein 3g; Fiber 2g; Sodium 330mg

---

QUICK PREP TIP MAKING A FOIL RACK
To make an aluminum foil rack to elevate your baking pan so water doesn't seep in, loosely roll a 24 by 12-inch piece of foil into 1-inch cylinder. Then bend in sides to form oval ring that measures 8 inches long by 5 inches wide. After adding water to slow cooker, place foil rack in center, then place pan on top.

Carrot Cake

Serves 6 • **Cooking Time** 2 to 3 hours on High • **Slow Cooker Size** 5½ to 7 Quarts

✔ **WHY THIS RECIPE WORKS:** Although carrot cake sounds like a healthy option, given all the oil it usually contains (not to mention the rich cream cheese frosting), it is anything but a healthy dessert. It turns out that the slow cooker makes it easy to produce a moist carrot cake without using all that oil. For a flavorful carrot cake with a moist, but not wet, texture, we tested different amounts of carrots and oil, both of which can weigh down the batter, and ended up dramatically cutting down the amount of oil to just 3 tablespoons and settling on ¾ cup of shredded carrots. In addition, we used just one egg, to replace the lost moisture, and included sour cream, which added the right amount of lightness and a welcome tang to the cake. To ensure that the cake had good lift and was light and fluffy, we used a combination of baking powder and baking soda. Finally, for the frosting we replaced traditional cream cheese and butter with neufchatel reduced-fat cream cheese and whipped it with some confectioners' sugar. You will need a 6-inch springform pan for this recipe, or you can substitute a 6-inch round cake pan. For information on making an aluminum foil rack, see page 276. This cake is great simply dusted with confectioners' sugar, or it can be topped with our Light Cream Cheese Frosting before serving.

¾ **cup (3¾ ounces) plus 2 tablespoons all-purpose flour**
½ **teaspoon baking powder**
½ **teaspoon baking soda**
½ **teaspoon ground cinnamon**
⅛ **teaspoon salt**
   Pinch ground cloves
½ **cup packed (3½ ounces) light brown sugar**
¼ **cup sour cream**
1 **large egg, room temperature**
3 **tablespoons canola oil**
¾ **cup shredded carrots (2 carrots)**
   Confectioners' sugar (optional)

1. Add ½ inch water (about 2 cups) to slow cooker and place aluminum foil rack in bottom. Grease 6-inch springform pan and line with parchment paper.

2. Whisk flour, baking powder, baking soda, cinnamon, salt, and cloves together in bowl. In large bowl, whisk brown sugar, sour cream, and egg together until smooth, then slowly whisk in oil. Stir in flour mixture until just incorporated. Gently fold in carrots.

3. Scrape batter into prepared pan and smooth top. Gently tap pan on counter to release air bubbles. Set cake on rack in prepared slow cooker, cover, and cook until toothpick inserted in center comes out clean, 2 to 3 hours on high.

4. Let cake cool in pan on wire rack for 10 minutes. Run small knife around edge of cake, then remove sides of pan. Remove cake from pan bottom, discarding parchment, and let cool completely on rack, 1 to 2 hours. Transfer to serving platter and dust with confectioners' sugar, if using. Serve.

Per serving: Cal 230; Fat 10g; Sat Fat 2g; Chol 35mg; Carb 34g; Protein 3g; Fiber 1g; Sodium 230mg

---

ON THE SIDE LIGHT CREAM CHEESE FROSTING
Using electric mixer set at medium-high speed, beat together 4 ounces softened ⅓ less fat cream cheese (neufchatel), 1 teaspoon vanilla extract, and pinch salt until smooth, 2 to 4 minutes. Reduce speed to medium-low, slowly add ½ cup confectioners' sugar, and beat until smooth, 4 to 6 minutes. Increase speed to medium-high and beat until frosting is light and fluffy, 2 to 4 minutes. Makes about ¾ cup.

Per serving: Cal 90; Fat 4g; Sat Fat 2.5g; Chol 15mg; Carb 11g; Protein 2g; Fiber 0g; Sodium 105mg

Blueberry Cornmeal Tea Cake

Serves 6 • **Cooking Time** 2 to 3 hours on High • **Slow Cooker Size** 5½ to 7 Quarts

✓ **WHY THIS RECIPE WORKS:** Fresh fruit is too often lost in heavy, overwhelmingly sweet desserts, so we set our sights on a versatile cake that would highlight the classically light combination of summery blueberries and moist cornbread. This low-fat cake is easy to assemble and works as both an afternoon coffee accompaniment and a welcome dessert for a summer meal. We used a quick-bread method of mixing, combining just 4 tablespoons of melted (instead of creamed) butter with sugar, egg, leaveners, and flour, which gave the cake good height and a substantial crumb. For soft and creamy results, we mixed in yogurt, which contributed a subtle sweetness and moisture for a delicate texture without excess fat. The addition of lemon zest gave our cake the final brightness that we wanted, pairing well with the juicy blueberries. Do not use stone-ground cornmeal here; it will yield a drier and less tender cake. If fresh blueberries are unavailable, an equal amount of frozen berries (do not thaw) can be substituted. You will need an oval slow cooker for this recipe. We recommend an 8½ by 4½-inch loaf pan for this recipe, but you can substitute a 9 by 5-inch loaf pan. For information on making an aluminum foil rack, see page 276.

1	cup (5 ounces) all-purpose flour
¼	cup (1¼ ounces) cornmeal
½	teaspoon baking powder
½	teaspoon baking soda
	Salt
½	cup plain yogurt
⅓	cup (2⅓ ounces) granulated sugar
1	large egg, room temperature
2	teaspoons grated lemon zest plus 4 teaspoons juice
½	teaspoon vanilla extract
4	tablespoons unsalted butter, melted and cooled
5	ounces (1 cup) blueberries
¾	cup (3 ounces) confectioners' sugar

1. Add ½ inch water (about 2 cups) to slow cooker and place aluminum foil rack in bottom. Make foil sling for 8½ by 4½-inch loaf pan by folding 2 long sheets of aluminum foil; first sheet should be 8½ inches wide and second sheet should be 4½ inches wide. Lay sheets of foil in pan perpendicular to each other, with extra foil hanging over edges of pan. Push foil into corners and up sides of pan, smoothing foil flush to pan. Lightly grease foil.

2. Whisk flour, cornmeal, baking powder, baking soda, and ½ teaspoon salt together in bowl. In large bowl, whisk yogurt, granulated sugar, egg, lemon zest, and vanilla together until smooth, then slowly whisk in melted butter. Stir in flour mixture until just incorporated. Gently fold in blueberries.

3. Scrape batter into prepared pan and smooth top. Gently tap pan on counter to release air bubbles. Set cake on rack in prepared slow cooker, cover, and cook until toothpick inserted in center comes out clean, 2 to 3 hours on high.

4. Let cake cool in pan on wire rack for 10 minutes. Using ends of foil as handles, lift cake out of pan and transfer to rack; discard foil. Let cake cool completely, 1 to 2 hours.

5. Whisk confectioners' sugar, pinch salt, and lemon juice together in bowl until smooth. Flip cake over and transfer to serving platter. Drizzle top and sides with glaze and let glaze set before serving, about 25 minutes.

Per serving: Cal 300; Fat 9g; Sat Fat 5g; Chol 55mg; Carb 50g; Protein 4g; Fiber 1g; Sodium 380mg

Lemon Cheesecake

Serves 8 • **Cooking Time** 1½ to 2½ hours on High • **Slow Cooker Size** 5½ to 7 Quarts

☑ **WHY THIS RECIPE WORKS:** To make a lemony low-fat cheesecake in the slow cooker, we started by replacing full-fat cream cheese with a combination of neufchatel cream cheese and 1 percent cottage cheese and cut down on sugar. We then added lemon zest and juice for a bright complement to the tangy sour cream. Finally, we pureed the filling in a food processor for an ultrasmooth texture. The result? A rich, creamy cheesecake with about half the calories and three-quarters less fat than the original. For the creamiest texture, we turned off the slow cooker once the cake registered 150 degrees on an instant-read thermometer, then let the cheesecake sit in the slow cooker for an hour so it could gently finish cooking. You will need a 6-inch springform pan for this recipe. Check the temperature of the cheesecake after 1½ hours of cooking and continue to monitor until it registers 150 degrees. To make neat slices, dip the knife blade into hot water and wipe it clean with a dish towel after each cut. For information on making an aluminum foil rack, see page 276. Serve with berries.

- **6** whole graham crackers, broken into 1-inch pieces
- **2** tablespoons unsalted butter, melted and cooled
- **⅔** cup (4⅔ ounces) plus 1 tablespoon sugar
- Pinch ground nutmeg
- Salt
- **2** tablespoons grated lemon zest plus 3 tablespoons juice (2 lemons)
- **12** ounces ⅓ less fat cream cheese (neufchatel), softened
- **6** ounces (¾ cup) 1 percent low-fat cottage cheese, drained
- **¼** cup sour cream
- **2** large eggs, room temperature

1. Pulse graham crackers in food processor to fine crumbs, about 20 pulses. Add melted butter, 1 tablespoon sugar, nutmeg, and pinch salt and pulse to combine, about 4 pulses. Sprinkle crumbs into 6-inch springform pan and press into even layer using bottom of dry measuring cup. Wipe out processor bowl.

2. Process remaining ⅔ cup sugar and lemon zest in food processor until sugar is yellow and fragrant, about 15 seconds. Add cream cheese, cottage cheese, and ¼ teaspoon salt and process until combined, about 15 seconds. Add sour cream, eggs, and lemon juice and process until just incorporated, about 15 seconds. Pour filling into prepared pan and smooth top.

3. Add ½ inch water (about 2 cups) to slow cooker and place aluminum foil rack in bottom. Set cheesecake on rack in prepared slow cooker, cover, and cook until cake registers 150 degrees, 1½ to 2½ hours on high. Turn slow cooker off and let cheesecake sit, covered, for 1 hour.

4. Transfer cheesecake to wire rack. Run small knife around edge of cake; gently blot away condensation using paper towels. Let cool in pan to room temperature, about 1 hour. Cover with plastic wrap and refrigerate until well chilled, at least 3 hours or up to 3 days.

5. About 30 minutes before serving, run small knife around edge of cheesecake, then remove sides of pan. Slide thin metal spatula between crust and pan bottom to loosen, then slide cheesecake onto serving platter. Serve.

Per serving: Cal 210; Fat 15g; Sat Fat 9g; Chol 90mg; Carb 9g; Protein 9g; Fiber 0g; Sodium 400mg

Spiced Pumpkin Cheesecake

Serves 8 • **Cooking Time** 1½ to 2½ hours on High • **Slow Cooker Size** 5½ to 7 Quarts

✔ **WHY THIS RECIPE WORKS:** For our lower-fat and seasonal pumpkin cheesecake, we found that the gentle heat of the slow cooker eliminated the risk of overcooking while also freeing up the oven. You will need a 6-inch springform pan for this recipe. Check the temperature of the cheesecake after 1½ hours of cooking and continue to monitor until it registers 150 degrees. To make neat slices, dip the knife blade into hot water and wipe it clean with a dish towel after each cut. For information on making an aluminum foil rack, see page 276.

6 **whole graham crackers, broken into 1-inch pieces**

2 **tablespoons unsalted butter, melted and cooled**

½ **cup (3½ ounces) plus 1 tablespoon sugar**

1½ **teaspoons ground cinnamon**
Salt

1 **cup canned unsweetened pumpkin puree**

12 **ounces ⅓ less fat cream cheese (neufchatel), softened**

½ **teaspoon ground ginger**

⅛ **teaspoon ground cloves**

¼ **cup sour cream**

2 **large eggs, room temperature**

1. Pulse graham crackers in food processor to fine crumbs, about 20 pulses. Add melted butter, 1 tablespoon sugar, ½ teaspoon cinnamon, and pinch salt and pulse to combine, about 4 pulses. Sprinkle crumbs into 6-inch springform pan and press into even layer using bottom of dry measuring cup. Wipe out processor bowl.

2. Spread pumpkin puree over baking sheet lined with several layers of paper towels and press dry with additional towels. Transfer puree to now-empty food processor, discarding towels (puree will separate easily from towels). Add cream cheese, ginger, cloves, ½ teaspoon salt, remaining ½ cup sugar, and remaining 1 teaspoon cinnamon and process until combined, about 15 seconds. Add sour cream and eggs and process until just incorporated, about 15 seconds. Pour filling into prepared pan and smooth top.

3. Add ½ inch water (about 2 cups) to slow cooker and place aluminum foil rack in bottom. Set cheesecake on rack in prepared slow cooker, cover, and cook until cake registers 150 degrees, 1½ to 2½ hours on high. Turn slow cooker off and let cheesecake sit, covered, for 1 hour.

4. Transfer cheesecake to wire rack. Run small knife around edge of cake; gently blot away condensation using paper towels. Let cool in pan to room temperature, about 1 hour. Cover with plastic wrap and refrigerate until well chilled, at least 3 hours or up to 3 days.

5. About 30 minutes before serving, run small knife around edge of cheesecake, then remove sides of pan. Slide thin metal spatula between crust and pan bottom to loosen, then slide cheesecake onto serving platter. Serve.

Per serving: Cal 240; Fat 15g; Sat Fat 9g; Chol 85mg; Carb 21g; Protein 7g; Fiber 2g; Sodium 390mg

Classic Brownies

Serves 6 • **Cooking Time** 3 to 4 hours on High • **Slow Cooker Size** 5½ to 7 Quarts

✔ **WHY THIS RECIPE WORKS:** Making low-fat brownies in a slow cooker is not only easy but yields great results, in part because the volatile compounds in chocolate can cook off in the dry heat of the oven. In the gentle heat of the slow cooker, this just doesn't have a chance to happen, a great advantage when you are using a smaller amount of chocolate (and less fat) but still want a rich, moist brownie. In our first attempts we tested many of the alternative ingredients commonly used in low-fat brownies like prune puree and applesauce to try to replace the missing chocolate, but they all yielded brownies with distracting flavors. We found that a combination of sour cream and brown sugar gave us enough richness and flavor that we did not miss the extra chocolate or butter. To make the batter, we melted the chocolate and butter and combined all the ingredients using a simple bowl method, which allows you to make homemade brownies with minimal work. You will need an oval slow cooker for this recipe. We recommend an 8½ by 4½-inch loaf pan for this recipe, but you can substitute a 9 by 5-inch loaf pan. For information on making an aluminum foil rack, see page 276.

2 ounces unsweetened chocolate, chopped fine

3 tablespoons unsalted butter

⅓ cup (1⅔ ounces) all-purpose flour

½ teaspoon baking powder

⅛ teaspoon salt

⅔ cup packed (4⅔ ounces) brown sugar

1 large egg plus 1 large yolk, room temperature

2 tablespoons sour cream

½ teaspoon vanilla extract
Confectioners' sugar (optional)

1. Add ½ inch water (about 2 cups) to slow cooker and place aluminum foil rack in bottom. Make foil sling for 8½ by 4½-inch loaf pan by folding 2 long sheets of aluminum foil; first sheet should be 8½ inches wide and second sheet should be 4½ inches wide. Lay sheets of foil in pan perpendicular to each other, with extra foil hanging over edges of pan. Push foil into corners and up sides of pan, smoothing foil flush to pan. Lightly grease foil.

2. Microwave chocolate in large bowl at 50 percent power for 1 to 2 minutes. Stir, add butter, and continue to heat until melted, stirring once every 30 seconds; let cool slightly. In separate bowl, whisk flour, baking powder, and salt together. Whisk brown sugar, egg and yolk, sour cream, and vanilla into cooled chocolate mixture until well combined. Stir in flour mixture until just incorporated.

3. Scrape batter into prepared pan and smooth top. Set brownies on rack in prepared slow cooker, cover, and cook until toothpick inserted in center comes out with few moist crumbs attached, 3 to 4 hours on high.

4. Let brownies cool completely in pan on wire rack, 1 to 2 hours. Using ends of foil as handles, lift brownies out of pan and transfer to cutting board; discard foil. Cut brownies into squares and dust with confectioners' sugar, if using. Serve.

Per serving: Cal 250; Fat 13g; Sat Fat 8g; Chol 80mg; Carb 33g; Protein 4g; Fiber 2g; Sodium 110mg

Rice Pudding with Dried Cherries and Cinnamon

Serves 6 • **Cooking Time** 3 to 4 hours on High • **Slow Cooker Size** 4 to 7 Quarts

✔ **WHY THIS RECIPE WORKS:** When it comes to simple yet sublime desserts, it doesn't get much better than rice pudding. For our slow-cooker take on this comfort classic we turned to short-grain brown rice as our starting point, since brown rice is a healthier choice and short-grain brown rice is starchier than long-grain, a plus when making pudding. Hoping to keep things on the healthier side, as rice pudding can often veer into calorie and fat overload, we took a hard look at alternatives to heavy cream and the amount of sugar needed. We wanted the most appealing balance of rice flavor and a rich consistency, which we achieved by using 3 cups of water, 2¼ cups of half-and-half, 1 cup of rice, and ½ cup of sugar. We tried using milk but it did not fare well, leaving unappealing flecks of curdled milk throughout the pudding. We found that the rice was more evenly cooked when we boiled the liquids before adding them to the slow cooker with the rice, and we also found that the rice cooked more evenly on high than on low. For flavor, we added dried cherries and cinnamon at the end of cooking and let them infuse the pudding with their warm notes and subtle sweetness before serving.

3	**cups water**
2¼	**cups half-and-half**
½	**cup sugar**
¼	**teaspoon salt**
1	**cup short-grain brown rice**
½	**cup dried cherries**
2	**teaspoons vanilla extract**
1	**teaspoon ground cinnamon**

1. Lightly spray inside of slow cooker with vegetable oil spray. Bring water, half-and-half, sugar, and salt to boil in saucepan over medium heat, stirring occasionally; transfer to slow cooker. Stir in rice, cover, and cook until tender, 3 to 4 hours on high.

2. Stir cherries, vanilla, and cinnamon into pudding. Turn slow cooker off and let pudding rest, uncovered, until fully set, about 20 minutes. Adjust pudding consistency as desired before serving; if too loose, gently stir pudding until excess liquid is absorbed or, if too dry, stir in hot water as needed to loosen.

Per serving: Cal 350; Fat 11g; Sat Fat 6g; Chol 35mg; Carb 55g; Protein 6g; Fiber 3g; Sodium 140mg

---

SMART SHOPPING VANILLA EXTRACT
Vanilla extract is sold in pure and imitation varieties. So which should you buy? If you're buying only one bottle of vanilla for cooking, baking, and making cold and creamy desserts, our top choice is a real extract—real vanilla has around 250 flavor compounds compared to imitation vanilla's one, giving it a complexity tasters appreciated in certain applications. Our favorite pure vanilla is **McCormick Pure Vanilla Extract**. But if you use vanilla only for baking, we have to admit there's not much of a difference between a well-made synthetic vanilla and the real thing (the flavor and aroma compounds in pure vanilla begin to bake off at higher temperatures, so the subtleties are lost). Tasters liked the "well-balanced and full" vanilla flavor and budget-friendly price of our top-rated imitation vanilla, **CF Sauer Co. Gold Medal Imitation Vanilla Extract**.

Coconut-Lime Rice Pudding

Serves 6 • **Cooking Time** 3 to 4 hours on High • **Slow Cooker Size** 4 to 7 Quarts

✔ **WHY THIS RECIPE WORKS:** For a creamy rice pudding with a tropical twist, we turned to rich coconut milk and tangy limes. To achieve a smooth, creamy texture from nutrient-rich brown rice in our slow cooker, we doubled the amount of liquid traditionally used and brought it to a boil on the stovetop to jump-start the rice. We found that the richest flavor and creamiest texture came from a combination of water, half-and-half, and light coconut milk. Full-fat coconut milk packed too much fat and created an overly thick pudding. The light coconut milk gave us some added sweetness, allowing us to cut down on sugar, and provided the coconut flavor we wanted, especially when we stirred in some extra at the end of the cooking time along with a little coconut extract. A final addition of lime zest and juice provided a bright complement to the coconut, resulting in a rich, summery rice pudding.

2½ **cups water**
1½ **cups half-and-half**
1   **(13.5-ounce) can light coconut milk**
¼   **cup (1¾ ounces) sugar**
½   **teaspoon salt**
1   **cup short-grain brown rice**
½   **teaspoon coconut extract**
½   **teaspoon grated lime zest plus 2 teaspoons juice**

1. Lightly spray inside of slow cooker with vegetable oil spray. Bring water, half-and-half, 1 cup coconut milk, sugar, and salt to boil in saucepan over medium heat, stirring occasionally; transfer to slow cooker. Stir in rice, cover, and cook until tender, 3 to 4 hours on high.

2. Stir remaining coconut milk, coconut extract, and lime zest and juice into slow cooker. Turn slow cooker off and let pudding rest, uncovered, until fully set, about 20 minutes. Adjust pudding consistency as desired before serving; if too loose, gently stir pudding until excess liquid is absorbed or, if too dry, stir in hot water as needed to loosen.

Per serving: Cal 260; Fat 10g; Sat Fat 6g; Chol 20mg; Carb 37g; Protein 4g; Fiber 1g; Sodium 230mg

---

SMART SHOPPING BROWN RICE
Brown rice is essentially a less processed version of white rice. Each individual grain of rice is made up of an endosperm, germ, bran, and a husk or hull. The husk is the protective outermost layer and must be removed. White rice is stripped of all but the endosperm, while brown rice also retains the germ and bran. After the husk is removed, brown rice is considered to be a whole grain and has more fiber than white rice. The bran and germ contain oils that shorten the rice's shelf life and require longer cooking to allow water to penetrate the bran. Brown rice tends to have a firmer texture and a nuttier, earthier flavor than white rice, thanks to the bran and germ.

Chocolate Chip Bread Pudding

Serves 10 • **Cooking Time** 3 to 4 hours on Low • **Slow Cooker Size** 5½ to 7 Quarts

✓ **WHY THIS RECIPE WORKS:** Bread pudding stays velvety and rich when made in a slow cooker without relying on an excess of cream and eggs. However, in this steamy environment, a new problem presented itself: soggy bread. Wanting to avoid the step of drying the bread in the oven, we turned to French bread for its firm crust and dry texture. We cut the loaf into cubes, then combined them with our custard (consisting of eggs, milk, sugar, cocoa powder, and salt). To cut fat, we used mostly whole eggs instead of exclusively egg yolks. Replacing some of the yolks with whole eggs gave the pudding a firmer structure and a significantly reduced calorie count. Cocoa powder was another essential ingredient, adding a chocolaty boost without too much sweetness. Pressing the bread into the custard ensured that every cube soaked up its share. We loved the addition of chocolate chips, which melted and added a decadent gooeyness that had tasters diving in for seconds. Finally, a topping of toasted almonds gave our chocolaty, rich dessert a crunchy bite. We prefer French or Italian bread here; avoid using rustic loaves with thick crusts, if possible. You will need an oval slow cooker for this recipe. Don't let this bread pudding cook longer than 4 hours or it will become dried out and rubbery. For information on making an aluminum foil collar, see page 169.

3½	cups 2 percent low-fat milk
¾	cup (5¼ ounces) sugar
6	large eggs plus 2 large yolks
2	tablespoons unsweetened cocoa powder
½	teaspoon salt
12	ounces French or Italian bread, cut into ½-inch pieces (10 cups)
¾	cup (4½ ounces) bittersweet or semisweet chocolate chips
¾	cup sliced almonds, toasted

1. Whisk milk, sugar, eggs and yolks, cocoa, and salt together in large bowl. Stir in bread and ½ cup chocolate chips and let sit, pressing on bread occasionally, until custard is mostly absorbed, about 10 minutes.

2. Line slow cooker with aluminum foil collar and lightly spray with vegetable oil spray. Transfer soaked bread mixture to prepared slow cooker, cover, and cook until center is set, 3 to 4 hours on low.

3. Turn slow cooker off and remove foil collar. Sprinkle bread pudding with remaining ¼ cup chocolate chips, cover, and let cool for 20 minutes. Sprinkle with almonds and serve.

Per serving: Cal 350; Fat 13g; Sat Fat 5g; Chol 155mg; Carb 47g; Protein 12; Fiber 3g; Sodium 420mg

---

SMART SHOPPING CHOCOLATE CHIPS
Nestlé first introduced chocolate chips to the public in 1939 in response to the chocolate chip cookie craze that swept the nation. Nowadays, you can find lots of different types and brands of chocolate chips on the market. We pitted eight widely available brands of semisweet and bittersweet chips against each other in a bake-off; when the dust finally settled, there was a clear winner: **Ghirardelli 60% Cacao Bittersweet Chocolate Chips** handily beat out the competition with their distinct flavors of "wine," "fruit," and "smoke" and lower sugar content, which allowed the chocolate flavor to really shine.

Flan

Serves 6 • **Cooking Time** 2 to 3 hours on Low • **Slow Cooker Size** 5½ to 7 Quarts

✓ **WHY THIS RECIPE WORKS:** Flan is a classic Spanish dessert, slightly sweeter than a traditional baked custard, with a crowning touch of thin, sweet caramel that pools over the dish once unmolded. To create our low-fat version we opted for low-fat sweetened condensed milk and 2 percent milk. Mixing the dairy with a combination of whole eggs, yolks, and sugar resulted in a tender, rich custard. We tried to make our caramel topping in the microwave but could not achieve the right texture or color, so we moved it to the stovetop. A water bath ensured that the custard cooked evenly. You will need an oval slow cooker for this recipe. Check the temperature of the custard after 2 hours and continue to monitor until it registers 180 degrees. We recommend an 8½ by 4½-inch loaf pan for this recipe, but you can substitute a 9 by 5-inch loaf pan. This recipe should be made at least one day before serving. Serve the flan on a platter with a raised rim to contain the liquid caramel.

⅔ cup (4⅔ ounces) sugar
¼ cup water
2 large eggs plus 3 large yolks
1½ cups 2 percent low-fat milk
1 (14-ounce) can low-fat
   sweetened condensed milk
¼ teaspoon grated lemon zest

1. Stir sugar and water together in medium saucepan until sugar is moistened. Bring to boil over medium-high heat, 3 to 5 minutes. Cook, without stirring, until mixture begins to turn golden, 1 to 2 minutes. Gently swirling pan, continue to cook until sugar is color of peanut butter, 1 to 2 minutes. Remove from heat and swirl pan until sugar is reddish-amber color, 15 to 20 seconds. Carefully swirl in 2 tablespoons warm water until incorporated; mixture will bubble and steam. Pour caramel into 8½ by 4½-inch loaf pan; do not scrape out saucepan.

2. Add ½ inch water (about 2 cups) to slow cooker. Whisk eggs and yolks together in medium bowl until combined. Whisk in milk, condensed milk, and lemon zest until incorporated, then pour into prepared pan. Set pan in prepared slow cooker, cover, and cook until center of flan jiggles slightly when shaken and registers 180 degrees, 2 to 3 hours on low.

3. Transfer pan to wire rack and let cool to room temperature, about 2 hours. Wrap tightly with plastic wrap and chill overnight or up to 4 days.

4. To unmold, run small knife around edge of flan. Invert serving platter on top of pan, then carefully flip pan and platter over. When flan is released, remove pan. Using rubber spatula, scrape residual caramel onto flan (some caramel may remain stuck in pan). Serve.

Per serving: Cal 390; Fat 8g; Sat Fat 4g; Chol 170mg; Carb 65g; Protein 11g; Fiber 0g; Sodium 125mg

Crème Brûlée

Serves 4 • **Cooking Time** 2 to 3 hours on Low • **Slow Cooker Size** 5½ to 7 Quarts

✓ **WHY THIS RECIPE WORKS:** We set out to simplify classic crème brûlée and lower the fat content while we were at it. Using the slow cooker yielded a creamy texture without the risk of overcooking. To lower the fat, we swapped the heavy cream for a combination of whole milk and half-and-half and reduced the number of egg yolks. We found that adding an ounce of white chocolate gave the crème brûlée a luxurious silkiness without too much fat. While we prefer turbinado or Demerara sugar for the caramelized sugar crust, regular granulated sugar will work, too, but use only 1 scant teaspoon on each ramekin. You will need an oval slow cooker and four 4-ounce (or 6-ounce) ramekins for this recipe. Check the temperature of the custards after 2 hours of cooking and continue to monitor until they register 180 to 185 degrees.

1	cup half-and-half
3	tablespoons granulated sugar
4	teaspoons cornstarch
1	teaspoon vanilla extract
⅛	teaspoon salt
1	ounce white chocolate, chopped fine
¾	cup whole milk
3	large egg yolks
4	teaspoons turbinado sugar

1. Whisk half-and-half, granulated sugar, cornstarch, vanilla, and salt together in small saucepan. Bring half-and-half mixture to simmer over medium-low heat and cook, whisking constantly, until thickened, about 1 minute. Place chocolate in medium bowl and pour half-and-half mixture on top of chocolate. Whisk until completely smooth, then whisk in milk, followed by egg yolks. Strain custard through fine-mesh strainer into 4-cup liquid measuring cup.

2. Add ½ inch water (about 2 cups) to slow cooker. Portion custard into four 4-ounce (or 6-ounce) ramekins and set in prepared slow cooker. Cover and cook until center of custard is just barely set and registers 180 to 185 degrees, 2 to 3 hours on low.

3. Using tongs and sturdy spatula, transfer ramekins to wire rack and let cool to room temperature, about 2 hours. Cover with plastic wrap and refrigerate until well chilled, at least 3 hours or up to 4 days.

4. Gently blot away condensation with paper towels. Sprinkle 1 teaspoon turbinado sugar evenly over each custard. Ignite torch and caramelize sugar. Refrigerate ramekins, uncovered, to rechill, 30 to 45 minutes. Serve.

Per serving: Cal 250; Fat 14g; Sat Fat 8g; Chol 165mg; Carb 26g; Protein 6g; Fiber 0g; Sodium 130mg

---

QUICK PREP TIP
CARAMELIZING THE SUGAR
After sprinkling sugar over surface of custard, tilt and tap ramekin to distribute sugar into thin, even layer. Pour out any excess sugar and wipe inside rim clean. To caramelize sugar, sweep flame of torch from perimeter of custard toward middle, keeping flame about 2 inches above ramekin, until sugar is bubbling and deep golden brown.

Vanilla-Cardamom Poached Peaches

Serves 6 • **Cooking Time** 3 to 4 hours on Low • **Slow Cooker Size** 4 to 7 Quarts

✔ WHY THIS RECIPE WORKS: This low-fat and fresh-tasting dessert makes an elegant ending to a meal with very little effort required. We've found that the slow cooker is the perfect way to poach many things, fruit included. Here, height-of-summer peaches are gently poached in a mixture of wine and water infused with vanilla and cardamom plus a little sugar. Once the peaches were cooked, we removed them from the slow cooker and reduced the poaching liquid on the stovetop, adding a tablespoon of butter to add complexity to the sauce. A sprinkling of pistachios for a nice crunch was a welcome finishing touch. For the best texture, look for peaches that are neither fully ripe nor rock hard; choose those that yield just slightly when pressed. For an accurate measurement of boiling water, bring a full kettle of water to a boil and then measure out the desired amount. The peaches can be served warm or at room temperature. If serving at room temperature, wait to sprinkle with pistachios until right before serving.

2	cups boiling water
1	cup dry white wine
2	tablespoons sugar
2	teaspoons vanilla extract
½	teaspoon ground cardamom
⅛	teaspoon salt
6	peaches (6 ounces each), peeled, halved, and pitted
1	tablespoon unsalted butter
⅓	cup shelled pistachios, toasted and chopped

1. Stir boiling water, wine, sugar, vanilla, cardamom, and salt together in slow cooker until sugar dissolves. Add peaches, cover, and cook until tender, 3 to 4 hours on low.

2. Using slotted spoon, transfer peaches to shallow casserole dish. Transfer cooking liquid to large saucepan, bring to simmer over medium-high heat, and cook until thickened and measures about 1 cup, 15 to 20 minutes. Whisk in butter, then pour sauce over peaches. Sprinkle individual portions with pistachios before serving.

Per serving: Cal 170; Fat 5g; Sat Fat 1.5g; Chol 5mg; Carb 22g; Protein 2g; Fiber 3g; Sodium 55mg

---

QUICK PREP TIP PEELING PEACHES

Using paring knife, score small X at base of each peach, then lower peaches into boiling water and simmer until skins loosen, 30 to 60 seconds. Transfer peaches immediately to ice water and let cool for about 1 minute. Finally, use paring knife to remove strips of loosened peel, starting at X on base of each peach.

Tea-Poached Pears

Serves 6 • **Cooking Time** 3 to 4 hours on Low • **Slow Cooker Size** 4 to 7 Quarts

✔ **WHY THIS RECIPE WORKS:** Poaching pears in tea creates a fragrant and delicate dessert that is naturally low in fat and calories. The key to this simple dessert was to create a tea-based poaching liquid that was strong enough to add flavor but not bitterness. We found that a ratio of 4 tea bags to 3 cups water worked best, and we steeped them for just 8 minutes. To add a subtle complexity to the liquid we added a cinnamon stick and star anise. After developing such a flavorful base, we decided to reduce the liquid on the stovetop and create a bold and spicy sauce to pour over the pears. For a rich and creamy topping we combined confectioners' sugar with 2 percent Greek yogurt and Grand Marnier, which complemented the warm spices of the sauce and the pears. For the best texture, look for pears that are neither fully ripe nor rock hard; choose those that yield just slightly when pressed. For an accurate measurement of boiling water, bring a full kettle of water to a boil and then measure out the desired amount. The pears can be served warm or at room temperature. If serving at room temperature, wait to dollop with the yogurt topping until right before serving.

3 cups boiling water
4 black tea bags
1 cinnamon stick
2 star anise pods
Salt
¼ cup packed brown sugar
6 Bartlett or Bosc pears, peeled, halved, and cored
1 tablespoon unsalted butter
¾ cup 2 percent Greek yogurt
3 tablespoons confectioners' sugar
1 teaspoon Grand Marnier

1. Combine boiling water, tea bags, cinnamon stick, star anise, and ⅛ teaspoon salt in slow cooker and let steep for 8 minutes; discard tea bags. Stir in brown sugar until dissolved. Add pears, cover, and cook until tender, 3 to 4 hours on low.

2. Using slotted spoon, transfer pears to shallow casserole dish. Strain cooking liquid into large saucepan, bring to simmer over medium-high heat, and cook until thickened and measures about 1 cup, 15 to 20 minutes. Whisk in butter, then pour sauce over pears.

3. Whisk yogurt, confectioners' sugar, Grand Marnier, and ⅛ teaspoon salt together in bowl until combined. Dollop individual portions with yogurt topping before serving.

Per serving: Cal 200; Fat 2.5g; Sat Fat 1.5g; Chol 5mg; Carb 40g; Protein 3g; Fiber 5g; Sodium 110mg

QUICK PREP TIP CORING PEARS
Halve or quarter pears from stem to blossom end and then remove core using melon baller. After removing core, use edge of melon baller to scrape away interior stem of pear, from core to stem.

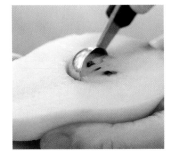

Warm Strawberry-Rhubarb Compote with Frozen Yogurt

Serves 6 • **Cooking Time** 1 to 2 hours on Low • **Slow Cooker Size** 4 to 7 Quarts

✔ WHY THIS RECIPE WORKS: Fruit compotes seem like an obvious choice for a healthy dessert option as they are naturally low in fat and simple to make. We set out to design a version for our slow cooker that would allow us to enjoy a warm summery fruit topping for frozen yogurt at the end of dinner without having to fuss with the oven. When developing our light recipe for this classic strawberry-rhubarb duo, we found that just a small amount of honey added to the slow cooker with the rhubarb provided a hint of sweetness and tamed the acidity in the rhubarb. The honey also thickened the fruit juice into a light syrup, while keeping the calories to a minimum. For big, distinct strawberry flavor we stirred the berries in at the end, which also prevented them from turning to mush. To finish the compote we stirred in just 1 tablespoon of butter for richness.

1	**pound rhubarb, peeled and sliced 1 inch thick**
¼	**cup honey**
2	**tablespoons water**
1	**teaspoon vanilla extract**
	Pinch salt
20	**ounces strawberries, hulled and quartered (4 cups)**
1	**tablespoon unsalted butter**
1½	**pints low-fat vanilla frozen yogurt**

1. Combine rhubarb, honey, water, vanilla, and salt in slow cooker. Cover and cook until rhubarb is softened, 1 to 2 hours on low.

2. Stir in strawberries and butter and let sit until heated through, about 5 minutes. Portion frozen yogurt into individual bowls, spoon warm compote over top, and serve. (Compote can be held on warm or low setting for up to 2 hours.)

Per serving: Cal 310; Fat 7g; Sat Fat 3.5g; Chol 70mg; Carb 53g; Protein 10g; Fiber 3g; Sodium 110mg

---

QUICK PREP TIP PEELING RHUBARB
After removing any leaves, trim both ends of stalk and then partially slice thin disk from bottom of stalk, being careful not to cut completely through. Gently pull partially attached disk away from stalk, pull back outer peel, and discard. Make second cut partway through bottom of stalk in reverse direction. Pull back peel on other side of stalk and discard.

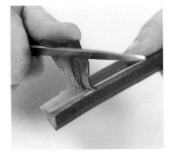

Warm Plum-Blackberry Compote with Frozen Yogurt

Serves 6 • **Cooking Time** 1 to 2 hours on Low • **Slow Cooker Size** 4 to 7 Quarts

✔ **WHY THIS RECIPE WORKS:** When the fruit piled high at local farmstands is so tempting, it's nice to have an easy way to transform it into a winning dessert that allows its fresh flavor to shine through. This warm fruit compote pairing fragrant plums and blackberries is as beautiful as it is delicious. To keep the flavor of the fruit front and center, we avoided using a thickener and instead relied on a little honey, which also provided a light, sweet floral note. The plums softened perfectly after a couple of hours in the slow cooker, at which point we added the sweet-tart blackberries, which softened just enough after sitting for only 5 minutes in the slow cooker. For richness and extra thickening we also finished the compote with a little butter. Look for plums of similar ripeness so that they cook evenly.

1½	pounds plums, halved, pitted, and sliced ½ inch thick
3	tablespoons honey
2	tablespoons water
1	teaspoon vanilla extract
	Pinch salt
10	ounces (2 cups) blackberries
1	tablespoon unsalted butter
1½	pints low-fat vanilla frozen yogurt

1. Combine plums, honey, water, vanilla, and salt in slow cooker. Cover and cook until plums are softened, 1 to 2 hours on low.

2. Stir in blackberries and butter and let sit until heated through, about 5 minutes. Portion frozen yogurt into individual bowls, spoon warm compote over top, and serve. (Compote can be held on warm or low setting for up to 2 hours.)

Per serving: Cal 320; Fat 7g; Sat Fat 3.5g; Chol 70mg; Carb 58g; Protein 10g; Fiber 4g; Sodium 105mg

---

QUICK PREP TIP STORING FRESH BERRIES

It just wouldn't feel like summer without a couple of quarts of fresh berries in our refrigerator. But when these juicy fruits are kept in their original basket, the berries on top crush those on the bottom. In the test kitchen, we safely store fresh berries by spreading them out on a dinner plate lined with paper towels, which absorb any excess moisture. The plate goes into the refrigerator, and we've got smush-free berries at the ready.

Apple-Oat Crisp

Serves 6 • **Cooking Time** 3 to 4 hours on Low • **Slow Cooker Size** 4 to 7 Quarts

✓ **WHY THIS RECIPE WORKS:** A great fruit crisp marries sweet, almost fall-apart-tender fruit with a buttery rich and crisp topping, so there is no wonder that it is an appealing dessert option. What's tricky about making a fruit crisp is ensuring that the filling and topping are perfectly cooked and ready to serve when dinner is over. Turns out that using the slow cooker makes this feat easier and more streamlined. We knew from the outset that we'd have to cook the topping separately—it would simply steam on top of the filling. But all that moist heat made the slow cooker the perfect way to make the apple filling: As the apples cooked, they were infused with flavor from the mixture of brown sugar, cinnamon, and cider. Cutting the apples into thick wedges ensured that they did not turn to mush during the long cooking time. And as they cooked and released their juice, they formed a delicious sauce, which was thickened by a little cornstarch that we added at the outset. Since our filling was naturally healthy, we wanted a topping that tasted rich but didn't tip the scales, so we turned to rolled oats, almonds, a little butter, honey, and spices. While the filling cooks, you can bake the topping and simply sprinkle it over individual portions at serving time—no last-minute rewarming required.

FILLING

- 1½ **pounds Granny Smith apples, peeled, cored, and cut into ½-inch-thick wedges**
- 1½ **pounds Golden Delicious apples, peeled, cored, and cut into ½-inch-thick wedges**
- ½ **cup apple cider**
- 2 **tablespoons packed light brown sugar**
- 1 **tablespoon cornstarch**
- 2 **teaspoons lemon juice**
- ¼ **teaspoon ground cinnamon**

TOPPING

- ½ **cup sliced almonds**
- ½ **cup (2½ ounces) all-purpose flour**
- ¼ **cup packed (1¾ ounces) light brown sugar**
- ¼ **teaspoon ground cinnamon**
- ¼ **teaspoon salt**
- ⅛ **teaspoon ground nutmeg**
- 5 **tablespoons unsalted butter, melted and cooled**
- ¾ **cup (2¼ ounces) old-fashioned rolled oats**
- 2 **tablespoons honey**

1. FOR THE FILLING: Combine all ingredients in slow cooker. Cover and cook until apples are softened and sauce is thickened, 3 to 4 hours on low.

2. FOR THE TOPPING: Meanwhile, adjust oven rack to upper-middle position and heat oven to 400 degrees. Line rimmed baking sheet with parchment paper.

3. Pulse almonds, flour, sugar, cinnamon, salt, and nutmeg in food processor until nuts are finely chopped, about 10 pulses. Drizzle melted butter over top and pulse until mixture resembles crumbly wet sand, about 5 pulses. Add oats and honey and pulse until evenly incorporated, about 3 pulses.

4. Spread topping evenly in prepared sheet and pinch it between your fingers into small pea-size pieces (with some smaller loose bits). Bake until golden brown, 8 to 12 minutes, rotating sheet halfway through baking. Let cool slightly.

5. Gently stir apples to coat with sauce. Sprinkle individual portions of apple filling with crumbles before serving.

Per serving: Cal 410; Fat 14g; Sat Fat 6g; Chol 25mg; Carb 70g; Protein 5g; Fiber 8g; Sodium 105mg

Conversions & Equivalencies

Some say cooking is a science and an art. We would say that geography has a hand in it, too. Flour milled in the United Kingdom and elsewhere will feel and taste different from flour milled in the United States. So we cannot promise that the loaf of bread you bake in Canada or England will taste the same as a loaf baked in the States, but we can offer guidelines for converting weights and measures. We also recommend that you rely on your instincts when making our recipes. Refer to the visual cues provided. If the bread dough hasn't "come together in a ball," as described, you may need to add more flour—even if the recipe doesn't tell you to. You be the judge.

The recipes in this book were developed using standard U.S. measures following U.S. government guidelines. The charts below offer equivalents for U.S., metric, and imperial (U.K.) measures. All conversions are approximate and have been rounded up or down to the nearest whole number.

EXAMPLE:

1 teaspoon = 4.9292 milliliters, rounded up to 5 milliliters

1 ounce = 28.3495 grams, rounded down to 28 grams

VOLUME CONVERSIONS

U.S.	METRIC
1 teaspoon	5 milliliters
2 teaspoons	10 milliliters
1 tablespoon	15 milliliters
2 tablespoons	30 milliliters
¼ cup	59 milliliters
⅓ cup	79 milliliters
½ cup	118 milliliters
¾ cup	177 milliliters
1 cup	237 milliliters
1¼ cups	296 milliliters
1½ cups	355 milliliters
2 cups (1 pint)	473 milliliters
2½ cups	591 milliliters
3 cups	710 milliliters
4 cups (1 quart)	0.946 liter
1.06 quarts	1 liter
4 quarts (1 gallon)	3.8 liters

WEIGHT CONVERSIONS

OUNCES	GRAMS
½	14
¾	21
1	28
1½	43
2	57
2½	71
3	85
3½	99
4	113
4½	128
5	142
6	170
7	198
8	227
9	255
10	283
12	340
16 (1 pound)	454

CONVERSIONS FOR INGREDIENTS COMMONLY USED IN BAKING

Baking is an exacting science. Because measuring by weight is far more accurate than measuring by volume, and thus more likely to achieve reliable results, in our recipes we provide ounce measures in addition to cup measures for many ingredients. Refer to the chart below to convert these measures into grams.

INGREDIENT	OUNCES	GRAMS
1 cup all-purpose flour*	5	142
1 cup cake flour	4	113
1 cup whole-wheat flour	5½	156
1 cup granulated (white) sugar	7	198
1 cup packed brown sugar (light or dark)	7	198
1 cup confectioners' sugar	4	113
1 cup cocoa powder	3	85
4 tablespoons butter† (½ stick, or ¼ cup)	2	57
8 tablespoons butter† (1 stick, or ½ cup)	4	113
16 tablespoons butter† (2 sticks, or 1 cup)	8	227

* U.S. all-purpose flour, the most frequently used flour in this book, does not contain leaveners, as some European flours do. These leavened flours are called self-rising or self-raising. If you are using self-rising flour, take this into consideration before adding leavening to a recipe.

† In the United States, butter is sold both salted and unsalted. We generally recommend unsalted butter. If you are using salted butter, take this into consideration before adding salt to a recipe.

OVEN TEMPERATURES

FAHRENHEIT	CELSIUS	GAS MARK (IMPERIAL)
225	105	¼
250	120	½
275	135	1
300	150	2
325	165	3
350	180	4
375	190	5
400	200	6
425	220	7
450	230	8
475	245	9

CONVERTING TEMPERATURES FROM AN INSTANT-READ THERMOMETER

We include doneness temperatures in many of the recipes in this book. We recommend an instant-read thermometer for the job. Refer to the above table to convert Fahrenheit degrees to Celsius. Or, for temperatures not represented in the chart, use this simple formula:

Subtract 32 degrees from the Fahrenheit reading, then divide the result by 1.8 to find the Celsius reading.

EXAMPLE:

"Roast chicken until thighs register 175 degrees." To convert:

175°F – 32 = 143°
143° ÷ 1.8 = 79.44°C, rounded down to 79°C

Index

P